Ple
ano

84

383

Human and Environmental Systems

Systems

A Geographer's Appraisal

Human and Environmental Systems
A Geographer's Appraisal

G. P. CHAPMAN

*Downing College and
Department of Geography
University of Cambridge, England*

1977

ACADEMIC PRESS

London · New York · San Francisco

A Subsidiary of Harcourt Brace Jovanovich, Publishers

ACADEMIC PRESS INC. (LONDON) LTD
24—28 Oval Road,
London NW1

U.S. Edition published by
ACADEMIC PRESS INC.
111 Fifth Avenue,
New York, New York 10003

Copyright © 1977 by
ACADEMIC PRESS INC. (LONDON) LTD

Library of Congress Catalog Card Number: 77—74364

ISBN: 0—12—168650—7

Text set in 11/12 pt. IBM Baskerville, printed by photolithography,
and bound in Great Britain at The Pitman Press, Bath

Preface

That I have written this book is obviously the result of many pressures and desires. If I am perfectly honest there have been some pressures: for many academics in the modern world "publish and be damned" has been transmuted into "publish or be damned". But I feel I can say quite honestly that this is only a small part or contributory factor. I have written it because I wanted to, because there were some things that I thought should be said, and because no-one else was saying them, perhaps at least I should attempt to do so. The success or failure of the attempt is for the reader to decide.

Originally I began to study the concept of "system" as the culmination of years of increasing irritation with much that went on in a subject vaguely known as Geography. But the irritations, about which I will say more in a moment, have been supplanted by more positive motivations. In particular it seems to me that the concept of system and the literature that surrounds it has much to offer in helping geography solve some of its methodological problems. There are indeed the first signs that the twilight world of geographical methodology is to be illuminated by some major conceptual changes. There has been no doubt a "Quantitative Revolution", but to my mind the real problem of the subject is that, notwithstanding the publication of books which would claim otherwise, there has been no "Conceptual Revolution". The failure of geographical methodology to inspire one mostly derives from the rather sterile way in which that aspect of the subject has been approached.

The most frequently adopted mode of analysis has been to compare the major schools of philosophy in an historical context with the methods that geography has used. Out of such discussion we may justify the present shift to phenomenology, away from logical positivism, but we cannot derive automatically the concepts of enquiry to make the new position operational. On the other hand it is possible to discuss concepts and their applicability without being weighed down by the history of ideas. In any case it seems to me that, on the whole, geography has not reached that level of sophistication where the adoption of a new school of philosophy is *a priori* rather than *a posteriori* justification of a less self-conscious evolution. To this remark there may of course be the beginnings of an exception in the current Marxist impulse.

The nature of the irritations which inspired this book are simply put. I first became acquainted with geography through the regional geography taught at school. I liked it because it said something about far-off places which were different from those of my own experience. But it also rapidly proved to be boring. This boredom emanated quite directly from the failure of the place to be alive on paper: activity, function, performance were written out of the study by the format used. It is now apparent that this failure to incorporate performance stemmed directly from the use of the concept of region as the base of these studies. But unfortunately I suspect that an uncritical use of the concept will still continue to fudge the real world for several more generations of students.

At University one learnt that there were other ways of looking at things. In my day as an undergraduate the new paradigm of the model had just been launched: the take-off was sufficiently fascinating that the basic question of where the trajectory pointed was for the time forgotten. But later it became clear that useful though the models were in many contexts, the fundamentally normative, static and positivistic approach precluded serious consideration of the movement as an all-embracing paradigm with sufficient power to achieve orbit, let alone escape velocity.

At about this juncture an attempt was made to incorporate greater power, greater generality, by adding systems theory to the existing framework. This was to me a very great irritation. Everyone talked systems, no-one thought systems. Authors could not explain, nor agree, what was meant by the panacea, but nevertheless extrapolated it to great altitudes. This book represents my attempt to pierce some of the jingoistic fog, and to clear up some of the muddles.

I may well succeed only in confusing people even more: but I hope not. Above all else I have attempted only to get to square two, knowing how I got there. I have not attempted an inexplicable quantum leap to square one hundred.

Having found that geography had nothing substantive to say about systems theory, I rapidly became embroiled in the literature of many other subjects, and several more minor irritations. Most of these concerned the proliferation of different names in different fields for the same ideas, or the use of the same name for different ideas. The literature was also full of accusation and counter accusation of incorrect borrowings of concepts. I feel sufficiently at home in the field now to know, I think, what is meant in each context. But it is almost certain that this present text will appear to have a sufficient number of inconsistencies and ambiguities in it to continue the process of irritation. It is clearly an open invitation.

July 1977   G. P. Chapman
                                               Downing College, Cambridge

Acknowledgements

The list of Acknowledgements in this book takes me some way back in time. I wish to acknowledge my debt to my geography teachers at Trinity School, Croydon. Mr G. A. Vincent first taught me what a fascinating subject it could be: Mr S. N. Meredith first taught me that learning was not the only thing in life, there was thinking too. At St. Catharine's College in Cambridge I was fortunate as so many geographers before me and since to have as my tutor and teacher Mr A. A. L. Caesar, whose razor-edged brain neatly cut through the successive woolly essays presented to him. As a postgraduate Professor R. J. Chorley's broad vision helped me enormously, and I was grateful that someone who, if titles have to be bestowed, is a physical geographer, would take a geographer of another kind under his wing. In Chicago Professor B. J. L. Berry's kind hospitality enabled me to learn how to use technique to advantage, and I was only able to attend the University because of the generosity of Miss Evelyn Pruitt and the Office of Naval Research.

Back in Cambridge I have been stimulated by conversations with many of my colleagues, among whom I must single out Jack Langton, Peter Dale, and Derek Gregory. But after them follows a large unnamed group, the many students who, wittingly and unwittingly, have taught me probably far more than I have taught them.

The production of a book obviously entails far more than just writing it. I owe a great debt to Mrs Carol Bussingham for typing and retyping, often many times, the manuscript which arrived on her desk in various degrees of confusion. Similarly, Mike Young, Bill Kirkland, Pamela Lucas, Roger Whittlestone and Arthur Shelley have translated my strange sketches into intelligible diagrams.

To all these people I owe a debt which demands more than formal recognition in a footnote.

Contents

For
L.R.R.P, Buller and Musen
who know the true cost

Introduction

The book in context

Despite what has already been said, I presume it may be of some help to put the book into some kind of context with respect to various philosophical viewpoints, if only to put my version before others do it for me.

It seems to me that the contemporary fashion, almost psuedo-dialectical in nature, is to start by stating one's opinion of logical positivism. The following diagram states the nature of the various reactions currently in play:

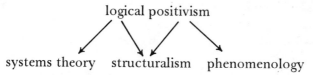

The logical positivists, also known as the consistent empiricists, which is probably a more telling name, insisted on the supremacy of verifiability: a proposition which could not be tested for its truth or falsity has no meaning. Further, the truth or falsity could only be established by the use of a consistent logical system, itself based on an axiomatic system, and this conditions the nature of the data which are acceptable in the testing procedure. Hence the positivists also insist on what one might call objective data, which usually means consistently observable or measurable, but certainly not subjective or intangible.

These two words, which have usually been uttered in the same breath, have nevertheless engendered slightly different reactions. The positivist element, insisting on cognitive rather than emotive meaning, even at times on a reductionist view that everything can be stated in the language of physics, was seen clearly to set up as an ideal the goal of value-free study. The spirit of psychometrics rather than psychoanalysis, of sociometrics rather than sociology, was abroad: the supremacy of observations and data before theory and speculation, and that it mattered more to do things correctly than to justify what was done, were the substance of the spirit.

These criticisms, if criticisms they be, can be levelled against much of what has happened in geography in the first stages of its revolution. But the second stage was not long in coming: the phenomenologists, the existentialists, the value-orientated have begun their task. It is an interesting one and a valuable one, and, as someone who has done a fair amount of field work in India, I think it an unavoidable one. But, I hope that the results of the positivist attitude will not be totally eroded.

On the logical side, there has been a reaction which is not necessarily anti-positivist. Confronted with complex wholes, biologists, and even sociologists, sincerely doubted whether the numerous languages of the logicians, whether verbal or mathematical, were adequate to the task of explaining observable facts. Although very disparate in kind, these languages did indeed form a single class which was inherently reductionist. All of them were the languages of relata, of the complex as the sum of simple parts, and none of them were languages of organized complexity. Clearly then it was necessary for some overriding new concept to be offered: a new class of language to make statements about these irreducible wholes. This new concept is the concept of "system". It is still young and still embryonic, but, I believe, with some promise within it.

Let it be clearly stated that the acceptance of this concept need not necessarily mean either the acceptance or the rejection of positivism. Yet it is an historical truth that most of the work that has been forthcoming on the concept of system has been accomplished in those sciences which almost by definition are committed to positivism. It will come as no surprise then, that this book is almost explicitly positivistic. In view of my own exceedingly limited capabilities I have dealt with only one issue in the reaction against logical positivism: indeed, in many ways this book is not even a reaction at all, but merely an attempt at an improvement of the power of the consistent approach. I have tried to walk before running.

It remains for me to explain why structuralism appears where it does. Structuralism, like systems theory, aims at the explanation of complex wholes, but its origins have been much more explicitly in the social and perceptual sciences, which were themselves far less committed to positivism than the sciences which gave birth to systems theory. Inevitably then, it has not *a priori* rejected as untenable data which are very often of the emotive rather than cognitive sort. If cognitive data are about beliefs, and emotive data about attitudes; if value-free statements embody propositions, whereas ethical statements embody exhortations; then the structuralist would admit that attitudes may be as firmly embedded in character and as effective in action as beliefs. But to this free attitude towards data it has added its commitment that there are such things as complex wholes which are explicable from underlying bases and which are not merely and superficially the sum of many two-way relationships.

To claim that the nature of the data is the only difference between structuralism and systems theory is of course misleading. There are many others — but many of them are, I think, not differences based on inherently different logical viewpoints, but merely the differences of the circumstance in which they have been applied. Systems theory in practice has been associated with the quest for defining order at the level of the data, and then the discovery of an arranging principle which will then in all likelihood be at a similar level. Structuralism has often abstracted heavily from its data before presenting the evidence of ordering and the accompanying principles. Thus systems theory has become associated with the scales of entities in the real world — from the atom through the molecule and cell upwards to the astronomical — with each entity providing the input parameters that are usually the motivation for the arranging principle of the next scale beneath it. In structuralism the rough analogy with scales of entities is scales or levels of abstraction. In practice there exists no methodology about these scales, and the resultant woolliness is a barrier to the understanding of many, and perhaps also symptomatic of the complete lack of knowledge about the mechanism of mind which is the ultimate judge of the value of the structure.

The distinction also explains why for many systems theory appears synchronic: that is, devoid of an ability to theorize about change, rather than the functioning of a changeless system. For these, the appeal of structuralism is its clearer concern with change as well as stability, although its critics would maintain that the ever-present chance of a meaningless collapse into ontology or dialectics makes the path too slippery. Quite simply, I do not believe that systems theory is merely synchronic: that would almost be a direct contradiction of its aim in studying complex *functioning* wholes. I would agree that its contribution to diachronic analysis is slow.

This then, is the context of the book. Not being frightened of the charge of eclecticism, I would simply say that on the whole, but not exclusively, this is a book which for operational reasons belongs to the category "systems positivistic".

The layout of the book

The book is quite simply based on an analysis of a definition of "system". This definition is not the only one possible, but is the one which I have found most productive. The definition is: "A system is a set of objects where each object is associated with a set of feasible alternative states: and where the actual state of any object selected from this set is dependent in part or completely on its membership of the system".

The pursuit of this definition gives rise one particular problem, that the definition can apply to itself, i.e. the state of the discussion of any part of the definition is dependent on the state of the discussion of the other parts simultaneously. To put this across less ridiculously, the treatment of the concept of the integrated whole ought to be itself an integrated whole in many dimensions. But language is one-dimensional and serial, and so it is impossible to talk about more than one aspect at any moment in the text. The breakdown of the definition into parts then means that we seek to recreate the whole by constant cross-referencing, while examining the parts sequentially. I might add that problems resulting from the single dimension of language are by no means new, as for example Darby (1962) has noted.

Given this caveat, the structure of the book should be intelligible from the accompanying diagram. The nature of objects is first examined, and this gives rise to considerations of kinds of objects, viewpoints of analysis, of measurement, of boundaries. Relative space and time are also introduced at this stage, although one can see from the diagram that these concepts overlap into the consideration of systems of objects. The discussion of the states of objects is never very explicit, although it becomes much more so in the section dealing with regulation. Study of a set of objects as a system brings us to a host of discussions, about complexions and ensembles, organizing principles, and redundancy. But then

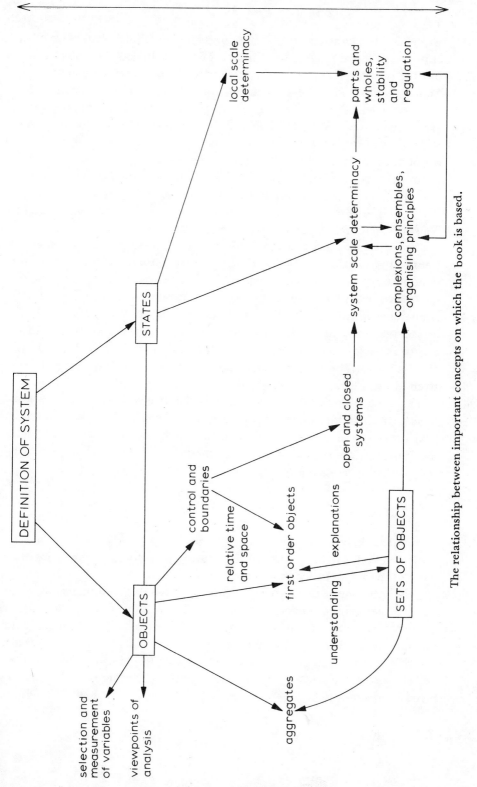

The relationship between important concepts on which the book is based.

we revert to a consideration of the parts in the wholes, and via the concepts of local scale determinacy, stability, change and regulation, we put the objects in context. Throughout the discussion, Information Theory is likely to appear, as the natural vehicle for the quantitative expression of the ideas involved. Now it occurs to me that many geographers do not have much backing in information theory, and indeed according to the work that has been published even those who use it often have some misconceptions, so a section explicitly on information theory is included. It is perfectly possible to read the book without knowing anything about it, and without bothering to follow that particular chapter. But to get the greatest benefit it would be a good idea to consult Chapter 8 at some early stage.

As a separate section I include some examples of practical applications. I am not altogether pleased with them — they are the result of research conducted at various times over the last 10 years while my ideas have been even more embryonic than they are now. But, I have determined that this will not be a book on systems in geography which does not at least try from time to time to go from theory to practice, and unfortunately there has been no fund of published work on which I can draw for examples. The gathering of data and practical analysis has therefore often slowed things up considerably.

The book is also very uneven in its detail in other respects. This is mostly the result of the fact that parts of it are based on a rich literature which I have been able to use for my own purposes, whereas in other parts I feel my contribution has been original. In these areas I have perhaps gone into more detail, presenting the background as well as the findings.

The conclusions

It might be helpful to include here some of the more important conclusions reached, to enable the reader to anticipate some of the points to which the argument leads.

Firstly, I do not think that the concept of system will have any great operational consequences in geography for a long time yet. It represents an ideal that the real world does not fully approach. On the other hand in conceptual terms I think the concept is extremely important and useful, and that it has a great and immediate role to play for those who are about to plan the strategy of their research. As a framework for analysis, it has no current peers.

Secondly, to my surprise, I find that though there are many super-ficially different definitions of system in various disciplines, all those of value do have a common meaning. Having started this work on the con-viction that system in human geography would be different from system in physics, I am delighted to find that I can make direct transformations from the definitions of social science into those of physics. This re-iterates the point made above, that system is a concept, a class of logic, and that its acceptance or rejection has nothing to do with the positivist or anti-positivist debate. Further, it echoes the remarks of the General Systems Theorists, which I have always found a little difficult to swallow, that the unity of science may be furthered by the isomorphisms of the systems they study.

Thirdly, it rapidly becomes obvious that we have given insufficient thought to the manner in which data are collected, and on what the observations are made. The *sine qua non* of systems theory is that there be parts in a whole. If the parts are arbitrary, then any arbitrary result may be proved. To quote what will be requoted later in similar context, "entitation must precede quantification". Geography has consistently and dismally failed to tackle its entitation problems, and in that more than anything else lies the root of so many of its problems. Its effects in the U.K. at least on the national data-gathering agencies has been mini-mal, and no wonder. There has been nothing even remotely resembling a consensus on what we are looking for. The procedure has been painful to watch. While the economists corner the economic variables, and the sociologists secure the social variables, the geographer has attempted to escape from what he has mistakenly conceived as his only and shameful refuge, that of synthesizer, by securing for himself paramountcy of the spatial variables. The spatial variables of what? Of measles and bronchitis, the price of chicken livers, of television sets and retail hosiery, of whole-sale big-end bearings, and propane gas. In the great technological wonder-land we are left with nothing but the smile on the Cheshire cat's face. Pattern. Observable and explicable in a simple Newtonian absolute space?

It seems important, therefore, that we begin to realize that we need some guiding lines, some theory of empirical enquiry. Much though I acknowledge the efforts of the new wave of theorists as being stimula-ting, I do not think that we have yet put our house in order, to the ex-tent that we know what we are trying to study, nor yet what we are trying to observe and measure. This is the last major conclusion: that we try effectively to develop some theory of empirical enquiry.

Part I

On Wholes

1

On Regions, Objects, and Hierarchies

"May the earth be filled with happy regions." (W. Bunge, 1973)

1.1 Introduction

Bunge's dream is a startling one, the more so since it is the concluding
sentence of a recent book on *new* directions in Geography. For him, the
region is back in strength. It is not difficult to see why he resurrects it —
he is asking for the opportunity to build a new Utopia, rather like
Moore's in many ways — and the only way in which this new Utopia
can be built is by the total integration of man, his neighbours, and
nature. To define this total integration he uses a unit of space, the
region, in which the integration is to be performed.

Much though I laud the idea, I doubt whether it is practical. I doubt
it because to achieve perfection within the boundaries of the region, the
inhabitants must have perfect control over all within their territories,
and to achieve perfect control their boundaries must be truly closed. If
not, then disease and pollution can diffuse into Utopia from the bad-
lands beyond.

Periodically the region, no doubt thought to be conclusively dead just
a few years ago, comes creeping back into the limelight. Perhaps it arrives
as an ill-defined force behind some "area studies" programme, or perhaps in some subject adjacent to geography, such as political science, it
is rediscovered. Perhaps it is diluted into some compromising apology,

as in Minshull's (1967) recent defence. But certainly, it has not gone
away completely.

On any logical grounds, it should have done. Its present stirrings of
life have nothing to do with what the region has been or is as a concept,
but with its aim. The *raison d'être* for the concept's existence was the
integration of many aspects of environment and society. That aim is
now the dominant pursuit of many studies within and between many
disciplines. But the worthiness of the aim does not guarantee the worthiness of the tool used to attain it, and because the aim has been resurrected
it should not mean that we resurrect an outworn idea.

And so I find a convenient starting point for this book to be a brief
analysis of the role that the idea of the region has played in geography,
and to see where this idea, as it has been framed, has led us into imprac-
tical or irresolvable problems. The way out of this impasse will be found
in a rigorous application of the concept of the first-order object of study,
and in a better understanding of the nature of time and space. The expansion of these themes will take us from the first into the second
chapter.

1.2 The regional impasse

Most geographers will agree that they are trying to study and understand
the patterns of interdependence and linkage between the phenomena
that cover the earth's surface. However, for the moment they are not
doing so at that grand scale of synthesis and integration that the regional
geographers have attempted. I feel that inevitably we will have to come
back to the problem of both describing and analysing the complex systems of human occupance of the earth's surface, and we will have to
consider real systems. Regional geography predated modern systems
thinking, and lacking the tools necessary for the fulfilment of its aims,
it has been abandoned by researchers suspicious of its format, or else it
has been written in modified form. There has been no real breakthrough
in regional geography. We are still awaiting a satisfactory methodology
to guide us in the analysis of large and incompletely known systems.

If geography merely wants to answer the question "What is within
this region" then we have no problems. But if we go beyond the realm
of description to the realm of performance and behaviour, if we wish to
answer the question "How do these things behave" then the definition
of an object is of great importance. Function is a term that can only be

applied to a discrete entity with form. Without form there can be no performance. To answer the question, "How do things behave?", we have to know what the "things" are.*

Previous definitions of an object of geographical study have usually attempted the definition within a region of space. Bunge (1962) has suggested that "place" is the individual of classification, while at other times "sites", "tracts", "stows", have all been suggested. If this "place" can be easily, unambiguously, and meaningfully identified then there is no problem. But if the definition is not clear and unambiguous, then we cannot have a true understanding of its behaviour. As an example we may take the Hampshire Basin, a well-known "region" of England. Within this region we know that there are many things, each of which is functioning, for example shipyards, schools, factories, etc. Some of these are closely interconnected, others are not. We can understand the behaviour of these taken as individuals, but we cannot understand the external (ecological) relationships of all of these with respect to other things within the Hampshire basin only. Nor can we understand the behaviour of the Hampshire basin as a single entity with respect to other similar regions of England. There is no complete understanding of the dockyards of Southampton with respect only to entities within the Hampshire basin; they just happen to be there. We cannot understand the behaviour of Cunard's Offices in Southampton with respect to other entities within the Hampshire basin, neither can we understand the Hampshire basin by talking of the north-east or the London basin. In the end definitions of place are seen to be arbitrary, and no behavioural study can be based on them. The Hampshire basin does not Perform.

We can also take a brief look at a typical piece of regional textbook writing. It might be claimed that this is not a fair target for criticism, but I am concerned with empirical analysis of what is outside my window. Regional textbooks attempt the same.

> The chief town of Charente is Angoulême, with a population in 1954 of 43 000, or if the whole agglomeration is included, of 53 368. It is situated in a

---

* It becomes apparent that to a great extent in this paper "object" and "system" will be virtually synonymous. I am aware that Ross Ashby (1956) has cautioned against the identification of a system with an object, but he does not define an object, though he does define a system, and his implicit intuitive definition of an object is more limited than the philosophical one advanced here. A careful and rigorous definition of object does in fact virtually define a system. I feel there will be little trouble in equating the two.

strong defensive position on a low limestone plateau, partly surrounded by the
Carente and its confluent, the Arguienne. Today Angoulême is a pleasant city,
very much the regional centre of the pays, "le centre d'une région très animée,
un véritable entrepôt commerciale'. Its industrial activity includes large paper
mills, breweries, flour mills, leather works and metallurgical manufacturers,
including agricultural implements.

(Monkhouse, 1959, p. 340).

First and foremost this is a description. There are some hints of an
explanatory nature, for example the defensive site, though we can guess
that this is of little relevance now. Secondly there is a list of the industries
that are found in the town. Such a list is not an integration.

In general, the point of view of most such textbooks is an attempt at
a synthetic statement and description of a countryside. Such books
seem to alternate between descriptions of specific functioning systems,
where there is one of interest, for example a port or an iron ore field,
and infilling which consists of lists of activities which are not very far
advanced from the days of capes and bays. These lists are in no way an
integration or a synthesis. Strangely, it is implied in the writing that these
activities are an attribute or property of Angoulême, although they are
the functioning entities which are the *raison d'être* of Angoulême. As it
stands, we do not know that Angoulême itself functions, although we
can guess that the factories do. In general we can say that at the next
scale level above that of the factories it has been accepted, but not
proved, that the town is a functioning entity, but its function cannot be
described, and the parts, factories, etc., of which it is composed are not
related to each other within the next higher entity, the town. The act of
listing has only one question attached to it: "What is within this area?".
To make a meaningful synthesis we have to ask the question, "How do
these functioning entities relate to each other in the functioning of the
next highest scale entity?". For the moment we should not assume that
the next highest scale entity is the town, nor should we assume that it
is any *a priori* defined place, since we have already decided that places
do not of necessity perform.

In empirical geographical writing, as opposed to methodological
writing, the concept nearest to that of an entity or an object, has
probably been the nodal system, or nodal region. The impression is
created of a complete sub system within the national system, and yet
there have always been difficulties in defining any nodal region precisely. Its boundaries are usually drawn in absolute space (this term is

explained further below) on the basis of some sort of "sphere of influence". But different criteria yield different spheres of influence and different boundaries. The garbage collection service does not have the same boundary as the readership of the local newspaper. Many such boundaries are often mapped in the hopes that there might be some coincidence suggesting a "real boundary".

This procedure is strange. Firstly, the definition of the nodal region does not depend on the whole region, but on part of it only, that is, the central nodal settlement. The subsystem is defined with respect to part of the subsystem. Secondly a sphere of influence does not define an object, but can only be defined once an object has been defined. An animal, having been defined, can have many boundaries drawn around it depicting many spheres of influence. It can be smelly to us within 3 feet, it can see 6 miles, and perhaps can smell the opposite sex within 10 miles. But none of these boundaries itself defines an object. Ultimately any object may have an infinite number of effects in an infinite number of ranges on a limitless number of other objects in a system, a principle which is obviously enshrined within Tobler's famous First Law of Geography — that things interact, but near things tend to interact more than far things. Thirdly it is assumed, but never proved, that the central settlement is an object. That this is so can be seen from a consideration of the most curious intellectual procedure of all. Real functioning objects are identified, for example the local newspaper printing house, and the local dairy. The properties of these objects in influencing other objects at a distance, that is the sale of goods to customers, are then assumed to be properties of the assumed object, the nodal town. There is a transfer of properties from several unconnected knowns to a single unknown.

The cataloguing and demonstration of these problems could continue almost for ever. I will content myself with one more detailed example, from one of the regional texts which is currently held in some esteem, Paterson's (1965) book "North America: A Regional Geography". He is not over-enthusiastic about the concept of region:

> Chapters VIII to XIX of the book deal with the regions of North America, and all of these regions are familiar to geographers. I have not, however, devoted much attention to their exact definition, on the ground, nor attempted to map them. Rather I have allowed them to define themselves, in terms of the regional problems which confront them. Among a forward-looking people like the North

Americans, the bonds of regional sympathy are tied less by topography or by
climate than by a shared concern for the future of the community.

(Author's note.)

In fact he has side-stepped the problem. Without defining region he
has used the adjective regional in association with the word problem, and
assumed that persons reacting to such problems are part of a region.
Whether these bonds that he speaks of as opposed to other bonds are in
fact strong enough to denote the region may be open to dispute. But it
is interesting to note that he is using people as the basic unit of his
regions, not space. People are functioning entities, and he has seen that
it is in terms of functioning that we can perceive some larger aggregate
unit.

We may also consider how he treats the actual problem of description.

Minneapolis, in turn, having the water power of the dalls of St Anthony at its
disposal, developed the early industrial core, participated as a mill town in the
Great Lakes lumber boom, and then settled down to a more stable career as one
of the continent's flour milling centres (its grain elevators' capacity of 115
million bushels is the largest in North America), with important manufacture of
machinery in addition.

(p.289)

With its fortunes so dependent on the sale of motor cars, it is essential that
Detroit and its satellites should create, and be able to show, clear locational
attractions to other types of industry in the future.

(p.281)

It is clear that Paterson is thinking in terms of functional entities.
However, it is doubtful whether the personification of the cities is a valid
way of presenting a functional entity. A city does not corporately
respond to lumber booms and car manufacturing. Individual companies
might respond, and they are the basic *raison d'être* of the city, which is
rather putting things the other way round. Moreover, even supposing
that Detroit were able to show clear locational attractions, it is not
possible to write of attracting industry to a place without regard for the
total amount of industry in the rest of the national system, and the places
to which it has gone. There are many "unbalanced" cities in America,
and why the personified "Detroit", as a place, should be competing with
other personified places is difficult to understand. If the people of
Detroit migrated to other better cities, would "Detroit" still be worth
saving? It is hard to put a finger on the personal essence of Detroit.

The problems that stand out all concern the nature of entities and their interdependence within a wider system. In order of priority, it would seem that first we must direct attention towards the question of what an entity is. If we do not do this we do not know what it is that is being interdependent within a system. Having defined it, we must understand not only what it is, but also what else it could have been. If we merely describe what it is, then we have achieved no explanation, for it is evident only that it is necessary because it exists, and a system of entities thus deterministically described cannot change. By analysing why it is what it is out of all the things it could have been, we seek to understand interdependence within the system and the methods whereby change can occur. Ross Ashby (1964) has observed how fruitful the concept of the "number of alternative states" has been in science.

We turn next, therefore, to a consideration of the definition of objects.

1.3 First order objects of study

(a) On objects

The idea developed by Rowe (1961) in ecology are based on Feibleman's concept of the Level of Integration of subjects (Feibleman, 1954). Basically Rowe attempts to classify individual disciplines according to the conceptual value of their subject matter as it relates to real objects functioning in the real world. It is in fact quite an old idea, that of ranking subjects according to the level of integration of their subject matter. To understand this, we first define an object.

An object is something which can be observed as a discrete entity by some perceptual mechanism, operated by man. Such a definition will serve as a starting point for those objects whose size falls between that of the atom and those of the stars. We can observe these objects because they have boundaries, that is exterior limits to their being which define their morphology. The fact that boundaries exist around objects does not mean that the objects are isolated systems, impermeable to any exchange of matter or energy, since, as Gerard (1957) observes, "Permeability to something — iron, gene, idea, person — in some degree is a property of all boundaries (indeed a boundary may be characterized as a zone of lowered permeability) . . . ". These concepts of boundary and permeability are important, and will be considered again below in relation to the question of control and systems closure.

Since objects exist in the real world, they have existence in three dimensions. Therefore objects are volumes, and, following Rowe's discussion, we will further characterize objects as volumes with structurally bound parts. The structure making the bonding strengthens our appreciation of the object as an object. On the other hand we may say that we can also perceive aggregates. A wood is an example of an aggregate, and it is known as an aggregative object because, if it is perceived close to, it is seen to be made up simply of many individual trees. Finally, we often abstract further and propose an intellectual class to be an object. A species may be an object of study, although its members may be scattered in many locations at any one time.

Three objects are thus defined. These are the structurally integrated object, known as the first order object of study (henceforth referred to as the object), the areal aggregate object, and the non-areal aggregate object, often known as a class. All such objects that are examined at any given scale are components structurally integrated within the next higher scale first order object of study, at the same time that they incorporate structurally within themselves objects of study at the next lower scale.

Working from a small scale to a higher scale, it can be appreciated intuitively that the atom is bound within molecules, the molecules are bound within the cell, the cell is bound within the organ, the organ within the organism (a plant or animal). At the same time that any one organ is bound within the plant or animal, there are many other organs of the same scale which are different objects, but which are also incorporated within the same whole. The inevitable question is what comes next, after the scale of the organism? For Rowe the only possible next scale structurally bound object is the ecosystem. The ecosystem is viewed as being the earth, the sky, and all the objects that link the components together, that is to say plants and animals. To make the point clear it is instructive to attempt to define some object at an intervening scale. Perhaps vegetation may be suggested. But vegetation is neither the complete environment of the individual plant, nor is it a structural object encompassed as a component of the ecosystem. It is not a whole.

(b) Tests of the first order object of study

A first order object of study can be analysed from several incommensurate points of view. If a given object cannot be analysed from all these viewpoints, it is not a first order object. The viewpoints from which the subject matter of the biological sciences are approached are taxonomy,

morphology, physiology, ecology, chorology, chronology and
composition.

Morphology is the basic recognition of the object and its shape as a
volume. It exists. It is also made of components, and the listing of these
components is known as composition. The classification of the components is known as taxonomy. The object performs, and its internal
functioning may be analysed in terms of physiology. Ecology is the
study of its relationships to the other objects of its own scale within the
next higher scale object of which they are all a part. Chorology is the
study of areal variation within the object, and chronology is the study
of the object in time.

We will test the concept of vegetation according to viewpoints. Vegetation is amenable to the viewpoints of composition, chronology, chorology, taxonomy. But it has no morphology, and without morphology it
cannot perform, hence neither physiology or ecology can be satisfied.
Hence vegetation may be mapped and classified, but study cannot
proceed further without involving the total ecosystem. The concept of
the community in vegetation studies should not be decried, but no more
should be asked of it as a conceptual tool than is inherent in its inferior
status as an aggregative object. Note, as an aside, how arbitrary the
mapping of vegetation communities often appears to be, whilst the
mapping of land use units is less difficult.

Rowe tests the concept of the ecosystem in similar terms. The ecosystem is a volumetrically inclusive whole with solid (earth), plastic
(air) and dowels (trees). A dissection and inventory of parts is possible.
These parts may be classified; thus we have satisfied composition and
taxonomy. The physiological viewpoint is the functioning of the whole
as a system with internal activity. Chorology is the areal variation within
the system, and chronology is sequential variation with time. Ecology
is the relationship with other ecosystems.

Rowe concludes that the ecosystem is a first order object of study.
I have some reservations about this, because although it is a structurally
inclusive whole, morphology is not easily satisfied, and hence ecology is
difficult to define precisely.

We can obviously define boundaries at rather large scales, for example
an ecosystem may be defined for any landmass surrounded by water
(the islands beloved of ecologists). Yet within a land mass such as the
Americas are many systems that we would like to define intuitively as
different ecosystems. All would seem well if we accept Von Bertalanffy's

notion of the wholeness of systems (Von Bertalanffy, 1962).

Wholeness can be exemplified by considering the ratio of the external trade of a country to its internal trade. If the ratio of the former to the latter is high, then the economic situation inside a country is to a great extent dependent on external conditions, and the economy of that country exhibits little wholeness. In general terms Ross Ashby (1960) states:

> When a set of subsystems [e.g. a set of national economies — author] is richly joined, each variable is as much affected by variables in other subsystems as by those in its own. When this occurs, the division of the whole into subsystems ceases to have any natural basis.

Such subsystems exhibit little wholeness.

But however much wholeness is accepted as a viable term in systems theory, it still leaves the definition of the ecosystem in any one place as a rather arbitrary matter.

(c) Objects and disciplines

Something of a controversy exists as to whether or not it is possible to associate different disciplines with different objects of study. We cannot possibly say that disciplines should have an object of study, but it often does appear that they can be associated with one, and equally we can claim that it is profitable within any one discipline to attempt to define an object of study.

Rowe suggests that at each successive scale of research there exists as the basis for that scale of research a structurally integrated first order object of study, and Boulding (1956) makes a categorical statement to the same effect:

> Another phenomenon of almost universal significance for all disciplines is that of the interaction of an "individual" of some kind with its environment. Every discipline studies some kind of individual — electron, atom, molecule, crystal, virus, cell, plant, animal, man, family, tribe, state, church, firm, corporation, university, and so on. Each of these individuals exhibits "behaviour", action, or change . . . .

The significance of this ascending scale lies not only in the fact that it exists, but also in the fact that there is a hierarchy of complexity in these systems, and hence there is in some rough correspondence a hierarchy of system concepts with which to analyse them. In the history of scientific development we have also seen a progressive development of our abilities to analyse such systems, from early mechanistic systems to later attempts at analysing complex animate systems.

Figure 1.1 is a suggestive illustration of the hierarchy of objects and the disciplines associated with them. Clearly the great difficulty in establishing first order objects arises at the scale where the individual plants and animals are to be grouped into the next highest object. Below this scale it is usually easier to identify disciplines with objects. Botany studies plants, zoology animals, microbiology the organisms within such plants and animals. Medical science studies man, mostly from the physiological viewpoint. Specialists study various organs within man. Psychologists study the mental physiology of man. Then we shift to the next scale up, and find fragmentation between disciplines. Sociologists study the mental ecology of man. Economists study the economic properties of man-orientated objects, including man himself. Often this is more successful than we might suppose, mostly because many of the institutionalized decision centres created by man which define objects of study have directives to interfere with economic parameters, and not any others. But even then, there are many areas they have overlooked. The objects created, factories and so forth, do in fact have other modes of performing than purely economic ones. Labour relations, which are not dictated wholly by rational economic processes, are a keenly studied new field.

Figure 1.1 shows a clear split at the level above that of the molecule. It is at this juncture that the complex inanimate objects such as buildings are seen to diverge from the ascending scale of objects which progresses into forms with life. If we extended Boulding's ideas we can say that it is at this point that the mechanistic frameworks become distinct from the "open system" frameworks of self-maintaining structure, a property first seen in the cell. Similarly we can find support for these ideas in some of Gerard's remarks. At the level above that of the molecule: "At the next level, however, is an unquestioned split into the complex inanimate orgs of geology and astronomy (and meteorology and oceanography, perhaps even of architecture and engineering) and the complex animate orgs of biology". (Org is a word Gerard uses for entities which are defined almost exactly as our first order objects of study.)

Clearly one of the problems facing geography in recent years, that of the split between human and physical sides of the subject, despite the fact that in the real world both human and physical environmental

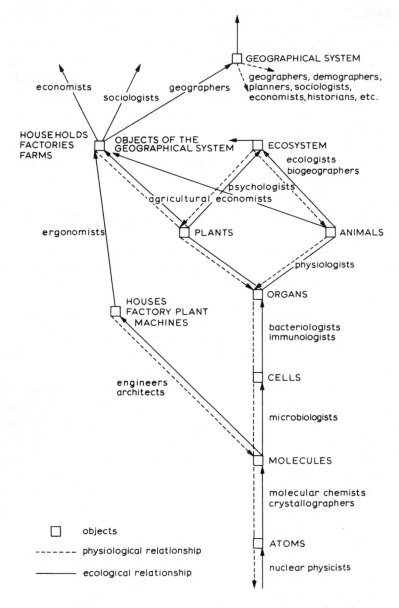

Fig. 1.1. Diagrammatic scheme of objects and areas of study.

factors are closely interrelated, may have its origins in this split between the complex inanimate object and the animate one. With the advent of systems theory and the realization that there is a hierarchy of systems of different complexity, it becomes apparent that the modes of analysis in physical geography may inevitably be far removed from the modes of analysis in human geography, and moreover the framework required for the analysis of the physical system is much better developed and can be used for empirical studies that are much more complete than their counterparts in human geography.

Having said that, it is also interesting to note that some facets of what is taught now conventionally as bio-geography concern a system, the ecosystem, with a high order place on the hierarchy. Nevertheless this system has proved to be much more amenable to a cybernetic framework of analysis than the human systems, mostly because the system has no image of itself and questions of choice and decision do not arise in a metaphysical sense. Hence the studies carried out in this field have been able to stay much closer to the mode of analysis used in inanimate systems.

A word of caution is needed in this section. The idea that subjects are associated with objects of enquiry is not supported by all writers. Abler *et al.* (1971) comment that sciences deal with constructs, and that often different sciences will deal with the same construct from different points of view. To their mind the difference is in the kinds of question asked. Figure 1.2 illustrates the construct "urban riot" and the related

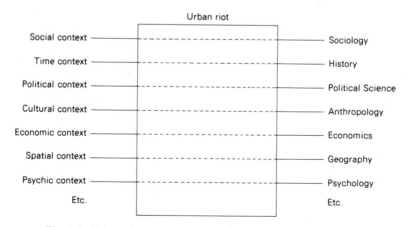

Fig. 1.2. Urban riot as a construct. (From Abler *et al.*, 1971)

contexts of questions and the disciplines involved. To a great extent one
has to agree with these writers that this is what does happen in the social
sciences. But note that the construct "urban riot" is something which is
related to systems of a high order in Fig. 1.1, precisely at that place in
the hierarchy where great confusion exists. Clearly no one single context
can explain an urban riot, and support for the notion that separate discipline should independently study different contexts is clearly close to
laying oneself open to the charge so often made today: that of fragment-
ing knowledge. To bring knowledge together again inter-disciplinary
centres, such as those for urban studies, are being established, which are
clearly centres devoted to the study of functional systems. One might
also ask, what, in the context of objects, is an urban riot. I would
answer such a question on the following lines, assuming for the moment
for the sake of the argument that a functional object such as an urban
system exists. Men are objects. As such they should be components of a
higher order object, the urban system, in which they are interrelated and
function together so that the whole may function. When an urban riot
occurs, some of the parts that should be functioning within the organized
whole cease to function normally, and come together in a loose assembly,
a form of aggregate object. (The term "loose assembly" is explained
below in the quotation from Furth).

Finally one can also mention Langton's (1972) excellent remarks on
the distinction between the morphological and functional aspects of
geographical study:

> Yet the system concept is essentially functional, whether applied to low
> order plant communities or to complex human groups, and much of what is
> construed as human geography is not concerned with functioning systems but
> with the artifacts of the system. That is, with the purely formal study of the
> distribution patterns of houses, shops, roads, factories and towns, and so on.

In essence, if we do not care about functional behaviour, then this
book and systems theory is irrelevant to geography. The same was said
above with respect to the format of regional geography. If we are merely
concerned with the description of what is, then we can continue as we
have done in the past. But in my view description is not enough.

(d) Some summary remarks on objects, regions and geography

The problem area of methodology that is becoming pinpointed more
and more explicitly revolves around two interlinked issues. Firstly it is

clear from the regional tradition outlined at the beginning of the chapter
that geography is concerned with studies at some scale, still hazily defined, above that of the individual plant or organism. But above that and
beneath what? Clearly the world represents an upper limit, but merely to
place these two limits *seems* to leave a large number of intervening scales
available. However, we are not sure yet whether this multiplicity of
scales is a methodological fact or an operational convenience. Secondly,
it is becoming quite clear that geographers have been imprecise about
the concept of region in relation to function and integration. What kind
of object is it? An aggregate one, an intellectual one, or a first order one?

From time to time the nature of the unanswered questions has been
half-perceived, and answers have been half given. In the next section I
wish to examine one particular paper which tried to move in this
direction.

1.4 First stirrings: Philbrick's attempt at escape

Over the years many people have voiced their own interpretation of the
relationships of function and area. But one of these attempts stands out
as clearly demanding some explicit comments. Philbrick's (1957) paper,
"Principles of areal functional organization in regional human geography",
represents a major attempt at escape from the impasse. I think it failed,
although gloriously, because throughout it retained an ambiguity about
objects and about the nature of space: that it did so was probably a
tribute even then to the mesmerizing effect that Central Place Theory
was to cast over the concept of hierarchy and scale in geographical
studies.

The aim of the paper was to provide scales of generalization of general
usefulness. This was deemed necessary because in making empirical
generalizations we need to know the various scales at which we can focus
our attention, while ignoring the details of the scale below. Thus, for
example, when making generalizations about fourth order central places,
we need not worry about individual farms of the lowest order. And if
we can erect such a hierarchy we can provide a consistent base for scales
of generalization.

Philbrick's starting point was explicit:

> Differentiation of areas is a distinctively geographical approach to the study
> of the world as the home of man: but differentiation alone does not provide an
> organization of the material of geography into a system of knowledge. Nor is the

classification of areas into any given system of regions a substitute for a body of principles upon which understanding of regions can be based!

The body of principles which he sought could be found in the Principle of Areal Functional Organization, where the several key words were considered in the following manner:

> The word area is used since geographers study phenomena in the context of their areal distribution. The word functional is used because the different yet associated purposes or functions of human establishments compose in the aggregate the different functional patterns of human activity which make generalization about society possible in the context of areal distribution. The word organization is used because human activity is interdependent and interconnected in area.

This passage is interesting because it contains within it the contradiction that makes the final paper implausible. He sees as the prime object of interest human establishments, and he recognizes their interdependence through the many interconnections that result from their functioning. Yet, *at the same time,* he acknowledges the geographer's interest in area *per se* and the idea of aggregates of areal patterns. As should be clear from above, aggregates are not the same as first order objects.

The basic building block of his landscape is the unit of occupance. At the smallest scale it is easily defined in functional terms. "The simplest unit of occupance is the single establishment occupied by a person or small group of persons. A farm, a store, a dwelling — all are simple examples which come to mind". He claims that these are focal in character — for example he shows that the farm has a core area, the farmstead, which is the focus of the fields, which constitute the peripheral area.

The building blocks are the units which interconnect: "The interconnection of establishments is responsible for the evolution of areal units or organization larger and more complex than the individual establishments." Again, note that the units may be responsible *for* the complex whole, but the complex whole is to be recognized *in* some areal pattern. But having said that, the obvious problem of the spatial discontinuity of such wholes cannot be avoided, and he states quite clearly that "When dealing with the areal organization of interconnected establishments in the structure of society such discontinuities become the rule".

If the argument had been left at this level I could hardly dispute it. But he then proceeds to define a nested hierarchy of areal functional organization based upon two kinds of relationships between units. Firstly there are parallel relationships, which are defined between similar kinds of establishments in a homogeneous area. For example, farms in an area are connected by a network of roads and telephones. But, this unfortunately represents a break with his principle of functional interconnection, since the existence of roads does not mean that they have to be used in any particular style at all, and the actual pattern of flows in a network may be very different from all the patterns of flows which are potentially possible. Secondly there are nodal interconnections between unlike units. Thus farmers and businessmen trade at central nodal points, expressing the principle of nodal areal organization.

Out of these two principles he is able to erect a hierarchy of units of areal functional organization, which displays alternating homogeneous and nodal forms, as shown in Table 1.I. The hierarchy becomes nebulous and difficult to display in real world terms. The basic functional establishments of the lowest rank give way at higher ranks to such concepts as a "settlement", or to ascending orders of central places. And at the higher orders such phenomena emerge as the "American manufacturing belt".

Table 1.I

Type of organization	Unit or order of areal functional organization
Homogeneous	Parcel
Nodal	Establishment
Homogeneous	Area of establishments
Nodal	Settlement, second order
Homogeneous	Parallel relationship of second order
Nodal	Third order area of functional organization
Homogeneous	Parallel relationship of third order areas
Nodal	Fourth order areas of functional organization
Homogeneous	Parallel relationship of fourth order areas
Nodal	Fifth order areas of functional organization
Homogeneous	Parallel relationship of fifth order areas (the American Manufacturing Belt)
Nodal	The American Manufacturing Belt as the core of the national unit
Homogeneous	Parallel relationship of national units in the integrated commercial world
Nodal	World organization of the uniform areas of the world: commercial, integrated, subsistence, and unoccupied

It is clear that the concern with area *per se* is never really lost. The alternating ranks of nodal and homogeneous organization display, to my mind, an enormous confusion between aggregate and first order objects. Because of this confusion he is able to maintain the fiction of nodal first order objects as inclusive spatial wholes up to high scale levels; by defining areal aggregates, the homogeneous regions, at each preceding level. Out of this fiction and confusion comes such a multiplicity of scales.

Similarly the extrapolation from the simple nodality or focal character of a farm or small village to an assumption of similar focal characteristics at larger scales is unfounded. Amongst many firms, establishments, and, as he would have it, towns, there is very rarely any marked consensus of focus in space — in fact there may be many, and these may not be consistent through *time*, an exceedingly important component of any functional connectivity, which receives not a single mention.

Thus, the attempt to define scales of generalization of global applicability fails. The major issues are still unresolved.

The real world might indeed not come as clean as we think. It might indeed just happen to be true that the resolution of the conflict between large scale generalization and excessive detail in a functional system is not to be avoided by such a hierarchy. It just might be that there is a very large jump from the establishment to the large system of which it is a part. The intervening scales, as we have seen, are based on the geographer's predilection for space and pattern. It might just be that space does not necessarily *contain* anything better than aggregate objects.

Certainly it is around the notions of aggregates, space, and time that the unresolved issues still turn, and these we sense in the next chapter.

2

The Object of Geographical Analysis

"Two conditions must be fulfilled in order that an entity may function as an object in a process of experiencing: (1) the entity must be antecedent, and (2) the entity must be experienced in virtue of its antecedence; it must be given."

(A. N. Whitehead, 1964)

2.1 Introduction

This chapter attempts to come to terms with the questions raised in the first. I have already given consideration to the concept of a first order object of study, but I have not yet said enough about the nature of time and space to make the concept explicit in geography. I therefore ask the reader's indulgence while the present chapter begins to wind its curious path through many fields of thought which should ultimately all appear to be relevant.

2.2 Space in geography

(a) Two kinds of space

There are at least two major ways to consider space — absolutely and relatively.

Absolute space is a space where position is defined in terms of some coordinate system with an interval scale of the coordinate axes. Any

position on the earth's surface recorded in terms of latitude or longitude
is recorded in absolute space. A set of objects may exist at defined locations in absolute space, and other members may be added or subtracted
arbitrarily without affecting the position of the members already in the
set, or the members left in the set after subtraction.

Relative space is that space within which position is recorded according to the relationship of the object being recorded with other objects
that exist within the space. There are many subjects in which relative
space is the obvious space to use for analytical purposes. If the analysis
of the human anatomy is considered, the position of the liver and kidneys
is not mapped according to some absolute space coordinate system, but
within the relative space of the body, wherein all the parts are mapped
in relation to each other. It is not possible to add or subtract members
without altering the total relative position of objects remaining within
the system. Fundamentally the definition of relative space presupposes
the existence and definition of the system and all its components. The
ecological viewpoint of Rowe is essentially one which is only possible
within such a relative space. The ecological viewpoint presupposes the
system.

Obviously anything which exists within a relative space can also be
said to exist within an absolute space and in fact can be measured and
recorded that way. Such measurement presupposes no knowledge of the
system within which the object exists. But it ought to be equally obvious
that it is impossible to derive from this absolute position knowledge of
the relative position until such times as the total system within which
the object exists is defined.

(b) Relative and absolute space in the geographical system

Clearly all objects within the geographic system, however that may be
defined, exist within the absolute space usually referenced by latitude
and longitude. The whole earth may be seen as the complete domain of
absolute geographic space. Subdivision of this domain into smaller parts
is quite possible, but still within the terms of geographic space, and hence
the smaller parts have no inherent connection with the ideas of object
or system. Only if an object or system is defined first can we then look
for morphology and map this morphology into the coordinate of absolute space.

The qualities of relative space can be appreciated intuitively. Consider first a normal map of the positions of New York, London, Brighton and Paris. Their positions are fixed absolutely by latitude and longitude. The addition of one more town does not disturb the picture presented. Now consider a map of their relative time distances from each other. On such a map the correct location of two points is simple, for example, the time distance between London and New York can be used to locate them both. A third point, say Paris, can be entered (providing that the time distance from Paris to New York does not exceed the sum of the time distances Paris/London and London/New York, etc.), as illustrated in Fig. 2.1., lower part. But if we try and add Brighton (see Fig. 2.1., upper part), it appears that to map all the relative positions accurately we have to move into another dimension. To maintain accuracy a shift in the referencing of all the members of the set is necessary.*

Usually in such cases the information is stored in matrices. But the addition or subtraction of a town changes the size of the matrix and accordingly causes a change in the set of relationships of any one town, and in the set of these sets, as both a column and a row are either added or subtracted.

Relative space also has the invaluable property of allowing multiples of the same location, where "same" has to be acknowledged in relative space terms. For example, consider Fig. 2.2., where six points are placed within a closed universe. No other information is given − no "north", no coordinate system. All six points are in the same place, that is all display the same set of distance values to all other points. From this distance information it would be impossible to make any kind of distinction between the places. If we say that we can see that the points are in different places, clearly we are only able to say this with an absolute space concept in mind, namely that locations are unique. To put it another way, in central place theory towns of a certain size are all the same, *because* they have the same position within a uniform plane. If

---

* Maps of the relative time distance of several places from each other are not drawn, because as pointed out here, an accurate representation in two dimensions is impossible. Maps of the relative time distance of several places from one place, are drawn, as in Bunge (1962, p.55). The distinction between these two cases is interesting. If the complete set of places constitutes the system, in both cases all the places will be recorded. But in Bunge's case the map represents the ecological relationships of one of the members of the system. In the alternative case the map is at the next highest object scale, and represents the physiological relationships of the whole system.

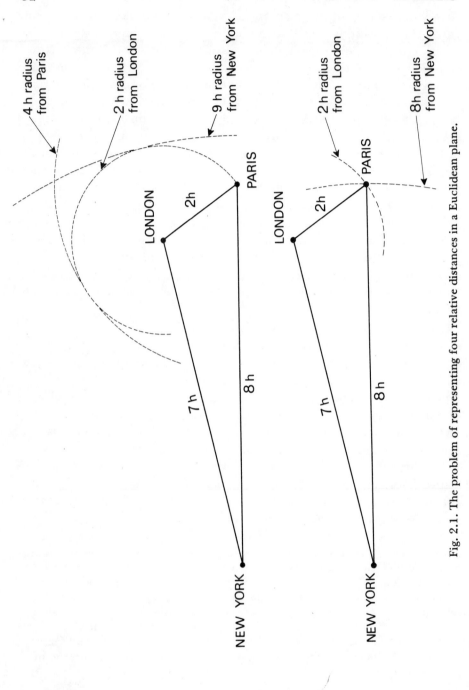

Fig. 2.1. The problem of representing four relative distances in a Euclidean plane.

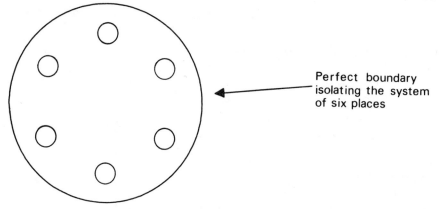

Perfect boundary
isolating the system
of six places

Fig. 2.2. Six towns in the same relative position.

their positions are not replicated then their functions cannot be replicated either.

This might be a simple and obvious point, as indeed it is. However, the
significance of the point has not been well received in geography. Clearly
what is of relevance to the geographic system is relative space, but
equally clearly this cannot be defined until the whole system has been
defined. To attempt to define units of absolute space within which it is
hoped we may be able to study objects in geography, or often in fact
define objects, is usually illogical.

It is at this point that I must take issue with Langton (1972, p.133).
Talking of systems closure he remarks:

> Solution of this problem is doubly difficult in geography because closure
> must be effected in two explicitly considered dimensions, the spatial and the
> 'phenomenal' — i.e. either social or economic or both. Although the variables
> occupy an area of earth-space which can be arbitrarily closed, the parameters
> almost always comprise expressions of the states of interacting phenomena
> which are irrelevant to the values taken by the variables — 'systems enclosures' —
> and many if not most of the interacting phenomena will be located outside it.
> The magnitude of the difficulty of achieving 'spatial closure' can hardly be
> exaggerated.

Langton sees this as a problem for two reasons: firstly he does not
differentiate between absolute and relative space; and secondly he
assumes automatically as a result of the recent history of geography,
that spatial closure is necessary and relevant, an implicit contention

which I explicitly reject. Further, one might query the meaning of a
variable occupying an area of earth-space.

We may characterize the basic problem as that of "overlap" where
overlap is defined as the non-coincidence of sets of objects grouped by
contiguity in relative space and absolute space. For example, at a large
scale in relative space West Berlin is grouped with West Germany, Alaska
with the U.S.A. and the former East Pakistan with West Pakistan. But if
these same objects in each two-object set are mapped in absolute space,
they no longer form a contiguous set. At this scale there are few such
examples, and most of those that do exist are two-object sets. But within
a national state overlap is the rule rather than the exception. The U.S.S.R.
exhibits a high degree of overlap because of the control by central
ministries of so many plants throughout the whole country. National
corporations weaken the "wholeness" of many "sovereign" states. Given
such a background we note two implications: firstly in the U.S.S.R. and
the U.S.A. regional development schemes are almost impossible to
implement smoothly — in recent years in the U.S.S.R. in particular there
have been many varied and unsuccessful attempts at decentralization of
power (the failure is as much due to economic problems as to political
considerations); and secondly (which amounts to the same thing), it is
almost impossible to draw a line round some region of absolute space and
call it an object. In Ross Ashby's view the richness of connection with
the environment so defined exceeds the richness of the internal connections; the boundary is not a zone of lowered permeability, and control
is thoroughly weakened.

In this context it is interesting to note that Harvey (1969) is unable
to make any firm recommendation for the object of enquiry. Instead he
substitutes the notion of resolution levels. Different problems are associated with different levels of resolution. He contends that geographers
have long been aware of a regional scale of resolution, and that it will
remain of central importance. The statement is weak, and comes as a
disappointment in the final chapter of a book that is dedicated to a
precise philosophical treatment of explanation in geography.

(c) Region, objects and classes

In Grigg's (1965) survey of the nature of classification and regionalization little comment is made in depth on the problem of the definition of
the geographical object. There have been many attempts to do so, all of

them concerned with the ultimate possible subdivision of the earth's surface. Most have worked down from the earth's unity towards the smallest definable unit. That there are an infinity of points on the earth's surface is well known. However, some authors have stopped at a scale which represents the limit of their capabilities of comprehension. This limit may be the site, the tract, the uniform slope surface. Probably we may surmise that these are all subjective figments of the imagination, but whether this is true or not, the significant point is that all of these attempts have tried to define a geographical object in absolute space.

Regionalization is analogous with classification or logical division. In either case when these terms are used in other subjects, the object of classification is well known and defined. This analogy should therefore not be made when objects do not exist; yet in geography there has been no successful attempt at defining an unambiguous areal object. Quite simply, space is not and never will be an object, but merely one part of the space—time domain within which objects may be thought of as existing. The study of areal variation is often cited as the prime aim of geography, but areal variation *per se* does not exist. Something moving within absolute space can be said to be changing its absolute coordinate position, but the coordinate axes and their interval scales do not of their own indicate any variation. Areal variation is only meaningful in that objects located in different places may be of different kinds, or that properties of similar objects differ from one object to another, and these objects of necessity occupy different locations to be distinct from one another. This is what we mean by areal variation. Therefore the grouping of area should be accomplished by the grouping of these objects and the space that each of them occupies. Space is thus an auxilliary characteristic, and a shift is accomplished from absolute space to that relative space required for the definition of object and system.

(d) Space as a property of objects

Space is clearly a property of an object if the object occupies some space to be an object. But we may also conceive of an object as occupying more space than its own physical volume indicates. A tree does not have pure space between its spreading branches, since this space is occupied by air, but it is in fact a supply of air that the tree must pre-empt for its own uses, and if we do not recognize this air as a first order object of study (it is in fact an aerial aggregate!) then we allocate it

to the tree. This we may do instinctively and philosophically. The air
space becomes a property of the tree.

Much as animals exhibit a rather similar behaviour (territoriality) so
human beings have space bubbles around them. Hall (1965) recognizes
several different bubbles around people. A person has his own volumetrically inclusive space, defined by his morphology. He has a space
within which his limbs are mobile, and which is essential for physical
development and psychological stability. He has various other spaces.
On average, in the U.S.A., if a person is introduced into a secretary's
office to await for an appointment, then the secretary will feel bound to
stop work and talk with him if he is within 10 feet, but will feel free to
continue with her work if he is further away. We also occupy space in
terms of living accommodation, or in terms of work, be it an office or a
farm. The definitions of such spaces are precise and usually legally
enforceable.

A map of the density of population is usually based on calculations of
the number of people within a defined area. This defined area exists in
absolute space independently of any specific objects. The density is given
as the number of people per unit space. However, correctly interpreted
it represents an average which should be expressed the other way round.
Each person or personal group (such as the family), will pre-empt such
space as he can for his various activities. If we measure these we will have
a set of data representing the amount of space per unit person (or
person group). This set can be averaged, and the figure we obtain given as
the average space per unit person. This figure is obtainable from the
usual density figures of people per unit space, but the thinking is
reversed.

It is in fact much more logical to perceive space as the property of
the persons using it, rather than the persons being the property of the
space. A tree in a desert may require a large area for its roots. A farmer
uses his fields, and the space that they occupy is defined relative to him,
or to whatever else is the prime decision maker affecting the status of
those fields. We can surmise that the central part of the analysis which
allocates space to people will in fact be use, and this implies some sort of
functioning system and control of the system. The constraint of areal
contiguity is not logically a part of this scheme. A farm may have several
units of land in non-contiguous locations, but all under the same decision
process.

2.3 Time

When time enters into any analysis in geography one rarely finds any justification for the philosophical basis of its conceptual use. Time is used in the simple sense of a scale locating objects of the three-dimensional world in a fourth dimension, so that we can speak of existence at a point in time, or duration over a given time interval. This dimension of time is a receptacle into which events are placed, much like the Kantian view of space as a three-dimensional receptacle. In short, time is usually considered in some sense as absolute time in the same way that we can conceive of absolute space.

This concept of time has done sterling service to science. It helps in the calculation of the motion of heavenly bodies and the rates of discharge of streams. But slowly the basic idea becomes more complex. Time in the Newtonian calculation of planetary orbits is reversible. The equations still hold good if the planets revolve the other way round, reversing their recent orbital histories. In fact the concept of history is irrelevant.

On the other hand one cannot arbitrarily reverse the discharge of a river and expect the water to rush up the tributaries and then pitter patter up into the sky to make clouds. So for many uses time is unidirectional — it has an arrow showing which way it is going. It is often said that entropy is time's arrow, meaning that it is entropy which shows which way the arrow points. For example, heat never spontaneously goes from a cold object to a hot one, although the reverse is true, and carbon dioxide and wood ash never spontaneously give up oxygen and form a log. Without for the moment worrying too much about thermodynamics, we can say that it is from this kind of statement that are derived the further statements that "the universe is running down" to a "universal heat death". Not every scientist believes it is profitable to make such statements about the whole universe, but on a more local scale we can take it that this is true of our solar system.

But thermodynamics, although pointing the arrow, does not say how fast anything approaches a thermodynamic equilibrium. So we find that the radioactive isotopes of different materials have different half-lives (the time it takes for radioactivity to halve itself). Now I am aware that I have said "the time it takes", which would at some stage have been measured by fractions of earth orbits, e.g. a minute is part of a day is part of a year. Such a standard datum is perfectly reasonable, indicating some length of elapsed time. But now we find that the Standard International Unit of time, the second, is defined as the duration of 9 192 631 770 periods of the radiation corresponding to the transition between two hyperfine levels of the ground state of the caesium-133 atom. More roughly, time is now measured according to the vibrations of the atoms of a certain element when it is in its energetically most stable state. If we substituted another element we would get another measure of time. In the end, time, like mass, is expressed in terms of the property of some concrete entity. It is related to something.

So we now know that time has direction, and that it is measured according to a scale which is relative to the characteristic behaviour of something. That is quite sufficient for the physical world on the whole, but it is not necessarily sufficient for the biological and human-social worlds, which as ever are apparently more complex and, shall we say, vaguer than the physical world.

Let us consider for the moment Murphy's (1965) concept of entropy time on the stock exchange. The first point he makes is that a normal calendar does not provide a useful time scale with which to make analyses of trading activity and capital gains and losses on the market. Obviously, since the exchange is closed on Saturdays and Sundays and on national holidays, any analysis which includes such days on the time scale will have an irregular spectrum of zero activity confused with the time trends of trading activity. The first stage of an analysis is therefore to equate entropy time only with those days when the exchange is open. However, this does not prove a sufficient change in scale to make the analysis clear and succinct. The activity rate varies not only for days of the week, but also for other reasons which occur at unpredictable intervals, such as the collapse of a major company, business cycles, foreign wars, civil disturbances, change of government, predictions of a change in government, etc. All these different events can be translated into an information equivalent, since we view an investor as someone who has to accept all this information and base his decisions accordingly. We then make an assumption that his decision rate has to equal the information rate, and it is difficult to prove such an assumption wrong since we can include "do nothing" as a subjectively sensible decision. The time scale thus becomes measured in received information bits, and the subsequent analysis of decision processes is based on this time scale. Within this view of time Murphy is able to achieve what can only be described as a beautiful analysis of the adaption process with respect to capital gains on the market.

Let us be quite clear what we are saying. In effect all of the activities referred to do occur in "normal" time. In fact we can think of "normal time" as being the general time into which all other times can be mapped, although the reverse is not necessarily true. But although activities may occur in normal time an analysis of the adaptive decision-making processes of the investor can be made best in entropy time. Here the key words are *analysis* and *process*. Process is a word we use for activity which accompanies change in some variables, and which can be stated in generalized terms. The generalization can be made qualitatively, as in the process of weathering, which degrades rock structure, or quantitatively, as when connecting given climatic variables with the rate of weathering of rocks. In Murphy's case entropy time provides the framework within which an adaptive process of an economic system can be quantitatively generalized. In this context time is measured in relation to the rate of reception of information by the investor. Note that it is quite possible for different investors to have different time scales, but within each person's time scale Murphy would apply the same model of adaptation. Note finally that the results of the analysis can always be mapped back into "normal time", that is the investor's portfolio at a given entropy time can be considered as the investor's portfolio at some point in "normal time" which is in a unique correspondence $(1:1)$ with the given entropy time.

Entropy time, as its name suggests, is a way of viewing time where there is some ongoing process with a definite time direction. A thermo-dynamicist would probably be appalled at the use of the world entropy, but never mind, that is Murphy's chosen name. Much of the physical world can be conceptualized in terms of entropy time trends and terminal equilibrium states of closed systems. But the world of animate systems is characterized by open systems which maintain themselves in some steady state. To a great extent, despite the fact that ageing occurs, we can consider the adult of some animal species to maintain itself in some steady state for a time period of some length. To do so it imports material which has chemical energy bound within it, and exports both material and energy (mostly as heat loss). This is a generalized black box cybernetic view of what consists of a complex of processes. The most important point is that the total processes do not form one general process that is continuous and unvarying with time. At different times animals are eating, sleeping, digesting, fighting, mating, etc. These activities are adapted to the conditions of the environment, and the environ-

ment against which the steady state is maintained shows during the
duration of that steady state a cyclic rhythm of activity due to the
diurnal revolution of the earth. The length of such cycles is bound — to
24 hours — in contrast to the unbounded nature of uni-directional
"normal" time. Instinctively we adopt a cyclic view of time when we
make generalizations about many animal activities. "In the day time the
owl sleeps; he hunts by night" is a generalization based on the repetition
of the diurnal cycle of night and day and a correlated repetition of
hunting and sleeping. Overlaid on this is the longer-term cycle of
seasonal change, when we observe different fur coats on animals (and
clothes on men) in different seasons, and different sleeping and eating
habits.

This might seem very obvious, but it is so obvious that we often ignore
the basis on which we think. As I write it is 3.13 p.m. on 25th September
1975. This means that since some arbitrary zero at the divide B.C./A.D. we
have had 1975 yearly cycles, eight moon cycles (we still have an approximation between months and moons, but it is weak), and 24 diurnal cycles,
and then a few divisions of a diurnal cycle. We have deliberately made
our measures of "normal time" coincide with that cyclic time which
affects us greatly. But any absolute time scale can be used. We can invent
a new scale of Temporals, and say 1 Temporal = 13.768 hours and then
record history in terms of Temporals. In fact of course earth time and
sidereal time are different, and because all our cyclic time intervals do
not fit perfectly together, we have leap years and add a 29th of February.
When Apollo rockets go to the moon we talk of hours into mission, not
days. And finally we note that now the standard international unit of
time is based on the activity of some atom, which knows neither night
not day, nor B.C. or A.D. But cyclic time is so dominant in our lives that
we have adopted a measure of absolute time which enables us to make
swift and accurate mappings between the two.

Much as an analysis of the stock exchange is made in terms of entropy
time rather than "normal time", we can note that there is also a dislocation between cyclic time by which biological man lives, and unidirectional time within which economic assets decay (building fabric
rots and machines rust) and within which we usually record the history
of economic development, as a process where the rate of accumulation
of assets exceeds the rate of their destruction. (We can note in passing
that during coal miners' strikes maintenance men are sometimes pre-
vented from working in the pits. Although "working time" stops "geo-

logical time" does not: the result is the collapse of many seams.)

A definition of economic development in the above terms is unrelated to the cultural fads of man. But men vary in their view of time, as in other things. Western (and predominantly atheistic) capitalist man has a highly egocentric view of time. On the whole it is his view that for him it ceases when he ceases. All economic development has to be seen in the terms of his individual gains. We consume now and do not invest for future generations. The Soviet Union ostensibly started out on the road to economic development with a social and not individualistic view of man, and consumption by the individual in his maturity was sacrificed in favour of consumption by the society in its maturity. Such an attitude may be breaking down there, but still would seem to be generally accepted in the Chinese republic. Ultimately we come to Hindu time, where life itself is cyclic. The doctrine of the present condition as the reward or punishment of a previous life, and a future life as a reward of punishment of the present has undoubtedly contributed to the docility of men in the face of adversity.

Whatever view a man takes, it is certain that every person has some concept of a commodity generally known as time. In economic terms Carter (1971) has pointed out that the present generation in the U.K. discounts future time much more severely than previous generations — in fact it would seem that the rate of discount of future time is dependent on the rate of change in society, which in turn is dependent on the rate of discount, a frightening example of positive feedback which will continually speed up the change (and hence stress and necessary adaptability) in our environment. Man also creates machines which often operate in a different time framework from our own biological time. Many industrial processes are continuous, and as a result we have to introduce night-shift working and the accompanying disorder in the private lives of workers. The computer operates at such a speed that to use its full capabilities we have to develop supervisor software that can manage disparate jobs at once, and we have to devote an enormous amount of research into producing high speed input—output peripherals. And we can note that those who accuse others of lack of urgency may find themselves accused of pointless haste. In general, we will have to expect that analysis within the social sciences of different activities may well take place within different time frameworks, and that an understanding of the functioning of "the national system" may require many time frameworks with an understanding of the accompanying mapping functions or interfaces.

Within the field of economics the conceptual problems of finding a suitable time framework for analysis have been considered at some length by both Shackle (1969) and Georgescu-Roegen (1971). The latter has some interesting remarks on the nature of entropy and time direction in thermodynamics in relation to clock-time (which we have referred to as "normal time"). The second law of thermodynamics states that the entropy of the universe is always increasing, and in any particular case the entropy of some closed system is always increasing. We will deal with these concepts in more detail later, but here what concerns us is the simple fact that in terms of clock time we cannot predict, using the second law of thermodynamics, how long it will take any given closed system to go to maximum entropy. Note that the discussion about entropy is more rigorous than the case of Murphy outlined above, and that here the discussion is in terms that should be acceptable to a thermodynamicist. The point is that if the only temporal law of thermodynamics, which is the second law, does not enable us to make predictions in terms of clock time, then it is still conceivable that we may be able to make predictions within some entropy time yet to be defined. (Murphy used the word entropy time in a context specifically related to information flow not heat flow). Georgescu-Roegen in fact is waiting for the discovery of a fourth law of thermodynamics. The present implication he sees as follows:

> ... the mechanistic dogma has been abandoned even by physical sciences. We should therefore regard as a sign of maturity the reorientation of any science away from the belief that all the temporal laws must be functions of clock-time Whenever it has taken place, the reorientation paid unexpected dividends. For instance, many biological phenomena which appeared highly irregular as long as they were projected against a clock-time scale have been found to obey very simple rules when compared with some biological phenomenon serving as a "Clock".
>
> ... However, the evidence of the phenomena that are not slave to the mechanical clock is so crushing that we must conclude that the laws of mechanics do not determine every mode of being in nature. Within what is thus left undetermined in nature, laws of a different essence may be at work without contradicting each other and, hence, without each one being able by itself to remove the whole indeterminacy.

Finally let me make a brief comment on a problem area which seems so daunting as to foredoom every assault on it to failure. Objects exist in time and space. The best spatial framework for analysis may be relative — and we have given as an example of relative space the concept of time distance. But if time is relative, if time in different places has different utilities, then presumably the best spatial–temporal framework may be relative in both space and time. The problem then of finding a mapping, unique and unambiguous, between that framework and a framework of absolute space and time might prove almost insurmountable.

2.4 Control

Any system is subject to some sort of constraint. This fact is so self-evident that we often overlook it. Ross Ashby observes that every law of nature is a constraint. He wonders what a world without constraint would be like. One can imagine cars leaping into the air for no reason, Niagara Falls suddenly going backwards, and people running upside down on their ears.

But constraint exists. A river system is dependent on elevation and gravity for an energy input, and water for the translation of potential energy into actual kinetic energy. These between them represent the constraints that limit the amount of work that can be done by transportation and erosion.

An animal system is subject to constraints. In any one area the population numbers of a given species are determined by its inherent reproductive rates, the food supply available, individual food requirements, and the action of predators and diseases. Garfinkel (1962) has used simultaneous equations to summarize this state of affairs, and Boulding (1955) has shown how these various parameters can affect the outcome of a Malthusian model. Note that the specification of these parameters controls the behaviour of the system.

Man is aware of the system within which he exists. On this basis he is within a system that is entirely different from those above. Man has the ability to change some of the parameter values of the constraints on his system, and by this process he can attempt to control it. (That the changes do not always control the system in the desired way is only too evident). He raises food production, and uses transport to change the availability of resources from one person to another. Control of the system depends upon control of the constraint parameters, but since man has the ability to change these we can think of control as resting in those centres where the decisions to change parameter values are made.

The questions of control, constraint, lead us back again to the definition of object and the definition of boundaries. Emery (1969, p.290) quotes an example of a management reorganization in a textile mill. Figures 2.3a and b show the management structure before and after the changes. The changes resulted in a clear improvement in efficiency and a reduction of accidental disruption:

> The significance of the difference between these two organizational diagrams does not rest only in the relative simplicity of the latter (although this does reflect less confusion of responsibilities) but also in the emergence of clearly distinct areas of command which contain within themselves a relatively independent set of work roles together with the skills necessary to govern their task boundaries.

The definition of boundaries has two purposes: the definition of the entities to be controlled by any one decision centre; and secondly, the definition of a boundary condition impermeable as far as possible to exchanges with the system environment other than those dictated by the control centre. (These two facets can be seen as two sides of the same coin.)

It is of course one of the weaknesses of the geographical objects that will be propounded below that many of them, particularly those in such fields as farming etc., have highly permeable boundary conditions. Pests, disease, ground water, floods, rain, do not necessarily respect the boundaries we have created. This does not invalidate the use of the object concept, but it does mean that for control to show any desired effect the regulatory capacity of the object must be very high in the face of all of these disturbances. It also provides the point of contact between empirical analyses of ecosystems and of geographical systems. Let us return to Emery for a moment;

> Whereas the former organization has been maintained in a steady state only by the constant and arduous efforts of management, the new one proved to be inherently stable and self correcting . . .

2.5 The object of geographical study

In the increasing scale of the first order objects of study from atom to plant or animal, no particular difficulty is found in distinguishing each level in turn. But above the level of plants and animals there hangs a question mark. Rowe (1961) claims that the next object is the ecosystem, and in some circumstances this may be acceptable.

The weakest part of this argument is that Rowe does not differentiate between absolute and relative space. His ecosystem exists in some arbi-

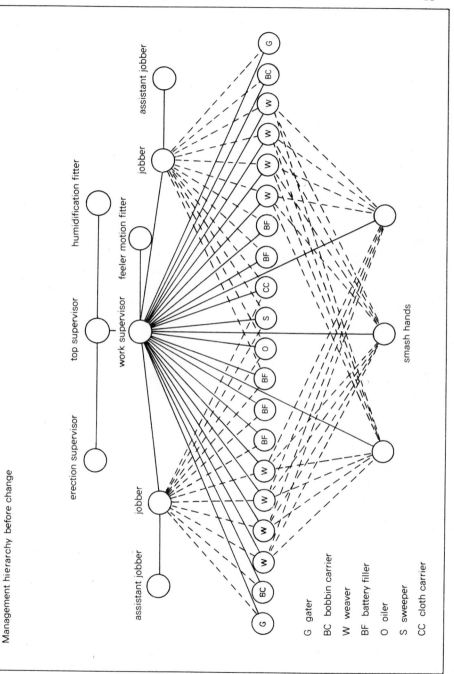

Management hierarchy before change

erection supervisor

top supervisor

humidification fitter

feeler motion fitter

work supervisor

assistant jobber

jobber

assistant jobber

jobber

assistant jobber

smash hands

G gater
BC bobbin carrier
W weaver
BF battery filler
O oiler
S sweeper
CC cloth carrier

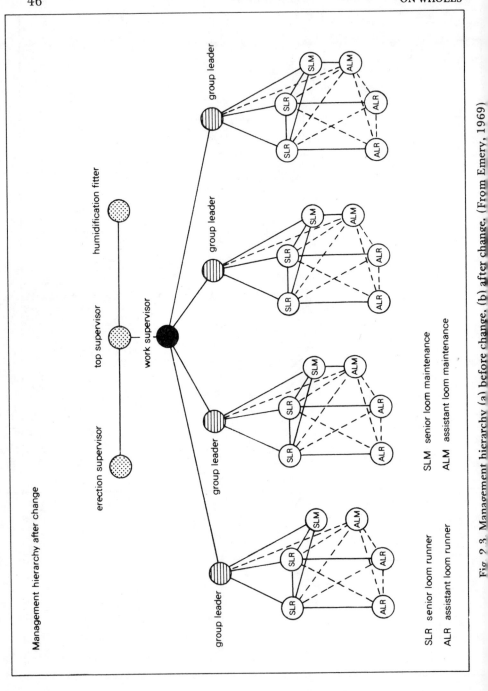

Fig. 2.3. Management hierarchy (a) before change, (b) after change. (From Emery, 1969)

trary region of absolute space. Space, which is not an object, delimits the ecosystem, but is not defined as being a property of it.

The approach followed here is not necessarily as complete philosophically as it might be, although it will be seen below that in practical terms it is more complete than appears at first sight.

We may take man as a first order object of study, and therefore a component of the next highest order. Within this next highest order object the reference space will of necessity be relative. Additionally parts of the absolute space domain can be seen to be properties of the component men that enable these men to operate within the next highest order object as components of the system. Man is an object and space is divided (though not necessarily exhaustively) amongst these objects,hence any grouping of these objects will in some way group some space together (though again no contiguity is implied of necessity).

Since every level of system has some control mechanism, we may look for control mechanisms to help in the definition of this elusive object. Since man has developed his reflective system (one of which he has an image) he has also created control or decision centres.

The smallest obvious control centre within western society that is bigger than the individual, is the family, or better still, the household. For census definitions a household can in fact be one person, e.g. a single pensioner, but nevertheless that person operates a significant household budget. At higher levels we move into concerns, and then government. Concerns are any corporate body with an institutionalized decision centre. These are thus everything from schools with headmasters, to shops with managers, and giant corporations with boards of directors. Control centres exist within government at both local and national level to monitor, or control, the actions of other decision centres, namely those of the concerns and of the households. There are obviously many scales of centres within concerns, within government, and even within households, and no method is suggested here for attempting to classify them.

We may now build a very simple model of the geographic system. At the first level above that of the individual exists the household and all its space properties. We may map these households and their accommodation (house and gardens). Consider next what we may envisage as a very small town, in ordinary terms. We see that this is composed of similar parts (households) and a few other sorts of parts, one manufacturing firm, one school, and some shops. Each of these has some space requirements and space properties, but these are ancillary to the definition of these components as objects in their own right to begin with. Above the level of the household, the shop, and the factory, the next level is then a composite of all of these, which incorporates their space requirements, and the additional space requirements of the connecting links, the roads and sewers. Since people can occupy both their own homes and their offices, though never two at the same time, the systems is always changing. But at any instant in time space is theoretically allocated unambiguously as the property of one decision centre, or of none. A house may cease to have any spatial significance for part of the day. Absolute space is not exhaustively allocated to persons, and, although in theory it is possible to be unambiguous about the assignment to those decision centres that are functioning, in practice it is not so. Therefore such an object definition will not produce as a by-produce an exhaustive and unambiguous classification of absolute space. As there are the many "gaps", it is possible to discern another feature of the definition. The next higher level may link objects that were previously widely scattered, owing to the inclusion of dissimilar objects amongst them. An increase in scale is not simply sideways areal accretion, but can include infilling as well. Figure 2.4 illustrates the observation of an object at the level one above that of households. It is interesting to note that this next higher level object is not always the same, changing from different times of the day, and that at any given time of the day there will be blanks where things which are at some time functional objects are, for the given moment, static and unused cogs. This immediately suggests that we could create some typology of movements, differentiating between those flows which maintain any given object as it is, i.e. flows of goods and power, a and those flows associated with the shift from one object state to another, for example the daily flow of commuting, which changes the object from that shown in Fig. 2.4d to that in 2.4c.

At a higher level we may include the decision centres of government, and link these into the object. However, the problem of wholeness is still not completely resolved. The national system would appear to be a reasonable whole, as would the individual factory or household. Intermediate levels are more difficult. It has often been suggested that cities are wholes, and it would appear reasonable to suppose that they might be. However, as the economy develops, then much of the decision making which we would expect in the city if it is a whole object, is in fact preempted by headquarters elsewhere, be they government or be they head

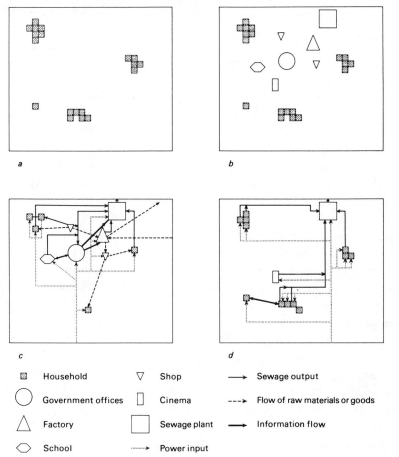

Fig. 2.4. A functional object comprising objects of the next lower level.
(a) an aggregation of similar objects;
(b) a set of dissimilar objects of the same scale;
(c) a functioning object using some of the components of (b);
(d) another functioning object using other components from (b).

offices of firms. It would appear that the small city as an effective whole might disappear, and such an interpretation is possible, especially of small cities near large ones, serving dormitory functions. There is no point in considering them as objects in their own right. They are areal aggregates of component objects of the next highest first order object of study. Wholeness in a developed economy is best exemplified by the total national system.

2.6 Tests of the geographical object

We may take the small objects first, that is households and factories.
They have morphology. They are organized to consume either finished
goods, or materials to produce goods; that is, they function. They are
subject to chronology, the mapping of their components, at any given
instant in time. They have ecological relationships with other components in the system, otherwise they fail to continue to function.

The national system is similarly amenable to all these points of view,
but not necessarily as obviously as the components, particularly with
respect to morphology and physiology. The form is the total form of all
factories, farms, buildings etc. and all connecting links between. The
object is thus physically continuous in the sense that there are continuous
physical links between all members, although there may be spaces between parts of the system, much as there are spaces between the legs of a
spider, or the leaves of a tree. These spaces may well be necessary, just
as the air between the leaves is necessary. Cohen (1964) has pointed out
that a super-power needs a large empty space. It might be thought that
this empty space is not a property of the larger object, the national system, but is instead the sum of the properties of all the smaller objects,
for example it is used by individual people for their recreation purposes.
However, this large empty space of which Cohen is talking can in fact be
seen as being directly connected with the national object, particularly in
its use for rocket research, atom bomb testing, army manouevres, and
even strategically empty border zones. All of these are national requirements. Thus even this largest geographical object is volumetrically inclusive yet may have space properties around it.

The morphology is curious compared with other objects, being long,
wide, but very thin. It is easy to study chorology in a collapsed form of
two dimensions, and it is easy to see that a lot of the relative space
variation may be in part explained by absolute space location. Hence it
has been possible to overlook relative space for a long time in the methodology of the subject.

It is possible to test the notion of the city as well. I have found that
most people are loath to abandon the concept of the city as a functional
entity, and there may be many cases of research where it is profitable to
assume that cities exist as functional entities. The dilemma probably
rests in the fact that many of the processes occurring within a national

system have different time frameworks, so that in a dynamic analysis it is easier to see cities as entities than in a static analysis of the functional links of a national system.

Within the static framework we can ask such questions as, "what is the morphology of the city?", using morphology in the strict sense defined above. To that question asked of modern western cities, there is no answer. If there were, we could given an unequivocal answer to the question, "how many people live in London?". Some people say 3 million, others 9. In Johnson's (1967) book on urban geography a diagram displays an almost perfect rank—size relationship for the urban hierarchy of England and Wales, but the top city, which one has to assume is London, has a population of 3 million. If one altered the definitions of a few cities one could produce a far from straight line. Berry *et al.* (1968) have produced a report on the definition of metropolitan regions for census purposes which suggests a definition but which points out that there is no such thing as the definition of a metropolitan area. We can contrast this case with that of the medieval walled city. Then, certainly, one could point to the morphology of the city. Note that it had morphology because it had a boundary, and this boundary was required for the purposes of control of who was in the city. Because control was wanted, the boundary was a zone of very greatly reduced permeability. The condition of boundary impermeability to arbitrary access by people still exists with respect to private homes, companies, and to national states, but no longer to cities.

If this is an insufficient argument, consider the viewpoint of ecology. If we look at a firm it is possible to define those functional units with which it has ecological relationships. These include the other organizations which provide it with materials, the people who provide work, and the other firms, wholesalers or retailers, who take materials from it. But if we ask for a similar listing of the ecological relationships of a city we are at a loss. We can only provide a list of the ecological relationships of all organizations which are arbitrarily placed within some set of organizations known as, for example, Southampton, and many of these relationships will be within the set anyway.

2.7 The city and time

Within a dynamic framework the considerations become more complex. Within the larger perspective of the whole national economy time is a unidirectional stream. "The *history* of the economic development of the Irish Republic" connotes the fact that there is a non-repetitive uni-directional time element in such development. However, being a member of the animal kingdom, man is also caught up in cyclic time. The fulfil-ment of cyclic activities such as sleeping dictates the amount of time available in any cycle for other activities such as commuting to work, and hence the time distance travelled to work. This time distance is one of the most severe constraints on the location of economic activity. It is often said that a firm can now locate anywhere in the U.K. What we mean by this is that a firm in any location in the U.K. can develop satis-factory ecological relationships. But the continued growth of the South East witnesses that this is not the whole truth. Most of the ecological relationships can in a dynamic sense be satisfied within a unidirectional time view: but the ecological relationship with labour cannot. Hence a firm has to locate where its extra incremental demand on a labour pool within a constrained time distance is not disruptive. This usually means that a location near a large population centre is chosen.

Suppose we take 1000 people at random in a country and follow every move they make over one month, and plot these moves on a map. We should get a result rather like Fig. 2.5. Clearly the dense clusters occur around what we call cities. These are defined by commuting. We

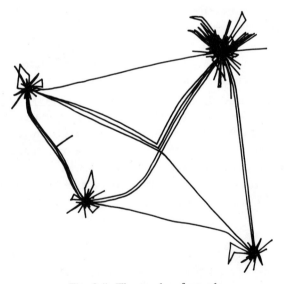

Fig. 2.5. The tracks of people.

can note that Berry *et al.*'s final definition of a metropolitan areas is based on commuting. The clusters are also linked by longer-distance travels. Such travels may be made for business purposes (the greater majority in Europe at present) or for purposes such as changing a job and moving to a new town, or for social purposes etc. If we look at the first two, where man is a producer, we can see that in most cases the time framework within which these trips are sensibly analysed is unidirectional. A salesman is travelling to make new market contacts at some time in a company's history of development. A man moves at some time in the course of his career. Indeed we may even characterize a career as work viewed in an unidirectional time stream. By contrast man as a consumer commutes from his workplace to his home. This essentially takes place cyclically, hence over shorter distances and more frequently. At cyclic intervals, therefore, the national economic system collapses into a myriad of home-based systems with much weaker interconnection than the national economic system shows.

In this we find why it is so difficult to relate satisfactorily the analyses of residential areas of cities with the role of the city in the national economy. Basically, when the central city is functioning, the suburbs are a collection of lifeless artifacts, and when the suburbs are functioning, most of the central city is lifeless artifacts. The nation-state as a whole is composed of many different systems operating at different times and within different time reference frameworks.

2.8 Traditional geographical ideas tested by viewpoint

The definitions of the first order objects of study in geography as listed above may not appear to be remarkably different from traditional concepts; however, the more traditional concepts can be shown to be inferior with respect to the concept of the first order object of study.

Geography is commonly split into analytical parts known as economic geography, social geography etc. Such parts are in fact taxonomic classes of the properties of some of the component objects of the geographic system, separated from the system by a combination of the compositional and taxonomic viewpoints. The result can be more or less successful. If a complete factory is taken for study, clearly this is a real object, and it can be analysed as such, although whether or not that is economic geography is another matter. If its location is taken into account, then perforce it is necessary to relate the plant to the total system, and to all decision makers within that system, and to all their social and cultural preferences. This has been realised only very recently. If a given industry is analysed for a whole country, as is often the case, then that industry is usually mapped. But the objects thus mapped do not create the next highest first order object. The map represents the absolute space locations of an intellectual class. This group taken together is not volumetrically inclusive and connected, it has no morphology, and it cannot perform. The analogy has to be with the concept of plant community, although it is even weaker than that, in that the group is not necessarily even an areal aggregate.

Agricultural geography can be seen to suffer from the same sort of dilemma. The crops and farms can be mapped, but such a map in no way represents a performing system. The comment on it is usually restricted to chorological interpretation of a static kind. Time cannot be built satisfactorily into a non-performing object.

The distinction between the kinds of object studied can be useful first-stage concept in many kinds of geographical research. A small urban unit is quite often selected for research in the field, and such centres are often surveyed by groups of students being introduced to field techniques. If such a town is more of an areal aggregate than an object, then research into it as a unit is necessarily restricted, static and incomplete. Dormitory towns and satellite towns near large cities suffer in this respect. Small rural service centres are usually far more satisfactory.

Clearly the great difficulty in establishing first order objects arises at the scale where the individual plants and animals are to be grouped into the next highest object. In general we may say that at the level of geography, economics, vegetation studies, sociology, no discipline has satisfactorily defined for itself an object of study, simply because they are all studying aspects of the same object. The proliferation of viewpoint studies masquerading as first order objects of study has caused considerable difficulty and some very biased examples of the effects of man on different compositional classes of lower scale objects, or vice versa: e.g. man and plant, man and animals, man and economic institutions, etc. But it is understandable in that the jump from the scale of plants and animals to the total ecosystem or the geographic system is rather large and for a long time was not recognized for what it really was.

This leaves a large question as yet unanswered. The words *ecosystem* and *geographic system* have both been used. Do these two systems exist independently of each other? It was suggested above that the geographic system is in fact not as narrow as its definition might imply. If the notion of control is reintroduced, then it is clear that on the whole ecologists prefer to study a system that is not reflective of itself. There are no active decision centres within the system that try and alter the parameters which effect the operation of the system. But the ecosystem and the geographic system coexist in space, and are often one and the same thing. Any change made by man in the controlling parameters of the geographic system ultimately affects those systems which are referred to as the ecosystems. This simple fact has caused ecologists to go to areas where the effects of man changing the parameters of the system are least. Isolated and uninhabited islands, be they the Galapagos or Aldabra, are often chosen. At the other extreme, the argument about man and the ecosystem has now in the U.S.A. reached political proportions.

2.9 Regions and areal classes

A region in geography to date has always been defined in absolute space, although with more or less reference to a system operating in that space. These regions are always contiguous, and ultimately defined by a line drawn on the ground without any explicit references to the volumetric edges of objects defined within the system. The best object definitions in regional geography are probably those that define political countries as units within a large land mass. Thus, for example, a regional geography of Europe that starts with a division by country recognizes the principle of decision and control within a system. But this principle is usually irrationally abandoned and the next smallest scale of division is often made on physical environment characteristics. Within this space, defined in absolute space, a compositional listing of the various intellectual classes of objects follows, which then is the subject of the mystical operation known as regional integrations. This integration is performed on arbitrary absolute space groupings of compositional classes, without any attempt to suggest the system within which the items and objects of the classes perform. The whole has never been and never will be simply the sum of the parts, unless the whole is an areal aggregate and not an object. The whole, the system, the object, the gestalt, exists in its own right as more than the sum of the parts. It defines its own space. The identification of the space within which it exists cannot precede the identification of the object. Regional integration is logically dead.

2.10 Logical division and classification as reversible procedures

Regionalization should ideally be possible both by logical division and by classification. That the two reverse processes do not necessarily achieve the same thing in geography is because they have started without a clear definition of object. The whole world is an object, but it also defines the absolute space within which the lower scale object exists. But division according to absolute space will not achieve, except fortuitously, the definition of lower objects. Yet such a division is often made, because it avoids the problem of the definition of object inherent in classification. Regionalization by classification is nowadays rarely attempted on the basis of an object of absolute space like the site or the slope. More often it is attempted on some approximation of an areal aggregate of individual objects (e.g. farms) to an intellectual class. That is, an areal aggregate which is mostly composed of one class of objects may be defined as a region. Thus *both* location *and* intellectual class are taken to be significant. But the use of intellectual classes in science is simply to list examples of case replication so that true generalization can be made. By the inductive leap a result applying to one ant is a general principle applying to all ants, if it applies to everything within the intellectual class *ant*. Case replication is the principle requirement of such classification.

Case replication cannot occur with objects defined in absolute space. Every location is unique. But a study of cities, or a study of suburbs presupposes that there is replication. A suburb is defined by reference to a city, that is in the space relative to the city. The word itself is inherently a relative space word. Thus if geography is to generalize, it must be able to replicate cases, and it has to use relative space.

Therefore it would appear illogical to insist, as regionalization based on classification has done, that absolute location is relevant to the definition of some composite of intellectual class and location. If this constraint is abandoned, and logical division is no longer achieved on the basis of absolute space, then we find that it is possible to produce a grouping procedure that is reversible, that is to say the same divisions are produced, whether we start by dividing from the top, or we group from the bottom. The whole earth can obviously be subdivided into the two major systems land and water, between which there is little overlap in space, and within each of which there is a reasonable wholeness of performance. Within the land system there are the large systems which are dominated by the largest decision centres — the decision centres of sovereign states.

At the next level it is admittedly difficult to know whether or not some cities are to be defined as objects, depending on the degree to which it is possible to say that local decision centres control the growth of the city. But at the next level again it is clear that households, factories and schools can be identified. Grouping from these lower level objects upward will achieve the same results.

The reverse process can be seen to be the simple extension of the reciprocal nature of physiology and ecology as defined by Rowe. Thus Rowe shows that the physiology of an organism, the functioning of the organism as a result of the functioning of its organs, is the same as the ecology of the organs that constitute the organism. The ecology of the households, that is their relationship, and functioning within the wider system, and the ecology of the factories and schools is thus the physiology of the national state.

A further comment on the usefulness of the scale sequence of objects may be made here. Feibleman (1954) has shown that in the study of any one object level, we may need to go only to the level above and the level below to achieve both understanding and explanation. Understanding of an object is achieved by observing its ecological relationships, that is one may see what its function and purpose is. How it is enabled to carry out this functioning is revealed by a study of its physiology.

2.11 Concluding remarks and a quotation

Once we were agreed that areal differentiation and spatial variation were the aims of geography. Subsequently Ackerman (1963) suggested that we should be interested in systems theory. This message was accepted in that we have begun to use the word system, but not the concept. And just to make our acceptance of the word appear geographical, we have added our identifying label, spatial. Now we study spatial systems. This chapter suggests that object and system come first, and space comes second, more or less relevant, but always ancillary, depending on the circumstances. No subject has ever made space or time its object of study, except of course for something abstract like geometry. Space and time are both infinite, and, *per se*, infinitely empty. The historian does not study time; he studies men and the development of ideas, which do not happen to take place in the present. The geographer does not study space; he studies real living systems, which to be different, happen to be in different places.

I wish to end this chapter with rather a long quotation from Hoffmann (1959):

> What, after all, are these mystic entities space and time? We imagine space to be so smooth and precise we can define within it such a thing as a point — something having no size at all but a continuing location. Now, that is all very well in abstract thought. Indeed, it almost seems to be an unavoidable necessity. Yet if we imagine it in the light of quantum discoveries, do we not find the beginning of a doubt? For how would we try and fix such a disembodied location in actual physical space as distinct from the purely mental image of space we have within our minds? What is the smallest, most delicate instrument we could use in order to locate it? Certainly not our finger. That would suffice to point out a house, or a pebble, or even, with difficulty, a grain of sand. But for a point it is far too gross.
>
> What of the point of a needle, then? Better, but far from adequate.
>
> It is much as if we sought to observe a detail in a newspaper photograph. We look at the picture more closely but the tantalizing detail still escapes us. Annoyed, we bring a magnifying glass to bear upon it, and lo! our eager optimism is shattered. We find ourselves far worse off than before. What seemed to be an eye has dissolved into a meaningless jumble of splotches of black and white. The detail we had imagined was simply not there. Yet from a distance the picture looks perfect.
>
> Perhaps it is the same with space, and time too. Instinctively we feel they have infinite detail. But when we bring to bear on them our most refined techniques of observation and precise measurement we find that the infinite detail we had imagined has somehow vanished away. It is not space and time which are basic, but the fundamental particles of matter or energy themselves. Without these we find we could not have formed even the picture we instinctively have of a smooth, unblemished, faultless, and infinitely detailed space and time. These electrons and other fundamental particles, they do not exist in space and time. It is space and time which exist because of them.

3

The Object Observed

"By measuring the universe, Vishnu also took part in its creation."

(V. Ions, 1967)

3.1 Introduction by way of an example

Consider two regions of equal size. One we might take to be the London Basin, and another we might take to be an area of similar size around Kano in North Nigeria. If we take the regions to exist *a priori* as meaningful units to be studied and analysed we can make summary statements about either of them at any level of detail, such that the descriptions of both are of the same length and contain the same amount of information. We could say that the London Basin was a gentle syncline drained by one major river, in which was situated the capital city of London, containing about 6 million people. The Kano region of Nigeria is a flat savannah region of Nigeria with no major rivers, but including the central trading and agricultural town of Kano, with a population of about 100,000. We might even go to a further extreme, and make some remarks with the same amount of information about another region of similar size in the tundra areas of Canada.

The amount of detail recorded is arbitrary, and the points of significance are arbitrary. Some points might be more or less justified according to the interests of the person writing the report, or the person reading the report.

However, we have an intuitive feel that the more complex case to be

studied is the case of London, more complex because there are more
things there, and because the interrelationships between the things is
more complicated. This is because there are more different types of
things. Around Kano there are pastoralist herders and a few agricultura-
lists. We can describe their interrelationships with the city of Kano
reasonably easily since there are many of the same sort of thing, and
hence few connections possible between different things. If there are
many different things as in London, then the number of connections
possible between different types of things constituting different types
of connections is correspondingly larger.

Now suppose we look not at the areas but at two different systems.
Let us be precise, and state that there are such things as objects of which
the larger system is made up. These objects are such things as households
and factories, being the next smaller scale of object below the scale of
system which we might here call city and region. If we look at the London
region, and try to identify all the parts of which it is made and their
interrelationships we find that we have a very big problem. We also find
that perhaps the London Basin does not contain all of the city and
hinterland system of London. Suppose, for the sake of the argument,
we identify this system, and all its parts and relationships. We have an
enormous amount of information.

If we do the same for the Kano region, again limiting the scale shift
to the level of the household and the factory, we find that we accumu-
late much less information. This system is much less complex, and its
structure much more easily defined. Thus the first and most obvious
difference resulting from the concentration on system rather than area
is in the amount of information we need to define the one as opposed
to the other, and this amount of information is itself the first step in
defining what the structure of the two systems is like. To gain as much
information from the Kano region as from the London one, we would have
to go into other questions and other details. For example, we could go
into problems of kinship and family structure, which explain why the
object household is like it is. In doing so we must make it very clear that
we have moved into another scale of enquiry, and that the amount of
information we now have about the Kano region is no longer comparable
with that we have about the London region, since we are dealing with
different scales of enquiry.

It would seem one of the great weaknesses of regional geography as it
is at present written that we migrate from one scale of enquiry to another

without any particular order, and without very often being aware of what we are doing. We then find ourselves enmeshed in the problem that all things are related to all things, and that we can expand and contract our enquiry in any direction we choose, losing as we do so all hope of balance in the study and all hope of producing studies that are made on a comparable basis from area to area.

Not surprisingly, therefore, we find that it is necessary to be able to make some measure of the information we have about systems, and to be able to relate this information to the successive scales to which it belongs. We have to know what information is, and to relate it to the nesting principle of the scales of systems.

Later in the book we will consider more explicitly ways in which one can try to estimate the amount of information one has about various systems. But for the moment it is necessary to look further at the relationship between entitation and quantification.

3.2 The act of measurement

There are at least two ways of considering measurement. Firstly we may conceive that we are to allocate some quantity as an assessment of an immanent property of a thing; secondly we may conceive of measurement as an interaction between an observer and an observed thing. This distinction is important for geography, because both have been used without clear discrimination.

But, in order of priority, we must first note that both definitions insist on things. To quote Gerard in Langton (1972): "this qualitative recognition of the important systems, which I find it helpful to call entitation, is far more important than their measurement. Entitation must precede quantification; only when the right things have been found to measure are measurements worthwhile". If this is not so, then measurement and definition become inextricably inter-twined.

An example of this should make it very clear. Suppose that in one of the Cambridge College quadrangles I observe a lawn, surrounded on all sides by a path. I can ask someone to measure the area of the lawn, and they can do so without any problem. Suppose then I ask them to measure the area of the centre of the lawn — note that I am not asking them to find the central point. The person cannot do so without further instruction from me. I propose the definition that the centre is all those places more than 6 feet from any edge. The task is now completed. But note that the figure which is given depends entirely on my definition, which itself was a quantification (6 feet) related to a pre-existing thing – the lawn. Definition and measurement are interlinked.

In the same way the concept "population of a city" is arbitrary if the city is an arbitrary unit of space. The results of arbitrariness are arbitrary, hence meaningless, analyses. Berry, in Haggett (1965) notes that the rank size distribution of urban populations for England and Wales is "intermediate", with a "primate" large city section grafted on a rank-size smaller city continuum. Johnson (1967) notes that England and Wales have a perfect rank size distribution. The contradiction stems directly from the fact that the definition of city is arbitrary, a point we touched on above.

Similarly the discussion that follows must equally be arbitrary, or, less delicately, meaningless.

We take it, then, as axiomatic that some thing must precede quantification. But here we then come across the two concepts of measurement which I have already mentioned.

The first view (see for example Ellis, 1968) necessary to science is that we measure an immanent property of a thing irrespective of the means of measurement. For example I may measure the mass of an iron bar, and the scales I use may work on springs, on gas pressure, on balances and fulcrums, but we accept that the measurement will in all cases be the same and that it will record the value of weight which existed before the procedure.

The second view is that measurement is an interaction, and that it is impossible to separate the act from the quantity. On such a view the measurement of mass by springs would be different from that by balances – and so we could dismiss the idea as absurd. But in the social sciences all observers are trained to realize that a questionnaire in the hands of two different interviewers may elicit different responses from the same subject, or that the same subject may give the same interviewer different responses at different times. In psychology there are many tests that attempt to measure intelligence, and the very multiplicity of assessments they can give necessitates a further step, often in the form of factor analysis, where we attempt to reduce this welter of evidence to some underlying factor or construct. Is this construct an immanent property? The answer to this question is not always clear.

3.3 An infinity of variables

Given any object, there are an infinity of variables that may be observed on it. For example, we may observe a house. We can measure its age, its height, its width, degree of fungal infestation, the electrical resistance of the roof, its acoustic deadening effects with respect to Concorde, the hardness of its bricks or concrete, the stresses induced in the structure at the window apertures.. . .

The number of variables which may be measured clearly compounds the problem of deciding what is an immanent property, what is a derivative of such properties, and what are "interactive" measurements. A typical example may be found in almost any book on empirical urban analysis or on empirical studies of development. A country may be assessed for the number of telephones per head, the number of washing machines, its G.N.P., the growth rate of its G.N.P., the number of people with higher education, the number of lactating cows, the number of bulls per cow, the number of tractors, the average age of tractors, the *per capita* output of steel. In fact the number of numbers seems to be very large indeed. Yet it is very hard to decide which are important to a study of development and which are not.

Presumably these measurements have been made for some purpose. But in fact the purpose is often very vague and general. National data collection agencies provide data for certain variables which they believe to be of general importance, although most analysts have great difficulty in obtaining exactly what they want in the right format, and a positive feedback relationship develops between what is used in one analysis and what is provided for the next.

It is clearly important to derive ways of classifying different kinds of variables, and, further, it is important to distinguish quite early between those that are to be used for a description of state, and those that are to be used for an explanation of the state.

3.4 Description, explanation: uniqueness and generality

This section contains several comments on the ways in which we can use data, and is, I think, illustrative of the confusion that often lurks beneath the surface where the precise roles of description, explanation, uniqueness, and generality have not been adequately specified. For convenience, three short sections are introduced separately before stating the general position they imply.

(a) Description and explanation in circular argument

The U.S.A. might well be described as being economically advanced. The economic explanation of its state of advancement is that it is economically advanced. Economies may be classified according to their economic advancement. The explanation of their membership of an economic class is in their economic advancement. Economies that are not as advanced as others are seen to be lacking those functions which have defined the advanced economies as being advanced. What it is that is advanced or not advanced can be seen as the area within which statistics have been collected, and the explanation and description of its state are one and the same thing. The essential nature of the economic system of the area is unknown and not described.

The same sort of circularity has been observed in ecology. Margalef (1958) has shown that if heterogeneity of an ecological unit is defined in terms of biocoenology, then biocoenology can hardly be explained in terms of heterogeneity in a satisfactory manner. His answer to this problem is the selection of a measure of heterogeneity which is independent of any biocoenotic concepts.

(b) Uniqueness and generality

Let us extend the above example to a two-country case, and compare the U.S.A. and the U.S.S.R. for three variables: size of population, number of business enterprises, and gross national product. The relative positions, low or high, for the two countries for these three might be: low, high; high, low; high, low. If then we wish to raise the low level of the G.N.P. in Russia, do we raise the number of business enterprises in the U.S.S.R., or lower the population or both or neither? The reactions to this question might be several. For example, the enterprises are not equivalent, being ministries and factories in U.S.S.R., and corporations and shops etc. in the U.S.A. Again, population may be an approximation for demand in the U.S.A., and an important part of growth, but consumer demand in the U.S.S.R. is not the final arbiter of the amount or kind of production. Or, to voice a simple objection, perhaps the environment of the U.S.A. is more genial and benign.

The crux of the issue here is that in attempting to make generalizations, we use variables which are so general as to be applicable to all countries — for example population, G.N.P. etc. But the generality is in the nature of the *variables,* and not necessarily in the nature of the *things* which are being observed. Hence if the level of advancement is *defined* in terms of these *variables,* we may find great difficulty in explaining the observed values except in terms of themselves. In short, we become circular because generality is incorrectly defined.

The example can be more graphic. Suppose we have two animals, an X and a Y. The X is seen to have the higher reproductive rate than the Y, and the Y is seen to have a fixed temperature whereas the X has an environmental temperature. Given this amount of knowledge, we can clearly say that the difference is that one has a higher reproductive rate and a variable temperature, and therefore if we are interested in raising the reproductive rate of the Y then we must make its temperature variable. This seems plausible, except that we do not know for sure whether the reproductive rate is dependent on the independent variable temperature, or whether the reverse is true, or whether neither is true. Given some extra information, such as that animals with constant temperatures are not the same kind as animals with variable temperatures, we might begin to wonder a little more. Perhaps X is a lizard, and Y a cow, and we cannot change the temperature of a cow, and even if we could the lizard is totally irrelevant.

(c) Input, output, and the non-unique system

There is a central tenet in systems theory which says, the input and the output of a system do not uniquely determine the nature of the system. In other words if we know the input and the output, then there are many ways in which the two can be linked. A radio signal can be the same to two radio sets, and each can produce the same sound as a result, but one might be a transistor and the other a valve set. The nature of the two is very different, though both perform the same function.

It would appear that the nature of the object cannot be determined from the input and output, and this may cause considerable rethinking of the present approaches to economic growth and development. That the lizard is the real animal cannot be proved from input and output variables, though, having seen and identified one lizard, then one might be able to guess that another set of similar variable measurements do also refer to a lizard.

This tenet is of course familiar to all who write computer programs. There are many ways that a program may be written to derive a certain output from specified input. That is true of simple programs which evaluate an algebraic expression, but the truth is even more graphic in those cases where an algorithm is needed for a solution to a problem. In network analysis there are now several algorithms available for finding the shortest path through the network.

It is also applicable to any model builder. The correspondence of model input and output with observed input and output proves nothing about the "truth" of the model. As De Bono (1969) puts it:

> One hates to admit it, but in the behavioural sciences, lack of imagination serves as proof . . .
> It is not that one is uninterested in some 'true story' that will allow one to make some predictions with confidence. The lack of any possible alternatives may indicate the excellence of your story, but it may also indicate the poverty of your imagination.

Those students who have examined the alternative explanations of the rank size rule may also be well aware of this tenet. Variables do not define the nature of objects.

(d) Some interim conclusions

I cannot at this juncture make sweeping observations which will eliminate all the above pitfalls; in so far as I can make any useful comments, they will have to wait until further material is presented.

Suffice it to say that it is quite clear that observation is not the simple task we usually pretend, nor is the selection of variables for use as state description and explanation simple. These problems are bound up in the nature of objects, their qualities as well as quantities, and our conceptions of uniqueness and generality. In the following sections I put forward one method that has come to my attention for classifying variables, according to two kinds of evolution, some comments on determinate systems in science, and other issues that seem to me to be relevant.

3.5 Specific and general evolution

In this section I put forward some ideas based on evolution, which divide variables into two categories. But it is important to note that the pre-supposition behind this is that we are observing complex functioning wholes, in their environmental setting.

The notion of evolution has been reintroduced into cultural anthro-

pology primarily through the exertions of White (1949). The significance
of this is seen by White as reuniting anthropology with the main stream
of science, since in science evolution has been a very successful concept,
and it can be a useful concept in Cultural Anthropology as well. He
applies the distinction to movements that result from evolutionary
change. In particular we may distinguish between general and specific
evolution. The latter may be expressed as being the change in an organism
to adapt it better to its environment, and as such the change is always to
be assessed relative to the environmental niche under consideration. On
the other hand general evolution is not concerned with a relative advancement by one organism with respect to its environment, but rather
with a general advancement whereby one organism may be seen to be
superior to another organism of a different type, in that it exhibits a
higher life form. Such evolution is not necessarily a strict unilinear change
through time. Protozoa still exist on earth, and so do reptiles and birds,
which evolved from the general vertebrate line before the origin of
man. But though all exist now, man is superior to a reptile, and a reptile
to a fish. The reason is to be found in that the higher life forms exhibit
differences in performance and structure. In performance, they have a
higher energy concentration per unit of weight, and they put it to work
in developing and maintaining their structure. In this way a man is
superior to a mouse, a mouse to a goldfish, a goldfish to a crab, and
a crab to an amoeba.

However, Sahlins and Service (1960) realize that this is difficult to
quantify accurately. They suggest that general progress may
be expressed in terms of organization. The greater the energy-harnessing
ability, the greater the complexity of organization. This is embraced
within the concept of the level of integration. However, it must be noted
that the level of integration is used here in a slightly wider sense than
Rowe's above, and is said by Sahlins to have three aspects. One object is
at a higher level of integration than another when it has more parts and
subparts; when its parts are more specialized; and when the whole is
more effectively integrated. Thus general progress in life proceeds in the
development of specialized organs and organic subsystems, such as res-
piratory, reproductive, digestive and the like, and also in the development of special mechanisms of integration, like the central nervous system and the brain. When organisms are compared on this basis, overall
progress is clearly seen in the evolutionary record. This thesis is developed and applied to human cultural systems, and the value of the

approach would seem to be justified. In particular here it may be noted that White (1949) typifies culture as the total man system, and specifies the main facts of the culture to be technology, social organization, and philosophy. Technology is the major determinant, in that it is this which is a permissive factor for the development of social organizations of one kind or another. Some cultures are of higher life-form than others in the terms of general evolution (although higher does not in any way mean good in a moral sense) and in the terms of the amount of energy they harness *per capita*. This does not determine the nature of the social organization, so that it is possible for cultures of high general evolutionary order to have different specific evolutionary social systems. This aspect is specific and not general. It can be seen in relative terms only, to the task of aiding the adaptation of that society to its own environmental and historical position.

Above all, it can be seen that the notion of general evolution is not related to time or place, nor to the sorts of parts and subparts a culture has to develop. It is related only to thermodynamic achievement and the number of parts, subparts, their specialization, and the development of the control mechanism. In short, the structure and functioning of the society.

In these ideas we find that some of the problems relating to the similarity and the difference between the U.S.A. and the U.S.S.R. can be partially resolved. The fact that one has private corporations and the other state ministries is ascribable to specific evolution — specific to the history and location of each country. These differences are unique, in the sense that there is no common variable which can be used to indicate merely differences in value between the two countries. On the other hand it is often remarked that the two countries are equifinal — i.e. going towards the same end state. They both have super-power status, and perhaps converging standards of living. In the sense that both these countries now possess and exert world-wide military and political power based on their own indigenous technologies, then both are at similar levels in terms of general evolution. In this context it may then appear that ideology is part of specific and not general evolution.

There is also one other facet of this distinction that is worth remarking. Specific evolution means that an organism is more highly adapted to a specific locality. General evolution, although defined in terms of complexity of organization, does also mean greater freedom from environmental constraint. The mammals have a wider terrestrial range than the reptiles because of their homeostatic temperature. Similarly the physical environments which advanced countries can profitably occupy are extending.

Lastly, it is important to note that the specific and the unique are mostly surface features, whereas the general are usually deeper aspects of organization which are capable of superficial expression in a variety of ways.

3.6 The determinate system

The reader might be forgiven for wondering when this text will get around to asking why one should make any studies of the object; what is the purpose of it all? The present section looks at the simplest aspect of this question and its answer. The object has been specified in terms of a functional whole — the idea of performance has been stressed. It follows then that study of the object must first of all concentrate on study of behaviour — that is change in time, or in some other interval that has correspondence with time.

No system in science is understood until it is single and determinate, as Ross Ashby (1956, p.40) has pointed out. Systems that appear to be multi-valued are usually so in appearance only, because we have not yet defined the correct variables for understanding the single transform operation. This can be illustrated quite clearly and simply. Suppose we have a swinging pendulum as the system to be determined. There is an infinite number of variables that can be measured for this system, as for any other. The pendulum has length, position, mass, temperature, electrical conductivity, crystalline structure, chemical impurities, reflecting power, tensile strength, bacterial contamination.

Suppose, to explain the swinging pendulum, we suggested the following variable and the associated transform of the variable over a given time interval, say half a second. The variable is the angular deviation. Now suppose the variable is first observed at $+30°$ at time $T1$, and at time $T2$ it is at $+10°$. From $T2$ we continue the observation and find at $T3$ the variable measurement $-15°$ (the other side). Thus so far the transforms are:

$$
\begin{array}{lll}
\text{from} & +30° & +10° \\
\text{to} & +10° & -15° \\
\end{array}
$$

To check the transforms we stop the pendulum and put it back to +10°, let it go, and observe it at the correct time interval again. This time the transform is

$$\text{from} \quad +10°$$

$$\text{to} \quad + 3°$$

The transform of the variable +10° is not single valued. We know that in the first case the pendulum was already moving fast, having come from +30°, whereas in the second case it was started with no speed at +10°. So we define a new variable, angular deviation: angular velocity. This one yields a single transform.

The discovery of missing variables has sometimes been of extreme scientific importance; Newton's discovery of momentum is one such. The discovery of vitamins in biology is another (Ross Ashby, 1956, p.40).

It may seem that these examples are too related to positivistic science to be of value to geography. Ultimately this may indeed prove to be the case, but for the moment the case is not proven. We have to be sure of the origin of the difference between geography and science to make such a statement, and at present I feel that the difference is more apparent than real. The number of variables used in geography — our peculiar multivariate problem — might appear to be what stands in the way of our search for determinate systems. But, on the other hand the difference may be in the fact that in science the distinction between general and specific has no value — that all variables can be "superficial". If there are hidden variables that might make our systems determinate, then it is not necessarily true that these will be surface manifestations, but, rather, they could be of the nature of general statements about levels of organization.

3.7 Structuralism

At this stage it is impossible not to introduce some example from structuralism of the notion of underlying comparability. Obviously I cannot go deeply into the literature at this juncture, but the points can be made neatly by example.

Lévi-Strauss, in Boudon (1971), has examined the relationship between the marriage rules of two different societies, the Kareira and

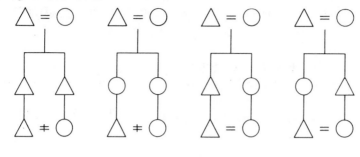

Kareira

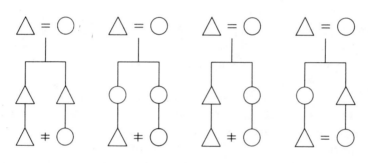

Tarau

Fig. 3.1. Marriage rules for the Kareira and the Tarau. (From Boudon, 1971)

the Tarau. The rules that govern marriage between first cousins in the two societies are as shown in Fig. 3.1. The two sets appear to be different, and certainly in both societies the verbal expression of the rules is also different. But if we delve deeply into the underlying order of these systems of relationships, it is possible to show that there is one way in which they can be given a common root.

We can derive a set of axioms that are expressed in general language. Quoting from the same source we can give the axiom set as follows:

1. Each member of a society S belongs to a marriage type.
2. Two individuals may marry if they belong to the same marriage type and only if they do.
3. The marriage type of an individual is determined only by his sex and the marriage type of his parents.

4. Two boys whose parents are of different type are of different type themselves. The same applies to two girls whose parents are of different type.
5. The permission or prohibition of marriage between two individuals of different sex depend only on the kinship tie between them.
6. No man can marry his sister.
7. It is always possible for some descendants of two individuals to marry.

This axiom set is interesting in that it has said nothing specific about any specific society. To make it specific we would have to specify what was meant by the word "type". It is also interesting in that the surface concept of axiom 5, which says that marriage is determined by kinship, is consistent because of the previous axioms 1—4. That is, rules may be expressed consistently with respect to kinship, because the previous axioms will always give the same marriage-type relationships to given kinship relationships.

The next step is therefore to give substance to the idea of marriage "type". Transition tables are prepared for the societies under observation, as in Table 3.1. Now it is important to note that for the axiom set to be valid these transition tables must be consistent with the set and not contravene them. But there may be many such tables which are consistent with a feasible set of axioms, giving rise to the possibility of defining not only those sets of transitions which have been observed, but also to a range of "alternative societies" which have not been observed but which do not contravene the axioms either.

Using Table 3.I we can demonstrate as in Fig. 3.2. that we can generate the correct rules for the two example societies. Note that the illustration is not complete, as it is also necessary to demonstrate that all other marriage type possibilities in Fig. 3.2. will give the same result, but that is left for the reader to confirm if he so wishes.

The significance of this is that what appear to be two arbitrary sets of marriage rules can in fact be shown to have a similar underlying base. Not only that, but an examination of this base reveals interpretations of it that make it easier to state general rules. From axioms 2 and 6 we know that sisters and brothers must always be of different types, and we also know that the definition of permissible marriages is dependent upon permutations of a person's parents' type. From this we can deduce that marriage between parallel cousins is always impossible, whereas

Table 3.I

Kareira transition rules		
Type of parents	Type of son	Type of daughter
1	3	4
2	4	3
3	1	2
4	2	1

Tarau transition rules		
Type of parents	Type of son	Type of daughter
1	4	2
2	3	1
3	1	4
4	2	3

marriage between non-parallel cousins is not necessarily impossible, and the actual rules which obtain in any particular society will depend upon the type transitions prevailing. (A parallel cousin is the offspring of a mother's sister or a father's brother.) In other words we know by an examination of the axiom set that certain kinds of transition situations are impossible for all societies, and the actual rules of marriage in these circumstances will all be the same. But in those aspects of the transition tables which do not have to be the same to comply with the axioms we may find different observances in different societies.

Without going into detail I would like in passing to mention that structuralism in linguistics in pursuing similar goals. In Chomsky's Transformation Grammar (see for example Lyons, 1970), a set of generative rules is invoked to explain the evolution from an underlying phrase structure to two or more surface structures of language that are different but convey the same meaning, for example "The man may have opened the door", and "The door may have been opened by the man". Quoting Lyons,

> The base rules generate an indefinitely large set of underlying phrase markers (which represent the deep structure of all the sentences characterised by the system); and these are converted into derived phrase markers (which represent the surface structure of the sentences) by the transformational rules, most of which (apart from "stylistic" rules) are now obligatory.

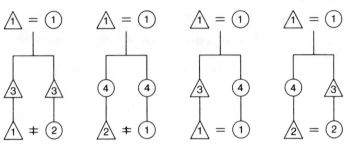

Kareira

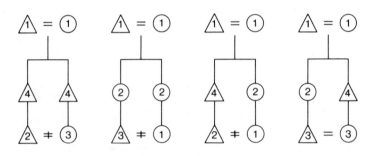

Tarau

Fig. 3.2. Marriage types for the Kareira and Tarau.

3.8 Summary

This chapter is almost bound to end in mid-air. There can be no neat conclusions, but some summary remarks and questions can be made.

We have seen that measurement is not necessarily always the simple act of assigning a quantity to some immanent property of a thing. Sometimes it is a property of an interaction between an observer and a thing. In the case of structuralism we might even be tempted to say that the structure is a property of the observer's understanding of the thing — that is that the set of axioms is neither a property of the Kareira nor the Tarau, but of the anthropologist. Certainly when we turn to Information Theory it will become abundantly clear that Entropy, as uncertainty, is a property of the observer and not the system. But there are areas of

doubt that remain. Psychologists take Chomsky's work seriously enough
to explore the hypothesis that it is not just a property of his understanding of the structure of language, but is the actual means whereby
people generate sentences — in other words it is a real property of
the human brain.

In the comments both on evolution and on structures we have seen
that the surface manifestation may be but one of many possible results
of an underlying order. We have therefore raised the possibility that, as
was stressed in earlier chapters, it is not only convenient but it is sometimes necessary to consider other things that do not exist, but could
exist, to explain what in reality we observe. Indeed we will find that
the only possible definition of the concept of organization will be made
in just such terms.

Covertly, too, we have slowly been drifting away from a concentration
on an "object" to sets of "objects", be they people in societies or
groups or societies. It is in relation to sets of things that we are able to
raise the questions of order and complexity, but these questions still
relate to clearly defined scale levels. It is, however, necessary to enter a
note of caution at this stage lest the reader confuse two kinds of hierarchies of scale levels. Firstly we have the hierarchy of objects, wherein
each complex whole is composed of a set of complex wholes of the next
lowest level. Secondly we have scale levels of abstraction in structuralism
and in the consideration of the problems of uniqueness and generality in
systems, which are often referred to by such terms as surface and deep
or underlying, which are concerned with the way that component parts
are put together, whether or not these component parts are objects or
rules or are simply ideas.

The greatest advantage of the pursuit of basic underlying order is that
we need not necessarily drop the goal of showing that systems are determinate in the same way as science attempts. We need not remain for
ever embedded in multivariate complexity, since most abstraction is in
fact simplification. Nor need we indulge in circular argument, where definition and explanation endlessly chase each other in circuits that are
obscured by the volumes of variables introduced, where first one then
another variable is taken as given and independent and the other dependent. Margalef's observation on this point is also a plea for deeper
understanding of structure.

As promised, the discussion here must end in mid-air; next we turn
to the problem of sets of objects and the definition of system.

Part II

On Systems of Interdependent Parts

4

The Definition of System

"The physical world consists of units of a small number of different kinds, and there are causal laws governing the simpler structures that can be built out of such units, causing such structures to fall into a rather small number of discretely differing kinds."

(Bertrand Russell)

4.1 The definition of "System"

Probably the most commonly quoted definition of a system is that of Hall and Fagen (1956): "A system is a set of objects with relationships between the objects and between their attributes". Hall and Fagen caution that their definition is not precise in the mathematical or philosophical sense and therefore expound at length on what is meant by object, attribute, and relationship. But those people who adhere to their definition have not been so cautious, and the definition has grown to mean all things to all men.

Chorley and Kennedy (1971) have defined a system as "a structured set of objects and/or attributes. These objects and attributes consist of components or variables (i.e. phenomena which are free to assume variable magnitudes) that exhibit discernible relationships with one another and operate together as a complex whole, according to some observed pattern". Specifically these two authors are considering the definition of "system" within the context of physical geography, whereas this book is concerned with human geography, but nevertheless some useful comment can be made on this definition. The phrasing, particularly by the inclusion of "and/or" implies that a structured set of attributes is possible. Hence one finds that a diagram appears such as that on their pages 156 and 157, reproduced here as Fig. 4.1, which raises a number of points.

Firstly, one asks, how can a set of unrelated (in this context uncorrelated) variables be grouped together as a subsystem? Why are they in the same box if they are unrelated? A different view of a subsystem might suggest a functioning whole within a larger whole, and one may think of cells within organs, braking systems in cars, the system of sap distribution in trees.

Secondly, many of the variables do not in fact refer to known objects i.e. this tree, that plant, but to sample properties of classes of objects. This kind of aggregation is a real problem in many sciences, but however one looks at it, the model based on aggregation is some distance removed from the ideal state of one:one correspondence between model and system. A simple illustration of the problem is the aggregation of data from many parts of a country to produce the model on a pin's head, so beloved of the economist, of the relationships between different sectors of the national economy, e.g. labour and employment, money supply and market demand. The information loss in this aggregation is enormous. The resulting model then cannot be compared too easily with the system from which the data was taken, and hence policy decisions which are supposed to bring about a desirable relationship between such sectors often have undesirable or unforeseen consequences in, say, one development region.

Thirdly, attributes are assumed to be variables of properties of classes of objects. But we know that there can be an infinity of variables measured on any object. Thus, if any real system is modelled in terms of variables, we can have an infinite number of models of that system, and then the model system behaves as much in response to its own definition as it does to the system being modelled.

The definition I most favour as being potentially useful for human geographers is largely taken from Rothstein (1956): "A system is a set of objects where each object is associated with a set of feasible alternative states: and where the actual state of any object selected from this set is dependent in part or completely upon its membership of the system. An object that has no alternative states is not a functioning part but a static cog."

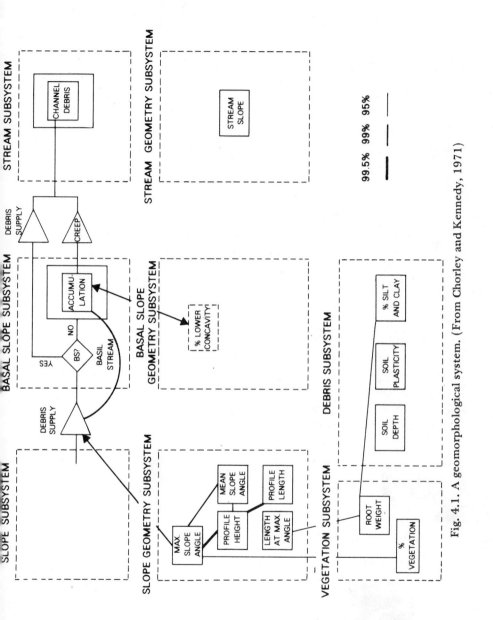

Fig. 4.1. A geomorphological system. (From Chorley and Kennedy, 1971)

Let us consider a farming landscape. Within this landscape there are many "objects" which we can call fields. Each field can be used for growing one of a variety of crops although one admits that it might be suitable for some rather than others by virtue of soil type and climate; nevertheless the extreme determinist view that a particular field can grow one and only one type of crop is not compatible with the facts of most landscapes, if of any. The farmer has to make a choice as to which crops to grow. He may require feed for animals, he may wish to avoid the disease risks involved with growing only one crop on all his land. He may wish to plant the crop that needs most care nearest to his farmstead. These kinds of influence we can call within-farm conditional influences. But there are also larger scale influences where, for example, if everyone in a country grew barley and nothing but barley the price for the crop would be too low and no farm could make a profit. So the farmer is also influenced in his choices by the amounts of various crops being produced by others and the market demands. Thus the actual state of a field is conditioned by the membership of the farm within a system of many farms, and by its own membership of a system of fields within the farm.

Within this same landscape we can typify the static cog as an immovable 30 acre intrusion of barren rock. There is no alternative set of uses for it and it plays no functional part in the system. It can indeed be an obstacle, around which tractors make daily detours, but it is certainly not a functional member of the farm system.

In ecology we find a similar definition of a system. Margalef (1968) states, "Every system is a set of different elements or components, or units, any one of which can exist in many different states, such that the selection of a state is influenced by the states of the components of the system".

4.2 System-scale and local-scale determinacy

This section introduces in a qualitative manner some concepts considered quantitatively in a later section below.

The components that compose a system must be in a state which is at least in part dependent upon its membership of the system. But we have not said how much the state of these component objects is determined by the system, and we have left open an avenue for the object to influence its own state. In fact, we are saying that determinacy can exist at two scales, the system scale, and the local (i.e. individual object) scale. Qualitatively we can assess the importance of each kind of determinacy in a system, and we find that we have a scale which runs from "no system determinacy — complete local determinacy" to "complete system determinacy — no local determinacy".

As an example of complete system-scale determinacy we can quote *Brave New World*. In that book the number of people incubated is controlled, and once "born" each is assigned to be a certain type, e.g. an Alpha or a Beta. Each person is then continuously trained to play his assigned role and no other. The basic unit, a person, is associated with a set of alternative state, but the society controls absolutely which kind of person he shall be. Another example of complete systems-scale determinacy is the Central Place Landscape (Fig. 4.2). According to the economic

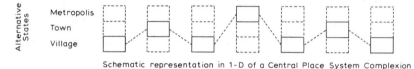

Schematic representation in 1-D of a Central Place System Complexion

Fig. 4.2. Schematic representation across a central place hierarchy.

demand functions built into the model, the division principle (i.e. the selection of $K = 3$ or 4 etc), and the site of the central metropolis, then the actual state of all other places is completely determined. Before the selection of the central metropolis, all places have the same chance of being villages, or the same chance of being towns, etc., so that we might in fact characterize an isotropic plain as a plain where all places had the same probability distribution over alternative functions. But once the metropolis is chosen then all places are determined to be villages or towns as the case may be.

An example of complete local determinacy would be a landscape where all places were exactly determined by their own local conditions. If all places that have harbours become port towns, and all gaps in the chalk become colonized by gap towns, and all snowy mountain areas develop ski resorts, then we would have such a landscape. Such indeed is the thesis of geographical determinism.

But of course it is nonsense. There is a limit to the number of ports a country such as the United Kingdom needs, hence many sea lochs in the highlands have not been developed as ports. Those harbours that are developed lie close to the centres of industrial production and demand. Thus a place becomes what it is both by its own local virtues and its relationship with the rest of the national system. The notion of geographical possibilism is, of course, a statement saying that some determinacy other than the local scale exists.

The concept of systems scale determinacy might seem to raise some serious issues about the freedom of will of an individual decision maker. Complete system determinacy could be paralleled with a Skinnerian view of absolute conditioning. However, I do not think that this has to be so: one can talk both of the free will to make a certain decision and also of the effectiveness of a decision. The state of the system may exert some pressures and influences on a decision maker; he may nevertheless choose his own course of action, but the results of his actions and those of many other decision makers do not necessarily achieve the desired objectives. In this context it is interesting to make some observations on the loss of a clear distinction between urban simulation models and urban gaming simulation models. In the former game-playing participants have never been included, in the latter the game-playing decision maker is the original distinctive component. But in the more sophisticated urban game it has become apparent that even with different players playing the same game on different occasions, the results can be replicated. Interested readers are referred to MIKEGASIMO (Milton Keynes Gaming Simulation Model) (Sarley, 1971). I have come to the same kinds of conclusions with a farming game (Chapman, 1973a) run at a high enough level of sophistication.

4.3 Change in systems

The concepts of system-scale and local scale determinacy can also give us an insight into the problems change in systems. In systems which are of concern to geography, the structure is usually evolving and changing over time. The doctor studying human bodies is in many ways more fortunate than we since the time scale of human physical evolution is so long that such change can be ignored. The study of this change is one of the most important aspects of a systems framework, but it is also one of the most difficult.

If we consider the system, such as a Central Place Landscape, where there is complete system scale determinacy, then every part is exactly and completely specified to be what it is by membership of the system. It is then obvious that change in this system is impossible. For change to occur in a part, for a moment it must go to some state other than that which the system has determined, but this is impossible. In the Christaller landscape a village cannot spontaneously become a town.

For change to occur some external agency must interfere. In a production line in a factory each machine, each man, has his place and his role; they are determined with respect to the production system. Companies therefore have an agency which is external to the production line, the board of directors and the management, whose job it is to introduce new machines and new productive processes when necessary.

Obviously we can very quickly get enmeshed in an argument here about the definition of internal and external, or indeed of system closure. But if we sidestep that for the moment, then we can see that a system which changes spontaneously must allow some degree of local determinacy, at the same time it must have some degree of system determinacy to be a system. We can note that in our own society we do not have complete system determinacy because the society can still exist with plus or minus 1000 railwaymen, plus or minus 1000 teachers etc. There is some latitude for change. Indeed, a latitude for change is essential not only in numbers in occupations, but in keeping alive for people within our society their original ability to be in alternative states. One of the problems of the comparatively long period of success by the same industries in our Development Regions has been that labour has become conditioned by and suitable for only one kind of occupation. Thus external agencies, either governmental or private firms, have had to develop retraining schemes in these areas.

The way in which change in one component will affect others is also important. If change in one almost immediately causes changes in all others, then we will have an unstable system which fluctuates rapidly in time. But if change in any one of any degree never changes any other then we have no system. Obviously the system changes by some controlled process, where we can ascribe the control to two aspects. Firstly, there are thresholds of change* which have to be reached by components before their change can affect others and secondly, there may be a re-

---

* In Chapter 6 the meaning of "change in a part which does not affect other parts" will be examined more deeply. From the system's point of view such changes cannot be recognized — it does not "know" of it.

stricted number of other components which they will influence. We can also turn this statement round and say that: given change in one component, other components will receive varying amounts of information about that change, and will regulate in various degrees their reaction to the receipt of that information. Thus systems change and system stability are closely tied up with the concepts of regulation to which we will return later.

Langton (1972) has rightly seen in this problem of system change the real reason why normative model building in geography has seemed to be so remote from empirical systems, "since the forging of links between studies of long term geographical change and theoretical locational analysis may be regarded as one of the major methodological puzzles of the subject". The same kind of concern with change is noted by Pahl (1965, p.222): "It is my view that mathematical and experimental models cannot be fully exploited in either geography or sociology until conceptual models of changing situations provide a better foundation from which to work".

4.4 Systems complexions quantified

This section demonstrated quantitatively the meaning of many of the terms we have used so far. The discussion is based on Fig. 4.3.

(a) The definition of complexion, ensemble, and organization

Suppose we have a society of five people. Each of these people, who are represented by the numbers 1–5 in Fig. 4.3, are associated with a vector of alternative states, in this case the states A, B and C. We could suppose that these states represented workers, teachers and bank managers. We take as given that there are certain demands created by the society for a certain number of people in each profession – here these are represented by the System Part Requirements, which are given at the right-hand side of the diagram. We assume that there will be a need for three workers, one teacher, and one bank manager.

These requirements are of course marginal constraints – in this case constraints on the vectors of probability of the alternative states of each of the parts. Note that the sum of the probabilities for A across all five people is 3, and that for B and C the sum is in each case 1. But note that the probabilities also satisfy the other marginal constraints – that they

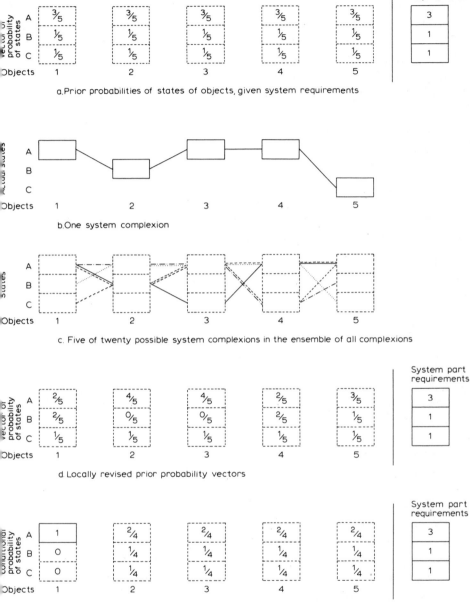

a. Prior probabilities of states of objects, given system requirements

b. One system complexion

c. Five of twenty possible system complexions in the ensemble of all complexions

d. Locally revised prior probability vectors

e. Conditional probabilities of state for objects 2, 3, 4, 5 after object 1 allocated as an 'A', probilities calculated from Figure 1

Fig. 4.3. Alternative states, complexions and ensembles.

sum to one. It is not necessary that all the probabilities for any given state across all people are the same — but we will introduce this complexity below.

Now at any one time the objects can only be in a single state. At any one time we will therefore observe a complexion — that is to say a selection, as in Fig. 4.3b — where all the five people are specified in one and only one state.

Given merely the knowledge we have so far, that is to say *a priori*, we can suspect that many complexions are possible. In fact we could surmise that 20 are possible, of which five are shown in Fig. 4.3c. The set of all alternative complexions is known as the system ensemble.

We are now in a position to define Organization. Organization is measured as the extent to which the *a posteriori* entropy of the observed ensemble is less than the *a priori* expected entropy of the ensemble:

$$O = H_E^* - H_{obs} \tag{4.1}$$

where O is organization, H_E^* is the *a priori* expected entropy of the ensemble, and H_{obs} is the *a posteriori* observed entropy of the ensemble.

We will tackle the meaning of these terms separately.

(b) The *a priori* expected entropy of the ensemble

Although Rothstein (1956) gives the same meaning for the word organization, his definition is superficially slightly different. He observes that organization is the extent to which the entropy of the ensemble is less than the sum of the entropies of the alternative states of the parts.

We find, then, that there is an equivalence between what I call the *a priori* expected entropy of the ensemble and what he calls the sum of the entropies of the alternative states of the parts. The difference indicates the two ways in which the quantity can be calculated.

In our example, Fig. 4.3c, we noted that there were 20 possible complexions, if we had no extra information to the contrary. We can calculate this figure in the normal fashion for combinations of C things taken at a time from P things.

Suppose we allocate in terms of the three As first. We find the first A can be allocated to any of five objects, the second to any of four objects, the third to any of three. But the order of choosing is not important since all will be As. Thus we have a combination of three things taken from five.

Number of ways of allocating three As $= \dfrac{5 \times 4 \times 3}{3 \times 2 \times 1}$

We then allocate a B from the 2 objects left. We then have the combination of one thing taken from two.

Number of ways of allocating one $B = \dfrac{2}{1}$

Lastly, the number of ways of allocating one C from the last remaining object is:

Number of ways of allocating one C from one object $= 1$

Overall the number of complexions is: $\dfrac{5 \times 4 \times 3}{3 \times 2 \times 1} \times \dfrac{2}{1} \times \dfrac{1}{1}$

which is 20.

Note that if we tried to allocate the B and the C first and then three As we would have:

$\dfrac{5}{1} \times \dfrac{4}{1} \times \dfrac{3 \times 2 \times 1}{3 \times 2 \times 1} = 20$, the same as before.

Given that there are 20 complexions in the ensemble of complexions, and given that there is no information to suppose that they are not equally probable, then since one complexion has to exist, and therefore the sum of the probabilities of the different complexions must be 1, the probability of the ith complexion is equal to all others and:

$$p_i = \frac{1}{20} = \frac{3 \times 2 \times 1}{5 \times 4 \times 3} \times \frac{2}{1} \times \frac{1}{1}$$

Now let us look at the question of the probability of the complexions from the viewpoint of the objects. We will go through an allocation sequence. We will allocate the objects in order 1 through 5 to be in the states indicated by the complexion in Fig. 4.3b.

Before any allocation takes place the probability that 1 is an A is $p(A : 1) = 3/5$.

After allocation we arrive at the situation in Fig. 4.3e. The probability that 1 is an A is now 1, and all the other probabilities have to change accordingly. All the remaining vectors of probability associated with the set of alternative states from the remaining objects now become vectors of conditional probability, that is conditioned by the information we now have that 1 is an A. As before the sum of each object's vector must be unity and, as before, the sum of the probabilities of objects being A must still be 3, and of being B and C must still be 1.

Figure 4.3e shows this situation where all these constraints are met. We note that the ratio of the probabilities of the remaining objects being in any given state is the same as before, in this case all are still equally probable.

At the next move we allocate 2 to be a B. We note that the conditional probability of 2 being this B is:

$$p(B : 2/A : 1) = 1/4$$

Having allocated 2, we now derive a new set of conditional probability vectors as follows:

$$
\begin{array}{cccccc}
A & 1 & 0 & 2/3 & 2/3 & 2/3 \\
B & 0 & 1 & 0 & 0 & 0 \\
C & 0 & 0 & 1/3 & 1/3 & 1/3 \\
  & 1 & 2 & 3 & 4 & 5
\end{array}
$$

If we continue with this for the whole complexion we find that the probability of the complexion is:

$$p(A : 1) \times p(B : 2/A : 1) \times p(A : 3/A : 1, B : 2) \times$$

$$p(A : 4/A : 1, B : 2, A : 3) \times p(C : 5/A : 1, B : 2, A : 3, A : 4)$$

$$= \frac{3}{5} \times \frac{1}{4} \times \frac{2}{3} \times \frac{1}{2} \times \frac{1}{1} = \frac{1}{20}$$

This result obviously agrees with the result given above. Note again that it would not matter in what order we allocated the objects, the probability p_i of one complexion will always be

$$\frac{\prod\limits_{i} (N_i!)}{N!} \tag{4.2}$$

and that therefore the number of such equally likely complexions is

$$1/p_i = \frac{N!}{\prod\limits_{i} (N_i!)} \tag{4.3}$$

Since these complexions are all equally probable we may write the *a priori* entropy of the ensemble as:

$$\ln \frac{N!}{\prod\limits_{i} (N_i!)} \tag{4.4}$$

which from Chapter 8 we know, for large N, to be equal to:

$$N \sum_i \frac{N_i}{N} \ln \frac{N}{N_i} \qquad (4.5)$$

It is necessary to remember that this is based on Stirling's Approximation which is not valid for small numbers.

From the opening remarks of his section we should expect Rothstein's
definition of H_E^* to give the same result. Now, we know from the diagram
that each of the vectors of alternative states has an entropy of

$$\sum_i \frac{N_i}{N} \ln \frac{N}{N_i} \qquad (4.6)$$

but there are N such vectors, one for each object. Therefore the sum of
the entropies of the alternative states of the objects is in this case

$$N \sum_i \frac{N_i}{N} \ln \frac{N}{N_i} \qquad (4.7)\ (4.5)$$

which is the same as (4.5). Both definitions give the same result —
remembering always that Stirling's Approximation is valid only for large
numbers.

It may be noted that H_E^* has been marked by an asterisk. Elsewhere in
this book the convention is used that an asterisk represents a compound
term, that can be divided into separate parts. Below in 4.4d we will
investigate the compound that it represents.

(c) The observed entropy of the ensemble

It has been made clear that the expected entropy of the ensemble is an *a
priori* quantity. The observed entropy of the ensemble is an *a posteriori*
quantity, one that comes from knowledge of the complexions that the
system actually does adopt. For the purposes of the argument the reader
is asked to accept an example which might seem unlikely in real life.
Suppose that the states of these five people were so interlinked that if
person number 5 were a bank manager, then it always happened that 2,
who might be a friend of his, was a teacher, and the other three were
workers — in other words that the complexion in Fig. 4.3b. was the only
one that ever happened. All I ask is that this is what is observed *a posteriori* — the reasons for it are not the important issue at the moment,

even if they are corruption, nepotism or simple friendship.

In such a case we know that the ensemble of complexions has only one member, with probability 1.0, and that therefore the entropy of the *a posteriori* observed ensemble is zero. Referring to (4.1) we therefore find that for a given H_E^*, O has been maximized and indeed equals H_E^*. We find that this is a maximally organized system.

We have to be quite clear about the source of this organization. It derives from coupling constraints between the parts, such that if one part is in a certain state we are sure of the states of other parts. In less organized systems we would find that we might not necessarily be sure of the states of the other parts, but would nevertheless have a better probability of defining the states correctly than in an uncoupled system.

We can take as a hypothetical example Fig. 4.3c, if we assume that *a posteriori* only these five complexions of the 20 *a priori* possible complexions are ever observed. The entropy of the ensemble *a posteriori* is then greater than zero, but still less than the sum of the entropies of the alternative states of the parts, so that there is indeed some organization.

Of course we can assume a case where

$$H_{\text{obs}} = H_E^* \qquad (4.8)$$

and where therefore organization is zero. Such would be the case if all 20 complexions of Fig. 4.3c were observed, with equal probability. The meaning of this must be clear in relation to the definition of system that I gave at the beginning of the chapter. The state of an object must at least in part be dependent on its membership of the system. If (4.8) is true, then clearly we are saying that for any combination of states of all other objects, any specific object can be in any state — which contravenes the definition of system.

We can comment on Central Place Landscapes as examples of organized systems. Firstly we find that the probability vectors of all places are the same — it is part of the theory that we have a uniform plain on which any place has the same chance as any other of being in a specified state. Secondly we find that if we know the location of the central largest city and the orientation of the landscape, then all other places are determined to be exactly what they are. These states are coupled across the landscape, as in Fig. 4.2, because of their adjacency in space.

However, let the reader be clear that, in order, we first define the organization and then secondly look to see its cause. There is an organizing principle in central place theory, and it happens that we can define this principle in spatial terms. There are many systems in which spatial terms are not necessarily important for organizing principles, and the diagrams of Fig. 4.3 should not be taken to mean that the five people are next to each other in space in the manner indicated. They may, for all I know of the reader's imagination, be next to each other in kinship.

(d) The two components of H_E^*

Let me define

$$H_E^* = H_{E_{max}} - I_{LS} \qquad (4.9)$$

whence we may calculate if necessary

$$I_{LS} = H_{E_{max}} - H_E^* \qquad (4.10)$$

where H_E^* is as before, $H_{E_{max}}$ is the maximum *a priori* value the entropy of the ensemble can take, given only knowledge of the System Part Requirements, and I_{LS} is local scale information.

$H_{E_{max}}$ occurs when, for the given marginal constraints, all the vectors of probabilities for the alternative states are the same, as in Fig. 4.3a, and as would be the case with the vectors in the central place landscape. The entropy of the ensemble will be reduced by any variation of the vectors of probability away from this state, for example as in Fig. 4.3d. Here we find that persons 2 and 3 are incapable of being a teacher; and hence we immediately know that now only 12 instead of 20 complexions are possible in the *a priori* ensemble. We also know that since some people are better suited to being workers than others, the complexions with these people as workers will be more probable than those where they are not, hence we also find that the complexions are no longer equi-probable, so again the entropy of the ensemble is reduced.

Ultimately it can of course be reduced to zero. If local scale deter-minacy is absolute, so that each part has an *a priori* probability of 1.0 for one state only, then clearly I_{LS} equals $H_{E_{max}}$, and then H_E^* is zero. It follows then that there can be no organization in the system.

It can also be shown that if any one part on its own is determined by local scale factors to be in only one state, that it is then a static cog that can contribute nothing to organization. If this is the case then the en-tropy of its own vector of alternative states is zero, and its contribution to the sum of the entropies of the alternative states of all objects is also zero, hence its presence has increased H_E^* not at all.

Finally, lest confusion result later, I would like to name H_E^* as the revised *a priori* entropy of the ensemble, and $H_{E\,\text{max}}$ as the absolute maximum of the *a priori* entropy of the ensemble.

(e) Some numbers attached as examples

In order to illustrate the figures one may derive from the kind of analysis suggested above, it is necessary to keep to simple examples, which there-fore usually involve rather small magnitudes. This immediately, in the present context, brings one up against the inaccuracies of Stirling's approximation with small numbers. It is wise to illustrate first the level of inaccuracies that can occur.

Equations (4.4) and (4.5) above have been equated with each other via Stirling's approximation. These two equations therefore give us two ways of calculating the entropy of the ensemble *a priori*. Taking Fig. 4.3 as the example we have

$$\ln \frac{N!}{\prod_i (N_i!)} = \ln 20 = 2.9957 \text{ nits (from equation 4.4)}$$

and

$$5 \sum_{1=1}^{M} \frac{N_i}{N} \ln \frac{N}{N_i} = 4.7514 \text{ nits (from equation 4.5)}$$

and clearly the discrepancy is large.

However if we increase N first to 50 and then to 100 but still main-taining the same set of (p_i) (in other words the relative frequencies of As, Bs, and Cs stay the same) we derive values as follows:

$N = 50$	$N = 100$	
43.6107	90.4400	equation (4.4)
47.5135	95.0271	equation (4.5)

and it can be seen that in relative terms the discrepancy becomes in-creasingly small.

For large numbers the approximation is acceptable. For the purposes of demonstrating the numbers involved in Fig. 4.3d the approximation is not acceptable and we will have to use one or other method of calcu-lation with consistency.

With reference to Fig. 4.3 we have already calculated the entropy of the ensemble, as 2.9957 nits. If *a posteriori* there is only one complexion and $H_{obs} = 0.0$, then the amount of organization in the system according to equation (4.1) is $2.9957 - 0.0 = 2.9957$ nits.

Suppose, however, that the *a posteriori* ensemble of complexions included the five which have been shown in Fig. 4.3c, then, since these are all equally probable, the entropy of the ensemble *a posteriori* is $\ln 5 = 1.6094$, and the amount of organization is $2.9957 - 1.6094 = 1.3863$ nits, which is less than half the amount previously measured.

We examine next the case presented by Fig. 4.3d, where the vectors of probability of alternative states are not all the same *a priori*. We may examine this case with reference to equations (4.9) and (4.10). Clearly some amount of local determinacy has been introduced, and we can attempt to find how much.

It is no longer possible to assume that the feasible complexions of the *a priori* ensemble are equally probable, and so it is not possible merely to calculate the number of such feasible complexions and take the reciprocal of this number to be the probability of any one of them. We must calculate the probability of each complexion that can occur.

It is now necessary to change the notation slightly. Let P_{ij} be the probability of the jth object being in the ith state. As before we must at all times observe

$$\sum_i P_{ij} = 1 \qquad (4.11)$$

and

$$\sum_j P_{ij} = R_i \qquad (4.12)$$

where R_i is the number of the ith object required by the system (the system part requirements).

Let us now assume that we are able to allocate a complexion beginning with object 1 is an A. P_{11} is then set to 1, and we now have to calculate the conditional probabilities for the other objects such that the constraints (4.11) and (4.12) above are met.

To do this we postulate two sets of scalars, a_i and b_j. We now write

$$P_{ij}^* = a_i b_j P_{ij}$$

where P_{ij}^* is the conditional probability at any stage that satisfies the marginal constraints, and where

$$a_i = R_i / \sum_j b_j P_{ij} \qquad (4.13)$$

and

$$b_j = 1 / \sum_i a_i P_{ij} \qquad (4.14)$$

(4.13) and (4.14) may be solved by reiteration at any stage of the sequence.

Using this technique it is possible to calculate the probability of each of the "20" complexions of Fig. 4.3c but using the initial probabilities as given in Fig. 4.3d. "20" appears in inverted commas because in fact eight of these complexions will have zero probability — those that involve either 2 or 3 being a B. The feasible complexions and their probabilities are shown in Table 4.I. The entropy of the ensemble is 2.43459 nits.

We are now in a position to state the degree of organization present in certain systems based on Fig. 4.3. Firstly, from equation (4.10) we can give the amount of local scale determinacy as $2.9957 - 2.43459 = 0.5611$ nits. Next we can say that if the *a posteriori* ensemble contains only one member of probability 1.0, then the amount of organization in the system is $2.4346 - 0.0 = 2.4346$. This is of course less than for the case above where there was no local scale determinacy. It is also interesting to note that it does not matter whether the observed complexion is one of the more probable ones, or one of the less probable ones; the amount of organization in the system remains the same.

We can also attempt to give an approximate estimate of the organization if the first five complexions of Table 4.I constitute the *a posteriori* ensemble. On the assumption that these five will occur with the same relative frequency as before with respect to each other, we can divide each probability by the sum of all five, to derive a set of probabilities that add to 1.0. The entropy of this set is 1.59061. Therefore the organization in the system then becomes $2.4346 - 1.59061 = 0.8440$, considerably less than in the case of the five complexion a posteriori ensemble of Fig. 4.3c which above was shown to have an organization of 1.3863 nits.

It is also beneficial to look at the other method of calculation of local scale determinacy based on the sum of the entropies of the vectors of

Table 4.I

Feasible complexions from Fig. 4.3d and their probabilities

0 0 1 1 1		1 1 0 0 1	
1 0 0 0 0	$P = 0.0814$	0 0 0 1 0	$P = 0.0788$
0 1 0 0 0		0 0 1 0 0	
0 1 0 1 1		1 1 1 0 0	
1 0 0 0 0	$P = 0.0834$	0 0 0 1 0	$P = 0.0910$
0 0 1 0 0		0 0 0 0 1	
0 1 1 1 0		0 1 1 1 0	
1 0 0 0 0	$P = 0.1054$	0 0 0 0 1	$P = 0.0730$
0 0 0 0 1		1 0 0 0 0	
0 1 1 0 1		1 0 1 1 0	
1 0 0 0 0	$P = 0.1291$	0 0 0 0 1	$P = 0.0437$
0 0 0 1 0		0 1 0 0 0	
0 1 1 0 1		1 1 0 1 0	
0 0 0 1 0	$P = 0.1265$	0 0 0 0 1	$P = 0.0455$
1 0 0 0 0		0 0 1 0 0	
1 0 1 0 1		1 1 1 0 0	
0 0 0 1 0	$P = 0.0758$	0 0 0 0 1	$P = 0.0643$
0 1 0 0 0		0 0 0 1 0	

probabilities of alternative states. As has been remarked several times, we cannot expect that this will give us the same absolute values for the small numbers, but nevertheless we can demonstrate that in relative terms we get approximately the same kinds of answer.

Based on (4.5), $H_{E_{max}}$ has a value of 4.7514 nits. The value of H_E^* for Fig. 4.3 is given by the sum of the entropies of the vectors, and is in this case 4.0609 nits. Expressing I_{LS} as a percentage of $H_{E_{max}}$ we derive local scale determinacy of 14.5%. By the previous method of calculating complexions, we have the values $I_{LS} = 0.5611$ and $H_{E_{max}} =$

2.9957, which gives a relative local scale determinacy of 18.7%. The order of magnitude are similar.

Much more can be said about the nature of the approximation procedure. The topic is dealt with in Chapter 8.

4.5   Some contemplations on the model of system complexions

Clearly the allocation sequences considered in the preceding section have purely arbitrary time bases. In other words, the concept of time implied in the serial order of an allocation is present by implication only, and nothing concrete is said about it. Indeed if it is to be introduced explicitly as a constraint, then the model would become exceedingly complex, and probably few quantitative statements could have been made.

This section muses on the model developed so far, but expressly introduces some temporal considerations in a purely qualitative manner. Rigour is abandoned for the sake of gentle speculation.

Firstly, it is obvious that a static cog, i.e. a part whose initial probability vector includes one entry of 1.0 for one state and all other states are 0.0, has to be allocated first, i.e. it is a non-functioning environment of the system. If this does not occur, then we may at a late stage in allocation of a complexion find that this part has to be something else, which would mean that the whole complexion was impossible. As an example, let us assume that there is some mountain whose only best possible state is to be left undeveloped, a wilderness for the enjoyment of citizens. Now suppose within this system we require a wilderness, a town, an airport and a farming zone. The environmental map shows three areas of low fertile land, and one barren mountain. If we allocate the farming zone and the town to two of the lowland zones, and then we decide to create a lowland wilderness park, then the airport has to be on the mountain. Such a complexion would be impossible. The only procedure that could be adopted would be to define the mountain as the wilderness zone first.

To make a more general case we can consider the possibility that although a part has many alternatives, there is some subset of alternatives for which it has zero probability. As an example I suggest the problem presented in Fig. 4.4a and b. Here we have nine states of object to be satisfied by nine objects, the squares on the map. The objection that the "squares" are not objects is completely valid, since they are arbitrary

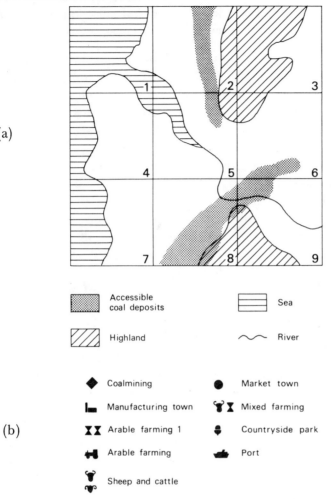

(a)

(b)

| | Accessible coal deposits | | Sea |
| | Highland | | River |

	Coalmining		Market town
	Manufacturing town		Mixed farming
	Arable farming 1		Countryside park
	Arable farming		Port
	Sheep and cattle		

Fig. 4.4. Alternative landscapes: (a) raw data, environmental information, (b) six
     land uses.

units of absolute space. But nevertheless the problem can highlight some
points. A square such as square 9 could be any of the nine states except
coal mining and possibly also a port. (A canal could be dug but we will
assume for the moment that it could not be a port.) If we had some
sequence of allocation which left square 9 to be the last to be allocated,
and the only state not yet fulfilled was coal mining, then clearly that

whole complexion would be impossible, even though square 9 was not a static cog by definition, i.e. it did originally have more than one alternative open to it.

In such circumstances it would appear that a model of an allocation procedure would best be built around the assumption that the allocation of objects to states would be most beneficially carried out in the order of the increasing entropies of the initial probability vectors. This would mean allocate those squares most constrained by local scale determinacy first to their most suitable functions. Of course historical accident in the real world would rarely conform to this principle, hence we may expect most real world systems to have less probable complexions than the most efficient possible.

This discussion still, however, hinges on some other assumptions. One of the critical ones is that the Part Requirements of the system are defined prior to the development of a complexion, and another is that they remain unchanged during the allocation sequence. Neither of these assumptions would seem valid, in the real world. If we were to ask how many airports, how many steel mills, how many railway men our system needed, we would probably find out by adding up the numbers of each in the system. Note that the system is arranged, and that by addition we derive aggregates which we can use for the Part Requirements, which, because they are aggregates, do not exhibit arrangement. We can then study arrangements that would satisfy these part requirements. The other arrangements might well be "adiabatically equivalent" to the existing arrangement, and have some intrinsic interest. But nevertheless, the procedure is notably circular. Clearly we need some way of deriving state requirements independently of the system being observed. Within ecology we might be able to do this by reference to some theory about the evolution of complexity in an ecosystem over time. Perhaps something similar could apply to the theory of economic development in geography.

But the assumption that the state requirements are unchanging would seem totally at variance with what we might expect from the real world, except in those cases of the perfectly conceived and executed Five Year Plans (which would seem to operate on this kind of principle). In all other cases time is not divided into neat time slices, and the entrepreneur's perception as to whether the system requires another car plant will certainly depend upon the time at which an existing plant becomes obsolescent and inefficient, and the conditions that exist in the market

and with his competitors at that time. Until that decision time arrives
the state requirement is undefined, and when that decision time does
arrive we can immediately see that the state requirement can hardly be
called a system one at all, but an entrepreneur's perception of such a
requirement.

Yet again, therefore, we find that the problem of change in the system, and the origins of this change, is difficult in the extreme. The difficulty is greater than that in such subjects as ecology, because of the self-
conscious perception and creation of man of his own man-extended
system. That is to say the evolution of new "species" in the human socio-
economic system is consciously directed in many instances. If a new car
plant is seen as a new species of man-machine, then clearly this new
species has evolved purposefully. In ecology the debate about the prior
existence of, as yet, unfilled niches in the ecosystem continues, but if
for the moment we do assume that such a concept as an unfilled niche
is tenable, even then the evolution towards occupancy of that niche by
some species would not be purposeful and self-conscious in the same way
that the development of the car plant would be. We might explain purposeful evolution in some wide "force of the ecosystem" terms, but
certainly not in terms of an animal species consciously perceiving an
opportunity and then purposely evolving new eyes, teeth, feet, etc. to
seize that opportunity.

4.6 Empirical subjective assessment of complexion probabilities

In one approach to the problem of assessing probabilities of system
complexions, participants in a game were asked to provide their own
subjective assessments of the probabilities at each stage in an allocation
process. The approach stresses immediately the old adage that order, or
pattern, or what-have-you, is in the eye of the beholder, that we are
assessing an observer's interpretation of a system rather than any objective property of an objective system. It is similar to Shannon's approach
to the assessment of redundancy (see Chapter 8), when he showed letter
by letter some text of English to a reader, and asked him to guess the
next letter. The technique was used because although one can measure
in simple terms, objectively, the various conditional frequencies of next
letters, a human text reader has use of much greater stores of information,
basing his guesses on spelling rules, idioms, clichés, styles, grammar,
context etc. (see Cherry, 1966, p. 118). A similar technique has been used

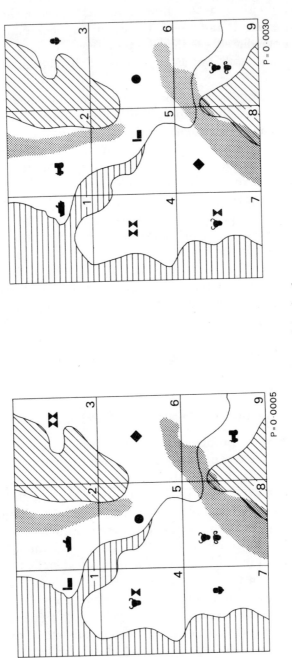

Fig. 4.5. Realizations from landscape game.

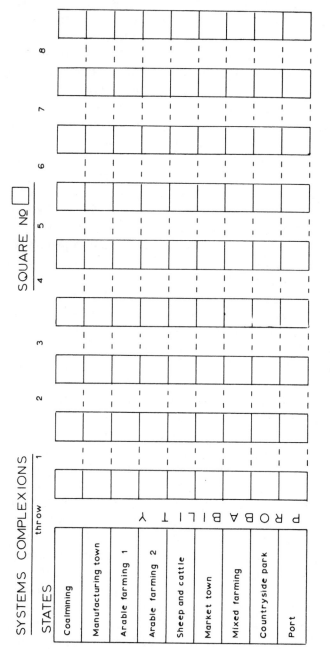

Fig. 4.6. Form of landscape game.

in geography in a slightly different context by Robinson (1974).

The map in Fig. 4.5 and the form in Fig. 4.6 were used in the game, presented here in as simple a version as possible. Any amount of extra information can be introduced into the maps and one could have two different kinds of allocation problem simultaneously e.g. allocation of each square to some areal state, such as arable or mixed farming, and allocate a point feature, such as a town, to a square.

In the game here nine people are allocated to choose the development probabilities of a single square each. They are asked to list in the first vector of the form shown in Fig. 4.6 the probabilities associated with the different states their square could be. For example, one person representing square 4 wrote down in the first vector, from coal mining to port, respectively 0.0, 0.3, 0.2, 0.1, 0.1, 0.2, and 0.1. These sum to one. A card is then drawn from a pack, designating the first square to be allocated to a state. On one trial square 8 came first. Square 8 is asked what is his most probable state and in this case his most probable state was coal mining and the probability was 0.4. All other squares then had to delete coal mining from their possibilities, and mark coal mining on square 8 of their maps. A single record sheet of the game is kept separately to work out the probability of the final complexion, and on this the first entry is coal mining, $p = 0.4$. Square 8 drops out and then the remaining squares still in the game, 1, 2, 3, 4, 5, 6, 7, and 9, write 8 against coal mining in the column under "throw 1" and then complete a new probability vector for the alternative states of their square, given the information of what has so far happened. The procedure is repeated until the map is completed, keeping a record of the last probabilities of the final state choice for each square as it is allocated.

Three results of the procedure can be studied. Firstly, there is the combined subjective probability of the whole complexion, obtained by multiplying together all the probabilities kept on the single record sheet and, secondly, there are the completed maps. Two maps and their associated complexion probabilities are shown in Fig. 4.5. Thirdly, we can compile charts of the subjective entropies of the individual decision makers as the game progresses.

The two landscapes that are produced here have probabilities of 0.0005 and 0.003. These orders of magnitude clearly indicate that the number of possible complexions was still thought to be high. But, nevertheless, these figures contrast markedly with the probability of one of the 9! complexions possible when the map is nine blank squares needing an arbitrary nine land-uses. We may note that 1/9! = 0.000003, and that Fig. 4.5b is 1000 times more probable than this, and Fig. 4.5a is 160 times more probable. The exercise seemed to stress, therefore, more than anything else, the enormous amount of information the participants (all geographers) seemed to read into a little mapping of the environment.

The third set of results for interpretation are the graphs in Fig. 4.7a. and b. Here the entropy of the probability vector at each stage for each square has been plotted. The entropies all go to 0.0 nits in the order in which they are allocated, but note that the last two are always allocated together, since if the penultimate is allocated then the last is also automatically determined (there being only eight degrees of freedom with nine squares). A priori I expected that the curves would show a continual gradual decline, such as that shown by 5 in Fig. 4.7a. In fact few do: most stay at some high level until allocation. This would suggest that people were responding slowly to the information generated by the allocation sequence, and not using the spatial information of what happened in adjacent squares. One would have thought that a coal mine in one square would increase the subjective probability assessment of a manufacturing town in an adjacent square etc., hence reducing the entropies. One could suggest that the people involved did not make good use of such information. There is another hypothesis though, suggested by one of the participants, which is rather interesting. He suggested that most people, given the base map and the nine functions to be allocated, would see not only their own square, but their idea of what the complete landscape ought to be like. They would then use not only the information from the history of the allocation as it proceeded, but also their anticipation of where things ought to go. In other words their information from the history of allocation might increase during the game, but at the same time the information from their anticipation of the future is being lost, so that overall no great information gains are being made.

We can further briefly consider the order of the starting entropies in the two cases, that is the order of the squares down the y axis from top to bottom before any allocation has been made. The orders in Figs. 4.7a and 4.7b are, respectively: 5, 3, 9, 4, 1, 8, 6, 7, 2 and 6, 7, 3, 2, 4, 8, 9, 1, 5. They are not at all similar. However, in the two cases the squares were not "owned" by the same people; they had been shuffled around amongst the participants. It would seem, therefore, that the subjective interpretation of the uncertainty associated with the use of some squares varies greatly from person to person. In Fig. 4.7a square 2 was

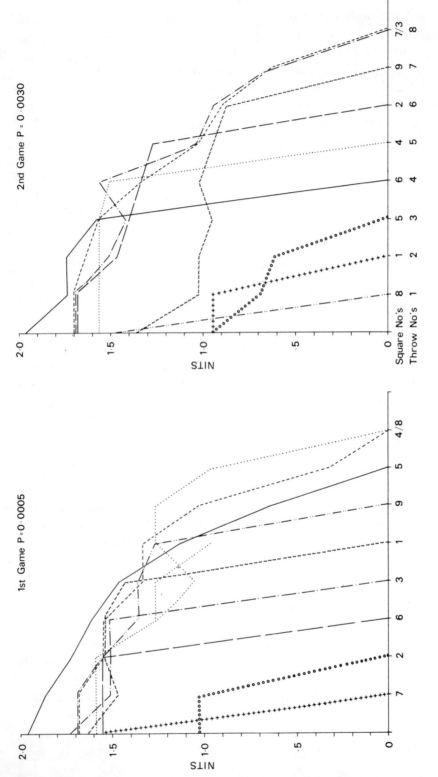

Fig. 4.7. Change subjective entropies (a) for 4.5a, (b) for 4.5b.

the most constrained, seen to be highly likely to be coal mining, a manufacturing town or a port. Square 5 was the least constrained, and anything was thought possible. But note that the two squares are not very dissimilar. Clearly one person thought that the presence of suitable resources such as coal fields and an estuary meant they had to be used for mining, or a port, or manufacturing, whereas the person considering square 5 with the same resources thought that the presences of these resources did not necessarily mean that they had to be used, but that they could be used. On his interpretation that square could also be anything to do with agriculture. Clearly his interpretation suggested that the presence of specific resources widened the range of possibilities, rather than narrowing the range of probabilities. In the second case the most constrained squares were 1 and 5, and the least constrained square 6. If one interprets resources as possibilities rather than as determining factors, then clearly 6 ought to be more constrained than 1 or 5.

The whole process is arbitrary and subjective but that, in a way, is its strength rather than its weakness. Given a map of a real landscape the average student of geography, particularly at school level, is probably persuaded first of the reasonableness, possibly even the inevitability, of what happened. It is there, it is correct, it happened. This is the basic premise, and once that is accepted then the task is to explain what happened. Because the past now seems to have been inevitable, it seems easy to bring at a deep subconscious level or at a conscious level a deterministic interpretation to the fore. The present is taken to be a functioning whole with its own rationale, the past and the myriad of subjective decisions is forgotten.

The exercise therefore emphasizes that the landscape is the result of many decisions made in highly subjective ways by many different people, each with a different amount of information as to what has happened so far, and with a different conception of the future. The information they have they interpret, ignore, or employ in different ways according to their past experience. There are many different things that could have happened. What could have happened is not relevant to a description of what is and how it works, but it is crucially relevant to any explanation of how what exists came to be. If a theory explaining the evolution of the present cannot cope with what else could have been, then it is worthless.

As a final comment in this section, I wish to draw the reader's attention to the discrepancy between the statements just made and the final paragraph of section 4.2 above. I think the discrepancy between the levels of effectiveness of individual decision makers on a system is obviously one of degree rather than of kind, but we have no sure guidelines as to a best expectation in any given circumstances of the amount of local rather than system scale determinacy. It would appear that there is a major problem area of research in the present unbridged gap between studies of perception and decision making, on the one hand, and studies of systems at large scales, on the other hand.

4.7 Empirical assessment of complexion probabilities: redundancy in time/space

If we accept that locations can be relative and replicable, then it is possible to make some attempt at measuring the redundancy in time-space of a series of objects in an evolving geographical landscape. If we think of locations as unique then such an approach is precluded.

In the next section I shall stress that the cooperation in a system which defines its degree of organization need not necessarily be fulfilled in a spatial manner. By this I mean quite simply that if one part influences the state of another, then this other one is not necessarily defined as an adjacent neighbour in space. However, if we are confronted with the problem of finding cooperation in some system when we have no idea of the manner in which this cooperation may be expressed, then it may well be that the best *a priori* hypothesis we can produce is that near things might tend to influence each other. As a result the empirical analysis in this section rests on definitions of neighbours in time-space. If we compare the procedure with Shannon's noted above (section 4.6), we are substituting the inferior strategy "the next letter statistical count" for the better strategy of "A person's guess of the next letter based on syntax, meaning, context, grammar, etc".

Suppose you receive a telegram which says "See you tomorrow mroning". The telegram contains a mistake, but you are in no doubt as to what the message should have been — namely, "see you tomorrow morning". We could quite simply say that the reason you know there is a mistake is that there is no word "mroning" in our language, but there is more to the recognition of this error than that. Suppose you came across a scrap of newspaper with part of a sentence on it ". . . which contained five tons of mron of high quality . . ."; even without knowing the context of the sentence, which might be scientific, you would suspect that mron was not the word intended, for the simple reason that the combination of letters "mro" does not occur at the beginning of words in English, even if it can occur when the "m" is preceded by a vowel as in the word "nimrod". All languages contain some kind of redundancy of this sort, that is, the linking of letters in words so that some combinations are more probable than others. Or, to put it another way, given one letter of a word, there is then a set of conditional probabilities of what the next letter is likely to be which is not the same as the unconditioned set of probabilities of the letters. So if we see the letters "tio . . ." in English the probability that the next letter is "n" as in the word "station" is much higher than the probability of finding "n" unconditionally in any particular position of the word.

Languages contain redundancy at several scales. We have now met intra-word or letter redundancy, but we can also meet inter-word redundancy. Suppose a newsflash on the radio is interrupted by noise, but you heard, "A spokesman for the butchers' federation said that the price of ****** was bound to rise in the next week", you would be very sure that the commodity which was about to rise in price was some form of meat, quite possibly beef.

Now we know from Information Theory that the maximum amount of information can be transmitted when the probabilities of transmitted symbols are all equal, and that the best coding methods for sources where the source characters are unequal probability produces a coded message in which the symbols used by the code appear equally frequently. In other words such codes have no redundancy. Yet we find that real-life languages have a considerable degree of redundancy and presumably for some purpose.

The purpose of redundancy has already been demonstrated with the first example of this section — it combats noise, helps us detect and eliminate errors, so that we read "morning" when we see "mroning". Its success in the realm of language depends upon the fact that human beings have immense store-houses of the conditional probability sets in their brains, so that instinctively they recognize probable and improbable combinations of letters and words.

Our interpretation of maps and our construction of spatial models depends upon redundancy in the series we create in two dimensions. There are also scale distinctions in the kinds of redundancy observable, as was the case with language. Thus we model a completely redundant inter-urban landscape with Central Place Theory, and a completely redundant intra-urban model with Burgess's concentric rings. By contrast, in language the intra-word and inter-word scales appear to be completely distinct. However, they are not wholly so, particularly with the spoken as opposed to the written form. Thus "a" becomes "an" in front of "orange".

In the real world we know that redundancy patterns in a landscape are not complete, nor are the two-scales mentioned above water-tight from each other. Thus part of London's industrial structure (intra-urban scale by most accounts) is influenced by the location of Birmingham and the M1. Figures 4.8 and 4.9 show an idealized two-scale redundancy

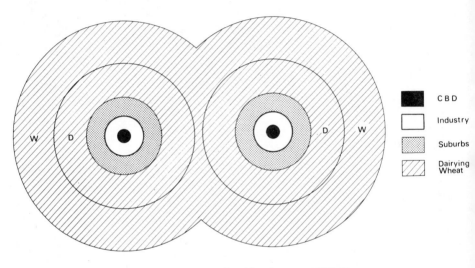

Fig. 4.8. An idealized landscape sentence.

model, and the reality of the real landscape of South Lancashire, which seems to hold some meaning, yet it does not represent complete sense. The intelligibility level of such a map may possibly be compared with the following sentence:

A big leakage of secret information which should help you cross the road to destruction is what must be inevitably the case of bacon and eggs for breakfast with the bishop who said we might go there next Thursday week is soon enough for me to understand the question of the hour hand of my watch chain swinging along . . .

(Miller, quoted in Cherry, 1966, p. 119).

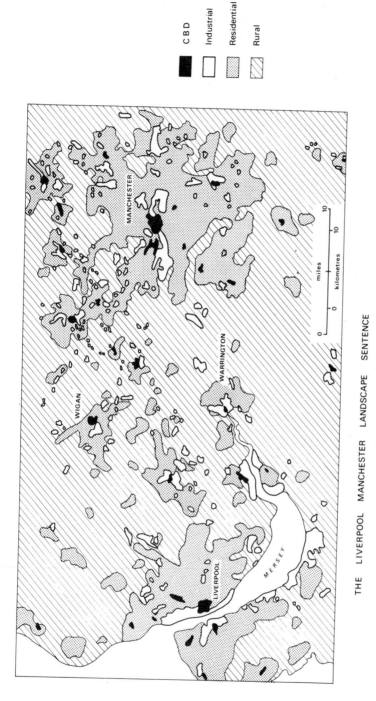

CBD

Industrial

Residential

Rural

THE LIVERPOOL MANCHESTER LANDSCAPE SENTENCE

Fig. 4.9. An actual landscape sentence.

The sentence was constructed by showing people just the previous two words of the text and asking them on the basis of that knowledge to put in what they thought to be the most likely following word. The result is a sentence which does have connections between words, but which eludes complete sense. We can also, by using the known letter redundancies of English, construct words and put them in sentences of a common grammatical structure:

> The ventious crapests pounted raditally.
> (adjective, noun, verb, adverb)

and then translate this into French:

> Les crapêts ventieus pontaient raditallement,
> (Cherry, 1966, p. 121).

So much for redundancy and its importance in pattern recognition. How do we measure it? In terms of information theory we can measure conditional entropies and unconditional ones, and we can do so for letter and word groups of any number of members. The possibilities are enormous.

Unconditionally we can measure the simple entropy of the frequency of letters as they are used in some language:

$$H(i) \text{ for } P(i), = P(a), P(b), P(c) \ldots P(x), P(y), P(z)$$

and often this is expressed relative to the maximum amount of information that could be portrayed by that number of letters:

$$\text{Redundancy} = 1 - \frac{H(i)}{H_{\max}} = 1 - \frac{H(i)}{\log 26} \tag{4.15}$$

Unconditionally we can measure the entropy of digrams:

$$H(ij) \text{ for } P(ij), = P(aa), P(ab), P(ac) \ldots P(zx), P(zy), P(zz)$$

Conditionally we can measure the entropy of letters given the preceding letter

$$H_i \ (j) \text{ for } P_i \ (j), = P_a(a), P_a(b), P_a(c) \ldots P_z(x), P_z(y), P_z(z)$$

We can express other conditional entropies such as H_{ij} (k) or H_i (jk) just as we wish.

The idea is very similar to those used in spatial forecasting (Curry, 1970) and in spatial autocorrelation (Cliff and Ord, 1970). Finally, we can mention Dacey's (1965) work on two-dimensional languages. His approach has connections with this, except that the problem he has set himself is slightly different. Just as entropy can be used as a measure and as the objective function of an allocation procedure in entropy maximizing model, so too we can use redundancy as a measure here, and we can also try to invent the grammar and redundancies of a deductively constructed spatial language and try to create some patterns similar to those we observe in reality. This is the kind of path that Dacey (1965) has taken: it is also remarkably reminiscent of Chomsky's ideas on transformation generative grammar.

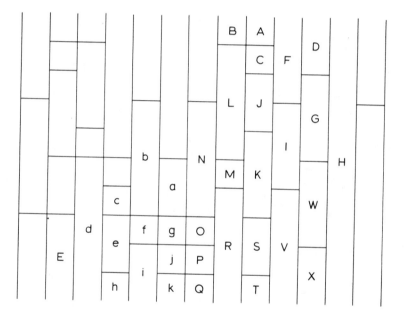

Fig. 4.10. A plane cut through time-space.

Figure 4.10 represents a plane cut through a time-space domain, where the x axis of the drawing therefore represents a line of land-use zones, for example, shop frontages on a street, and the y axis of the drawing represents time. Each rectangle in the drawing represents an object, for example R may be a laundry, and the next object on that site, M, could be a butcher's shop. Thus, the diagram illustrates changes of objects by

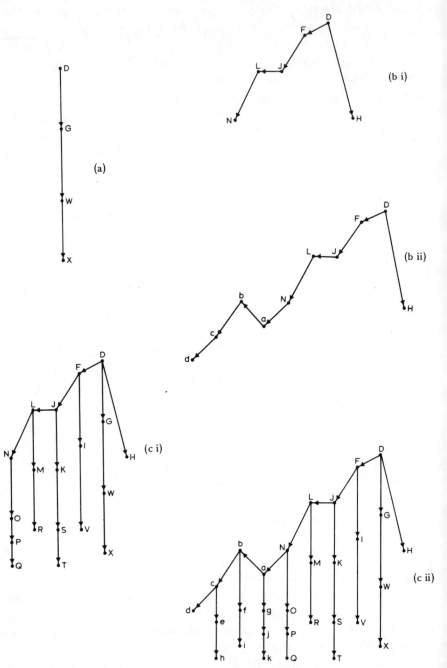

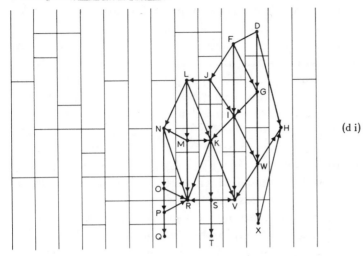

(d i)

(d ii)

Fig. 4.11. Antecedence relationships between objects in Fig. 4.10:
    (a)   non-spatial antecedence;
    (b i) spatial antecedence without simultaneity;
    (b ii) spatial antecedence with simultaneity;
    (c i) a and bi combined;
    (c ii) a and bii combined;
    (d i) ci with recontact;
    (d ii) cii with recontact.

kind, and not changes by degree. These objects constitute the basic data set within which we can attempt to analyse redundancy.

The first step is to define the meaning of "next" in the same way as we can define the next letter of a word. There are basically two ways in time that we can do this, although it rapidly becomes apparent that there are many possible complications. Given any object as a starting point we can find its antecedents or its descendants. Basically an antecedent is some object which begins its existence prior to the given object and which terminates its existence after the given object has begun its existence: in other words an earlier object which exhibits some temporal overlap. A descendant is an object which starts to exist after the beginning and before the end of the existence of the given object. But, unfortunately, a purely temporal definition yields so many descendants or antecedents, that the concept of "next" is also bound in space. Thus the previous conditions apply, plus a further condition that the objects under consideration are spatially contiguous.

The illustrative charts, Figs 4.11a—d, give various antecedent patterns that can be defined from the data set in Fig. 4.10. The cases are as follows:

(a) Historical antecedence only;

    (b.i)   Spatial antecedence without simultaneity;
    (b.ii) as (b.i) but with simultaneity;
    (c.i)   Spatial and historical without recontact of previously contacted locations, without simultaneity;
    (c.ii) as (c.i) but with simultaneity;
    (d.i)   as (c.i) but with recontact;
    (d.ii) as (c.ii) but with recontact.

Most of the definitions are clear from reference to the diagrams. Note that simultaneity means a slight relaxation of the temporal rules above to enable two objects that begin to exist at the same time to influence each other, presumably through knowledge of intentions by, for example, planning applications.

There are some implications of the diagrams that are worth mentioning. Firstly, there is no way in which we can define a purely spatial redundancy. Any such attempt, as in (b.i) and (b.ii) produces a pattern in time as well. Secondly, in terms of contact numbers some past events might be very significant, e.g. R in (d.i). Thirdly, in the case (d.i) and (d.ii) an object may occur at the next, and the next but one location as well, from a given object. In (d.i) for example I occurs at one step from F and at two steps from F either via J or via G.

Perhaps one of the best implications, however, is the complexity of defining cause and effect. If as in Fig. 4.11d.ii we define all the causes of D, one of which is Q some time in the past, and then we examine all the effects of Q, as in Fig. 4.12, we can see that there is no simple

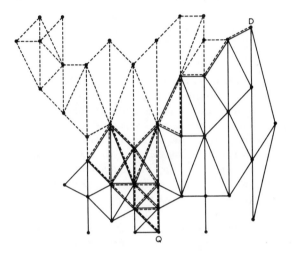

Fig. 4.12. Cause and effect.

one:one correspondence of cause and effect between Q and D. To abstract partial explanations out of the total explanation of the whole might not only be less sound but might also in the long run prove more difficult if this is done for all pairs of objects in turn.

Empirical analysis based on these ideas has been attempted for changes in small businesses in the Acton area of London. A report of the analysis is included in Chapter 12.

4.8 Part requirements and organization in geography

The view that geography is a science of spatial relationships is widely held. The philosophy behind this view is not often explicitly given, the assumption being that the matter is self-evident. In Chapters 1 and 2 I have tried to show that much of the analysis in geography is implicitly relying on a concept of absolute space rather than of relative space. Recently with the development of techniques for the analysis of spatial autocorrelation, the strength of spatial relationships, still usually expressed in units derived from an absolute space framework, is being quantitatively assessed. We find more often than not that we can make no general statement about the strength of these relationships other than at the simplistic level made famous in the context of Tobler's First Law of Geography: "everything is related to everything else, but near things are more related than distant things". We find similar reasoning in Furth's (1952) discussion of the Physics of Social Equilibrium:

> For loose assemblies under the action of external forces it is possible to calculate from general theorems of statistical mechanics fixed probabilities for a particle to be found in certain positions and orientations, irrespective of the position and orientation of the rest of the assembly. But in close assemblies these probabilities depend on the configuration of all other particles, *and in the first place, of course, those in the immediate neighbourhood of the considered particle.* This cooperation may either enhance or reduce probabilities for certain configurations. Phenomena mainly in solid and liquid matter which are the outcome of such processes are called cooperative phenomena.
>
> Communities of animals and human beings are clearly also assemblies in which the interaction between the individual members is very considerable . . . .. Thus we are almost forced to adopt the model of a close assembly and in doing so we must expect to find the features of the cooperative phenomena of statistical mechanics in many social processes. For the fundamental assumption made is only that there exists a strong interaction of some sort between members of the community: whether this interaction is of a physical or non-physical, conscious or non-conscious nature is unessential.

We have already shown that cooperation of this type is what defines organization in a system, indeed the extent to which we can consider the phenomena to have system determinacy. But the way in which this cooperation arises can be the result of any kind of interaction. Tobler and Furth both recognize a spatial element in this cooperation, but it is not the only basis nor necessarily the most important basis for interaction. The importance will vary from case to case.

We have seen that the satisfaction of a system's Part Requirements does not guarantee that there is any cooperative organization in the system. We know that an analysis based mostly on these requirements is an analysis of aggregate values and, as such, the model based on aggregates, like those of the economists "pin's head", does not give a one:one correspondence with the real world. If we believe that some organization does exist, where and in what form does it exist? Clearly, the interaction which "enhances or reduces the probabilities of certain configurations" can be of many forms. Perhaps Furth's correct use of the word cooperative is a little misleading, since there is a connotation of voluntary activity in a situation which may cut across our notions of free will. At the atomic scale cooperation and coercion are indistinguishable. But clearly in his broad meaning of the word this cooperation exists most strongly.

In a temporal sense we know that there is a greater probability that a son will follow a father in a similar occupation than go into a very different one, and it is on the basis of this fact that we find social class a mostly hereditary phenomenon even today. We similarly recognize "industrial inertia" to mean that the existence of an industry in some location is the result of a tradition for that industry in that place.

Similarly, there is an element of spatial cooperation. Not all the bakers in England are located on the south coast. Nor are all the sewage farms for the whole of Britain located on the Isle of Skye. We know that there is a replication of most service activities throughout the whole country. But such cooperation is often very loose. At a detailed scale the knowledge of the use of one particular unit of land is usually not a very good predictor of the use of the next (in a developed and densely settled society). If one unit of land is used for a house, the next could be used for a road, for another house, a garden, a petrol station, a school, a field, a gravel pit, etc. This happens simply because everything cannot coexist on a pin's head, and the expression of the spatial cooperation between phenomena thus becomes a study in such surfaces as population potentials and income potentials. But the generalization involved at the scale at which most such studies are pursued is very great. Usually it is only at these scales that the cooperation in a spatial sense is really evident. Consider the problem of trying to correlate a map of six supermarkets with eight women's clothing stores. If they are separate shops they cannot coexist in space and the observations cannot be given in pairs. We surmise that the two are not completely independent of each other, but each might be influenced by other factors as well, and different factors in each case. The interpretations of any relationship may only be possible through the use of some variable such as total sales turnover correlated in each case with sample values from the same general surface such as an income potential. Warntz (1965) has taken this viewpoint to the extreme.

But there are other forms of organization in the geographical system, and it is because other forms exist that it would seem necessary that the subject of geography is orientated around the study of a system rather than just spatial relationships, and that having become system orientated it does indulge both in spatial and non-spatial analyses. The trend is already clearly evident. The dependence of Ford's Halewood on Ford's Dagenham, of Rolls Royce in Scotland on Rolls Royce in Derby are the kinds of examples given of long-distance links included in "linkage analysis" studies. Such studies in effect merely consider the relationship of a plant to everything that affects it in a direct and observable link (observable even as it is in information terms, such as face-to-face management contact). Another form in which the trend is visible is in such studies as Wärneryd's (1968) urban interdependence, and the study of diffusion "down the hierarchy" as well as contagiously through space.

In effect many of these links can be thought of as spatial, but spatial in a relative, not absolute sense. In many ways two high-order urban centres may be informationally and monetarily nearer to a metropolitan centre than a rural zone which in simple mile or kilometre terms is nearer than either of them. We are now close to welding together many attitudes and definitions of systems. Angyal (1941) defines a system as a distribution of members in a dimensional domain. We began this chapter by defining system as a collection of parts where the state of one part could influence the state of another. We then said that this influence often has a strong spatial component, that is, nearness is important, and we have then generalized nearness to mean not simply nearness in a single three-dimensional frame of reference within a concept of absolute space defined in terms of miles, but nearness in many dimensions in a relative space — Angyal's dimensional domain. We have, too, considered the problem of allocation, and clearly any analysis of distribution in a dimensional domain is closely linked to an analysis of some allocation mechanism. We will touch on this again later.

4.9 Conclusions

There is only one major conclusion from this chapter that I wish to stress yet again, even having pointed it out in passing several times.

This is quite simply that to theorize merely about what does exist is not very useful. If we restrict ourselves to that alone, all explanation will be merely historical accidental. At all stages it is most important to include consideration of what else could have been. The definition of organization in a system even explicitly requires the assessment of what else could have been. This same message runs through every aspect of systems theory, and through structuralism as well. From control theory to regulation, from marriage rules to linguistic generative grammar, what has been seen to exist is such a small subset of all those things that could have existed.

It is also clear that if we have to discover what else could have existed, we have to consider the present as an arrangement made out of parts. This chapter has been devoted to a consideration of this issue; but the story of the part and the whole has not yet been finished, and I continue with it in the next chapter.

5

On Emergence, Degrees of Freedom, and Other Related Topics

Pooh was playing Pooh-sticks, dropping fir cones in upstream of a bridge, and watching them come out downstream:
"So the next time he dropped one big one and one little one, and the big one came out first, which was what he had said it would do, and the little one came out last, which was what he has said it would do, so he had won twice . . . "

(A. A. Milne)

5.1 Introduction

This chapter attempts to bring together a number of diverse strands of thinking about a number of diverse issues. That there is a reason for bringing them together I hope will become apparent — they do so awkwardly and often feel ill at ease together, but it is clear that they are all part of an incomplete answer to one basic question. The question is: what is the relationship of parts with the wholes to which they belong? There are many reasons for thinking that this question should never be asked. Quite clearly, if a whole is more than the sum of its parts, then there is no way in which we will create the whole by studying its parts. Laszlo (1971) has a long comment on the priority of parts versus wholes which also suggests that the question is irrelevant.

> Holistic evolutionists tend to regard the totality as ontologically prior to its parts: the parts are viewed as deriving their significance (and perhaps also their

reality) by participation in the whole. Analytical and mechanically orientated investigators view the parts as prior to the whole, considering the whole as an outcome of certain systemic interactions of the parts. In the pure structuralist view, however, neither position is tenable, since a structure proper is a totality defined in reference to the transformations and self-regulation it manifests, i.e. it is a whole which is neither above, nor in addition to, its parts, but is its parts in systemic interconnection. Hence that what we define as a characteristic law of the whole is likewise capable of definition as a recurrent factor in the related-ness of the parts. The whole is necessarily a totality, however, and not a mere agglomeration of its parts, because the systemic interrelatedness of its parts emerges only when all interactions are considered simultaneously.

Nevertheless, despite this view, I think the question can still be meaningful. It is meaningful because the structures defined by Laszlo are in a sense too pure. As we have seen in Chapter 4 there are degrees of system organization. There are some which are loosely interconnected, and some which are more completely interconnected. We have both good and bad gestalts. Few people would deny some kind of wholeness to the concept of Britain as a nation: few would care to deny that within that nation most individuals had a considerable freedom in their actions. It is this kind of looseness which makes the question of the priority of parts over wholes askable, even if it remains unanswerable.

I shall ask for the reader's patience while the diverse strands of thought are introduced and explained in their own contexts. The attempt to bring them together is left till later.

5.2 Gestalts

The gestalt is usually defined as meaning a whole, where "the whole is more than the sum of the parts". The concept is unintelligible to some people, intelligible but irrelevant to others, intelligible and relevant but empirically useless to others. But one aspect of the concept is important: although there is great ambiguity over the matter from circumstance to circumstance, the whole that is more than the sum of the parts is so in the observer's understanding and perception of the whole. The concept probably rightly belongs in perception. This clearly has links with the subjective view of information theory: that when we talk of the entropy of a system, the entropy is a property of the observer's understanding of the system and not of the system itself.

A watch is more than the sum of all the component parts. The parts have to be arranged in some specific manner, and when they are so arranged they can do something — tell the time — which it is not possible to surmise from the sum of the cogs, springs and wheels. Such things exist in aircraft instruments and clockwork trains. It is interesting to note therefore that for many people the stumbling block in understanding what a gestalt is lies in the fact that they expect it to be something outside their experience, whereas in fact our whole lives depend upon instinctive recognition of gestalts that surround us. When meeting a friend we do not count the hairs on his head, measure the assymetry coefficient of the eyes etc., to recognize him. We are aware of him or her as a totality; and interestingly enough, as a totality that is recognizable even although the arrangement of the parts may vary, as the hair blows in the wind, or the legs and arms move.

Similarly, we understand the purpose and functioning of a watch as a whole, and do not consider it or see it as a collection of parts. But in both these examples we can suspect that there is something near complete system-scale determinacy. In systems of interest to geography such determinacy does not necessarily exist, hence there may be no clear and certain way, no single function or purpose, by which we can see a definite gestalt property. This is not a trivial stumbling block, and is why the basic question is admissable. Thus we may have to conceive of gestalts which are of a lower order than the simple examples above.

But we also live within the system we are studying. We also have our own local-scale determinacy and can regulate against many of the influences in our system. It is therefore difficult to conceive of the whole to which we belong having any quality which is greater than the sum of the parts. But, if one assembles many regulators together, each with its own defined properties, and then stands back to see the group as a new whole in whose behaviour we are interested, we can see that we have indeed created something with a behaviour pattern characteristic of itself: by itself, we mean that there is some specific arrangement of the parts so that one behaviour pattern is apparent. The same parts could be arranged in other ways to create a new whole which behaved differently from the first. Take a close look at a city. See that it is made of many parts — factories, shops, schools, houses. If the parts are rearranged then one can see that the city will function in a different way. For this reason we admit the occurrence of uniqueness, that cities apparently composed of the similar parts are nevertheless different and behave differently. It is obvious that we have to accept the uniqueness of phenomena, but this does not mean that we shall automatically have stumbling blocks in the way when we construct theories, as we have already discussed in section 3.4.

Thus one of the first considerations of the system as a gestalt must be to see if we can find and understand any specific arranging principle which determines how the parts fit together (see Chapter 4). Secondly we can look at the many components of which the system is made, and see how they behave individually and how they behave when put together in the arrangement discovered.

In a sense we are looking for explanation at two scales: the system scale and the local. One of the great mistakes in the application of systems theory in geography to date has been to consider the local scale only while talking of systems. We list the parts, and show how they affect each other, either by correlation bonds, or by boxes and arrows of positive and negative feedback — *but* the statement of how the resulting whole behaves in time is missing, and the principle underlying the arrangement which is observed is neither sought nor discussed. We end with a list of parts, some connections, and the statement "things are thus".

5.3 Aggregates, system, and arrangement

It is helpful in clarifying the notions of gestalt and arrangement to consider Angyal's "Logic of Systems" (1941). He writes:

> The problem of the integration of part processes in the total organism is the most important and at the same time the most difficult problem for a science of personality. The difficulty lies not alone in the paucity of usable factual data, but to an even greater extent in the inadequacy of our logical tools. Such a handicap is felt not only in the study of personality, but in the study of wholes in general. . . . Here an attempt will be made to demonstrate that there is a logical genus suitable to the treatment of wholes. We propose to call it *system*.

The most developed logical genus that science has used to date has been the genus of relationships. The part processes that Angyal mentions are those that have been defined in terms of relationships.

> A relationship requires an aspect out of which the relationship is formed. Two objects can be related to each other for instance, with regard to their colour, size, or weight. Therefore before a relationship can be established it is necessary to single out some aspect of the relata which serves as a basis for the relation. The attribute of the relata on which the relationship is based is an immanent quality of the object, like size, colour or weight.

The point to be stressed is that the objects have some immanent quality which is the basis for the relation, such a quality being an attri-

bute of that object, a property which is part of the complete description
of what that object is. In a system according to Angyal an object does
not participate by virtue of an immanent quality, but by virtue of its
position within a dimensional doman: "It is immaterial for a linear system whether points or stars or crosses or circles or any other objects be
the members, if only in the arrangement the positional values remain
the same." In a relationship the positions of the two objects merely have
to be different in order that the objects be different so that a relationship can be made, but in a system the distribution in the dimensional
domain defines the system. But it is important to note here that although
use is made of geometrical analogies, this dimensional domain can be
any kind of space in which the objects are located, for example in a
Markov chain the distribution of objects in an initial probability vector
coupled with the transition probability matrix will determine the distribution of objects between states at a later time period irrespective of
what the objects are. The behaviour of the system is characterized by
these distributions, and the nature and immanent qualities of the objects
can only enter the system in a secondary way.

A similar point is made by Angyal with a diagram of four points on a
line (Fig. 5.1.). The relations *a* to *b*, *b* to *c*, *c* to *d*, can be expressed, but
do not specify a line. We can have any possible configuration of linked
short straight lines as a result. The only way to fix *a, b, c* and *d* on a line
is to express their membership of this larger whole, the line itself. "In a

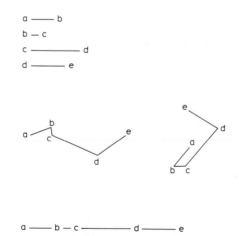

Fig. 5.1. A shaped line as a system.

system the members are, from a holistic viewpoint, not significantly connected with each other except with reference to the whole." But from the line we can compute $a-b, b-c, c-d$.

In the example quoted earlier (Chapter 4) from Chorley and Kennedy this expression of connection with the whole is missing. The "system" is composed of many two-way relationships, and thus the significance of the total arrangement is not known or expressed. We are left with explanation without understanding. Indeed it is interesting to note that Angyal links his discussion of relation and system to the distinction between explanation and understanding, since Feibleman (see section 2.11) finds a scale distinction between explanation and understanding in terms of the physiological viewpoint of the individual part and the ecological viewpoint of the part within the whole.

In pursuit of this understanding and the significance of the arrangement of the parts we can see a simple clear distinction between a mere summation of parts in an aggregate and the arrangement of the parts in a whole, or system. "In aggregates it is significant that parts are added; in a system it is significant that the parts are arranged." If we take a wood as an aggregate, then quite clearly one wood can be larger than another simply by having more trees. The way in which the trees are arranged is not of any significance to the identification of either as a wood. If we return again to national statistics of imports and exports, the mere statement of a total does not define the nature of the system which gave rise to them. The whole export figure could come from one industry, or from many, and it is of peculiar importance to prediction of future trends that we know which industry contributed what, and how these industries are related to each other.

The summation of many things, even the summation of many two-way relations, thus does not give us understanding. For this we must look to arrangement and the significance of the whole. But there are many areas in which distinctions are not clear and easy to make. Some properties of the objects in a system, their immanent qualities, may be essential for them to occupy their position in the system, and these we may term "leading" properties. Others may be "accompanying" properties. In this we find a concept of "degree of organization"* of the whole.

---

* The term "degree of organization" is used here in Angyal's sense, as defined here. It is not the same as the measure "degree of organization" defined by Rothstein and examined in Chapter 4.

The greater the organization of the whole, the more the inherent properties of parts are utilized as co-determinants of positional values. The human organism is for example, highly economical in this respect: it carries a minimal load of irrelevant properties of parts; most of the properties of parts are utilized, that is, are co-determinants of the positional value of the part.

Since this was written medical research has begun to produce evidence which suggests the paramount importance of relative position within the body. For long we have been puzzled as to how cells arriving at, for example, the position of the future hand in an embryo should "know" that they should grow a hand rather than a foot or a knee. The most likely reason seems to be that cells carry with them a "map" of the body and know by their position in the body to what form of growth they should contribute.

Unfortunately for us, however, Angyal has not produced a complete new genus of logic that would enable us to handle the problems we wish to study, and there are problems in the application of those ideas that have so far been expressed. He suggests, for example, that in every system there is one and only one arranging principle, but whether this statement is a matter of definition or empirical truth is unclear. Furthermore, the application of the principle may, he suggests, be incomplete. There are wholes, in which not all positional values are occupied, rather as if in an ecosystem some niches remained unoccupied, and there may indeed be so few that are occupied that it is impossible to guess the outline of the principle. Where above we talked of "gestalts" in geography of lower order than an animal or a watch, in system terms Angyal recalls the ideas of good and bad gestalts, of open and closed gestalts. The good gestalt expresses complete conformity between system parts and the arranging principle, the open gestalt expresses one where there are positional values still vacant. When we search empirically through the real world for central place hierarchies we are assuming that by deduction we know the arranging principle of the urban system. That we do not find perfect hierarchies might be ascribable to the fact that in the real world the gestalt is a bad one, with some members out of position, and other positions unoccupied. But of course, given the factor of time, and the presence of pointly bound and areally bound places, the two other classes of urban places Christaller named but explicitly excluded from his theory, it seems more likely that we need a more complex arranging principle, including some of the other notions such as complementarity expressed in basic/non-basic ratios, which would produce a more com-

plex set of interrelationships. Equally, of course, we are constrained by
the nature of data, which rarely define our objects of study in any positional sense. If job classifications list people as "labourers", "architects",
"company directors", we have only a crude aggregate approach to
understanding the roles of people in our system. What we need are data
where we know whether the "architect" designs lavatories for the Town
Hall, or runs a large practice designing opera houses, and where we know
that one company director runs ICI and another a three-man lamp-shade
emporium.

The last and most worrying deficiency of Angyal's logical genus is that
it is specifically restricted to static forms of systems. In these the parts
have a positional value derived from their membership of the system. He
suggests that in a dynamic whole, the parts function differently according
to the whole to which they belong. But as yet there is no firm methodology for the study of dynamic wholes.

Instances of the use of arranging principles are not easy to find. This
may well be because given the problem of change in the system, which
later we show to be something that probably cannot be analysed theoretically but only empirically, there never is a complete application of a
single arranging principle to the system. Secondly, in thermodynamics
the idea of an arranging principle is applied to closed systems, and in
geography the few examples that do exist have all been applied to closed
systems, e.g. the work by Wilson (1970), and in deductive models such
as the Central Place Theory where competition in a closed system produces a time-independent state. The problem then is that the cases where
we can use a closed system as a realistic approximation of reality are few,
and nearly all of them are concerned with what one can call flows or
structures of system maintenance, and not flows of information or goods
producing system change.

In essence Anygal's work is stimulating, but leaves one wondering
how one can approach a new genus of logic when so little is known
about it.

5.4 Emergence

Implicit in the forgoing discussion, but not yet explicitly named, there
is a concept of emergence — that is the emergence of properties at the
level of the whole which cannot be surmised from the parts. In the usual
treatment of systems theory, emergence is given due attention as demon-

strating the need for a system viewpoint. Quite simply, it is construed that a set of individuals behaving together demonstrate behavioural forms which are distinct from those of the individuals separately and which cannot be predicted from the individuals' properties on their own. A crowd of people at a football match behave in ways which could not be predicted from study of their individual behaviour: "the crowd mentality". The concept of entropy in thermodynamics is itself an emergent one: the individual atoms retain their characteristic velocities, but a property of a group of atoms changes in the direction of minimal energy available for work.

Clearly, since we are considering groupings of individuals, behind the idea of emergence we may find yet again the concepts of hierarchies. The laws of physics pertain at a certain level in the hierarchy of objects, and the laws of biology at another. Futher up, we find that the laws of sociology may apply to sociological organizations. The atoms in groups may behave according to the laws of thermodynamics, the groups of cells according to genetic laws, and groups of people according to social custom.

Here we are touching on one of the great and continuing debates of scientific method: the horny problem of the reductionist and the holist. We can contrast the two following quotations.

> According to these holist schools which, phoenix like, are reborn in every generation, the analytical attitude (reductionist) is doomed to fail in its attempts to reduce the properties of a very complex organization to the "sum" of the properties of its parts. It is a very stupid and misguided quarrel, which merely testifies to the "holists'" total lack of understanding of scientific method and of the crucial role analysis plays in it. How far could a Martian engineer get if, trying to understand an earthly computer, he refused on principle to dissect the machine's basic electronic components which execute the operations of propositional algebra?
>
> (Monod, 1974)

> Physical laws are inadequate by themselves to account for organized complexity on the biological level. Biological laws may likewise be inadequate to account for organized complexity on the sociological level. But social anthropology need no more be reduced to biology than biology to physics. Irreducibility does not mean a break in the uniformity of organized nature, for it does not suggest contradiction. Biological organisms do not violate the laws of physics, even if they are not adequately explained by them. And social systems do not violate the laws of biology although they, too, cannot be explained in purely biological terms.
>
> (Laszlo, 1971)

Monod's fascinating book is the most persuasive argument against a systems viewpoint that I have read. I cannot hope to catch the essence of it here, but suggest that the reader studies it for himself. Suffice it to say that in the end he has an apparent holistic view of the whole biosphere: that the biosphere, as a whole, is one single accident. But this accident and the whole biosphere with it are compatible with physical laws, whence we find that the apparent wholeness evaporates. But, again, we find that he acknowledges that because of our genetic as well as social inheritance, we have an innate need for concepts such as God and Soul; in other words he admits that we will have to put up with use of enveloping attitudes towards understanding even if they are not based in objective reality. It is a begrudging acceptance of the existence of ideas which he nevertheless feels are untenable.

What then of Laszlo's comments? Clearly in his view the essence is not merely explanation, but also understanding. Understanding depends upon the level at which we observe the phenomena in the first place. If we observe a riot at a football match, then ultimately, even if in the chain of logic we descend to an analysis of the physical properties of the atoms in the cells of the neurons of the brains of the individuals, we shall phrase the understanding of that riot in scales of thought adjacent to the original phenomenon. In other words, yet again we find that the analysis of emergent properties depends upon our observation and understanding. It is a property of an analysis which belongs in the structures of understanding.

Let me conclude this section with another return to Monod's world. In considering the quest for a universal theory, to explain everything, he states:

> A universal theory would obviously have to extend to include relativity, the theory of quanta, and a theory of elementary particles. Provided certain initial conditions could be formulated, it would also include a cosmology which would forecast the general evolution of the universe. We know however . . . that these predictions could be no more than statistical. The theory might very well contain the periodic table of the elements, but could only determine the probability of the existence of each of them. Likewise it would anticipate the appearance of such objects as galaxies or planetary systems, but would not in any case deduce from its principles the necessary existence of this or that object, event, or individual phenomenon — whether it be the Andromeda nebula, the planet Venus, Mount Everest, or last night's thunderstorm.
>
> In a general manner the theory would anticipate the existence, the properties the interrelation of certain classes of objects and events, but would obviously not

be able to foresee the existence of the distinctive characteristics of any particular
object or event.

There are two comments to be made on this quotation. Firstly, the
last paragraph amounts to almost the best succinct statement of the aims
of the structuralists, to derive general theory based on such concepts as
the group etc., which would be the basis of their holistic understanding
of the principles underlying social phenomena. The irony of taking
Monod out of context in this manner is obvious: in context perhaps it
highlights the misunderstanding generated by the assumption that reductionist viewpoints never lead to universal truths. Secondly, the fact
that the universal theory will predict classes of events, but not the actual
unique events, means that those who are concerned with real systems
are allowed the necessity of explaining some actual events in terms of
some other actual events. The basis of comparative sociological studies
is the existence of different actual societies. Monod's physical laws may
indeed explain anything that does happen, in that it is physically possible
for "this" to result from a previous state, but we may equally be
interested in explaining some present unique event in relation to a previous unique event or events. That is, there are many studies which begin:
given x, then what will happen to y, where x is not a law but an event.

We are now explicitly distinguishing between the laws that govern a
system and its actual history at any one time between, for example, the
laws which undeniably are not contradicted by evolution, but which do
not account for the specific form it takes. (Monod would insist that the
specific form is a consequence of random processes.) Let us stay with
the latter for a moment.

Rothstein (1958) has some pertinent comments on the relationship
of information about the universe to time. Our information about an
isolated system can only decrease. To increase our information about it,
we must interact with it — this is simply the same principle as Brillouin
used to exorcise Maxwell's demon. As a consequence, the entropy of the
universe as a whole increases as a result of the energy involved in the
interaction. To put this somewhat inaccurately and loosely, while we
concentrate on learning about some particular thing, our information
about the rest of the universe gets out of date. It is a lesson well learnt
by academics whose usual course is to know more and more about less
and less. In general we may summarize as follows: because of the limitations imposed on us by the degradation of information, we cannot hope

to base our understanding on detailed observation at all levels; we have to be able to make valid general statements which subsume the parts within the whole. Statistical aggregation is one way of doing this and systems theory is another. Because the latter explicitly seeks to accommodate arranging principles and the associated problems of degrees of freedom (see below) it is superior to the former.

What of the laws that govern a system, invariant through time? Gödel (in Piaget, 1971) provides the answer to this question. He demonstrated "that no consistent formal system sufficiently 'rich' to contain elementary arithmetic, can, by its own principles of reasoning demonstrate its own consistency". It may be that there is a higher formal system that can explain the lower, but then again the higher cannot prove itself consistent. There are systems within systems within systems. Even Monod acknowledges this proposition. His whole thesis rests on the assumption of objectivity. But as he admits, objectivity itself is initially an arbitrary choice.

> It is obvious that the positioning of the principle of objectivity as the condition of true knowledge constitutes an ethical choice and not a judgement reached from knowledge, since, according to the postulates own terms, there cannot have been any true knowledge prior to this arbitrary choice.

I am aware that the line is sometimes blurred in the above between a discussion of the time-invariant laws underlying a system and the actual behaviour of the system in time. But it does seem that we can in fact make some general conclusions by analogy. The amount of information necessary to specify the total universe is vast: each man is but one part of that universe, and constitutes part of its total information: the information that he contains logically cannot specify the whole universe. The little system cannot "know" completely the greater. Thus, as Langton observes that the human system is composed of both things and images of things, the images of the things are necessarily crude representations. The holistic approach is a necessary part of any attempt at understanding the world about us.

I also think Monod's reductionist viewpoint results from his failure to make similar distinctions. It is one thing to say that we know how *a typical cell transmits* its genetic message to a successor cell: it is another to say that we know all the cells in an animal, and can work out from these parts how the animal in total will behave. The amount of information needed is too vast: the limits of observation and comprehension work at the macroscopic as well as the microscopic level. In essence he tacitly admits the same.

> A given species' 'teleonomic level' may then be said to correspond to the quantity of information which, on the average and per individual, must be transferred to assure the generation to generation transmission of the specific content of reproductive invariance. . . .
>
> It is the degree of complexity of all these performances or structures, conceived as having the function of serving the teleonomic purpose, that we would like to estimate.
>
> This magnitude, while theoretically definable, is not measurable in practice. Still, it may serve as a rule of thumb for ranking different species or groups upon a 'teleonomic scale'.

5.5 Degrees of freedom

To the average student of geography in the 1960s I have no doubt that degrees of freedom means $N - 1$. But the origin of the concept is wider than that!

When a set of some objects, each of which has some number of alternative states, does not exhibit in combination all the permutations of states that are possible, the set has some degree of constraint that we can describe in terms of degrees of freedom. Ross Ashby has an example of traffic lights. British traffic lights have three colours, each of which can be in one of two states — on or off. Since $2^3 = 8$, there are eight permutations of lights possible. But only four of these are used, as in the sequence illustrated in Fig. 5.2. Four of the possible permutations are unused. Thus some kind of constraint exists, linking the states of the individual lights, so that they are not completely independent of each other. We can find a number to express this constraint: we hypothesize the number of objects, each with two states, but able to act independently of each other which would give the same number of states as are observed. Two lights can provide four combinations, as in Fig. 5.2c. Thus we say that the British traffic light with three colours has two degrees of freedom.

Suppose we have a set of numbers (x_i) $i = 1 \ldots 10$. Suppose for the moment I do not know their total. Then clearly any of them can have any value. All of them are assumed to be independent of each other, since we know no better. There are 10 degrees of freedom in the set — that is all 10 members are unconstrained. But now let me introduce a constraint. Let me say

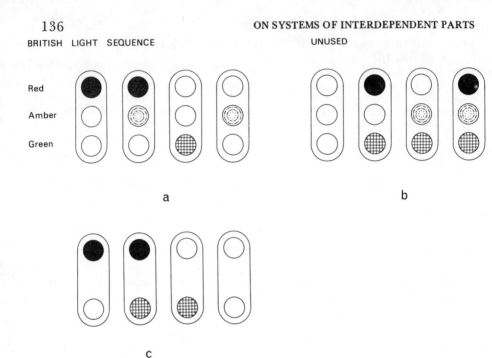

Fig. 5.2. Degrees of freedom and traffic lights.

$$\sum_{i=1}^{10} x_i = 2305$$

I have specified one constraint on the set, and we now have $10 - 1 = 9$ degrees of freedom. Only nine of the members are completely free. It does not matter which are the nine: remember that with the traffic lights we said that we could hypothesize a number of independent lights which would have the same range of states as the constrained lights. Now it is easy to show that there are nine degrees of freedom. When we know the values for nine of the x_i then the tenth is

$$x_{10} = \sum_{i=1}^{10} x_i - \sum_{i=1}^{9} x_i$$

that is to say that when we have allocated nine values completely freely, we can derive the tenth with respect to the constraints. We can try the nine numbers 23, 54 678, 24, 290, 56, 3456, 34, 65 778, −3889. Their total is 120 450, so we conclude that the tenth number is 2305 − 120 450 = −118 145. In general, we will need one constraint for every one unknown before we can derive all the x_i: in other words before we can remove all degrees of freedom.

There are more complex ways of handling the concept. In a chi-square test where the numbers have been laid out in a contingency table, the degrees of freedom are expressed as $(p - 1)(q - 1)$, where the table has p rows and q columns. It is not my purpose here to explain the test, but to show why the degrees of freedom are expressed that way. Suppose we have a table where we are analysing the habits of shoppers, where we have recorded the number of shoppers in a two way classification, by age group and by shop used, as in Fig. 5.3. Each of the rows and each of

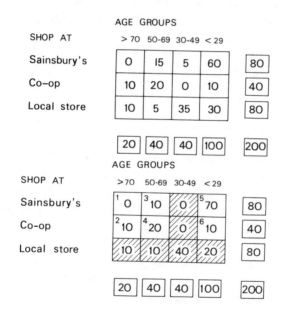

Fig. 5.3. Contingency tables.

the columns has its own total, a sub-total of the grand total. There are three such row subtotals and four such columns subtotals.

The analysis then proceeds by making use of these subtotals to work out an expected number of shoppers for each cell of the matrix. The test is then made comparing the number of actual shoppers in each cell with the expected number. But for there to be any statistical validity to the test, we have to work out the degrees of freedom in the calculation of the chi-square statistic. Were there no degrees of freedom then the very idea of a statistical test, of chance deviation, is nonsense: where there is a deterministic solution there can be no statistical result.

According to the above there are $(3 - 1)(4 - 1) = 6$ degrees of freedom. In Fig. 5.3 (lower) I attempted to fill values into the matrix as I thought fit. In cell 1,1 I placed a 0. That was one degree of freedom — there were no difficulties about assigning that number. In cell 2,1 I place 10 — no difficulties, so far I have had two degrees of freedom. But now that cells, 1,1 and 2,1 are completed, I know by the subtotal of column 1 that the cell 3,1 must contain $20 - (0 + 10) = 10$. There was no freedom in this. The cell has been shaded accordingly. I can proceed — next I assign 10 to cell 1,2, and then 20 to cell 2,2, and then I find that 3,2 is determined, so again it is shaded. Next I assign 70 to cell 1,4 and 10 to cell 2,4. It is easy to verify that the remaining four cells are then all determined with respect to one subtotal or another. The diagram indicates that six of the 12 cells are shaded and six unshaded. There were indeed six degrees of freedom.

Consider the mobility of a piece of wood. How many degrees of freedom does a free piece of wood have? Let us represent its position by a vector of six coordinates (v_1, v_2, v_3, x, y, z), where v_1 is its angular position with respect to a specified orientation in one axis, v_2 its angular position with respect to its second axis, v_3 with respect to the third, and x, y, and z are its position in a three-dimensional grid. The piece of wood thus described has six degrees of freedom — they have been indicated in Fig. 5.4. Here we see that the piece can be rotated around any of three orthogonal axes (the circles represent the 360° rotation in each plane) and translocated or transported or moved in any of three orthogonal directions — for simplicity we could say left or right as one direction, forwards or backwards as another, and up or down as the third. Similarly for the angular case we have the familiar words other way round, other way up, turn it end to end.

Suppose a chair is made from six pieces of wood — four legs, a seat, and a back. While these pieces are unattached to each other they have in total $6 \times 6 = 36$ degrees of freedom. If we glue and screw them together rigidly, the chair that results has only 6 degrees of freedom. The constraint that the chair represents has absorbed 30 degrees of freedom. More accurately, if each of the pieces is indicated by a vector of six

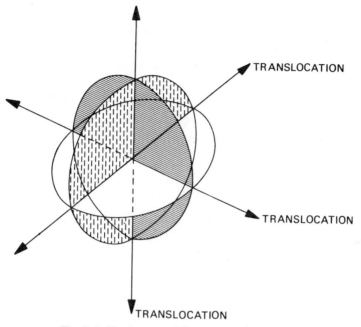

TRANSLOCATION

TRANSLOCATION

TRANSLOCATION

Fig. 5.4. Six degrees of freedom in space.

variables arranged in matrix form as in Fig. 5.5., then there are consistent transformations that relate each row to each other, such that if we know the values for any row a, b, c, d, e, f, then we will know those values for all other rows.

In this sense the chair does represent a system. The degrees of freedom

Variables

		V_1	V_2	V_3	X_1	Y_1	Z_1
	1	a_1	b_1	c_1	d_1	e_1	f_1
	2	a_2	b_2	c_2	d_2	e_2	f_2
	3	a_3	b_3	c_3	d_3	e_3	f_3
Pieces	4	a_4	b_4	c_4	d_4	e_4	f_4
	5	a_5	b_5	c_5	d_5	e_5	f_5
	6	a_6	b_6	c_6	d_6	e_6	f_6

Matrix of observed values

Fig. 5.5. A matrix of the degrees of freedom for six components.

in the whole are less than the sum of the degrees of freedom of each part considered separately; the parallel between this and the definition of the degree of organization in a system in Chapter 4 is readily apparent.

For all that, chairs are not very interesting systems. Let us move onto something a little more subtle.

Let us again take a set of numbers, (x_i), $i = 1 \ldots 10$, only this time we will, for the sake of the logarithms that follow, assume that all x_i are non-negative. Let us place a constraint on them

$$\sum_{i=1}^{10} x_i = Z$$

We now have nine degrees of freedom. Now let us place the further constraint,

$$\sum_{i=1}^{10} \frac{x_i}{Z} \ln \frac{Z}{x_i} = K$$

Now we know from Chapter 8 that the maximum value of K is $\ln 10$, and the minimum value is $\ln 1 = 0$. And we know if $k = \ln 10$, then $x_i = Z/10$ for all i, and that if $k = 0$ then for one i $x_i = Z$, and for all other i $x_i = 0$. Quite clearly the one extra constraint has absorbed nine degrees of freedom. The constraint produced by using an entropy expression is remarkably powerful. The same is true for all other values of K, where K is specified to be a known degree of accuracy. We have to say this because $\ln q$ produces an irrational number, that is one that does not terminate nor recur after the decimal point. We can for the purposes of the argument hypothesize the function $\ln*$ which truncates $\ln$ at six decimal places. Thus if then we write

$$\sum_{i=1}^{10} \frac{x_i}{Z} \ln* \frac{Z}{x_i} = K$$

and we know the values of K, we will also know the value of all 10 numbers x_i although the permutation of those values amongst the subscripts i would be arbitrary. More is said about this in Chapter 8.

The point I wish to emphasize here is that I believe the peculiar importance of the entropy expressions in systems theory hinges almost exclusively on this attribute. The inherent additivity of the algebraic expressions is most helpful, and makes manipulation and interpretation much easier, but the basic reason why we get numbers out that are useful indicators of inequality or uncertainty is that the relationship between the value K and the set which gives rise to it is almost determinate. We have a measure of arrangement. All parts are fixed by it within the whole.

5.6 Solid chairs and creaky chairs

The solid chair has but six degrees of freedom. The parts are rigidly locked with the whole, and in fact for the purpose of a person interacting with the chair, he need consider it merely as one thing, and not as a complex of six parts. But what of creaky chairs? In such chairs, although they are assumed here to be recognizable as such, it nevertheless remains true by definition that some of the parts are less than rigidly fixed in relation to the whole. Yet when a person interacts with such a chair, it is highly probable that the way in which one part goes will influence the way in which other parts go, even if not completely so.

The systems of the world of interest to us are creaky chair systems: those in which the parts, though influenced by the whole, are nevertheless to some degree free. These are of interest to us not only because they are the kind of system we find in reality, but also because the intellectual challenge they represent is so much greater than for perfectly organized systems. Perhaps it would be fair to say that the challenge is daunting, but if a systems approach to geography is to be adopted these issues cannot be avoided.

This chapter has covered a number of topics, which can all be illustrated by reference to our apocryphal chairs. Very creaky chairs make bad gestalts, and have too many degrees of freedom. If the situation degenerates too far, we may not even recognize the chair as such at all. Again a creaky chair may lose one or two pieces: and then in Angyal's terms the organizing principle has been unfulfilled — there are unoccupied positional values. Well organized chairs should also be comfortable ones: in such chairs the leading characteristics of size that enable a part to fill a position are accompanied by characteristics that co-determine that position — for example the seat is sculptured for rumps to fit it. Chairs made of drift-wood are usually not well organized.

The characteristic "chair" is also an emergent one, that derives from the way that the parts have been put together. The emergent characteristic cannot be explained solely in terms of the aggregation of those parts, but in their arrangement. Understanding of this emergent property, "chairness", cannot be attempted without acceptance of the chair as a whole with a purpose, rather than as an aggregation of parts. But the creakier the chair becomes, the greater the degrees of freedom we allow, then the less likely that there will be any emergent property "chairness" of interest or value. As progressively we become left with a mere heap of parts, so progressively the significance of any particular form diminishes.

However, these analogies do not cover all the grounds of contention, and there are further areas still to be explored. Figure 5.6 summarizes much of what we have covered so far in this book, and also touches on the issues which have yet to be resolved. In the upper diagram of Fig. 5.6 I have sketched the relationships between the perfectly organized system and time. Since all parts are perfectly determined to be what they are at any point in time, all that we need to explain change of the whole through time is to define change in the parameter that governs the organizing principle. In this sketch I have an entropy-maximizing example in mind, where we have some cost constraint that totally determines the pattern. Because part-to-part links do not exist through time, I have moved the component parts in space as well as changing the strength of links between them, to symbolize the extent to which the external constraint explains the whole.

In the lower diagram of Fig. 5.6, by contrast, there are part-to-part links through time, and the successive constraints, $C1-C3$, explain possibly the size and colour of the parts, but not their position. I have in mind the idea of the location of service industries. Ideally, at each stage in time urban locations should be mobile to maximize the efficiency of distribution at each point in time: but in reality urban locations are fairly fixed, and the allocation of services takes place within a fairly rigid framework.

This does of course beg many questions; most importantly of all we have to ask what is the system we are trying to explain, what are the givens that are external to it, and what are the internals to be assigned. If the location of the towns is to be a given, then the part-to-part links through time are not an issue which clouds the search for an explanatory model. But an even bigger question, which cannot be avoided so easily, is what happens if the part to part links through time are strong but not immutable — in other words there are lags in the system such that change in response to the C states does occur, but never quickly enough for an

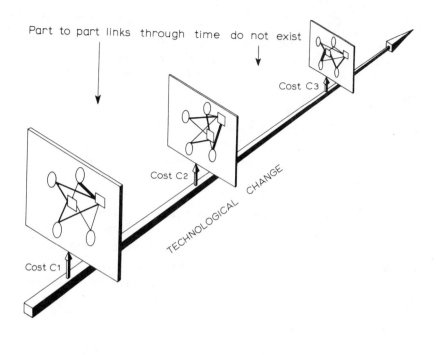

Part to part links through time do not exist

Cost C3

Cost C2

TECHNOLOGICAL CHANGE

Cost C1

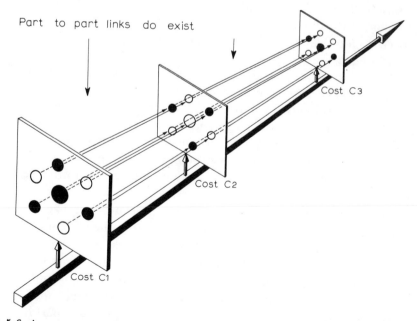

Part to part links do exist

Cost C3

Cost C2

Cost C1

Fig. 5.6. Arrangement and change (a) in a completely organized system, (b) in a system with historical lags.

equilibrium to occur between a current C and the system. Such an equilibrium has been assumed in the upper part of Fig. 5.6.

Lastly, I wish to consider again the problem of the creaky chair, but to look at it from the point of view of a loose leg. If I wobble the leg, there is a certain amount of freedom of action before I begin to move the chair with it. There are thresholds of change which have to be crossed before the rest of the system knows of its change of state. We need to know if this is a phenomenon to be explained by our theories or not. It might appear that it is simply local scale determinacy; but, in the sense that this was defined in Chapter 4, this is not possible since local scale and system scale determinacy jointly defined the states of the part. In this example the change can occur without the system ever "knowing" about it, hence it must be unrelated to any concepts of system organization, since the rest of the system is never influenced by these small changes of position of the part. This problem can be explained and amplified, and I will do so in the next chapter. Suffice it to say for the moment that the definition of "state" for the part has to be one that can cause change in the system. It is a term relative to the system, and not to the observer. All those positions which the leg can occupy without changing the state of anything else are a single state from the system viewpoint. In the next chapter we shall find that it is possible to calculate a quantity for this freedom of the part, which will be termed "overspecification", and which is analogous with equivocation in communications theory.

Not all problems have as yet been resolved. Clearly, within the framework of six degrees of freedom and translocation and rotation in space, there is something that can be said about this example. There are movements which one part can make within bounded regions of the six-dimensional coordinate space, without affecting the chair. This implies that the chair has more than six degrees of freedom overall. However, I have not as yet pursued this issue further, and leave it for the reader to puzzle over.

From the system's point of view it is important to realize that we define a change of state in a part in some way that the system can "know" of it. In other words something else in the system must have a potential for change as a direct result. But we have also seen in Chapter 4 that if change always occurred, then the system would be erratic and unstable. If, however, this potential change is not always fulfilled, and if we sometimes have lags as suggested above to account for part-to-part links through time, then clearly we need some way in which to determine the idea of potential change that is blocked in effectiveness.

To this issue of Regulation, I turn in the next chapter. It is, I think, probably the central part of the part—whole relationship.

6
On Regulation

6.1 Introduction

At the risk of seeming to be obscure, I wish to retain an abstract approach to the definition of regulation. This is necessary not just to be general, but, most importantly, the ideas are generated from an abstract base, and cannot be applied indiscriminately without regard to this base. For example, it is quite common to read of extraordinary applications of the Law of Requisite variety, without realization of the manner in which variety should be defined for the law to hold. To say that only variety can destroy variety is only true if the right forms of measurement have been used both times. Without such a limitation statements such as the following convey no unambiguous meaning:

> It is called the Law of Requisite Variety, and in simple terms it states that for effective regulation in any system, the variety in the control device must be at least equal to that of the disturbances. . . .
> Let us begin by considering a typical planning office. In order to cope with the control of an area, some massive reduction of the very high variety of the human environment must be attempted and this is done by means of a development plan. We must think here in a comprehensive way, where 'plan' includes all the policy statements, committee resolutions, etc., or additions to the formal plan and its legal amendments. Even though plans have been criticised for becoming too complicated (planning Advisory Group 1965) they obviously represent a huge reduction in variety by comparison with the real world. But as we know British planning control is based on 'accord with the plan'; so here we have a

situation in which the attempt is made to control a very high-variety world using
the low variety tool of the development plan.

(McLoughlin, 1969)

I think the utter vagueness of the passage needs no detailed comment.
Let us assume that we are observing some object, and that this object
can be in a number of different states. Let us denote the full range of
states by the letters *a, b, c, d, e, f, g, h*. Now let us assume that this object is in an environment, and is not completely isolated from it (the
first condition really means the second as well). Therefore if it is not
isolated from the environment, if the environment is subject to a distinguishable change, the object itself will also change in state.

I have said, a distinguishable change. It is this point that is most
readily ignored in popular and vague application of the idea. Something
is not inherently distinguishable on its own: it is distinguished by something. In this case the distinguishable states of the environment are those
which cause a change of state in the object: and are therefore limited by
our ability to observe changes in the object. We will denote the environment by *D*.

Now suppose that it is possible to operate a machine *R* with a number
of states such that its effect on the object is to vary the state of the
object as its own state changes, and to do so in conjunction with the
changes possible in the state of the environment.

6.2 The simple case

What we have supposed can be illustrated by a matrix, as in Fig. 6.1.
The environment is denoted by *D*, and the response by *R*. The environment has the five states 1, 2, 3, 4, 5 and the response the four states α,
γ, δ, and β. As a result of these compound environment—response states

D

	1	2	3	4	5
α	a	d	e	f	g
β	d	c	b	a	h
γ	e	a	c	d	b
δ	b	f	a	g	h

R

Fig. 6.1. Matrix example of regulation.

the object adopts the states indicated by the lower case alphabetic letters which comprise the set E.

Can anything useful be said about this matrix, the set of outcomes, and their relation to D and R? We can say some useful things, provided that we make a few more assumptions. First let us assume that there is a purpose in R's moves, and that that purpose is to maintain E as far as possible in one state. Let us assume that D may adopt randomly or purposefully — it does not matter which — any of its five states. Let us suppose that R's purpose is to maintain an "a" as the outcome. We can pair D's moves and R's moves as follows:

$$
\begin{array}{lccccc}
\text{if} & D: & 1 & 2 & 3 & 4 \\
\text{then} & R: & \alpha & \gamma & \delta & \beta \\
\text{outcome} & E: & a & a & a & a
\end{array}
$$

and we see that for these four states of D, R can always maintain E at "a". R is acting as a regulator to maintain the state of the object. But if D adopts 5, then R cannot score an "a", and the resultant set of states from E that the object exhibits has to contain at least two members. The variety in R was not sufficient to eliminate all the variety in D.

At that statement the protests burst out. The objections probably centre around the apparently arbitrary way that the matrix was constructed. Let us be less arbitrary about how it was constructed and impose two conditions on it. Firstly let us say that no member of the set of outcomes E may be repeated in any row of the matrix. Secondly let us say that each row must be different from all other rows. If this were not true, if all rows looked the same, then we would be distinguishing between R states for no apparent reason.

It is clear that the matrix in Fig. 6.1. complies with these conditions. It is also clear that the only way we can hope to reduce the variety in outcomes from two states to the state "a" only is to have another R move with an "a" in the last column. It is of course perfectly possible to define an R move which obeys the above two conditions (that it contains no repeated outcome, that it is not identical with any other R move) but which does not have an "a" in the last column. And so it is that the Law of Requisite Variety as defined by Ross Ashby is expressed in terms of an inequality. Later, we will define it in terms of an equality. In a table which obeys the two set conditions, the variety in the outcomes cannot be less than the variety in D divided by the variety in R. In this case the variety in outcomes cannot be less than 5/4. Since in this case we are dealing with a simple approach and variety is expressed in the number of states, but not in their frequency, the nearest whole number above 5/4 is of course 2, which was the variety we observed in the outcomes. Below we will deal with the frequency case where 5/4 does have meaning.

In effect our table was one such that the minimum variety in outcomes was attained. Still obeying the two set conditions and using the same number of states in *D, R* and *E*, we can construct a table such as Fig. 6.2. in which *R*'s moves have no effect on the outcome of *D* moves

D

		I	2	3	4	5
	α	a	d	e	f	g
R	β	a	d	e	f	b
	γ	a	d	e	f	c
	δ	a	d	e	f	h

Fig. 6.2. A non-compliant matrix.

1, 2, 3 or 4, but do have some effect on *D*'s fifth move: but the outcomes in column 5 do not occur in any of the other columns. The variety of outcomes is clearly five if *R* has a consistent response to *D*'s move 5. This variety is much greater than 5/4, but such a possibility was not excluded by the law, which was expressed as the minimal variety that could be attained in the most favourable circumstances, i.e. those where *R*'s moves are most effective, and each row of the matrix is as dissimilar as possible from all others.

The implications of the law are simple. If the minimum has been attained in the variety of outcomes, and assuming that the number of *D* states is constant then the only way to reduce variety further is by increasing the number of *R* moves. If we express the law as

$$\text{var } E \geqslant \text{var } D / \text{var } R$$

and for convenience take logs:

$$\log \text{var } E \geqslant \log \text{var } D - \log \text{var } R$$

then when the minimum has been reached only an increase in *R* will make it possible to reduce *E*. This leads to what Ross Ashby calls his picturesque version of the law: only variety can destroy variety. Put like that, and used without fulfilling any of the above stringent conditions, we could verbally use it to prove anything. But we must always remember that there are conditions which have to be fulfilled for the statement to have any meaning.

It is primarily, as Ashby remarks, a statement about permissible arrangements in a table. It is a problem in matrix degrees of freedom. For it to have any meaning in reality, reality must fit such a table: if it does not, then we must re-define reality. That might sound absurd; in fact it is not so absurd. What we are asking is that such ideas as "distinguishable" should have accurate meaning and that such meanings are interrelated among all the states D, R, and E which are the subject of study. They may have states which are not distinguishable in the context of each other but which an outside observer can distinguish; but such precision can be superfluous and redundant in the study of regulation. It would be like indulging in calculations with rounded numbers, where some number were rounded to five significant figures and others to eight, despite the fact that the answer can only be given to the same number of significant places as the number with fewest such digits.

When using more sophisticated frequency formulations these various strictures do not have to be observed early in the construction of empirical studies. In such cases it is possible to use formulae which compensate for the kinds of redundancy and over-specification which we have noted. I will deal with these considerations below. Here I wish to consider some of the other points that may be drawn from our example so far.

Let us give the abstract some concrete reality. Suppose that the E are the states of a crop, that D are the states of the environment, and that R represents the activities of a farmer who uses sprays and pesticides and irrigation etc. What is the system that we are considering? In other words where are the boundaries around the system of concern. They can of course be where we define them to be. Suppose as in Fig. 6.3.a we define the farmer and his farm to be one system. In reality we know that this system has subsystems such as those in Fig. 6.3.b, and that the farmer can maintain his crop in a good state by making the correct response to environmental states. This means that the farmer has to exhibit variety as the environment does: hence, if our model of the system is as in Fig. 6.3.a, then the system of interest is not invariant, it changes state as the environment does. *One part,* a subsystem, the crop, is invariant. Thus we can see that regulation necessitates change in order to prevent

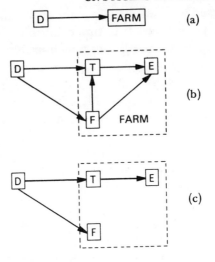

Fig. 6.3. A farm as a regulator: (a) the farm as a system; (b) the subsystems of the farm; (c) in effective management.

change: that there must be some order of priority in a system exhibiting regulation such that some variables may be considered "vital" and others as supportive. In the human body the dilation of sweat glands is supportive to the maintenance of an even temperature.

Secondly, we may note that there are in effect two ways of limiting the effect of the environment on an individual. One way is by adopting more responses, by regulating more — this is the law as we have seen it. The other way is of course to redefine the environment so that it does not have so much variety. We have said that distinguishability should have relative meaning. In the case of the farmer it has meaning with respect to his crops; if the environment does not alter in such a way that we can see this in the crop, without observing the environment, and assuming for the moment the farmer does nothing, then for our purposes nothing has changed in the environment. The only changes that are of concern to us are those which can potentially transmit information about their change to the "vital" variables. Let us suppose that one day upon the earth the first humble proto-tortoise evolved, but without a shell. The species is in acute danger, and needs some protective response. Conceivably it could have evolved into a more acutely seeing tortoise, a more acutely hearing tortoise, a more athletic tortoise, i.e. one that could monitor all the nuances of the environment, and adopt any of a vast range of responses based on variety of speed and direction change (known as agility) and the commensurate degree of sensing to enable it to calculate the state of the environment accurately (the sabre tooth is leaping at me at 33.56 m.p.h., not 31.34). But as we know, this species did not do that. It withdrew into a shell. The variety in the environment is immediately reduced to three states: no attack, shell-breaking attacks, non-shell-breaking attacks. The tortoise's response is of course in or out of the shell. The tortoise has redefined the environment.

In the course of evolution this kind of response has been less and less favoured. In general it has been found better to admit to a greater amount of variety in the environment and develop a full response capability. This enables animals to adapt and react better to changed environments, but also of course can usually be done with better energetic efficiency. The trouble with a thick heavy shell is that whether or not you are being attacked, you have to lug the thing round with you, which is a high price to pay for simplifying the environment.

Thirdly we can consider the case portrayed in Fig. 6.2.3.c which has returned to the case of the farmer. In this illustration either the farmer has a low aspiration level, and does nothing, or else he indulges in activity which bears no true meaning in terms of effective regulation. We could include ritual slaughter of animals, rain dances, and copulation in a recently sown field, as activities of this kind. The crop in either case exhibits the full range of environmental influence, and the farmer is most definitely not part of the system. In other words there is no information in E as a result of R.

If we now make the algebra more sophisticated then we can express all these things succinctly. I shall have to request the reader unfamiliar with information theory to read Chapter 8 before continuing with this section. Where the occurrence of D states, E states and R states is given in frequency form we can use entropy measures to indicate the degree of uncertainty in each set, and to measure uncertainies in each set given certain conditions. We will define the values of H as follows:

$H(D)$ is the uncertainty in D

$H(R)$ is the uncertainty in R

$H(E)$ is the uncertainty in E

$H_D(R)$ is the average uncertainty in R remaining after we have gained knowledge of D. Typically we would hope that for a certain D state R

would have a determinate response. If this is true then this value $H_D(R)$ is zero.

$H_R(D)$ is the uncertainty in D given knowledge of the R state, again averaged over all R states.

$H_E(R)$ is the uncertainty, or equivocation, in R given E.

$H_R(E)$ is the uncertainty in E given that we know which R occurred, again expressed as an average over all R states.

$H_{RE}(D)$ is the uncertainty in D given which R was used and which E resulted. If the environment is not over-specified, if it has no equivocation, then this value will be zero.

$H_{DR}(E)$ is the degree of uncertainty in E given which R and D have occurred. In the cases we have portrayed so far this is always zero, that is D and R give rise to a determinate result. We can, however, use a probability distribution over the E states if we wish for any D and R combination, and this of course will be necessary where the situation studied is not determinate.

$H(DRE)$ is the total uncertainty in the whole system.

6.3 Ross Ashby's specific case of the law of requisite variety

We are interested in $H(E)$, the variety of outcomes in E, and the conditions under which it can be minimized.

Ashby starts his generalization by applying a condition:

If $$H_R(E) \geqslant H_R(D) \qquad (6.1)$$

The condition has a simple interpretation. If the outcome for a given R move is at least as uncertain as the environment for that same R move, averaged over all R moves of course, then it is necessary that R actively responds to D to reduce uncertainty in E. To put it another way, there is no one R move that can be permanently adopted by the regulator which will also reduce the variety in E compared with that in D — there is no blanket move. In reality there often are such moves, *at a price*. For example, the move "build a greenhouse with a controlled environment" would effectively be a blanket move against the outside environment. The condition is also equivalent to the first condition governing tables in the Simple Case — namely that no outcome is to be repeated in any row.

By algebraic necessity we can write:

$$H(D) + H_D(R) = H(DR) = H(R) + H_R(D) \qquad (6.2)$$

whence

$$H_R(D) = H(D) + H_D(R) - H(R) \qquad (6.3)$$

and by substitution into (6.1) above we have

$$H_R(E) \geqslant H(D) + H_D(R) - H(R) \qquad (6.4)$$

whence

$$H(RE) = H(R) + H_R(E) \geqslant H(D) + H_D(R) \qquad (6.5)$$

but again by algebraic necessity we note that

$$H(E) + H(R) \geqslant H(RE) \qquad (6.6)$$

whence by substitution into (6.5) and (6.4) we obtain

$$H(E) \geqslant H(D) + H_D(R) - H(R) \qquad (6.7)$$

This statement can be interpreted as follows. If the condition (6.1) holds, then there is a minimum to $H(E)$, and if that minimum holds it can only be reduced, for a given $H(D)$ by an increase in $H(R)$ and a decrease in $H_D(R)$. This means that only by increasing the variety in R and the accuracy with which R responds to D, can variety in D be reduced. If R's move is a determinate function of D then $H_D(R) = 0$, and there is only one way left to reduce the minimum of $H(E)$, and that of course is by increasing $H(R)$ alone.

This is a restatement of the law of requisite variety. But it is unsatisfactory particularly with respect to the final statement equation (6.7), because of the use of inequalities instead of equalities. We are not left with a statement which shows how $H(E)$ is determined, but only with a statement which shows what governs its minimum value. If in any analysis we find $H(E)$ to have a value greater than this minimum, what can we then say or do? We cannot then say that only an increase in $H(R)$ will reduce $H(E)$, since clearly some other factors will be involved. We can also note that this restatement has implicitly assumed that $H_{DR}(E) = 0$, that is the outcome is a determinate function of R and D, and again this might restrict application in fields where we were unable to assume such accuracy.

These faults can, however, be remedied.

6.4 The general case of the law of requisite variety

We will start by examining the condition (6.1) above. This is designed to prohibit consideration of those cases where there are blanket moves. Ross Ashby offers a kind of corrective ability to the condition by saying that if all outcomes are repeated exactly K times in each row in which they occur, then we may write:

If $H_R(E) \geqslant H_R(D) - K$ (6.8)

from which the solution equation (6.7) becomes

$$H(E) \geqslant H(D) + H_D(R) - H(R) - K$$ (6.9)

I think that in fact for K in both of these we should substitute $\log K$ to make the mathematics consistent. However, that is not the main point. Problems arise if outcomes are repeated in a row, not all of them K times, but by some variable amount, and again if they are repeated but not by an exact integer amount. This might sound nonsensical, but it is not. If we allow $H_{DR}(E)$ to be other than 0, that is we do not have a determinate outcome in E for any R and any D, then clearly we have only a probability of a certain E state. If we have only probabilities, then we cannot state that repetition of the outcome will occur an exact integer number of times.

For the correction K which is applied in (6.8) we therefore need something more general. The quantity is $H_{RE}(D)$, or the equivocation in D which remains even although we know both R and E. This is the amount of information in D which cannot be transmitted — it is the extent to which, to use our previous terminology, D has been overspecified, or given a distinguishability which is greater than the distinguishability we have observed in E. If this is the exact amount of such overspecification, then we can simply subtract it and write a new condition:

If $\qquad\qquad H_R(E) \geqslant H_R(D) - H_{RE}(D)$ (6.10)

But we may note that

$$H(DRE) = H(R) + H_R(D) + H_{RD}(E)$$ (6.11)

and

$$H(DRE) = H(R) + H_R(E) + H_{RE}(D)$$ (6.12)

in which case instead of inequality (6.10) we may write the equality

$$H_R(E) = H_R(D) - H_{RE}(D) + H_{RD}(E)$$ (6.13)

This simply says that inequality (6.10) is true if $H_{DR}(E)$ is greater than zero. $H_{DR}(E)$ is of course the uncertainty which remains even if we know R and D, and is therefore that amount of uncertainty in E which belongs to factors other than those that we are studying, to factors that cannot be eradicated by R, and which may not have been initiated by D.

Using (6.13) we may proceed with substitutions from (6.3), and (6.6) above, and we still then arrive at the solution as given in equation (6.14), which still contains an inequality.

$$H(E) \geqslant H(D) + H_D(R) - H(R) - H_{RE}(D) + H_{DR}(E) \qquad (6.14)$$

We therefore ask ourselves two questions: what has happened to condition 2 of the Simple Case (that no two rows should be exactly the same), and under what conditions does the equality of (6.14) hold?

To discover the conditions under which the equality does hold we note that

$$H(E) + H_E(R) = H(ER) \qquad (6.15)$$

and recall inequality (6.6)

$$H(E) + H(R) \geqslant H(ER) \qquad (6.16)$$

whence by subtracting (6.15) from (6.16)

$$H(R) \geqslant H_E(R) \qquad (6.17)$$

This is reasonable enough, since it states that uncertainty in R given some knowledge about E can never be greater than uncertainty in R when we have no helping knowledge whatsoever. But if the equality of (6.17) holds, then by (6.15)

$$H(E) + H_E(R) = H(E) + H(R) = H(ER) \qquad (6.18)$$

and the solution becomes

$$H(E) = H(D) + H_D(R) - H(R) - H_{RE}(D) + H_{DR}(E) \qquad (6.19)$$

Our suspicions about $H_E(R)$ are aroused. Starting completely from scratch we can find the determinate solution to $H(E)$ very quickly. We may write by algebraic necessity

$$H(DRE) = H(E) + H_E(D) + H_{RE}(D) \qquad (6.20)$$

whence

$$H(E) = H(DRE) - H_E(R) - H_{RE}(D) \qquad (6.21)$$

but

$$H(DRE) = H(D) + H_D(R) + H_{DR}(E) \qquad (6.22)$$

by substitution we conclude that

$$H(E) = H(D) + H_D(R) + H_{DR}(E) - H_E(R) - H_{RE}(D) \qquad (6.23)$$

on recombining terms we may write

$$H(E) = (H(D) - H_{RE}(D)) - (H_E(R) - H_D(R)) + H_{DR}(E) \qquad (6.24)$$

and if we define

$$H(D)^* = H(D) - H_{RE}(D) \qquad (6.25)$$

and

$$H(R)^* = H_E(R) - H_D(R) \qquad (6.26)$$

then 24 becomes

$$H(E) = H(D)^* - H(R)^* + H_{DR}(E) \qquad (6.27)$$

Equation (6.27) is a completely general statement of the Law of Requisite Variety. It can be applied to any three-dimensional table of probabilities, and will have meaning if the table refers to some system which can be modelled in terms of regulation.

The terms have simple meanings. $H(D)^*$ is the distinguishable uncertainty in the environment, that is $H(D)$ corrected for equivocation (which therefore guarantees compliance with condition 1 of the Simple Case). $H(R)^*$ is the worthwhile or effective regulation that can be achieved. It is composed of $H_E(R)$, a term which eliminates overspecification in R, or in other words useless R moves (and in conjunction with other terms already in the equation guarantees compliance with condition 2 of the Simple Case), and $H_D(R)$, the term which refers to the accuracy with which R responds to D. The last term is $H_{DR}(E)$, which, as we have pointed out, is a term referring to factors outside the definition of the study; it is a passive term which appears consistently in each and every equation as the equilibrating factor to account for the otherwise missing information.

It may seem strange that equivocation in D is eliminated by a double conditional entropy $(H_{RE}(D))$ whereas equivocation in R is eliminated by a single conditional entropy (the use of $H_E(R)$). However, given that this is a table, we know from the analysis of degrees of freedom above that conditions in one dimension will reduce possibilities in the other dimension. In other words some of the conditions are interlinked. Additionally, there is some asymmetry in the equations, reflecting the fact that there is an initiator (D) and a responder (R). There is nothing to stop the algebra being applied the other way round: that is transpose the matrix so that R becomes D and D becomes R, or any other way, including with E. The asymmetry of the solution implies that there is a direction in the process and that this direction should be sensibly applied.

To illustrate how all these terms operate we will consider three illustrative matrices. The first two are limiting cases of arrangements in tables, to transgress the two conditions of the Simple Case as far as possible. The last is an ideal case which transgresses nothing. In all we assume that $H_{DR}(E)$ is zero for the sake of clarity. Since in all equations $H_{DR}(E)$ is a passive term, this does not alter the general interpretations that follow — but we can mention in passing that if $H(DRE) = H_{DR}(E)$, then R and D have no part in the system. (My mind conceives of witch doctors confronting witch doctors with rival spells.)

Table 6.I
D

	a	a	a	a
	b	b	b	b
R				
	c	c	c	c
	d	d	d	d

This table transgresses condition 1 of the Simple Case. We can see that there is complete equivocation in D at all times, and therefore $H_{RE}(D) = H(D)$, so that $H(D)^* = 0$. But we may also note that there is no equivocation in R for any E, and therefore $H_E(R) = 0$. It follows that $H(R)^* = -H_D(R)$ so the solution becomes $H(E) = H_D(R)$. This is entirely reasonable. It says that the variety in E is completely conditioned by R's activity. D has no part in this system.

Table 6.II
D

	a	b	c	d
	a	b	c	d
R				
	a	b	c	d
	a	b	c	d

This table transgresses condition 2 of the Simple Case — that is a row is repeated. But E is a determinate function of D, and for E at any stage we may substitute D. In the solution, equations (6.27) and (6.24), we note that $H_E(R) = H_D(R)$ for this case, and that $H(R)^*$ is therefore zero. But $H_{RE}(D)$ is also zero, since for any R and any E, there is no equivocation in D. Thus $H(D)^* = H(D)$ and we conclude that $H(E) = H(D)$. R has no part, therefore, in this system.

Table 6.III

In this table $H_{RE}(D) = 0$, which is the only firm statement we can make without further assumptions. If however we assume R's behaviour to be consistent and rational, and that $H_D(R) = 0$, then the solution becomes $H(E) = H(D) - H_E(R)$. It may be of interest to note that in this example $H_E(R) = H(R)$, but that were any row of the table repeated, $H(R)$ would be greater than $H_E(R)$.

The interpretation of the terms in real-life situations is also of interest. We can illustrate this by returning to the example of the tortoise.

The purpose of the tortoise as evolution has taught it is to survive. To minimize the uncertainty of outcomes means to maximize the certainty of survival. We will take the outcome to mean survival or otherwise.

$H(D)$ is the uncertainty of the environment: this is the variety of moves which the environment can make, the variety of ploys that tigers can perpetrate on tortoises. $H_{RE}(D)$ is the variety of such ploys which is irrelevant to tortoises and the tortoise with a shell increased this value compared with a shell-less proto-tortoise. Unless the tigers increase their $H(D)$ in such a way that $H_R(D)$ does not also increase simultaneously, that is unless tigers make meaningful increases in $H(D)$, the tortoise is reducing $H(D)^*$ and hence $H(E)$ also. Many animals do not change their $H_{RE}(D)$. Instead they increase their $H_E(R)$ — or flexibility of effective response, and simultaneously their $H_D(R)$ — the correctness of the response. Decreasing $H_D(R)$ is associated with better monitoring through sight sound and smell of the environment, and computation of the best response, and $H_E(R)$ is associated with the number of effective responses.

It is also quite obvious that if an animal achieves perfect regulation, then, for the moment assuming death does not occur through old age, to all intents and purposes it no longer belongs to the ecosystem. As evolution has progressed each animal has striven to achieve better regulation, but its environment has likewise been striving to achieve better success against it. We could reverse the tables and analyse the tiger's success and failure against its environment. The process of regulation treats as a whole two parts in behavioural conjunction.

The last term $H_{DR}(E)$ is the uncertainty of outcome for the given moves. Suppose we have a state Tiger-Attacks/Tortoise-in-shell. Perhaps

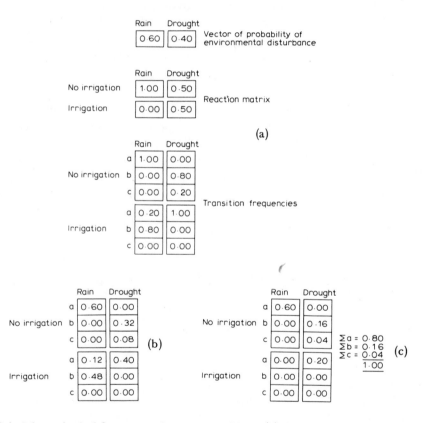

Fig. 6.4. A hypothetical farmer—environment problem: (a) the three data matrices; (b) the result of multiplying the transition frequencies by corresponding elements of the vector of probability of environmental disturbance; (c) The resultant matrix derived from the multiplication of the elements of the matrix in (b) by the elements of the reaction matrix.

this might be supposed to give a single outcome — tortoise survives. However, let us suppose that some tigers have stronger jaws than the average, and some tortoises weaker shells. Then some tortoises would not survive: $H_{DR}(E)$ would measure the extent to which such other factors has been omitted by the analysis.

To put flesh on the bones, I will now work through an example, taken from Chapman (1974). We will assume an environment of two states, rain and drought, and a response by a farmer in two states, irrigate and do not irrigate. We will assume a crop of three permissible states, a, b and c, meaning good, average, and bad. We will now assume that we can measure the frequency of the two environmental states, the frequency of the farmer's responses to each of the states, and instead of assuming that we know exactly what will happen at each cell of the matrix representing a given D state and given R state, we will replace the single determinate outcome by a frequency distribution over the three states a, b and c.

The three relevant sets of data are displayed in a fictitious case in Fig. 6.4. By multiplying the D vector values down the respective columns of the Transition Matrix we arrive at the situation in Fig. 6.4.b, and then by multiplying each set of a, b, c, frequencies of this by the corresponding frequencies of the matrix R, we arrive at Fig. 6.4.c, a matrix in which we have all the information about D, and R, and the resultant E states stored.

Within our Resultant Matrices we can then calculate the following values:

$$H(D) = \sum_j P.j . \log \frac{I}{P.j.}$$

$$H(R) = \sum_i Pi.. \log \frac{1}{Pi..}$$

$$H(E) = \sum_k P..k \log \frac{1}{P..k}$$

$$H_D(R) = \sum_j \sum_i Pij. \log \frac{P.j.}{Pij.}$$

$$H_E(R) = \sum_k \sum_i Pi.k \, \log \frac{P..k}{Pi.k}$$

$$H_{RE}(D) = \sum_i \sum_k \sum_j Pijk \, \log \frac{Pi.k}{Pijk}$$

$$H_{DR}(E) = \sum_i \sum_j \sum_k Pijk \, \log \frac{Pij.}{Pijk}$$

$$H(DRE) = \sum_i \sum_j \sum_k Pijk \, \log \frac{1}{Pijk}$$

In all these formulae the dot . refers to summation over the index that is replaced. For example:

$$P.jk = \sum_i Pijk$$

Table 6.IV

Calculation of H values

$$H(D) = P_{.1.} \log \frac{1}{P_{.1.}} + P_{.2.} \log \frac{1}{P_{.2.}}$$

$$= 0.6 \log \frac{1}{0.6} + 0.4 \log \frac{1}{0.4} \qquad\qquad = 0.6730 \text{ nits}$$

$$H(R) = P_{1..} \log \frac{1}{P_{1..}} + P_{2..} \log \frac{1}{P_{2..}}$$

$$= 0.8 \log \frac{1}{0.8} + 0.2 \log \frac{1}{0.2} \qquad\qquad = 0.5004$$

$$H(E) = P_{..1} \log \frac{1}{P_{..1}} + P_{..2} \log \frac{1}{P_{..2}} + P_{..3} \log \frac{1}{P_{..3}}$$

$$= 0.8 \log \frac{1}{0.8} + 0.16 \log \frac{1}{0.16} + 0.04 \log \frac{1}{0.04} \qquad = 0.6005$$

$$H_D(R) = P_{11.} \log \frac{P_{.1.}}{P_{11.}} + P_{21.} \log \frac{P_{.1.}}{P_{21.}} + P_{12.} \log \frac{P_{.2.}}{P_{12.}}$$

$$+ P_{22.} \log \frac{P_{.2.}}{P_{22.}}$$

$$= 0.6 \log \frac{0.6}{0.6} + 0 \log \frac{0.6}{0} + 0.2 \log \frac{0.4}{0.2} + 0.2 \log \frac{0.4}{0.2} \qquad = 0.2773$$

$$H_E(R) = P_{1.1} \log \frac{P_{..1}}{P_{1.1}} + P_{2.1} \log \frac{P_{..1}}{P_{2.1}} + P_{1.2} \log \frac{P_{..2}}{P_{1.2}}$$

$$+ P_{2.2} \log \frac{P_{..2}}{P_{2.2}} + P_{1.3} \log \frac{P_{..3}}{P_{1.3}} + P_{2.3} \log \frac{P_{..3}}{P_{2.3}}$$

$$= 0.6 \log \frac{0.8}{0.6} + 0.2 \log \frac{0.8}{0.2} + 0.16 \log \frac{0.16}{0.16}$$

$$+ 0.0 \log \frac{0.16}{0.0} + 0.04 \log \frac{0.04}{0.04} + 0.0 \log \frac{0.04}{0.0} \qquad = 0.4499$$

$$H_{DR}(E) = P_{111} \log \frac{P_{11.}}{P_{111}} + P_{112} \log \frac{P_{11.}}{P_{112}} + P_{113} \log \frac{P_{11.}}{P_{113}}$$

$$+ P_{121} \log \frac{P_{12.}}{P_{121}} + P_{122} \log \frac{P_{12.}}{P_{122}} + P_{123} \log \frac{P_{12.}}{P_{123}}$$

$$+ P_{211} \log \frac{P_{21.}}{P_{211}} + P_{212} \log \frac{P_{21.}}{P_{212}} + P_{213} \log \frac{P_{21.}}{P_{213}}$$

$$+ P_{221} \log \frac{P_{22.}}{P_{221}} + P_{222} \log \frac{P_{22.}}{P_{222}} + P_{223} \log \frac{P_{22.}}{P_{223}}$$

$$= 0.6 \log \frac{0.6}{0.6} + 0 \log \frac{0.6}{0} + 0 \log \frac{0.6}{0}$$

$$+ 0 \log \frac{0.2}{0} + 0.16 \log \frac{0.2}{0.16} + 0.04 \log \frac{0.2}{0.04}$$

$$+ 0 \log \frac{0}{0} + 0 \log \frac{0}{0} + 0 \log \frac{0}{0}$$

$$+ 0.2 \log \frac{0.2}{0.2} + 0 \log \frac{0.2}{0.0} + 0 \log \frac{0.2}{0} \qquad = 0.1001$$

$$H_{RE}(D) = P_{111} \log \frac{P_{1.1}}{P_{111}} + P_{121} \log \frac{P_{1.1}}{P_{121}}$$

$$+ P_{121} \log \frac{P_{1.2}}{P_{112}} + P_{122} \log \frac{P_{1.2}}{P_{122}}$$

$$+ P_{113} \log \frac{P_{1.3}}{P_{113}} + P_{123} \log \frac{P_{1.3}}{P_{123}}$$

$$+ P_{211} \log \frac{P_{2.1}}{P_{211}} + P_{221} \log \frac{P_{2.1}}{P_{221}}$$

$$+ P_{212} \log \frac{P_{2.2}}{P_{212}} + P_{222} \log \frac{P_{2.2}}{P_{222}}$$

$$+ P_{213} \log \frac{P_{2.3}}{P_{213}} + P_{223} \log \frac{P_{2.3}}{P_{223}}$$

$$= 0.6 \log \frac{0.6}{0.6} + 0 \log \frac{0.6}{0}$$

$$+ 0 \log \frac{0.16}{0} + 0.16 \log \frac{0.16}{0.16}$$

$$+ 0 \log \frac{0.04}{0} + 0.04 \log \frac{0.04}{0.04}$$

$$+ 0 \log \frac{0.2}{0.2} + 0.2 \log \frac{0.2}{0.2}$$

$$+ 0 \log \frac{0}{0} + 0 \log \frac{0}{0}$$

$$+ 0 \log \frac{0}{0} + 0 \log \frac{0}{0} \qquad\qquad = .0000$$

$$H(DRE) = P_{111} \log \frac{1}{P_{111}} + P_{112} \log \frac{1}{P_{111}} \ldots$$

$$\ldots + P_{222} \log \frac{1}{P_{222}} + P_{223} \log \frac{1}{P_{223}}$$

$$= 0.6 \log \frac{1}{0.6} + \ldots 0.16 \log \frac{1}{0.16} + \ldots 0.04 \log \frac{1}{0.04}$$

$$\ldots + 0.2 \log \frac{1}{0.2} + \ldots \qquad\qquad = 1.0504$$

Analysis

$$H(E) = (H(D) - H_{RE}(D)) - (H_E(R) - H_D(R)) + H_{DR}(E)$$
$$0.6005 = (0.6730 - 0.0) - (0.4499 - 0.2773) + 0.1001$$
$$H(E) = H(D)^* - H(R)^* + H_{DR}(E)$$
$$0.6005 = 0.6730 - 0.1726 + 0.1001$$

The computation is carried out in Table 6.IV, and the results for analysis are also displayed at the bottom of this table. We can see that little of the environmental disturbance is eliminated, and that in large parts this is the result of an inaccurate response to D, that is the corrective value of $H_D(R)$ is quite high. This follows from the fact that only half the farmers are able to irrigate their land in response to a drought.

Although the results of this analysis seem to be valuable, and the whole approach most promising, there are some problems with it that have yet to be resolved, and it is only fair that they are mentioned now. The prime problem results from the fact that the resulting E states are not given any associated measurements of value. That is, in terms of regulation, we could analyse a table showing a high degree of regulation in which every farmer consistently scored a "c" crop. All that we are doing is measuring the reduction in variety, and a consistently bad crop will have a variety of zero. This is a problem that I have not yet solved, but I am sure that there will be a sensible solution to it. In part of the work reported below there is one interesting result which shows sensitivity to this problem.

This section on regulation has attempted to show one way of considering a part that is to some degree tenacious within a changing whole — that is a part which does not fully respond to a change of state in its environment. We have illustrated this with the simplest system — a two-part system of initiator and responder. Clearly most systems of interest to us will be far more complex. In the next chapter we will consider a small ecosystem of seven animal species, which eat each other in various food-web patterns.

7

On Many-part
Wholes

7.1 Introduction

In Chapter 4 system was defined as comprising several parts which inter-
acted with each other. But in the ensuing discussion it became necessary
to define the way in which each part could influence another, or by the
way in which each part might respond to a disturbance in another, and
for the purposes of the introductory examples it was also necessary to
restrict the analysis to simple two-part systems.

In this chapter we consider many-part systems, and we will do so by
considering such a system built of the kind of regulators that we have
discussed in Chapter 6. Such an approach is of course not the only one
possible: I propose in fact to start the chapter with what is a simpler
approach to a many-part system, and to work from there towards the
reintroduction of regulation.

My starting point will be the work of Williams (1972) and Margalef
(1968). Margalef comments on the modelling of ecosystems through the
use of sets of simultaneous differential equations. Suppose we have three
animal species N_1, N_2 and N_3, and an environment E. Suppose we are
interested in the rates of change of the species with respect to each
other; then we can use differential equations to describe the system.

For example:

$$
\begin{array}{cccc}
& E & N_1 & N_2 & N_3 \\
\end{array}
$$

$$\delta E/\delta t = \qquad\quad aEN_1 \;-\; bEN_2$$

$$\delta N_1/\delta t = +eEN_1 \;-\; fN_1{}^2 \;-\; qN_1N_2 \;-\; hN_1N_3$$

$$\delta N_2/\delta t = \qquad\quad +\, iN_1N_2 \;-\; jN_2{}^2 \;-\; kN_2N_3$$

$$\delta N_3/\delta t = \qquad\quad +\, lN_1N_2 \;-\; mN_2N_3 \;-\; nN_3{}^2$$

Such a set of equations describes a system behaving in time. Its validity with respect to an ecosystem will clearly depend upon such concepts as species, being handled as one unit, and on the value of the coefficients and the way in which the equations are formed. The model demonstrated is probably defective, as Margalef clearly states, because a more realistic model would require leads and lags, non-linear effects, higher cost interactions etc.

But, accepting all of this, we can still see some value in the idea. Because the set of equations is simultaneous, then no part can be considered without the whole — a solution will have to be found simultaneously. And the whole set should describe a system which will reach an equilibrium. This is because we can visualize the equations as an interactive procedure, whereby the next values of the variables depends on their present values, rather akin to a Markov model, and if we allow it to reiterate a few times an equilibrium will result. As an aside, to demonstrate the need for care in applying these ideas to an ecosystem, we may consider the following. Although any two such systems may reach an equilibrium, the energetic costs of the equilibrium may vary considerably If the rates of change of the species with respect to each other are higher in one case than in the other, then the rate of exchange of matter and energy is also higher as a proportion of the total biomass. But since in a real ecosystem no exchanges are perfect, and in general there is considerable wastage at each exchange, then the total energy input into the faster changing system is also higher — it is a less efficient system.

We can add substance to the discussion by considering Williams' work. He is concerned with an analysis of the usefulness of such sets of equations relating to models of ecosystems which have from 2 to 5 species which are coupled in various ways and under varying sets of assumptions. We can start with the simplest case, a two-compartment system, with an input from the environment and leakage to the environment.

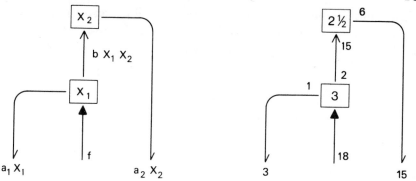

Fig. 7.1. A two-compartment system with forced inputs. (From Williams, 1972)

Such a system is displayed in Fig. 7.1., and the equations which relate to it are as follows:

$$\dot{X}_1 = f - a_1 X_1 - b\, X_1 X_2$$

$$\dot{X}_2 = b\, X_1 X_2 - a_2 X_2$$

where $\dot{X}_1$ is the differential increment of X_1.

Now, these equations could be of any form; here they have been written to have a form which has a feasible explanation in ecological terms. The basic form is one of rates of flow times mass. For example, the flow from X_1 to X_2 is proportional to the product of their masses times a constant. This is so obviously analogous to the gravity model in geography that I hope I am not irritating the reader by pointing it out.

To find the equilibrium values we set both equations to zero and solve simultaneously, because at equilibrium, by definition, the rate of input will equal the rate of loss for either compartment. The solutions are:

$$X_1 = a_2/b \qquad\qquad (3 = 6/2$$

$$X_2 = (fb - a_1 a_2)/ba_2 \quad (2\tfrac{1}{2} = (18 \times 2 - 1 \times 6)/2 \times 6$$

At equilibrium X_1 will always be positive and finite so long as a_2 and b are positive and finite. X_2 will be positive and finite if all coefficients are positive and finite, and so long as $fb > a_1 a_2$. If $a_1 a_2 \geqslant fb$ then there are solutions to the equations which are mathematically feasible, but ecologically meaningless, since we would have a negative compartment value for X_2.

This first example has used a forced input function, that is f has a fixed value irrespective of X_1. Most species will eat less if there are fewer animals, and it is therefore desirable to replace the forced input with one that is self-generating. This has been done in Fig. 7.2., where the input

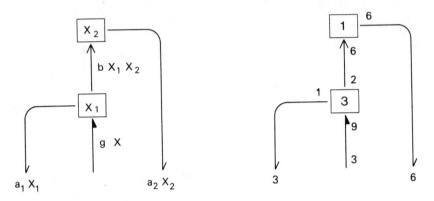

Fig. 7.2. A two-compartment system with self-generated input. (From Williams, 1972)

function is now mass times a coefficient. Williams finds that this system does have feasible steady states, but that a simulation model of the system produces wildly fluctuating compartment values unless it is started at the steady state. This is not revealed by an analysis of the equations themselves, but only by experimentation.

The three-compartment branching model with forced input is displayed in Fig. 7.3. The equations that govern the system are:

$$\dot{X}_1 = f - X_1(a_1 + b_{12}X_2 + b_{13}X_3)$$

$$\dot{X}_2 = X_2(b_{12}X_1 - a_2 - b_{23}X_3)$$

$$\dot{X}_3 = X_3(b_{13}X_1 + b_{23}X_2 - a_3)$$

with solutions

$$X_1 = \frac{fb_{23}}{b_{12}a_3 - b_{13}a_2 + b_{23}a_1}$$

$$X_2 = \frac{a_3 - b_{13}X_1}{b_{23}}$$

$$X_3 = \frac{-a_2 + b_{12}X_1}{b_{23}}$$

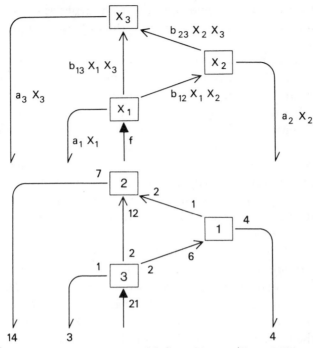

Fig. 7.3. A three-compartment system with forced input. (From Williams, 1972)

It will be noted that the solutions are becoming more complex. In fact, not only are the solutions, but so is the behaviour. Table 7.1 gives the sensitivities for the variables in the system; that is, how a change in any one variable, the independent, will cause a change in any other. While for most of the pairs there are algebraic solutions, this is not true for all pairs. There are five question marks in the table, and for these there are only numeric solutions. For example δX_3 will respect to δb_{12} will have a form $k - c$, where k and c are functions of some of the bs and as of the system — in other words functions of the coefficients. So,

Table 7.I

Sensitivities of the forced three-compartment
system as a closed network

Independent variable	Dependent variable		
	δX_1	δX_2	δX_3
δf	+	−	+
δb_{12}	−	+	?
δb_{13}	+	−	+
δb_{23}	?	?	?
δa_1	−	+	−
δa_2	+	−	?
δa_3	−	+	−

whether $k - c$ is a positive or negative term depends upon the numerical values of k and c, which depend upon the numerical value of the coefficients.

As the systems become more complex, so it is increasingly difficult to define by analytical algebra whether or not they have feasible equilibria positions, and if so, under what conditions. Williams has examples of systems that do not have unique steady-state solutions for any given set of coefficients, and others that do not have steady-state solutions for any set of coefficients at all. At the same time the sensitivity becomes increasingly explained in terms of numerical values rather than algebraic relationships. How many times have we seen diagrams of systems where the relationships between components are accompanied by a + or a −? It is almost certain that the value of such diagrams is extremely low. The cumulative effect at one node will not depend on the simple summation of several +'s and −'s, but on numerical values.

I would like to summarize this section by stressing several points. Firstly, although the systems are mathematically closed, that is all terms are included in the equations and they are solved simultaneously, in other senses the systems modelled are open. Diagrammatically we have shown the basic input from the ground, and returns to the ground. But the ground is an unknown mass which does not enter the equations. The losses can be to anywhere − the atmosphere, high entropy heat, etc. − and not necessarily back to the ground. Alternatively the ground could be construed to be one of the compartments. In the Markov model which features briefly below, some kind of closure will be necessary.

Secondly, the way the flow values are derived would look suspect to a geographer trained in gravity models. There are in the second example three flow functions involving two masses each, and one coefficient each. These coefficients are not related to each other, but are given arbitrarily. The equivalent coefficient in a gravity model would be of the form: $O_i D_j A_i B_j$, where O_i and D_j are the masses and the coefficient is a double term $A_i B_j$. This is done for consistency, to make the total flows correct, but nevertheless it does entail also some overlapping of coefficient values from one interaction term to the next. In the ecosystem case we can imagine that through the effects of competition etc. that the coefficient relating X_2 to X_1 in the three-compartment model should have some function relating it to the coefficient linking X_3 and X_1. I am aware that in the three-compartment model there is only one "destination" for each "origin" and that these remarks would not therefore make much difference to this particular case, but where an animal is eaten by several others, and there are several destinations for each origin, then the form of the coefficients should be more complex.

Thirdly, the principle of simultaneity needs to be looked at very carefully. It is necessary to solve the equations, and find an equilibrium for the system, but it is not realistic enough. It is on this point that Margalef has already observed that real systems have leads and lags. If for example X_1 increases, it may be some time before X_2 increases in response to it, and then as it corrects X_1 it does so excessively, and depletes X_1 so that it is forced to decrease excessively itself. Such a system is full of overshoots and undershoots, over- and under-correction, delays and lags, is often reasonably realistic, and is prohibited here by the principal of simultaneity.

Fourthly, and in some ways related to the third point, the system as Williams portrays it is modelled in one variable only, presumably biomass. But there are many features of the population of one species that are number dependent: reproduction habits, territory per individual, and so forth. These effects are excluded by the one variable approach, which is again necessary to yield a set of equations which can be expected to lead in some circumstances to a solution.

These are defects of which Williams would seem to be aware, and so these criticisms are not directed at him for pursuing this line of enquiry as far as it can go to see how well the approach can work, but are merely illustrative of the kinds of problem which may ensue when the method of modelling comes first, and the reality second. It is a black box approach, where the results may be made to approximate to some real system by calibrating the coefficients, even though these coefficients may be given little substantive interpretation in terms of real world phenomena.

This section has been phrased in terms of equilibria and other words implicitly connected with the general ideas of stability. In a dynamic system the equivalent of the creaky chair problem (actually of course "creaky" seems to have connotations of dynamism) is that although the parts do not fluctuate exactly in phase with each other, neither are their fluctuations of state completely unrelated. The mathematically derived equilibria of Williams' ecosystems are specifically the equivalents of rigid chair models. All parts are locked with the whole, and the system is completely determinate at the system scale: it represents the other extreme from the case where the parts are completely unrelated in their behaviour in time, and to use the phraseology adopted elsewhere in this book, where complete local scale determinacy exists.

7.2 Stability

Stability is clearly to be defined in terms of some kind of constancy in time. But what it is that is to be constant needs careful definition. Indeed many authors now insist that there is no general concept of stability, but rather that for each circumstance it must be given an operational definition. The United Kingdom has often been cited as probably one of the most stable societies in the world over the last two or three hundred years: but during that time the economic, social, political and physical character of the country has changed enormously. So what is it that is constant? Since I would not care to make the statement in the first place, I cannot offer an authoritative answer, but it does seem clear that what is meant by stability in this case is that there have been no abrupt revolutions in the society, that it has been constantly rather than erratically evolving: hence it is possible that in this case stability means that the rate of change has been constant. The concept of stability has moved into first differential form.

This is not a trivial point, since it is quite clear that in complex societies the concept, if of any use at all, will be seen to be more subtle than in the case of an ecosystem, where the rate of evolution is so slow that we can give meaning to the term stability in non-differential form, in other words in terms of the orginal functions of the system. Constancy then means constancy in the number of animals in each species in the ecosystem.

Margalef claims that there are two distinct kinds of stability in an ecosystem, although both involve the same basic notion of constancy of numbers. First he hypothesizes the constancy of numbers in an ecosystem at equilibrium under set conditions — which we have just covered in the case of Williams's equations above. This also corresponds to the common notion of the trajectory of a system in phase space staying in one small area of that space, perhaps even a point of the space.

Secondly he considers the stability which is represented by the capacity of a system to resist change. "If such parameters change often (climatic changes, destruction of organisms by unforeseen agents, and so on), then the term stability is frequently used to designate the ability of the system to remain reasonably similar to itself in spite of such changes." Stability is then an inherent property of the structure of the system. But it is unclear what is meant by "reasonably similar to itself", whether this means that most animals maintain roughly similar numbers, or whether it means that the same animals are still there, although in altered numbers, i.e. that the constancy is in the number of species not the number of individuals. To go any further would stretch "reasonably similar" too far.

The source usually cited in discussing this "inherent" stability is MacArthur (1955), to which I will turn next. But first let me mention the curious fact that though it is one of the more frequently quoted articles in ecology on this subject, in the 20 years since it was published the idea seems to have remained as it was, and no-one has done any practical work in using it with real systems.

MacArthur defines stability as the stability of other species in their numbers even if one species changes its abundance remarkably. The principle implication of the definition is thus seen to be flexibility. If one species is over-abundant then a great number of energy paths from it (a great number of predators) will minimize the effects on other species. Similarly, if one species becomes uncommon then it is necessary that its predators have alternative sources of food supplies. The variable that must be maximized to make the system maximally stable is thus associated with the number of paths through the system. The concept has to be made quantitative, and according to MacArthur has to satisfy equality conditions such that the web A in Fig. 7.4. is as stable as web B. If further we define abe in A as a separate community then the stability of A may be defined additatively as $S(abe) + \frac{1}{2}S(bcd) + \frac{1}{2}S(efg)$. These conditions lead us to define stability as

$$S = \sum_i pi \log \frac{1}{p_i}$$

where p_i is the proportion of energy passing through the ith path of the system. Maximum stability would be associated with maximum S, or in terms of information theory, maximum entropy or maximum uncertainty. That this is the most stable system is easy to see: at any one time not all paths are operating, and to specify which animal is eating which source at any time would require greater information than in a system with lower S value.

The deductions we can make are as follows. Stability increases as the number of links increases. If the number of species preyed on by each

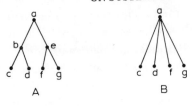

Two Animal Communities

Fig. 7.4. Two animal communities. (From MacArthur, 1955)

predator remains constant, then an increase in species increases stability. Therefore it follows that a given stability can be achieved by a large number of species with restricted diets or a small number of species with wide diets.

In relating parts to the whole in this way a number of interesting considerations come up. Most importantly there is a paradoxical relationship between efficiency and stability. The more restricted a diet the more efficient the processing animal. But the more restricted the diet the less stable the system. Clearly there has to be a balance between individual efficiency and system stability, which we could characterize as efficiency of the whole.

The point has only recently really struck home in industrialized society. Henry Ford attempted to make the factory more efficient, and standardized everything, or in other words restricted the input variety. Now we find that car plants in the U.K. and elsewhere are extraordinarily sensitive to trouble in component supply factories: they cannot arbitrarily switch from one supplier to another. The same is true in nearly every other aspect of our system: dependence on one source of energy supply above all others has caused us acute problems in recent times. By designing for efficiency at the local scale we have devised a system which is inherently unstable. Anybody can make political capital out of doing his little bit of dislocation, and where the plaintiff sees too much flexibility in the response of the target, a little "blacking" is used to reduce the flexibility of response.

Flexibility is the principal implication. In noting this we are repeating in effect what was stated above about the Law of Requisite Variety. In the stable system each part will have a variety of responses capable of dealing with a variety of disturbances. We are now in a position to try and join together the ideas of the part as regulator within a whole of measurable stability.

7.3 A system of regulators

Before arousing the reader's expectations too far, let me say that we have reached the point of thought which stimulated this chapter, but which has given rise to several problems as yet unsolved. Nevertheless I think it has been useful to write the foregoing, and it is useful to commit to paper my attempts at a solution so far.

Let me first sketch the tempting goal. MacArthur's measures of stability assess an ecosystem in terms of the proportion of total energy flowing in each path through the food web. The index derived is based on information theory, and the concept involved is implicitly one of flexibility. But we have also analysed the behaviour of a part in terms of regulation and its assessment in terms of information theory, based on an underlying concept of variety. The closeness of these two seems to suggest that we ought to be able to model a system of parts in terms of regulation, and assess simultaneously both the regulation achieved by the parts and the stability of the overall system. It may well be that the attempt to derive both kinds of measurement from one model is philosophically unsound. At the system level, stability may be an emergent property that cannot be broken down into component contributions. But, nevertheless, if it is possible to derive both scales of measurement simultaneously I think it right to see just how far we can get using one level to explain the other.

From here on this section will narrate the development of a series of ecosystem models, each one being a modification of a preceding one to overcome some difficulty that had been encountered.

The basic structure of an ecosystem and its energy paths can be visualized in terms of a venn diagram, such as Fig. 7.5., where a three animal and plant mass ecosystem is portrayed. Energy in the form of the potential energy of consumed matter can pass up from the plant mass D into the animals B and C, and from them either back to D or up to A. To avoid excessive complication the conversions are assumed to be totally efficient, and no energy is lost from metabolic processes, and no energy is input from the outside into D.

From such a venn diagram we can construct a flow chart of energy flow through the ecosystem. The flow chart associated with Fig. 7.5. is

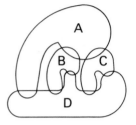

Fig. 7.5. Venn diagram of a simple ecosystem.

shown in Fig. 7.6. Clearly in this scheme, there are divergent flows leaving the animals as well as convergent flows as matter and some energy returns to "earth" and as it flows to predator animals. Figure 7.6 thus contrasts with Fig. 7.4 showing two of MacArthur's webs and the latter are seen to represent a simplification. This simplification is adopted for subsequent work here, although I do not think it affects the deductions about the conditions of stability which MacArthur made.

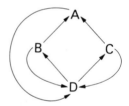

Fig. 7.6. Flow chart of the system of Fig. 7.5.

The first calculations were performed on an ecosystem of the type shown in Fig. 7.7., where A, B, C, D, E, F, and G are animals, and H represents the plant mass. We need first to find the probabilities of exchanges of matter between the various prey and predator species, defining these in terms which will enable us to study the regulation of each animal within the system.

A procedure for doing this is illustrated by Fig. 7.8. It is essentially the same as in the case illustrated above for farmers who could irrigate against drought. Starting from the "top" of the ecosystem, animal A is

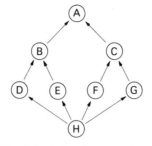

Fig. 7.7. A simple ecosystem.

the environment to animal B. A is given certain probabilities of attacking B, which represents B's vector of probability of environmental disturbance. B has a reaction matrix, showing what he does if A attacks or does not attack, where his reactions are given in terms of attacking D or E or of adopting a defensive attitude towards A, represented by the case "B not eat", if he is attacked by A. We also have a table of transition frequencies, showing what happens to B under the various possible compound conditions. The frequencies are given for two outcomes — that the matter stays at B, or that the matter goes to A. Multiplication for the elements of these vectors and matrices in the order shown above produces an outcome vector over the two outcome states, shown by the summations, which give the final probability of matter staying at B or being transferred to A. The same procedure is followed for C.

When we come to calculate D we find the first of the conditional links that have to operate in the model. The probability of B attacking D is conditional on A's attacks on B and B's responses to A. In this example B's probability of attacking D is given by $0.2 \times 0.05 + 0.8 \times 0.3 = 0.25$. This rigid linking seems undesirable, and is eliminated in a model introduced later, but the elimination requires much more complex construction procedures. The same kind of linking also affects B's attacks on E and C's on F and G.

At the end of these first calculations we know the probabilities of the various transitions except for the transition from H to D, E, F and G. H is passive and has no response to attacks from these four animals, and so is not illustrated by a similar set of matrices. Although we can calculate conditionally the attacks that D, E, F and G make on H, since H does not regulate we can give arbitrary probabilities for input from H to any of these four. In Williams' terminology we have a forced input

A

Probability of attack from B's environment

	eat B	not eat B
	0·2	0·8

B's reaction matrix

	eat B	not eat B
B eat D	0·05	0·3
B eat E	0·15	0·5
B not eat	0·8	0·2

Transition matrix

		eat B		not eat B
B eat D	P_B (A)	0·6		0·0
	P_B (B)	0·4		1·0
B eat E	P_B (A)	0·6		0·0
	P_B (B)	0·4		1·0
B not eat	P_B (A)	0·2		0·0
	P_B (B)	0·8		1·0

Resultant matrix

	eat B		not eat B	
B eat D	0·006		0·00	
	0·004		0·24	
B eat E	0·018		0·00	
	0·012		0·40	
B not eat	0·032		0·00	
	0·128		0·16	

$\Sigma \rightarrow A = 0·056$
$\Sigma \rightarrow B = 0·944$
$\overline{ 1·000}$

B

Probability of attack from D's environment

	eat D	not eat D
	0·25	0·75

D's reaction matrix

	eat D	not eat D
D eat H	0·2	0·4
D not eat	0·8	0·6

Transition matrix

		eat D		not eat D
D eat H	P_D (B)	0·9		0·0
	P_D (D)	0·1		1·0
D not eat	P_D (B)	0·3		0·0
	P_D (D)	0·7		1·0

Resultant matrix

	eat D		not eat D	
D eat H	0·045		0·00	
	0·005		0·30	
D not eat	0·060		0·00	
	0·140		0·45	

$\Sigma \rightarrow B = 0·105$
$\Sigma \rightarrow D = 0·895$
$\overline{ 1·000}$

A

Probability of attack from C's environment

	eat C	not eat C
	0·1	0·9

C's reaction matrix

C eat F	0·1	
C eat G	0·1	
C not eat	0·8	

Transition matrix

C eat F	P_C (A) 0·7	P_C (C) 0·3	0·0	1·0
C eat G	P_C (A) 0·8	P_C (C) 0·2	0·0	1·0
C not eat	P_C (A) 0·1	P_C (C) 0·9	0·0	1·0

Resultant matrix

C eat F	0·007	0·003	0·00	0·36
C eat G	0·008	0·002	0·00	0·45
C not eat	0·008	0·072	0·00	0·09

$\Sigma \to A = 0·023$
$\Sigma \to C = 0·977$
1·000

B

Probability of attack from E's environment

	eat E	not eat E
	0·43	0·57

E's reaction matrix

E eat H	0·3	0·5
E not eat	0·7	0·5

Transition matrix

E eat H	P_E (B) 0·8	P_E (E) 0·2	0·0	1·0
E not eat	P_E (B) 0·1	P_E (E) 0·9	0·0	1·0

Resultant matrix

E eat H	0·0301	0·0258	0·000	0·285
E not eat	0·1031	0·2709	0·000	0·285

$\Sigma \to B = 0·1333$
$\Sigma \to E = 0·8667$
1·0000

Probability of attack from F's environment

C

	eat F	not eat F
	0.37	0.63

F's reaction matrix

	eat F	not eat F
F eat H	0.4	0.8
F not eat	0.6	0.2

Transition matrix

F eat H	P_F (C) 0.9	P_F (F) 0.1	0.0	1.0
F not eat	P_F (C) 0.3	P_F (F) 0.7	0.0	1.0

Resultant matrix

F eat H	0.1332	0.0148	0.000	0.504
F not eat	0.0666	0.1554	0.000	0.126

$\Sigma \to C = 0.1998$
$\Sigma \to F = 0.8002$
 1.0000

Probability of attack from G's environment

C

	eat G	not eat G
	0.46	0.54

G's reaction matrix

	eat G	not eat G
G eat H	0.3	0.9
G not eat	0.7	0.1

Transition matrix

G eat H	P_G (C) 0.6	P_G (G) 0.4	0.0	1.0
G not eat	P_G (C) 0.4	P_G (G) 0.6	0.0	1.0

Resultant matrix

G eat H	0.0828	0.0552	0.000	0.486
G not eat	0.1288	0.1932	0.000	0.054

$\Sigma \to C = 0.2116$
$\Sigma \to G = 0.7884$
 1.0000

Fig. 7.8. Regulation tables for Fig. 7.7.

model. Similarly we can give an arbitrary value to the probability of return from A to H.

With these values the calculation becomes a closed one. We have the probabilities of transfer from any state to all others, and can construct a Markov transition matrix. The matrix is powered to give us the masses of each animal species at equilibrium, which, under the Markov theorem, we know will be attained regardless of any assumptions about initial masses. Multiplication of the mass of each species at equilibrium by the transition probability of a transfer of mass to its predator will give us the values of the flow of matter through the ecosystem.

Using the values derived in Fig. 7.8 we attain the equilibrium state shown in Fig. 7.9.a, where both the equilibrium masses and the flows at

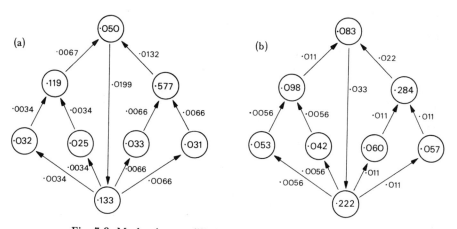

Fig. 7.9. Markovian equilibrium values (a) case a, (b) case b.

equilibrium are displayed. We can also calculate if so desired the regulation achieved by each animal against its predator's attacks.

Next, some of the parameters of the model are changed. A's attacks on C become more frequent, C's attacks on F and G of necessity decrease, and C's defence against A is made more effective. The revised data are processed in the same way as before, and we reach the equilibrium states shown in Fig. 7.9.b. These values are different from those of Fig. 7.9.a, and we conclude that changing the regulation data has produced a new solution. But in one very important respect the solution has not changed at all.

It will be recalled that the purpose of the model is to enable us to

evaluate MacArthur's S measure at the same time that we evaluate the
regulation achieved by each animal individually. But MacArthur's
measure S is the same for both solutions.

This can be demonstrated simply. The flows from B and C to A in
solution 1 are 0.00067 and 0.0132, or in a ratio of 1 : 2. In solution 2
the flows are 0.011 and 0.022, a ratio of 1 : 2. The ratio of the flow
values in the two solutions is exactly the same, and hence if we convert
all flow values into fractions of the total flow values this set of fractions
will be the same in both cases, and hence the measure S will also be the
same. The difference between the two solutions is in terms of their equilibrium masses, which are not in the same ratios, and in the absolute
values of the flows through the system. They are therefore different in
the respect which Margalef noted — the stability is the same, but the
solution with the higher throughput is achieving that same stability at
higher energetic cost, since all interactions are inefficient in the real
world and degrade some energy.

The reason why the two solutions are the same can be easily seen. At
equilibrium the inflow of matter must equal the outflow for each mass.
But the probability of transfer from H to D, E, F and G is the same in
both cases, the same forced input probability was used in both cases,
from H to D, E, F, and G as follows: 0.025, 0.025, 0.050, and 0.050.
These four figures fix the ratio of the flow values through both ecosystems, although the actual flow values will be derived from these probabilities multiplied by the equilibrium mass of H.

We may fairly ask what went wrong. The answer is, of course, that the
model is too simple. Firstly, we have used a single-variable model — in
this case biomass. As we have seen above, this allows little sophistication
in the expression of the relations between animals. Secondly, the model
has been restricted by the principle of simultaneity, and we have already
seen one result of this in that the actions of A and the responses of B and
C dictate the activities of B and C with respect to D, E, F and G. These
two problems are in a sense related. We have simple transfer functions
from one animal species to another, in this case probabilities, because we
are dealing with the single variable biomass. Because we are dealing with
probabilities of exclusive activities, i.e. B defend against A *or* B eat D *or*
E, for consistency the activities of A and the responses of B will dictate
to the rest of the system etc. If we choose to make the response probabilities non-mutually exclusive, i.e. we will allow B to eat D with some
probability unrelated to A's attacks on B, the whole system will become

completely arbitrary and we will have no conception of time. So far the probabilities have been restricted by the conditional associations, which has implied that in any one iteration of the model no animal can simultaneously do two things. If we remove the restrictions on the probabilities then we have removed the idea of simultaneous restriction, and hence have removed the concept of a finite amount of activity allowed in any unit iteration.

It may also be noted that the discussion alternates between consideration of a typical animal of any species, and a consideration of the species as a whole. As we saw above the Williams model also restricted itself to consideration of "compartments", i.e. a species *en masse,* but as a result some of the features of a species behaviour which are number-dependent were not included in the model.

The next step in the development was therefore to move from the one-variable concept to the two variables — mass and number. This also enabled the principle of simultaneity to be abandoned in favour of a loser set of conditional restriction between the species. We will illustrate the new model based on Fig. 7.10. by considering the sequential activities of A attacking B and B attacking D.

ECOSYSTEM 3

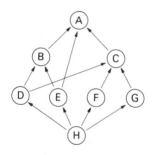

Fig. 7.10. A modification of Fig. 7.7.

A is typified by individual mass and by number, so we also know at any time the mass of the species as a whole. A has a "propensity" to attack B, which is expressed like a probability, but since it is modified in the process of attack it is initially termed a propensity. Suppose A has a propensity to attack B of p and there are N_A of A, then the number of attacks on B is $N_A p$. There are N_B of B, so thus far we have a probability that any B will be attacked of $P_{AB} = N_A p/N_B$. The next step is somewhat *ad hoc*, but nevertheless justifiable. If B becomes extremely common, then the probability of an attack as expressed so far becomes very small. And yet in most ecosystems if a species becomes very common the propensity of the predator to attack it increases, although there are of course levels of satiety which may place an upper limit on this effect (see Lassiter and Hayne, 1971). We assume no such upper limit in this case. If we multiply the probability so far by the number of B then we derive $P_{AB} = N_A N_B p/N_B = N_A p$, in which case in this model N_B no longer has any effect. Thus we need a more complex function of N_B to introduce. To do this we hypothesize a threshold value of N_B at which the propensity of A's attack is as the input data p specifies. By writing the modifier as $(1.0 + (N_B - T_B)/T_B)$ we derive a function which will increase P_{AB} if N_B becomes very large and reduce it to zero if N_B becomes very small. A cut-off is placed at $P_{AB} = 1.0$, which is necessary for consistency in the computation.

B has a response matrix as before, but the responses are differently expressed. B can either evade or not evade. As before there is also a transition matrix which specifies whether for any A move and any B move B is consumed by A or not. If we consider the resultant outcomes, clearly there are only two: B is consumed by A or not consumed: but the second category, not-consumed, is reached by two different routes, i.e. evading A but not-consumed, and not evading A but still not consumed. These three groups of B in terms of probabilities can be denoted by P_{B-A}, P_B, P_{B*}, which are in order the probability that B will go to A, the probability that an evading B is unconsumed, and the probability that an unevading B is unconsumed. By multiplying these three by N_B we know the numbers of B in each category. By using the individual masses we know then the mass that A consumes, and we assume that this turns into A's at A's individual mass value. The number of B's which attack D are then assumed to be on $P_{B*} N_B$, that is only unevading surviving B's are allowed to attack D, and the actual probability of such attacks is again modified by the number of D and the D threshold value.

It can be seen that in this sequence of events the principle of simultaneity is abandoned because it is necessary to know the number of attacks by A on B and their outcomes before we can calculate the number of attacks on D. This procedure would seem entirely reasonable in this respect, and does of course mean that there will be leads and lags between the various species. Indeed an impulse starting at one point will pass through the whole system sequentially.

The calculations are nevertheless closed. All accounts are made to balance. A is returned to the ground mass H by a "propensity" to die, which is modified by the number of A with respect to an A threshold. The lowest animals D, E, F and G graze H, modified by the amount of H available.

Because there are lead and lags and because the system is not solved simultaneously, it is quite clear that there is no analytical method to find out if the system will reach an equilibrium. But the system has been framed in such a way that each animal's interaction with another can be analysed by use of the model of regulation, and to that end the inter-actions have been specified in terms of the matrix representation of regulation. It was also hoped that these regulation values could be com-pared with MacArthur's measure S, but quite clearly that particular measure does need average or equilibrium values for the passage of matter through the various paths of the ecosystem. For these reasons the next step was to run the simulations long enough to see what kind of pattern of regulation emerged, and whether or not the system as a whole reached equilibrium.

Since the calculations progress sequentially from animal to animal, it would be possible to start the calculations at any point. They are in fact started with A's attacks on B. When the sequence returns to this point one iteration is deemed to be complete. All calculations are made in real numbers: if integers had been used it would have been more difficult to make sure that the model was consistent. As it is, it is possible to make sure that the biomass at the end of a run is the same as at the beginning. It does of course mean that an animal species still exists when there are only 0.45 animals, which may appear illogical. There are several instances in the runs when numbers do drop to these levels, only for the species to recover again later. We could excuse this on the grounds that the numbers are only representative of much larger ones possible, or that a species may be reintroduced into an ecosystem from a neighbouring system. If such contingencies were not allowed for, I have an intuitive suspicion that the equilibrium solution would in each case involve only one animal, or perhaps just the plant mass.

The first three runs were for 400 reiterations each, and the last was for 1000, in an attempt to see if patterns did recur. The runs differ from each other in input data as follows. Run 1 used the data displayed in

A Propensity to H   0.2
   Propensity to attack B 0.2
   Propensity to attack C 0.2
   Propensity to attack E 0.1
A Threshold number 100

B Propensity to attack D 0.2
   Propensity to attack E 0.2
B Threshold number 200

B reaction matrix

A

	attack	Not attack
B No evasion	0.1	1.0
Evasion	0.9	0.0

B Transition Frequencies

B No evasion	eaten 0.9	0.0
	not eaten 0.1	1.0
Evasion	eaten 0.3	0.0
	not eaten 0.7	1.0

C Propensity to attack E 0.1
   Propensity to attack F 0.2
   Propensity to attack G 0.2
C Threshold number 150

C reaction matrix

A

	attack	Not attack
C No evasion	0.3	1.0
Evasion	0.7	0.0

Fig. 7.11 Regulation Tables for Fig. 7.8

C *Transition Matrix*

No evasion	eaten	0.9	0.0
	not eaten	0.1	1.0
Evasion	eaten	0.3	0.0
	not eaten	0.7	1.0

D Threshold number 4000
D Propensity to eat H   0.7

Reaction Matrix

	B only attack	C only attack	B and C attack	No attack
No evasion	0.3	0.2	0.1	1.0
Evasion	0.7	0.8	0.9	0.0

Transition Matrix

No evasion	eaten	0.9	1.0	1.0	0.0
	not eaten	0.1	0.0	0.0	1.0
Evasion	eaten	0.5	0.7	0.8	0.0
	not eaten	0.5	0.3	0.2	1.0

E Threshold number 4000
E Propensity to eat H   0.6

E reaction matrix

	A only attack	B only attack	A and B attack	No attack
No evasion	0.5	0.3	0.1	1.0
Evasion	0.5	0.7	0.9	0.0

Fig. 7.11 continued

E Transition Matrix

No evasion	eaten 0.9	0.9	1.0	0.0
	not eaten 0.1	0.1	0.0	1.0
Evasion	eaten 0.8	0.5	1.0	0.0
	not eaten 0.2	0.5	0.0	1.0

F Threshold number 7000
F Eat H   0.2

F reaction matrix

	C attack	C Not attack
No evasion	0.4	1.0
Evasion	0.6	0.0

F Transition Matrix

No evasion	eaten 1.0	0.0
	not eaten 0.0	1.0
Evasion	eaten 0.6	0.0
	not eaten 0.4	1.0

G Threshold number 6000
G Eat H   0.3

G reaction matrix

	C attack	C Not attack
No evasion	0.5	1.0
Evasion	0.5	0.0

Fig. 7.11 continued

G *Transition matrix*

No evasion	eaten	0.8	0.0
	not eaten	0.2	1.0
Evasion	eaten	0.4	0.0
	not eaten	0.6	1.0

Fig. 7.11. continued

Fig. 7.11, for a system structured as in Fig. 7.10 with the starting positions as shown in Fig. 7.12. For Run 2 Fig. 7.13, only the starting numbers of the animals were changed. Since in both of these runs C is reduced to minimal levels early on, and F and G bloom, in Run 3 Fig. 7.14 there are several changes. C's threshold number of animals is increased from 150 to 300, and the starting number from 200 to 400. The likelihood of F adopting evasive action against C is reduced from 0.6 to 0.5. The effectiveness of C's attacks on G are increased, with the likelihood of a transition from G to C during an unevaded attack being increased from 0.8 to 0.9. For Run 4 Fig. 7.15 only one change is made to Run 3: F's propensity to eat H is reduced from 0.2 to 0.1.

We may first pay attention to Run 1. The system seems to adopt some kind of consistent pattern quite quickly: A and B oscillate about each other, with A's peaks and troughs following B's with a neatly lagged display. C's seems to disappear, and G and F without attacks from C quietly increase. D and E and H oscillate due to the predations of B. But by iterations 150–190 the oscillations seem to come into phase, with the result that there is a curious smooth section in the graph. It terminates violently with the reappearance of C and the demise of B. A and C then oscillate in the manner that A and B had shown before. The graph enters a phase in which it looks superficially as if an oscillating equilibrium has been achieved, i.e. one in which although the numbers of the animals do change, they do so in a consistent and repeated manner. In fact this is not so, since F is increasing slightly, G decreasing slightly, and D increasingly slightly. Further, following the reappearance of C at about reiteration 220, I would not bet that B will not reappear in a similar manner some time in the future. The fact that they seem to be alternatives is quite curious – this is not programmed into the system, it is quite simply an emergent property of it.

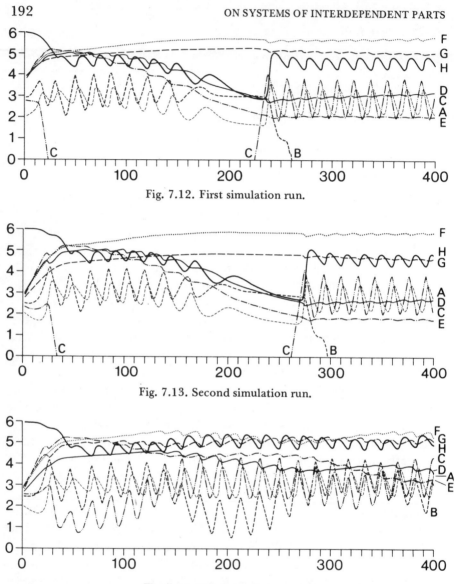

Fig. 7.12. First simulation run.

Fig. 7.13. Second simulation run.

Fig. 7.14. Third simulation run.

In Run 2 the starting positions were changed, in an effort to see if there was any kind of equifinality in the process. Some of the major features of the previous pattern are repeated: the disappearance of C, then its recovery and the disappearance of B. The oscillations of A and B, the smooth phase, the oscillations of A and C are also repeated. But

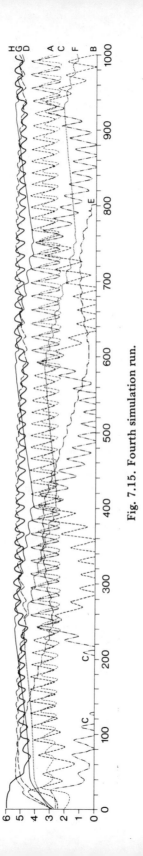

Fig. 7.15. Fourth simulation run.

they all occur about 40 iterations later than before, and the numbers of the animals are not the same at the end: in Run 1 G terminates with a higher number than H, but this is not true in Run 2. In Run 2 the value of E is lower. Thus it appears that the process is not equifinal, although some gross pattern aspects are repeated. How do we express such gross pattern features rigorously and quantitatively? I certainly do not know.

Another feature worthy of note is the periodic sudden upheavals, as with the reappearance of C and the disappearance of B. An observer at iterations 40–120 studying such an ecosystem in the field might be forgiven for concluding that it is relatively stable, within the limits of his observations. If later he observed a sudden upheaval of the kind portrayed, he might conclude that some external force had suddenly upset his ecosystem: but no force has intervened from the outside. The upheaval of iterations 180–260 is determined by the values we see in iterations 40–120; it is an inevitable outcome of them. Such behaviour is, to borrow a phrase, counterintuitive.

The changes made for Run 3 attempted to limit F's somewhat excessive growth, and to introduce C on a more permanent basis. C certainly does enter the picture, and towards reiteration 400 A, B and C all appear to be locked together in a complex lagged set of oscillations. But it will be noted that at 400 the system shows no signs of repetitive pattern. C is gaining the upper hand again, and B is in secular cyclic decline. F still seems to have a large value.

In Run 4 an attempt was made to restrict F further by limiting its intake from H. This was the only change in the whole set of input data. The effect is quite dramatic. By 400 D is much larger than before, and F much smaller. This effect is achieved as follows. Because of the smaller number of F, C is severely affected, and again virtually disappears. When C becomes small, predation on D also decreases, since D is eaten by both C and B. D therefore increases. When C recovers, the gross pattern is again repeated. But note that we have to use the word gross: as the system moves towards 1000 the disappearance of C and the increase in F and D is repeated three times, and F and D have almost parallel lines. Yet the lines are not quite parallel, and the two species appear to be divergent in detail although their gross patterns are the same. Another curious feature is that although G like F is preyed on solely by C, G has a much more consistent population than F, and oscillates in sympathy with H although F's line is alternately oscillating and smooth. E seems to have a fate of its own, and diminishes throughout, although it seems to take a long time dying. Whether it reappears again at some time in the future I do not know.

Overall, the system displays complex behaviour. Knowing any one section of the graphs would make it very difficult to predict the next, and yet as I have said the future is determined by the past in this model. Similarly the sensitivity of the system to parameter changes varies according to the parameter chosen: purely by empirical experiment it would seem likely that one sensitive pressure point is the link between the plant mass and F — changing this can cause great changes in the rest of the system.

It would seem a reflection on the state of the science that it is an art. Our best known method of controlling such systems is to build a model of them, and then play intuitively with the data input to the model. No amount of sophisticated mathematics will summarize the behaviour of the system by analytical methods, none, that is, at our current level of ability.

The analysis of regulation at each stage did not produce any neat summary of the activities of the animals which would explain the behaviour of the whole system. The reasons for this are not hard to determine. Firstly the numbers of each animal are plotted on the graphs, as a single species, but the analysis of regulation will summarize the activities of any animal in two distinct interfaces. For example, B can be analysed in its defence against A, that is the degree to which it can avoid the predations of A, and also as the environmental disturbance to D and E. With respect to both of these it is not the only source of "disturbance" since D is also attacked by C and E by A. The numbers of any one species are therefore the result of the balance between the regulation achieved at these two levels of interfaces, and of course at some levels it is not possible to consider one animal at a time only. This really enforces Margalef's view of an animal species as an energy gate. This view puts the interactions of the species to the fore, and the interactions become the basic event or phenomenon of interest, not the species on their own. The significance of this is quite far reaching: "The energy gates at the places where species interact — or where they interact with environment — are the organs by which selection is achieved and evolution occurs, the rate of evolution depending on the efficiency of the gate." (Margalef, 1968, p. 81).* The second reason for the failure of the analysis of regulation is

---

* See also the comments quoted from Laszlo in Chapter 5.

again concerned with the non-value-orientated nature of information theory. Although the desired outcome of any animal is to survive, and to survive is "better" than not surviving, the theory outlined above is concerned with minimizing the uncertainty of the outcome. If this uncertainty value reaches a peak at the point where survival v. death is 50/50, any increase in the likelihood of death and consumption by a predator will then reduce the uncertainty $H(E)$.

Overall, the analysis has shown several things. It has shown one way of building a model system in which components are not simply linked by single coefficients, but in which they have some behavioural connection. It has shown that such a system is very sensitive to input data, and that even with the simple form shown here it would seem that they are not equifinal, and achieve an equilibrium, if ever, only after a large number of iterations. In terms related to ecosystems in particular, it has stressed the fact that species act as energy gates with at least two interfaces. Evolutionary tendencies are not the property of the individual species alone, but the property of the ecosystem. To put it another way, in such systems the context of the component is essential to understanding the component. Finally, it has proved difficult to derive summary statistics to describe the behaviour of the system.

The sensitivity of these systems is great. It supports the views of Williams, noted above. As the system becomes more complex then so it becomes more and more difficult to propose any analytical solution. The necessary corollary of this is that it becomes more and more important to define variables which are meaningful in any real system, and to model their relationships accurately. The above model was an attempt to use a framework that gave meaning to the derivation of the relationships between species, instead of using simple coefficients. But since I am not an ecologist I doubt very much whether such concepts of attack and defence are adequate for empirical use or that they are in fact measurable. Others have attempted to make models in which the variables are empirically useful and meaningful, and I wish to quote at some length from the conclusions of Lassiter and Hayne (1971) after their detailed study of an ecosystem model in which they have attempted to do just that.

> It is apparent from this investigation that sufficient biological information to simulate a real community accurately is not available at the present time . . .
> At the same time we feel the model to be heuristically useful, in that it has required us to set down specific information and identify areas of greatest deficiency . . .

This model emphasizes contingency as determining population change. Population dynamics may be described as a set of potentials for action, with final action contingent upon the set of factors instantaneously influencing the population. What happens next is contingent on the present status . . . Of no real importance is the position the population should take at some future date on some mathematical curve of expected growth. Such a curve may have great descriptive and predicted usefulness; used with caution it can enhance understanding. But what the population does at the moment must be determined only by the set of influences at that moment.

In computer simulations of the model, whenever the same set of initial conditions, rates and characteristics, are provided the same output follows. But if a single effective condition is changed, the resulting series of population fluctuations differs to some degree. Even with the vastly simplified description of nature . . . it seems quite unlikely that exactly the same sequence of events will happen twice in a simulation. How much less likely is the enormously more complex natural system to return exactly to the same set of conditions, to predispose it to generate exactly the same set of responses. Any degree of predictability seems remarkable under these circumstances.

We could almost add, history never repeats itself.

These authors also identify some of the major methodological problem areas: and one that they highlight is the need for better methods of describing and comparing the results of ecosystem simulations. It was to this end that the attempt at analysis of regulation was aimed, but with little success.

7.4 The phase space: or, alternatively, the state space

As far as I can make out, there are many situations in physics where these two names are interchangeable — so I have given the subtitle two names as well. At all events, what I mean by either of these terms should be clear from what follows.

So far, the general drift of the argument has been towards finding a system which is reasonably realistic, which reaches some kind of equilibrium, and which can then be summarized by a descriptive statistic, as for example, with MacArthur's S. So far, this has not been achieved, and we have looked at some of the reasons why.

To go further, I wish now to introduce the idea of the phase space or state space. Let us consider a system with two variables. Suppose an island exists in which there are farmers and cowboys, and nothing else. We can draw a graph in two dimensions with one axis labelled "number of cowboys" and the other "number of farmers". At any one time the actual state of affairs on the island may be summarized by marking a single point in this phase space, which defines exactly the number of cowboys and number of farmers at that time. If over time the numbers of these two change, then the point can be extended into a line which is the trajectory of this particular system as in Fig. 7.16.

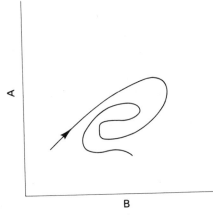

Fig. 7.16. A phase space.

Many times I have come across this idea of the phase space; Murphy (1965) mentions it, Melton mentions it in geomorphology (1958), and of course countless books in statistical thermodynamics mention it. Each time I have been left with the basic attitude "so what?". As usual the answer to such a defeatist question only comes when one finds for oneself a situation in which the idea is needed. In considering summary statistics for the system stimulated above, somehow the emphasis always seemed to be on finding a reducing statistic, or a summary by the process of information loss, much like a standard deviation loses information from the original set of values. Let us suppose that instead of trying to find such a summary statistic we retain all the information.

Let us create an eight-dimensional space, each axis of which demarcates the number of one of the species of animals A to G of the plant mass H. At any one time the state of the system can be represented exactly by a single point in this space, defined by the eight coordinates which are the numbers of the seven animals and plant mass at any single point in time. As the system changes through time then this point becomes a line which represents the trajectory of the system in its state space.

The usefulness of this approach can now become clear. We have lost no information in the summary statistic (the point or trajectory); and, most importantly, we can make definitions about "stability" and the behaviour of the system with respect to such stability by defining behaviours in the state space.

To go back to the mythical island, suppose harmony is achieved when the number of cowboys and farmers remains constant over time, because for some mythical reason they stop fighting over land and barbed wire, then the phase space trajectory may have followed a path such as in Fig. 7.17. It reaches a fixed point and stays there. If the trajectory is the

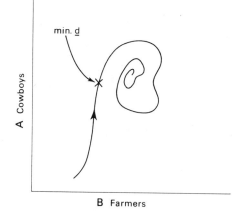

Fig. 7.17. A possible central value in a phase space trajectory.

first definition we have achieved, and to make it more appealing, I will repeat the same again in more sophisticated form, by quoting from Kowal (1971):

An equilibrium state ("steady state", "equilibrium point", "critical point", "singular point") x_e is any state in which the system remains indefinitely with the passage of time, i.e. at which $\dot{x} = 0$. Stability is usually defined with reference to the equilibrium states.

The distance between two points (x_1, x_2) in state space is measured by the Euclidean "norm", $|x_2 - x_1|$. Thus, one may consider the concept of a "neighbourhood" (or "open ball") of an equilibrium state x_e. A neighbourhood is the set of all points which lie less than a fixed distance d from x_e, i.e. all points for which $|x - x_e| < d$.

We are now in a position to define stability, as it is usually treated, in engineering and differential equations, i.e. in the "Lyapunov sense". An equilibrium state
is "stable" if an initial state within a small neighbourhood of the equilibrium
states results in a trajectory which remains within another small neighbourhood
of the equilibrium state. The initial state is thus a perturbation from the equilibrium states, e.g. the result of some sudden disturbance to an ecological system
in equilibrium. An equilibrium state is "asymptotically stable" if (1) it is stable,
and (2) the initial state within a small neighbourhood of the equilibrium state resul
in a trajectory which approaches the equilibrium state as time approaches infinity.
Obviously the latter is a much stronger type of stability.

This quotation contains much that can interest us. Firstly, stability
which always leads a system to the same equilibrium is of a special
strong kind, although it is perhaps the most commonly conceived kind.
In Fig. 7.18 an outbreak of lead poisoning reduces the number of

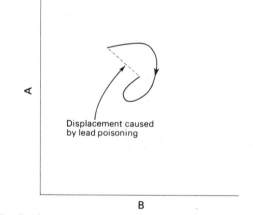

Fig. 7.18. An outbreak of lead poisoning in phase space.

farmers and the cowboys increase, but then the same equilibrium is
reached as before. A more general kind of equilibrium would also be
vaguer; for example the neighbourhood concept can lead us to define a
small region for an initial state and another small region for the subsequent trajectory, such as the two regions A and B in Fig. 7.19. We are
left with a knowledge of the system's behaviour, but less precise than
before.

This idea can also take us back to the problem of the creaky chair.
The ecosystem simulated in the sections above is not a creaky chair
system; it is deterministic at all times: subsequent values are contingent

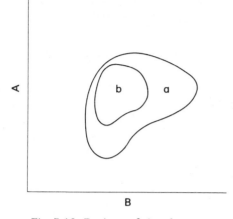

Fig. 7.19. Regions of the phase space.

upon prior values completely. This too can be discussed within the phase space framework. Suppose we follow the trajectory of some ecological system of two animals A and B in Fig. 7.16. This trajectory does not cross itself at any stage, and for this reason we presume that the system is determinate. That is, for any point on the trajectory, the next point representing a future state of the system is determined. If the trajectory crosses itself, then this is no longer true. Under the assumption that the model has no memory other than the current number of A and B, and under the further assumption that these are the only two variable quan-

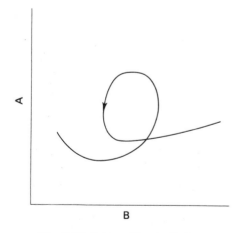

Fig. 7.20. Intersecting trajectory.

tities of the system, then if we find a system which has a trajectory such as in Fig. 7.20 we know that there are at least two trajectories which follow from the point of intersection, x_i. Thus with respect to x_i at least, the system is not completely determinate, and there is some freedom in the system. If we then apply the neighbourhood concept to some point x_i, or some set of points (x_i), with the same property of intersection, and say that the trajectory of the system which passes through any of the (x_i) will remain within a defined neighbourhood, then such a system would exhibit a creaky chair form, provided always that the neighbourhood so defined was smaller than the total phase space itself. Such an idea is demonstrated in Fig. 7.21.

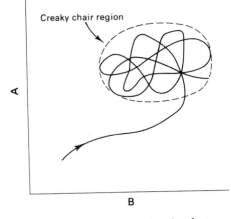

Fig. 7.21. A creaky chair region in phase space.

It remains for me to define a few more terms. By "total phase space" I mean that space which is defined as a rectangular volume or hypervolume by the maximum value each of the coordinate axes could attain. For example in the ecosystem model the total number of units of biomass is at all times constant at 917 500. The maximum value of each of the eight axes is therefore 917 500, and the volume defined by these eight axes is the "total phase space". At any time the system will be within it; if, however, having been started at any arbitrary point x_i there are some regions of the total phase space which could never be reached, clearly the system is operating with some degree of constraint. If, within the region of phase space which is reached, intersections occur, then

clearly the system is operating both with constraint and with indeterminacy. Such a system is a creaky chair system. This leads to some interesting conjecture, which the reader must realize is conjecture, and as yet
nothing more. Heisenburg's Principle of Indeterminacy is often illustrated
by the phase space defined by the axes q and p for the velocity and position of a particle. In such a phase space it is never possible to define a
point representing the state of a particle: that is the principle of indeterminacy. As much as we can do is to define a region of space within
which the representative point may occur. There are specific grounds
for this, tied to energetic limits to our acquisition of information, so
that the principle is one which belongs to atomic physics. But, nothing
says that the mathematics of such theories is sacrosanct: Wilson (1970)
has borrowed statistical thermodynamics and applied its methods to
other phenomena. My conjecture is that for us many systems in geography are creaky chair systems, about which we have imperfect information such that for us they are never determinate, and that the mathematics of indeterminacy may serve us well in the future. It bears looking
at.

Next I turn to my first attempts to analyse what happened to the
ecosystems modelled above, in terms of a phase space. All the calculations were performed on the results of Run 4, since this visually seemed
to be the most stable (in that most of the species were present for most
of the time), and since this was run for the greatest number of iterations.
The first task was to find whether or not the trajectory of the system
intersected itself at any point in the phase space. Intuitively one ima-
gined that it would not: this is a determinate system by design in that
the eight variables are the only source of variation, and all of their variation is due to deterministic calculation and none of it to random numbers generators. A straightforward approach was adopted for the calculation: assume a given point x_i, specified by eight coordinates. For all
points j along the trajectory, calculate their Euclidean distance from x_i,
by

$$d_{ij} = \sqrt{a^2 + b^2 + c^2 + d^2 + e^2 + f^2 + g^2 + h^2}$$

where a, b, c, d, e, f, g and h are the differences in each of the eight
dimensions between the coordinates of x_i and x_j. If any one of these
distances is zero when $i = j$, then clearly there has been an intersection.
The procedure was carried out for x_i, $i = 1, \ldots 1000$, and, as expected,
no intersections occurred. The smallest value for any d_{ij} on the large

sample output on the lineprinter was 8800, which was the distance of iteration 49 from iteration 50, and the largest d_{ij} was iteration 1 from iteration 750, with a value of 1 000 776. For any i we can also compute the mean distance to all j, simply by $\bar{d} = \sum_j d_{ij}/1000$. The following table gives some values:

iteration i	$\bar{d}$
50	516 200
150	286 500
250	469 500
350	357 000
450	358 500
550	311 900
650	350 300
750	372 200
850	301 100
950	398 600

This shows that the system is behaving in its eight dimensions rather like the two-dimensional system in Fig. 7.18. The start is the furthest away from all the other points, and for that reason the smallest value occurs early, at iteration 150, rather like the hypothesized min $\bar{d}$ in Fig. 7.18, is pulled towards the origin. The remaining values tell us little about the behaviour of the system: we do not know from them whether it is converging to a point or not. To attempt to find this out we have to examine the distances from one of the later is to all the js. Imagine in Fig. 7.18 that the i is the central equilibrium point: then the distances to all the js from the first to the last will show a general secular decline, even if obscured from time to time by wavelike fluctuations. If this secular decline is more pronounced in this last i than in any other, then we may presume some tendency towards equilibrium. Ten graphs of the distances to all j for the same i as in the table above were prepared and examined for this tendency.

These 10 graphs do represent a collapse from eight-dimensional information to the one-dimensional information of simple distance in a Euclidean space. This is a demerit — but the great merit is in the visual impact that they give. The 10 were very similar, and one of them showed a secular decline which might suggest an approaching equifinality. What they all showed, however, was a predominant long-term fluctuation: the

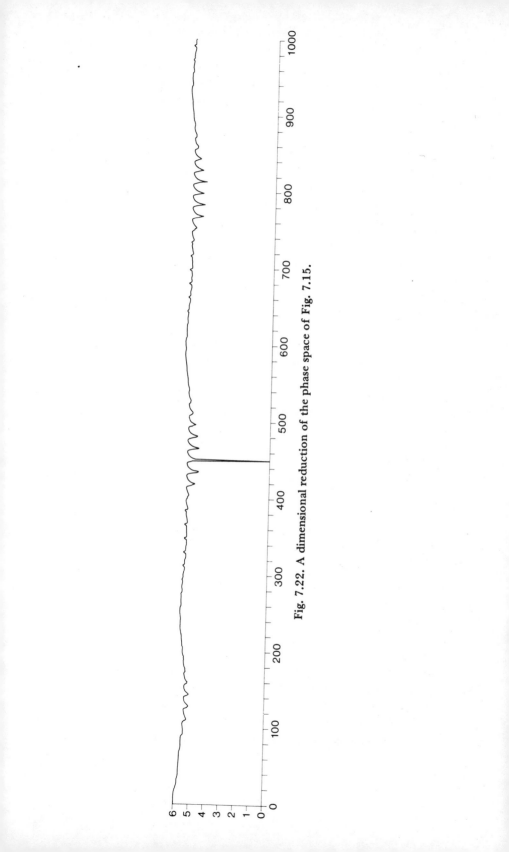

Fig. 7.22. A dimensional reduction of the phase space of Fig. 7.15.

graph of distances from iteration 450 is shown in Fig. 7.22 as an example. The period of the long-term wave should appear to be about 330 iterations, and corresponds with the time interval of the periodic upheavals and major changes of dominance amongst the animal groups perceptible on the previous graphs. The graph in Fig. 7.22 is appealing, in that it suggests a major description of the animal populations which is repetitive, but which does not dictate exactly which species are involved in it. A further idea was to see if a neighbourhood could be defined within and smaller than the total space, which contained the trajectory of the system. Unfortunately the techniques for defining such spaces do not seem to exist. The simplest manner would be to describe an eight-dimensional sphere, but this is prone to exaggerate the volume occupied.

The likelihood of defining a sphere of volume greater than the total phase space also increases with the number of dimensions, for the simple reasons that the ratio between the maximum distance definable in a space and the maximum length of any coordinate axis increases considerably with the higher dimensions. For example in a two-dimensional space with sides of unit length, the diagonal across the square is 1.414. In three-dimensional space the length of the longest diagonal is 1.732, and in eight-dimensional space it is 2.828.

7.5 A definition of system which is different but the same as before

A system is often defined simply as a trajectory in phase space. This might seem very far removed from the definition which was given in Chapter 4. However, they come to the same thing in the end, and I shall attempt here to show the equivalence of terms.

The phase space represents the sum of the alternative states of the parts: any point in the phase space represents a system complexion, and therefore the total phase space represents the total of all possible complexions *a priori*. It is the *a priori* ensemble of feasible complexions. We know that a system is organized if the *a posteriori* ensemble is less than the *a priori* ensemble — in this context we mean if the neighbourhood of the system trajectory is less than the total state space. If this neighbourhood shrinks to a point, then the system is completely organized, and can exhibit no behaviour without external inputs.

A static cog is a part with no alternative states: in the phase space representation it is a part with an axis of length zero — in other words it does not increase the volume of the space. Over-specification of the freedom of a part occurs if for any axis or axes referring to any one part, displacements of position are possible which do not affect the values in other axes. Finally, of course, I wish to repeat and re-emphasize the definition of the creaky chair system given above. It is one where the trajectory does intersect, but only within a restricted region of space. Such a system is not completely determinate, but neither is it completely unorganized.

7.6 Some more deliberations

The reader might be forgiven for wondering by now whether he is reading a book on ecology or geography. The reason why so much of this material is connected with ecology is simply that ecologists have done more work in the analysis of "creaky chair" systems than other groups of which I am aware. Their systems are also similar in scale to ours, and in some respects much simpler, which is a good reason for using this approach as an introductory sketch of the behaviour of dynamic systems. Above all they are simpler in that matter and energy flow together in the same network, and there is no "image" of the system guiding decision making. Industrial society energy paths to factories and homes are usually separate from flows of materials. This means that the energy gate concept becomes much more complex. And predation, or let us say consumerism, is dependent greatly upon the flow of information and the circulation of images of things, of fashion and idea.

But within our industrial society the importance of understanding the dynamic systems is also great. I ask you to look at the diagram in Fig. 7.23 reproduced from the *Times* of September 23 1974, which accompanied an article on inflation. There are three curves which are related to each other, but which are also supposed to lag behind each other. First the rise on OPEC oil prices causes a surge of inflation in the commodity markets but this suddenly flattens out. So much is historical fact at the time of writing. At some time after the surge in commodity costs, there is an increase in wholesale costs, as the material is processed and released into the warehouses of the country: the lag has been caused by the time it takes for material to pass through the system. Then following that, the retail prices finally start to surge as well. Now it is quite obvious at the point in time at which the graph stops that retail prices are rising, but it is most important to the policy maker to know whether they are going to go on rising. Will there be a lagged plateau as a result

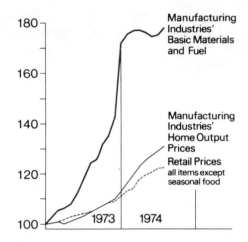

Fig. 7.23. Price behaviour in the U.K. economy. (From *The Times*, September 23, 197'

of the plateau some time earlier in commodity prices? If we can expect one, it would make sense to tie wage agreements to threshold clauses, because we could then expect wage increases to slow down as the retail price reaches the plateau. But if the government does not believe in the coming plateau, then they will probably not consider threshold agreements desirable, since they will build inflation into the system. Thus the behaviour of these curves over the following few months is important. But none of them can be predicted accurately by mathematical extrapolation: to borrow Lassiter and Hayne's remarks, the system is contingent on the totality of present influences.

Those readers who are interested in the analysis of dynamic system in the fields of urban studies or of world affairs can pursue the matter further by reading Forrester's books (1969, 1971), which are simulations of systems of reasonable complexity. Again, I think it worthwhile mentioning some of his conclusions:

> Complex systems have many important behaviour characteristics that we must understand if we expect to design systems with better behaviour. Complex systems: (1) are counterintuitive; (2) are remarkably insensitive to changes in many systems parameters; (3) stubbornly resist policy changes; (4) contain influential pressure points, often in unexpected places, from which forces will radiate to alter system balance; (5) counteract and compensate for externally applied corrective efforts by reducing the correspondingly internally generated action (the corrective program is largely absorbed in replacing lost internal action)

(6) often react to a policy change in the long run in a way opposite to how they react in the short run; (7) tend toward low performance.

(Forrester, 1969)

Obviously these points are not all mutually exclusive. The fact that complex systems may be insensitive to some parameter changes does not mean that they are insensitive to all: Forrester's points 2, 3 and 4 should be taken together. The interesting feature with respect to sensitivity is of course that if pressure points exist, from which forces radiate out through the system, such outward radiation of changes can only occur in time: ergo, to achieve some future desirable state may require the manipulation of a pressure point which occurs far before it. To extrapolate rather wildly to an obvious extreme case, and ignoring aesthetics, the problems which confront many city planners in England were generated by the Elizabethans.

Point 1 is a general statement to the effect that although within any one system we can see what will happen to B as an immediate consequence of A, by the time that change has passed through many feedback loops through the whole system, the final effect at B may be the opposite of what we intended. Limiting the rate of interest building societies may pay investors will cheapen a mortgage for a borrower, but will reduce the funds available to borrowers as investor's deposits fall, which will cause a fall in building new houses, which will cause a house shortage, which will cause house prices to rise, which will make housing more expensive for new borrowers, by an amount more than likely greater than the initial savings due to low interest rates. In reality of course, the situation is more complex than that, which is only to say that counterintuitive may be more "counter" in reality than we suspect.

Point 5 can be illustrated with reference to an ecosystem: although some species may be in undesirable abundance, nevertheless there will be some control in the ecosystem over its numbers. Suppose we then eradicate the pest chemically: we may also damage the natural control system. We therefore have to redouble our own effort to control the pest: the system resisted the change — that is as we attempted control over the species, the system control disintegrated. Forrester gives an example of a programme to eliminate unemployment: 19 000 people were retrained and provided with jobs, while the jobless total fell by only 11 000. Obviously the training programme was not purely additive on top of other avenues back into employment: it attracted into it people who would have gone by other routes. The private industrialist will not finance his own retraining scheme as the government decides to do it for him. Point 6 is also fairly well known, but not necessarily well received. Among the many suggestions made for the poor growth rate of the U.K. economy since the Second World War compared with that of France there is one that corresponds exactly with this point. The budgetary system of the U.K. and the so-called Regulator, the Chancellor's ability to change Purchase Tax up to a specified amount without reference to Parliament, provided the government of the day with a quick response to balance-of-payments and unemployment problems. The result was the familiar stop-go. By comparison, France had no such fine control, and the only effective response to her situation was to stress growth at all times: in the fifties it may have appeared that she had more problems than the U.K., but by the late sixties it became apparent that the long-term benefits greatly outweighed the short-term difficulties.

Point 7 demands a paragraph to itself. This is a feature not of complex systems of any kind, but of complex social systems, those created by the human being who has an ability to create images of his system, and to attempt conscious control over it. It depends for its validity on all the foregoing. The point can be simply posed: if complex systems are counterintuitive, with varying long- and short-term responses, it becomes certain that at any one time less than optimal choices are made: these inevitably lead to further complex situations in which further less than optimal choices will be made. The effects are cumulative, and the whole performance drifts to a low state.

7.7 Uncertainty as a limit

It is quite clear that from the point of view of a participant in a complex system, the environment (i.e. the totality of all other participating components) may often behave in an uncertain way. From the participant's point of view one reaction to the uncertain environment may take the form of regulation and the elimination of uncertainty: we have already dealt with this topic at some length. However, this is not the only way to approach problems of this kind, nor is the case of regulation against uncertainty the only kind of problem at the part-whole scale. There are other requirements for parts within wholes to pursue in other circumstances. Of these, growth is often an obvious requirement, so too is the capacity to "learn" the environment. It is to an illustration of these two aspects within a deductive framework that I turn next.

Murphy (1965)'s problem is centred around the behaviour of investors in a stock market where future prices of stock are unknown to them. They have to make investment decisions against a background of uncertainty. His approach is built up through a series of models, each one relaxing some of the assumptions of the previous models, so that he develops more general cases at each step. He is concerned with the growth of capital value, not with interest or dividends. He starts by considering a decision variable, which is defined as the proportion of his capital an investor ought to invest, in relation to the expected maximum growth rate of capital in a situation of risk. Risk is defined as the probability of making a gain or a loss as the price of the stock rises or falls, and where these probabilities are known and are stationary. In other words, even with perfect knowledge about the probability of a rise or a fall, and where such probabilities do not change over time, the investor faces some degree of risk. Later, he introduces the notions of adaptive processes where in addition to a rise there is also uncertainty from the investor's point of view. In this model uncertainty arises from the fact that the investor does not know what the probabilities of a rise or fall are, and he has to adapt to and learn his environment, until he reaches a stage of "enlightenment", when he knows what the true probabilities of a rise or fall are. By then he has eliminated uncertainty, but is still left with residual risk which cannot be removed so long as the environment continues to behave stochastically. Clearly this latter model will involve consideration of subjective information about the behaviour of the market.

We will start by following the risk model in some detail. As in many growth processes we may use the constant e to derive the value of some commodity subjected to proportional growth. Suppose we are interested in considering the growth of capital stock whose value is K, that we start with K_0 capital and that by stage t we have K_t capital, and that by stage t the overall growth rate has been g_t. The exponential growth equation is then:

$$K_t = K_0 e g_t{}^t \qquad (7.1)$$

We may express g_t in terms of the other members of equation (7.1) as follows:

$$\frac{K_t}{K_0} = e g_t{}^t$$

$$\therefore \ln K_t/K_0 = g_t{}^t$$

$$\therefore g_t = \frac{1}{t} \ln K_t/K_0 = \frac{1}{t}(\ln K_t - \ln K_0) \tag{7.2}$$

Now, if we are interested in future events we wish to maximize the expected growth rate, denoted by $\bar{g}_t$. If we use E to denote expectation from (7.2) we have:

$$\bar{g}_t = E\left\{\frac{1}{t}(\ln K_t - \ln K_0)\right\} \tag{7.3}$$

In this equation K_0 is fixed and given as the starting capital. Therefore to maximize $\bar{g}_t$ we need only consider maximizing $E(\ln K_t)$ for any given t.

We now consider the way in which this objective function may be maximized, in relation to the decision variable. Suppose we have an investor who wonders how much of his capital he ought to invest in a given stock, and that we designate the portfolio ratio "a" as his decision variable. "a" is defined so that $0 < a < 1$. To begin with we will assume that the investor decides upon the value of a at time 0 and then keeps his investment ratio fixed and illiquid. Later this assumption may be relaxed, but the results remain the same. The investor's value of stock is therefore aK_t at time t, where K_t is the total value of his invested stock and uninvested cash at time t. We now define a unit of time in such a way that one unit of time passes every time the value of the stock rises by r_1 points or falls by r_2 points, where r_1 and r_2 have values which are fixed for the duration of the whole process. This is what Murphy called entropy time, and we have already met some of his ideas on this in Chapter 2 (Section 2.3).

Therefore the value of his capital at time $t + 1$ will be either

$$K_{t+1} = ar_1 K_t + aK_t + (1 - a)K_t \tag{7.4}$$

if the price rises, or

$$K_{t+1} = -ar_2 K_t + aK_t + (1 - a)K_t \tag{7.5}$$

if the price falls.

These may be reduced quite simply

$$K_{t+1} = K_t(1 + ar_1) \text{ for a rise} \tag{7.6}$$

$$K_{t+1} = K_t(1 - ar_2) \text{ for a fall.} \tag{7.7}$$

Suppose we consider a total time period of T, during which the price rises n_1 times and falls n_2 times, so that $n_1 + n_2 = T$. Then from (7.6) and (7.7) above, at the Tth stage the investor's capital is

$$K_t = K_0 (1 + ar_1)^{n_1} (1 - ar_2)^{n_2} \tag{7.8}$$

Comparing this with equation (7.2), we note that we can write this in the form of a growth equation by taking logs and dividing by T.

$$\frac{1}{T} \ln \frac{K_t}{K_0} = \frac{1}{T} \ln (1 + ar_1)^{n_1} (1 - ar_2)^{n_2}$$

$$= \frac{n_1}{T} \ln (1 + ar_1) + \frac{n_2}{T} \ln (1 - ar_2) \tag{7.9}$$

Now, of course we do not know what the values of n_1 and n_2 will be in the future, but over some long time period if the environment behaves in a stationary stochastic manner then it is true that the probability of a rise, p_1, and the probability of a fall, p_2, may be defined as:

$$p_1 = \frac{n_1}{T} \tag{7.10}$$

$$p_2 = \frac{n_2}{T} \tag{7.11}$$

By substitution into equation (7.9) we derive:

$$\bar{g}_t = \frac{1}{T} E \left\{ \ln \frac{K_t}{K_0} \right\} = p_1 \ln(1 + ar_1) + p_2 \ln(1 - ar_2) \tag{7.12}$$

We now have an equation which may be used to maximize $\bar{g}_t$ with respect to the decision variable "a". To do this the right side of equation (7.12) is differentiated with respect to "a", and the result set to zero and solved, at the same time testing the second derivative to make sure we have a maximum and not minimum solution. The first differential is

$$\frac{\delta \bar{g}_t}{\delta a} = \frac{p_1 r_1}{(1 + ar_1)} + \frac{-p_2 r_2}{(1 - ar_2)} \tag{7.13}$$

which when set to zero, and remembering that $p_1 = (1 - p_2)$, may be solved by simple algebra to define "a" as follows:

$$a = \frac{p_1 r_1 - p_2 r_2}{r_1 r_2} \tag{7.14}$$

We may note in passing that the maximum has been obtained so far without constraint.

The next step is to put the investor's best "a" value, equation (7.14) back into equation (7.12) to give:

$$\bar{g}_t = p_1 \ln\left(1 + \frac{(p_1 r_1 - p_2 r_2)}{r_1 r_2} r_1\right) + p_2 \ln\left(1 - \frac{(p_1 r_1 - p_2 r_2)}{r_1 r_2} r_2\right)$$

$$= p_1 \ln p_1 + p_2 \ln p_2 + p_1 \ln \frac{(r_2 + r_1)}{r_2} + p_2 \ln \frac{(r_1 + r_2)}{r_1} \quad (7.15)$$

if, as elsewhere in this book we define $H = -\sum_{i=1}^{2} p_i \ln p_i$

$$= -H + \ln(r_1 + r_2) - p_1 \ln r_2 - p_2 \ln r_1$$

and by adding and subtracting $\ln 2$

$$= H_{max} - H + \ln \frac{(r_1 + r_2)}{2} - p_1 \ln r_2 - p_2 \ln r_1$$

if further we denote the last three terms by Y, then (7.15) reduces to

$$= H_{max} - H + Y \quad (7.16)$$

We can see that $\bar{g}_t$ is a function of the uncertainty of the environment, and of the asymmetry of the values r_1 and r_2. If there is no asymmetry in these two values, then Y will disappear. If however asymmetry is present, then these values must enter the calculations. In real life such asymmetry is not uncommon. For example, investors in Chicago's grain exchange often say that they have many more losses than gains, but that the size of the average loss is much smaller than the size of the average gain.

It is, however, quite obvious that I have left something out from the analysis. As equation (7.16) stands then any particular value of H can be derived from two values which may be assigned either to p_1 or to p_2 at random. If, for example, p_1 equalled 1 we would have the same gain as if p_2 were equal to 1. Clearly this is nonsense. In this case we would have failed to introduce some values into the analysis. The nature of the problem is very similar to the value problem recognized in other places in this book.

As in other solutions of this kind of problem, the answer here lies in

the placing of constraints on the maximization process. We noted that
(7.12) was maximized without constraint, and clearly this is not good
enough. Murphy imposes conditions on r_1 and r_2, and permits consideration only of those values of these two variables which result in $0 < a < 1$.
If r_1 and r_2 are allowed beyond these values then "a" will "lock" either
at 1 or at 0, and become undiscriminating as a decision variable.

If we substitute the investor's optimum value of "a" as defined in
equation (7.14) into this constraint, we obtain the conditions of r_1 and
r_2 which must not be violated in the analysis:

$$0 < \frac{p_1 r_1 - p_2 r_2}{r_1 r_2} < 1$$

$$\therefore\ 0 < p_1 r_1 - p_2 r_2 < r_1 r_2 \tag{7.17}$$

The left side of the constraint has a simple interpretation. We restrict
our examination to those cases where there is a positive expected pay-off,
that is $p_1 r_1 - p_2 r_2 > 0$. The other side of the constraint is more difficult, but it can be given meaning by considering extreme values of p_1.
Basically it prohibits those cases where there is a possibility of a total
loss.

If these conditions are fulfilled, then the maximum rate of gain by an
investor is defined as in equation (7.16). It is therefore apparent that
risk places a limit on the rate of gain — only by reducing the value of H
can the gain be increased. Only if risk is eliminated and $H = 0$ can gain
be maximized totally. Intuitively this is a most reasonable result, and it
can of course lead to a policy choice to eliminate risk wherever that is
feasible, about which I shall say more in a moment.

So far we have only dealt with risk. In the case of uncertainty it is
necessary to consider the subjectively defined probabilities of the environment as seen by the investor with imperfect knowledge. Suppose
we define his expectations of a rise or fall as $\hat{p}_1$ and $\hat{p}_2$, where these
sum to 1 as before. In this case, quite clearly the assumption of stationarity cannot hold. The investor will change his assessment of the environment probabilities as time passes, and his best estimate of the probabilities
of a rise or a fall will be subjective conditional probabilities, conditional,
that is, on the history of the environment as he has observed it up till
then.

The derivation of the final results that Murphy gives for this case are
more complex than the above derivation of the risk case, but they follow

an exactly comparable line of argument and development. I feel therefore that the reader will be able to recognize the form of the conclusions
if I present them directly. Murphy is able to show that the maximum
expected rate of growth of capital for the investor from the *market
point of view* is

$$g_t = H^* + Y - \frac{1}{T} \sum_{r=1}^{t} \hat{H}\,(R_r \mid R_{r-1} \ldots R_1) \qquad (7.18)$$

where the entropy term for the tth stage is defined as

$$\hat{H}(R_r \mid R_{r-1} \ldots R_1) = -p_1 \ln \hat{p}_{1r} - p_2 \ln \hat{p}_{2r} \qquad *(7.19)$$

The reason for the averaging of the sum in equation (7.18) is of course
that the uncertainty is not stationary, but at each stage it changes as a
result of experience. This is shown in the definition in equation (7.19).
Again, for these equations to hold, it is necessary that the condition

$$0 < \hat{p}_{1t} r_1 - \hat{p}_{2t} r_2 < r_1 r_2 \text{ for } t = 1, \ldots T \qquad (7.20)$$

is not violated.

What is most fascinating for the information theorist is the definition
of the market view of the investor's uncertainty, the weighting by the
probabilities p_1 and p_2 of the information contents of the probabilities
$\hat{p}_1$ and $\hat{p}_2$. I can only describe this as quite beautiful. It summarizes quite
exquisitely the fact that the investor's perception of the environment
alone does not give the resulting gain in capital; rather we must deal with
both the investor's perception of the environment and the actual behaviour of the environment; the first conditioning the move that the
investor will make, the second conditioning the results of his move.

This kind of situation has been considered in an entirely different
light, by, amongst many others, Sommerhof (in Emery, 1969), who
has formalized the concept of directive correlation in goal seeking behaviour. For a full understanding of what is involved I would direct the
reader to consult the reference, but briefly I may note here his area of
concern. If at some stage t the operator of a system S at stage S_t in an
environment E at state E_t desires that at $t + 1$ he will obtain the defined

---

* It is interesting to note that Brillouin (1962) proves that $\sum_i p_i \ln q_i \leqslant \sum_i p_i \ln p_i$,

where $\sum_i p_i = 1 = \sum_i q_i$.

state S_{t+1}, then whether or not he obtains that state will not only depend upon his action at time t but also on the state of the environment at time $t + 1$. For example, suppose a man with a bow and arrow wants to shoot a wild dog that is running very fast; if at time t he aims his arrow at where the dog is at time t and lets it fly, he will miss the dog. To achieve his desired effect, the impact of the arrow in the dog at time $t + 1$, he must aim his arrow at where the dog will be at time $t + 1$. The result of an action now upon the future depends upon what the state of the environment will be in the future. Directive correlation of this kind may be illustrated by Fig. 7.24. In the diagram we assume that the hunter is always able to shoot perfectly accurately at the spot at which he expects the dog to be at time $t + 1$. But he cannot always calculate this position accurately, because the dog is not determinately controlled by him. In (a) the position has been calculated wrongly and the dog lives; in (b) the dog is hit and dies; in (c) the position is calculated wrongly but by fortune the dog still dies. In dynamic systems it is of course quite common that the desired result is achieved for the "wrong" reasons, that a firm located by the manager's wife's prejudices may nevertheless survive because of a change in central government grant policies.

That there is such a directiveness in time is of course essential to the whole concept of risk, and uncertainty. Were we always able to wait until we knew the state of the future environment before doing now what we need to do to achieve a future goal conjointly with the environment, then there would be no risk.

In a sense, all of this thinking is summarized in equation (7.18) above, and it is for that reason that I find it so appealing. We may also, of course, examine the investor's view of his own capital growth. Murphy demonstrates that we can only give an indication of his expected maximum capital value for the $t + 1$ stage, given his position at the tth, in a process of T stages. This is given by

$$f_{T-t}(K_t) = \ln K_t + (T-t)H^* + \sum_{r=t+1}^{T} \hat{Y}(R_r \mid R_{r-1} \ldots R_1)$$

$$- \sum_{r=t+1}^{T} \hat{\hat{H}}(R_r \mid R_{r-1} \ldots R_1) \quad (7.21)$$

where

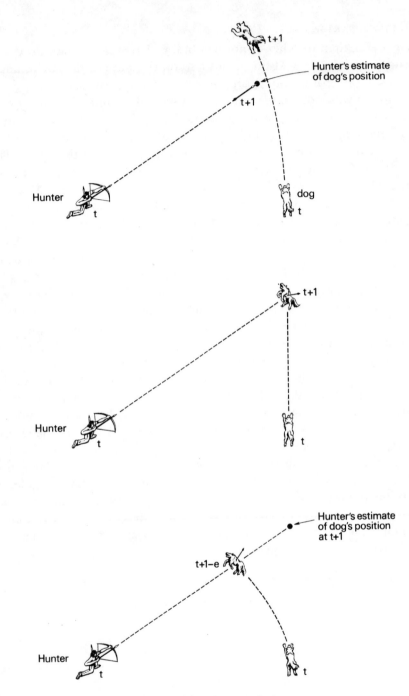

Fig. 7.24. Directive correlation.

$$\hat{Y}(R_r \mid R_{r-1} \ldots R_1) = \ln \frac{(r_1 + r_2)}{2} - \hat{p}_{1r} \ln r_2 - \hat{p}_{2r} \ln r_1 \quad (7.22)$$

and where

$$\hat{\hat{H}}(R_r \mid R_{r-1} \ldots R_1) = -\hat{p}_{1r} \ln \hat{p}_{1r} - \hat{p}_{2r} \ln \hat{p}_{2r} \quad (7.23)$$

Here, therefore we have his own expectations, and the market probabilities do not enter into the analysis, unless he has reached that stage of enlightenment at some stage t where $\hat{p}_{1t} = p_1, \hat{p}_{2t} = p_2$.

In these equations we may note subjective probability by the use of $\hat{p}_i$, but we do not know what the arithmetic values for these probabilities will be. Nevertheless we can suggest the form that they may take. We can assume that the investor has some initial convictions, and we can assume that he will finally learn his environment, so that as in Fig. 7.25

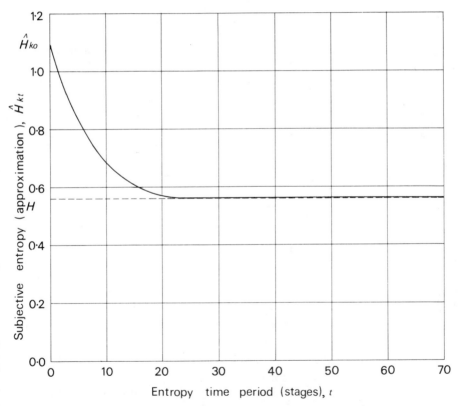

Fig. 7.25. Subjective entropy. (From Murphy, 1965)

his subjective entropy approaches the real entropy as a limit, that is uncertainty is eliminated and only risk remains. Murphey suggests a function
which will model suitably this process of adaptation, and although its
form can clearly be the subject of great debate, I do not wish to digress
into that field. We may accept for our purposes here that the function
may be calculated in the same manner for different input parameters,
and that the parameters of interest are the initial subjective information
(called the conviction vector), and the amount of capital. Using this data
base the comparative history of three investors is shown in Figs 7.26

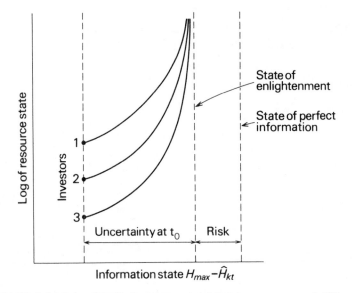

Fig. 7.26. Three investors' behaviour: same initial resource state and different
        information rates. (From Murphy, 1965)

and 7.27, and in Fig. 7.28 the history of the resource state of one
investor compared with the ideal resource state of an investor with
perfect knowledge of the environmental behaviour. Dealing with the last
of these first, we find that the rate of growth of the investor's capital
lags some way behind the optimum in the first time periods, but then as
he gradually learns the true probabilities of the environment his rate of
capital growth approaches the limit set by risk. At this stage in Fig. 7.25
the optimum line and the achieved line become parallel, indicating the

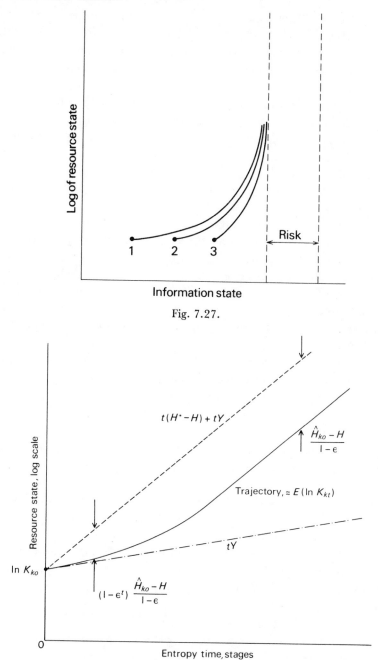

Fig. 7.27.

Fig. 7.28. The irreversible loss. (From Murphy, 1965)

same overall rates of growth in both, but the unfortunate investor lost some potential growth early on when he was poorly informed, and he is never able to recover these losses to his total capital. The poor information and his *uncertainty* result in an *irretrievable capital loss*. The irreversibility of time thus described is most exciting. In the world of the investor we can attribute to uncertainty a phenomenon which is clearly analogous to entropy in thermodynamics and the "arrow" or "direction" of time. Equilibrium economics is as reversible as Newtonian mechanics, but if we relax one of the most usual assumptions of equilibrium economics, that of perfect information, we discover irreversibility.

In comparative terms the fortunes of three investors under differing input conditions are shown in Fig. 7.27 and Fig. 7.28.

In the first case the three curves are the same, but displaced downwards with successive reductions in the starting capital. After some large number of time periods the difference between the investors' total resources narrows in relative terms. In the second case, where the investors start with the same capital but different initial conviction vectors (different subjective information states) the investors with less information suffer an irretrievable loss compared with the investors with better initial information. Although the lines approach each other, they never intersect, so that some degree of difference is always maintained. Additionally I would caution the reader that although the trajectories are shown, the time scale t is not shown, so that it is not clear from the Figures at which time the investors reach the stage of enlightenment, that is when their information state is within some arbitrarily small defined distance from the line of $H^* - H$.

It is of course possible for the lines of two investors to cross each other if they have, for example, access to differential amounts of information. In Fig. 7.29, just such a case is portrayed. In this case Murphy assumes that the investor with a smaller initial resource state, who catches up and overtakes one with a better resource state, has access to more information than the other investor, and thus learns his environment faster. In the real world this has to be true for investment advisory agencies to exist: they make their profits on the basis of the fact that superior information makes money.

Murphy's contribution is to formalize the extremely complex nature of adaptive processes in uncertain and risky environments. In this he may only have confirmed what we think we know intuitively, but within the limits of deductive thought, he has shown what we think we know to be

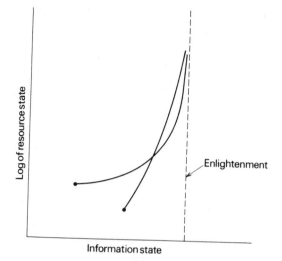

Fig. 7.29. Intersecting trajectories, with different learning rates. (From Murphy, 1965)

something indeed worth knowing and a demonstrable conclusion from realistic assumptions. We find that uncertainty itself is a limit on the optimal behaviour of a part in a stochastic environment, and that this uncertainty lies at the root of irreversible losses. This must obviously have profound effects on the way we view complex dynamic systems, and the behaviour of parts within them. Since in such systems it may well be that the environment does not exhibit stationarity, we can envisage the parts acting all the time in a state of less than full enlightenment, suffering continually from irreversible losses and, from the system viewpoint, suboptimal results. In a complex developing economic system such a conclusion must surely lend credence to Forrester's view of the drift to low performance. It is not a comforting thought. But, unless we get too pessimistic, we must remember that the "second" industrial revolution, following a century and a half after the first revolution in the application of inanimate energy, is of course the "information revolution" that we are witnessing today. The advent of computers and data processing is a necessary stage in economic development to combat the inevitable poor performances which can develop in the complex system. This is no less true in the U.S.S.R. than in the U.S.A., and so it is independent of ideology. The alternative to such a state of affairs must either be to reduce the complexity of the system, or to reduce the uncertainty of the environment, which may amount to the same thing.

So far we have merely assumed a part and its stochastic environment. I have not said how the part and the environment came to be defined. In the case of the investor it may be obvious: in fact that it is not obvious can be deduced from the rules that are laid down about collusion on the stock exchange, and leakage of information amongst members. In the case of large companies it is even further from the obvious. I mentioned above that one response to uncertainty may not be to optimize in the face of it, but to eliminate it. It is therefore no surprise to find Galbraith (1970) and others hinting that the removal of uncertainty is one of the major driving forces in the development of corporations in the modern state. In *The Affluent Society* he says: " . . . the development of the modern business enterprises can be understood only as a comprehensive effort to reduce risk. It is not going too far to say that it can be understood in no other terms". And one of the clearest ways to do this is to grow, to eliminate the competitive environment, to form monopolies or cartels, to research markets and manufacture wants, to buy up technological change and innovation. Galbraith styles it as the logical pursuit of security.

In itself this concern for security is basically amoral, or conceivably moral. Such issues are not really my concern: what is of concern is that theory based on profit maximization and the competitive management of prices is at serious risk itself of being completely irrelevant. Such matters may still be taught in that spatial branch of economics known within geography as "locational analysis", but they sit uncomfortably beside our experience of the real world. What matters is organization:

> Organization replaces individual authority: no individual is powerful enough to do much damage. Were it otherwise, the stock market would pay close attention to retirements, deaths, and replacements in the executive ranks of the large corporations. In fact, it ignores such details in tacit recognition that the organization is independent of any individual.
>
> (Galbraith, 1970)

The ultimate extension of the corporation into its erstwhile environment is of course the foundation of the Multi-national Corporation. Nation states, each busy securing its own borders and extending control beyond them by Empire, by Common Market, by Commodity Agreement, and by Controlled Currencies, comes into conflict with them, and the stage is set for the ultimate dissolution of economics into politics.

Part III

On Information Theory

8

The Definition of Information

8.1 Introduction

Information as defined by Information Theory and information as defined by common usage of the word in everyday life are not the same thing. The statistical quantity defined in the theory is much more restricted in meaning, and cannot so far handle what is known as the "semantic value" of a message. For example, there is an agent in the Palace of Heaven in Peking waiting to explode a bomb on hearing the word "Blurb" broadcast on some normal radio wavelength. When he hears it, he explodes the bomb. But there may be many other people who also receive the radio message, but to them "blurb" essentially is meaningless. The semantic value of the word, its contextual meaning, varies between the different recipients. But in the context of the statistical theory the amount of information transmitted to each person was the same.

Ackoff (1957) in a paper in which he attempts to develop a more general theory of information, summarizes Weaver's classification of the general information problem into three stages. These are:

Level A. How accurately can the symbols of communication be transmitted? (the technical problem).

Level B. How precisely do the transmitted symbols convey the desired meaning? (The semantic problem).

Level C. How effectively does the received meaning affect conduct in the desired way? (The effectiveness problem).

The work of Shannon and Weaver has been directed to answer Level A problems, and in this one could say they have been completely successful. Ackoff's paper is exploring Level C problems, but is tentative.

Clearly one could make a distinction between the physical and social sciences on the basis of the fact that the division between Level A and Level B problems is almost irrelevant for the physical sciences but very relevant for the social sciences, which deal with systems where the circulation of symbolic information is fundamental to the operation of the systems concerned. One hardly need be reminded that Gordon Childe (1936) identified writing as one of the major concomitants of the urban revolution, and that the importance of transmitted information has increased to the extent that the industrial (energy-based) revolution of the last century has in the last decade been matched with the information revolution, some say explosion. However, no matter how desirable it would be within this test to use a theory of semantic information, none is firmly established yet, and we will make only occasional forays in that direction from a base established in the statistical theory. Moreover the latter theory is very useful, as Levels B and C depend on Level A, and since in many cases the objectivity of Level A can be pertinent.

8.2 The statistical theory of information

The statistical theory of information can be approached from more than one viewpoint, although all lead to the same general definitions and theorems. But because the approaches can be different, so are some of the interpretations placed on the definitions and theorems, and some interpretations that would be inadmissible from one viewpoint are admissible from another viewpoint. It is because of this that there is often so much controversy and misunderstanding in the literature on information theory. An author will attack from one frame of reference an analysis carried out in a different frame of reference. I shall accordingly introduce the theory of information from two viewpoints, and I hope that if one of these is not understood, then the other will be. But I hope that the basic philosophical differences between them will be clear.

8.3 First approach

(a) The information content of a message

Telecommunications engineers needed a measure that would enable them to work out how much information could pass through a given channel. This quantitative measure ignored the value put on information by human beings, since, whether some transmitted information is useful or useless, it is still transmitted.

The transmitted measure comes from an information source. Suppose this source is an alphabet of 8 letters, a, b, c, . . . h. Now a message is sent from this source to a receiver, indicating one of these letters. We wish to know how much information has to be transmitted in order that the letter is correctly identified. We assume, for the moment, that all the letters have an equal probability of being transmitted. Thus we have a uniform range of doubt. To begin with we decide to use simple binary questions, requiring either a "yes" or a "no" for an answer. We can count how many such questions we need in order to identify the letter. The first question can divide the uniform range of doubt into two halves. Is the letter in this half or that half? Whether the answer is "yes" or "no", we know which half the letter is in. A second question will divide the remaining uniform range of doubt into two halves, that is into two quarters of the original range of doubt. The answer to the second question identifies which quarter the letter is in, and the answer to a third question will identify which eight the letter is in, i.e. the actual letter. We require three binary questions. Figure 8.1 shows the branching

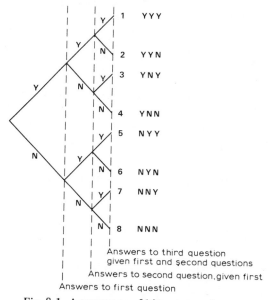

Fig. 8.1. A sequence of binary questions.

effect of successive binary questions, and we can see that with three questions we could identify one of $2 \times 2 \times 2 = 2^3 = 8$ possible outcomes. If there are eight possible alternatives in the source then we need

$$\log_2 8 = 3 \text{ questions}$$

It appears that $\log_2 N$, where N is the number of equally likely alternatives in the source, might serve as our definition of information for the selection of one of the alternatives. The information is measured in binary units, or bits. We can test the definition in other circumstances as well. Suppose we have three separate messages, each of which selects either H or T (for example heads or tails on a coin). We would like the information content of the three messages added together to equal the information content of the single message which told us of the results of all three selections. For each separate message we have $\log_2 2 = 1$ bit, so the three messages added together give us 3 bits. How many alternatives does the message telling us of the results of all three selections have in its source? The number of permutations possible is $2 \times 2 \times 2 = 8$, which are

HHH	*THT*
HHT	*THH*
HTH	*TTT*
HTT	*THH*

and we find that the single message that gives us the results of all three selections is $\log_2 8 = 3$ bits, the same as before. Information is additive in the sense that we require it to be.

So far we have two conditions necessary for the correct use of the definition. One is that the number of alternatives is a power of two, the other is that the alternatives are equally probable, i.e. there is a uniform range of doubts. Under such conditions we have shown that there will always be some *whole number* for any *single selection* of one alternative. This makes sense, since it is not possible to have part of a question.

(b) When the alternatives are equally likely but not a power of 2

It is often said that $\log_2 N$, where N is the number of equally probable alternatives, is the average of yes/no questions one would have to ask to identify one of the alternatives. Strictly speaking, this is not correct, and can lead to some puzzling misunderstandings by the student who wishes to build up his knowledge of information theory from first principles. $\text{Log}_2 N$ is in fact a limit that a certain average will tend towards, under specified conditions. If the conditions are not met then the use of $\log_2 N$ has to be justified on grounds other than "the average number of yes/no questions".

Let us first present the puzzle. A source of three equally likely characters a, b and c is being questioned at each stage to identify one character from the three. The questioning can be represented by a tree diagram as in Fig. 8.2. It is obvious that no matter how the tree is arranged, 1/3 of

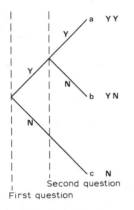

Fig. 8.2. Binary questioning of a three-member source.

the time we will have to ask one binary question to identify the character, and for 1/3 + 1/3 = 2/3 of the time we will have to ask two binary questions. The average number of binary questions would therefore be:

$$\tfrac{1}{3} \cdot 1 + \tfrac{2}{3} \cdot 2 = 1.666 \text{ bits per character selection}$$

Now the value of $\log_2 3$ is 1.586, so that if we simply use the $\log_2 N$ function we will have underestimated the number of binary questions we will have to ask on average.

Suppose instead of sending single character messages we wait and store messages of longer length. If we sent two character messages there would be 3 x 3 possible messages = 9 messages, all equally probable. If we sent three character messages we would have 27 possible messages to choose from, still made up of a, b and c, and on average the frequencies of a, b and c would still be the same. Now study the following table of powers of 2 and powers of 3.

3^x	x	2^x
3	1	2
9	2	4
27	3	8
81	4	16
243	5	32
	6	64
	7	128
	8	256

An eight bit binary code could be used to transmit one of 256 equally likely alternatives. We note that if we had a five letter message length, then since there would be 243 equally probable messages based on the three character source, an eight bit code would be more than sufficient for selecting one of the messages. Now if we use an eight bit code to transmit a five letter message, then the average number of bits per character is:

$$8/5 = 1.600 \text{ bits per character.}$$

This is a reduction from 1.666 although we have not quite reached 1.586.

What we have done is to introduce a coding system. We have decided that to transmit each character down the channel independently using a binary code is inefficient, and that if we wait and transmit messages of many characters with each message identified by the binary code, then we can be more efficient.

In the limit the best that we could achieve, assuming unlimited delay time, is $\log_2 1.586$. We show this with an argument from Cherry (1966).

We have N equally likely characters. We will send a message T characters in length. There are $S = N^T$ equally likely such messages. Now on the definitions above, the information content of selecting one of these S equally probable messages is

$$I = \log_2 S \qquad (8.1)$$

but I may be fractional, and we cannot have fractional questions. Therefore we will have to increase I to the nearest whole number. The nearest integer R has the value

$$R = \log_2 S + d \qquad (8.2)$$

where d is the increment to make I up to the nearest whole number. We therefore have to ask R questions in a binary code to identify one of S messages. But these messages are T characters long. The average information per character is therefore

$$I_{char} = \frac{1}{T} R$$

$$= \frac{1}{T} (\log_2 S + d)$$

$$= \frac{1}{T} (\log_2 N^T + d)$$

$$= \frac{1}{T} (T \log_2 N + d) = \log_2 N + \frac{d}{T} \qquad (8.3)$$

and if T goes to infinity the limit is $\log_2 N$.

This point has been put at some length because it is not always appreciated in writing in geography. Shannon's definition of entropy in Information Theory in fact defines a quantity which is a limit. The limit is useful, since a communication channel may approach the limit, although usually it is too costly to make it reach the limit, but we can quote efficiency in terms of the extent to which the limit is approached. There is a rough analogy here with engines, which may approach 100% thermal efficiency, but which in fact are usually some distance from that. As Ramsay (1971) points out, engines are allowed to be inefficient because we want power from them — that is, a large amount of energy in a short time interval. In information theory there are cases where we can only afford a maximally efficient coding system if we can afford to wait to infinity before transmitting.

Since we now know that $\log_2 N$ is a satisfactory measure of the amount of information on average even when N is not a power of two, and hence $\log_2 N$ is not necessarily a whole number, we find that we are at liberty to change from one base of logarithms to another. There is a series of constants which relate logarithmic functions of different bases to each other. For example:

$$x \log_2 2 = \log_{10} 2$$

Therefore $x = \log_{10} 2 / \log_2 2 = \log_{10} 2$
Similarly $y \log_2 2 = \log_e 2$
Therefore $y = \log_e 2 / \log_2 2 = \log_e 2$

Information units measured by logs of base 2 are called bits, those by logs to base e (Natural or Naperian logs) are usually called nits, and those by logs to base 10 dits or sometimes decits.

Note that $\log_e$ is usually written as ln.

(c) When the alternatives are not equally likely

The second problem relating to the definition of information so far is that we assume that the alternatives in the source are equally likely. If this is not so, then the range of doubt is not uniform. We can then profitably structure our questions towards some expected minimum number. The proofs of the answer to this problem in communications theory are based on what has been given above, namely that the information content of a selection from N and equally likely alternatives is still $\log_2 N$ bits even when N is not a power of two. But we have to remember that if the proof is based on the foregoing, then we have to retain the assumptions which refer to the limiting average case.

Suppose we have an experiment which has N equally likely outcomes, but these outcomes are in two groups which are not equal in number. For example, a development project might have N equally possible outcomes, which are divided into two groups, profit and loss, which are not equal in number (Fig. 8.3.). Suppose that all we require is the information

PROFIT

LOSS

Fig. 8.3. Unequal grouping of eight equally probable source states.

as to which of the two groups the outcome is in. The number of equally likely outcomes is N split between the two groups with N_1 and N_2 alternatives each so that

$$N = N_1 + N_2$$

and
$$p_1 = \frac{N_1}{N} \text{ and } p_2 = \frac{N_2}{N}$$

(8.4)

If we know exactly which of all the alternatives has occurred we receive $\log_2 N$ bits of information. But this is more than we want. The message may have been selected from the alternatives of group 1, in which case we still have $\log_2 N_2$ bits of information that we did not want. If the alternative was in group 2, we will have $\log_2 N_2$ bits of information that we did not want. From $\log_2 N$ we therefore subtract the average amount of information that we did not want. The average we subtract is a weighted average, since it is obvious that if p_1 is greater than p_2 then the excess $\log N_1$ is more likely to occur than the excess $\log_2 N_2$. Hence the information we receive when we know from which of the two groups the outcome has been selected is, *on average*

$$\log_2 N - p_1 \log_2 N_1 - p_2 \log_2 N_2 \text{ bits}$$

$$= \log_2 N - 1/N(N \cdot p_1 \log_2 N_1 + N \cdot p_2 \log_2 N_2)$$

in general $= \log_2 N - 1/N \sum_i N_i \log_2 N_i$

$$= \log_2 N - \sum_i \frac{N_i}{N} \log_2 N_i$$

*(8.5)

Now, since $\sum_i \frac{N_i}{N} = 1$, then $\sum \frac{N_i}{N} \log_2 N = \log_2 N$

Hence we may write from the above

$$= \sum_i \frac{N_i}{N} (\log_2 N - \log_2 N_i)$$

$$= \sum_i \frac{N_i}{N} \log_2 \frac{N}{N_i}$$

$$= \sum_i p_i \log \frac{1}{p_i}$$

(8.6)

---

* Some readers may not remember much about logarithms. However, when using log tables as a short cut to multiplication they will remember the procedure as follows: take the log of both numbers, add the logs together, take the anti-log. That is making use of the relationship $\log (2 \times 4) = \log 2 + \log 4$. Similarly other relationships are $\log(2/4) = \log 2 - \log 4$, and $\log 2^4 = 4 \log 2$.

This is the basic equation for the calculation of the entropy of the information source of n characters with probabilities $p_i, i = 1 \ldots n$; and $\sum_i p_i = 1$. We will note this by H.

Note that the log of 1 in any base ($\log_2$, $\log_e$, $\log_{10}$ etc.) is 0.

Thus
$$H = \sum_i p_i \log \frac{1}{p_i}$$

$$= \sum_i p_i \log (1 - \log p_i)$$

$$= -\sum_i p_i \log p_i \qquad (8.7)$$

(8.6) and (8.7) are the two common expressions for H, the entropy of a source. Where there is a possibility of confusion we will refer to information entropy as distinct from thermodynamic entropy, but in other places the context should make the distinction clear. Wherever a formula of the form of (8.6; 8.7) above occurs, or of a multiple summation such as

$$H = \sum_i \sum_j p_{ij} \log \frac{1}{p_{ij}} \qquad (8.8)$$

we will call this the entropy of the probability set defined by $\sum_i p_i = 1$ or $\sum_i \sum_j p_{ij} = 1$ as the case may be.

Not surprisingly we can also derive the definition of H in ways analogous to the multiple character message used above, but for those cases where the characters of the source have unequal probabilities. The following is Fano's approach, quoted in Cherry (1966).

Let the characters of the source have the probabilities $p_a, p_b, \ldots p_n$. We send a message of T characters. There are S possible messages of length T, and all S of these messages are equally probable if T is of great enough length, since in all such messages a, b, and c will appear with the frequencies as defined above. Therefore in a message of T characters there will be $T \cdot p_a$ occurrences of the letter a, and $T \cdot p_n$ occurrences of the letter n. Since the probability of the message of T characters is the product of probabilities of all the characters in the message, the probability of one message of T characters is:

$$p(T) = p_a{}^{T \cdot p_a} \cdot p_b{}^{T \cdot p_b} \dots p_n{}^{T \cdot p_n} \tag{8.9}$$

But we also know that if there are S equally probable such messages then

$$p(T) = 1/S \text{ and therefore } S = 1/p(T) \tag{8.10}$$

and the information content of one of these messages is

$$\log_2 N = \log_2 1/p(T) \tag{8.11}$$

and on average the information per character is

$$1/T \log_2 1/p(T)$$

$$= \frac{1}{T} \log_2 \frac{1}{p_a{}^{T \cdot p_a}} + \frac{1}{T} \log_2 \frac{1}{p_b{}^{T \cdot p_b}} + \dots \frac{1}{T} \log_2 \frac{1}{p_n{}^{T \cdot p_n}}$$

in general

$$= \sum_i \frac{1}{T} \log_2 \frac{1}{p_i{}^{T \cdot p_i}}$$

$$= - \sum_i \frac{1}{T} \log_2 p_i{}^{T \cdot p_i}$$

$$= - \sum_i \frac{T \cdot p_i}{T} \log_2 p_i \tag{8.12}$$

$$= - \sum_i p_i \log p_i$$

$$= H$$

I shall now present yet another way of achieving the above result. In the above Fano approach we found the number of possible equally likely messages S by saying $S = 1/p(T)$, and then calculating $p(T)$. Here we will derive S by another method.

Suppose we have an alphabet of two letters, a and b. In a very long message of T characters, there are T_a of a and T_b of b, so that we may write

$$p_a = \frac{T_a}{T}$$

$$p_b = \frac{T_b}{T}$$

The problem is considered in terms of combinations and permutations. Suppose we conceive for the moment of all the letters L_i, $i = 1, \ldots T$, as being individual letters. Then clearly the number of messages that these individual letters could send would be $T!$ However, we are not interested in their individuality, merely whether they are in correspondence with an a or a b. As an example we will consider a short message in which we shall for the purposes of the example hypothesize that p_a and p_b have the same value as they would for a very long message. In the example $T = 10$, and L_i, $i = 1, \ldots 10 = 1, 2, 3, 4, 5, 6, 7, 8, 9, 10$. The correspondence between these 10 "letters" and the letters a and b will be as follows

$$2, 3, 7, 8, 10 \text{ are all a}$$

$$1, 4, 5, 6, 9 \quad \text{are all b}$$

The number of possible messages that the 10 letters could give is $T! = 10!$ which is a very large number. *Two* of these 10! possible messages are

$$10\ 4\ 3\ 5\ 6\ 8\ 9\ 7\ 1\ 2 \qquad\qquad (8.13a)$$

and

$$2\ 4\ 5\ 8\ 9\ 7\ 6\ 3\ 10\ 1 \qquad\qquad (8.14a)$$

which would be interpreted according to the correspondence we have set up as follows

$$a\ b\ a\ b\ b\ b\ a\ b\ a\ b\ a \qquad\qquad (8.13b)$$

and

$$a\ b\ b\ a\ b\ a\ b\ a\ a\ b \text{ respectively.} \qquad (8.14b)$$

But we note that (8.13b) and (8.14b) could have been transmitted by other individual letters as well. For example (8.13c) and (8.14c) as follows

$$8\ 5\ 7\ 6\ 9\ 10\ 1\ 3\ 4\ 2 \qquad\qquad (8.13c)$$

and

$$3\ 5\ 6\ 8\ 1\ 10\ 9\ 2\ 7\ 4 \qquad\qquad (8.14c)$$

would give the same pair of a and b messages. The question which follows is obviously: "by how much has the number of possible messages S been reduced below $T!$ because we only have letters a and b?" Note that there are five of a and five of b, and that it does not matter at all from the point of view of the receiver of the message in "a"s and "b"s in what order the individual letters corresponding to a and b arrive. The letters 10, 8, 7, 3, 2 corresponding to "a" can come in 5 x 4 x 3 x 2 x 1 = 5! ways, all of which would still mean five of "a". And it does not matter where in the string of 10 letters these five come, they still could arrive in 5! ways: in other words for any given specific message in terms of "a" and "b", for example message 8.13.b, the letters corresponding to the "a"s, even although not necessarily together, could still have come in 5! different ways. The same is true for the "b" letters, and the same is true also for the message in 8.14.b.

To return to the initial problem, the number of different messages possible given a message length of 10 characters, composed of five "a"s and five "b"s, is:

$$S = \frac{10!}{5!5!} \tag{8.15}$$

in general

$$S = \frac{T!}{\prod_i (T_i!)} \tag{8.16}$$

and in terms of a two character alphabet

$$S = \frac{T!}{T_a!T_b!}$$

Now the information attributed to the selection of one of these S equally probable messages is

$$\log_2 S = \log_2 \frac{T!}{T_a!T_b!} \tag{8.17}$$

If we convert from bits to nits and use natural logarithms we may use Stirling's approximation as follows

$$\ln S! = S \ln S - S$$

Thus $\ln \frac{T!}{T_a!T_b!} = \ln T! - \ln T_a! - \ln T_b!$ (8.18)

$$= T \ln T - T - (T_a \ln T_a - T_a) - (T_b \ln T_b - T_b)$$
$$= T \ln T - T - T_a \ln T_a + T_a - T_b \ln T_b + T_b$$

(but $T_a + T_b = T$)

$$= T \ln T - T_a \ln T_a - T_b \ln T_b$$

$$= T \left(\ln T - \frac{T_a}{T} \ln T_a - \frac{T_b}{T} \ln T_b \right)$$

$$= T \left(\frac{T_a}{T} \ln \frac{T}{T_a} + \frac{T_b}{T} \ln \frac{T}{T_b} \right)$$

or in general

$$= T \sum_i \frac{T_i}{T} \ln \frac{T}{T_i}$$

Therefore the average information per character is

$$\sum_i \frac{T_i}{T} \ln \frac{T}{T_i}$$

and since

$$\frac{T_i}{T} = p_i$$

$$\sum_i p_i \ln \frac{1}{p_i} \tag{8.19}$$

which is H as before.

The point of introducing this method is that the combinatorial approach is very common in many fields, and particularly in statistical thermodynamics and analogous applications such as the work of Wilson in geography. An equation such as (8.16) above is very common in the literature indeed. If the reader has not fully grasped the way in which the combinatorial term is derived, he can wait till Chapter 9 (Section 9.3), when the term appears again and is explained again in an example with a slightly different slant. The reader is also cautioned that some authors on entropy and information theory maintain that only when a factorial term of the kind given can be used in analysis is the subject matter fit for the correct use of these techniques.

There are, however, some obvious problems of interpretation arising. If we work back from (8.19) to (8.18) we derive

$$N \sum_i p_i \ln \frac{1}{p_i} = \ln \frac{N!}{\prod_i (N_i!)} \qquad (8.20)$$

Whereas, if we work back from (8.12) to (8.10) we derive

$$N \sum_i p_i \ln \frac{1}{p_i} = \ln \frac{1}{\prod_i \left(\frac{N_i}{N}\right)^{N_i}} \qquad (8.21)$$

Obviously the right-hand sides of (8.20) and (8.21) are not equal, but approximate each other under defined conditions, which I shall now identify. The quantity behind the ln on the right-hand side of (8.21) is the number of messages of length N characters which come from a source of m letters of frequency $p_i, i = 1, \ldots m$. It is clear that we are dealing with a message sampled from a stationary statistical source with replacement, hence there are no conditional probabilities.*

The alternative formulation is to make sure that the frequencies of the various letters do represent their true frequencies, by sampling from a finite source of N characters *without replacement*. In effect this is not a sample at all, but the sequential selection of a population. To do this we use the conditional probabilities implied by the factorial expression.

Therefore the extent to which the approximation is true depends upon the extent to which sampling without replacement (8.20) approaches sampling with replacement (8.21). We can discuss this problem further with reference to some multi-nominal distribution. If we resume the problem posed by section 4.4, we can specify a Trinominal distribution, with $m = 3$, there being the three letters A, B and C to consider, with associated probabilities $p_A = .6, p_B = .2, p_C = .2$ and a message length $N = 5$ characters. We can now compute not only the probability of a message such as AAABC but also of AAAAA or CCCCC etc. The probability of a message of a specified number N_i of each of the m letters is given by

$$\prod_{i=1}^{m} (p_i^{N_i}) \times \frac{N!}{\prod_{i=1}^{m} (N_i!)} \qquad (8.22)$$

* With reference to Chapter 4 (Section 4.4), this means that the system "marginal" requirements are met purely because the frequencies of the m letters in a very long message are arbitrarily close to their "true" frequencies.

For a message of $N_A = 3, N_B = 1, N_C = 1$ the probability according to formula (8.22) is only 0.1728. Clearly there is a very large error possible in obtaining the system part requirements, and therefore the approximation is not useful with such a small N. But for large N the standard error of the estimates of the m letters becomes very small, until for infinite N the probability of receiving a message with infinitely small errors in the estimates of p_i approaches unity.

(d) Some coding implications

Not surprisingly we can comment on the implications for coding which result from the definition of H. I say not surprisingly since the derivations of H given all depend on the fact that the information content of one message taken from N equally likely ones is $\log_2 N$ bits, and this as we have shown implicitly assumes a coding system, if necessary.

Ross Ashby (1956) gives a neat demonstration of the coding problem in a case where the source characters are not equally likely. Suppose we have the characters A, B, C and D, which are emitted by a source. If they were equally probable they would need a 2 bit code, since $\log_2 4 = 2$, and the code could be as follows:

A	B	C	D
00	01	10	11

But suppose they are not equally probable, but have the frequencies 1/2, 1/4, 1/8, 1/8 respectively. We find

$$H = \frac{1}{2} \log_2 \frac{1}{1/2} + \frac{1}{4} \log_2 \frac{1}{1/4} + \frac{1}{8} \log_2 \frac{1}{1/8} = 1\tfrac{3}{4} \text{ bits}$$

which is less than two bits. There exists therefore a code which will reduce the average amount of information per character to less than 2 bits.

First code the message   A   B   C   D

with this correspondence   0   10   110   111

Take a sample message and code it accordingly

A	A	A	A	B	B	C	D
0	0	0	0	10	10	110	111

the lower line can be grouped in pairs which for convenience we will call E, F, G and H

00	01	10	11
E	F	G	H

Clearly these are two bit codes, and so it does not matter how often the E groups or G group occur, the average information to transmit these will always be two bits.

Now we can find a correspondence between the original message above and this new two bit code, which is unambiguous we may add, as follows

A	A	A	A	B	B	C	D
0	0	0	0	10	10	110	111
	E		E	G	G	H	F H

Note that the ratio of letters is 8 in the top line to 7 in the bottom, therefore we have a reduction in a ratio $2 : 1\frac{3}{4}$, as was predicted by H, simply by using a bit code of 0 and 1, but using a single binary digit for the most common letter, A, and three digit number for the least common, C and D.

Note that in this example no delay in transmittion is necessary, because the probabilities of the letters are all reciprocals of some power of two (e.g. $\frac{1}{2}, \frac{1}{4}, \frac{1}{8}$ etc). If they were some odd values such as 1/53, 5/49, etc., then some delay would be necessary as well.

8.4 Shannon's theorem 11

Shannon's theorem 11 is a coding theorem.

Let a discrete channel have capacity C and a discrete source the entropy per second H. If H < C there exists a coding system such that the output of the source can be transmitted over the channel with an arbitrary small frequency of errors (or an arbitrarily small equivocation). If H > C it is possible to encode the source so that the equivocation is less than H − C + e, where e is arbitrarily small. There is no method of coding which gives an equivocation less than H − C.

(quoted from Laming, 1968)

There are several aspects to this theorem. Firstly, we are dealing with a limit which assumes a coding possibility. Secondly mention is made of a rate per unit time. Thirdly there are some extra components such as C and equivocation.

The assumption of the coding possibility was expected after the demonstration of coding above, and the fact that the proofs have been based on the information content of one message taken from N equally probable ones. But the rate is something new. Let us for a moment consider a river channel. The capacity of that channel is given as cusecs, or in other words cubic feet per second. It does not make sense to say that the capacity of a river is 10 gallons. The capacity of a *store* of water, be it tank or lake, may be 1000 gallons, but the capacity of a *channel* is given as a rate. Now, *any* channel can empty a 1000 gallon reservoir. But a small channel will take longer to empty it than a large one, hence the size of the channel affects performance in time. Suppose however, we took a channel of a fixed size, and varied the height of the controlling sluice on the reservoir. The rate at which the water emitted from the reservoir could build up until such time as the channel overflowed. By now we are measuring both the rate of emission and the capacity of the channel as rates. The same is true of the information channel. The source emits at some rate, and the channel has a rate capacity. If the rate of source emission exceeds the channel capacity some information gets lost, no matter what coding we use, and we say equivocation has occurred. This is the loss of information due to channel overload.

The reason we have gone into these problems in some detail is to make clear the basic assumptions underlying an information approach to a communication channel. These assumptions will only be important when we are applying information theory in some situation where we believe the channel model of communication is relevant, and a suitable model for analysis. One can imagine many cases where it might be useful in the social sciences, particularly in diffusion studies, but in fact in many communication situations it is impossible to identify unambiguously the components of the system that correspond to the communication system.

Many writers on psychology have developed an information theory approach to the analysis of choice reaction times. Laming (1968) has criticized this approach on a number of grounds. The experiment is normally set up as follows. The subject is confronted with a number of lamps, any of which may be illuminated for some brief period. Depending on which lamp is illuminated at any given stage, he has to press a corresponding key or button. The subject receives a signal and presses a chosen key out of a range of alternatives, and the whole process is timed — hence the name choice-reaction time experiments.

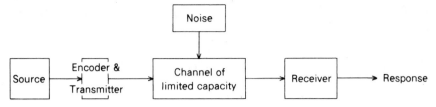

Fig. 8.4. An information channel.

Now an ideal communication system can be shown as in Fig. 8.4. The components are, as is consistent with the comments on Shannon's theorem above, a source, a transmitter, the channel, a noise source, and the receiver. The transmitter can encode if necessary the basic message from the source, and the noise source is a hypothetical way of considering interference (although the source of noise is in many cases understood and not merely hypothetical). Figure 8.5. shows the kind of

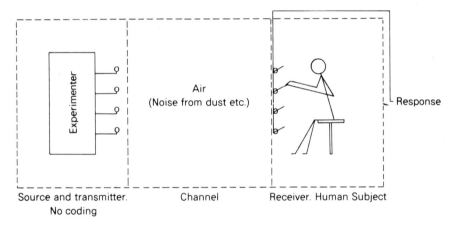

Fig. 8.5. An information channel incorrectly drawn.

correspondence which has been made by Hyman between the ideal system and the experiment, but which has been criticized by Laming. The control (the source) and the transmitter are one and the same and are locked together, that is the transmitter sends a given signal, by illuminating one of the lamps, for any given control move. The transmitter does not encode. The frequencies of the source do not change the way in which the lamps are lit, whereas we know from the example from Ashby above that the frequencies of the source should affect the coding.

Additionally, since there is no delay possible in transmission, none of the limit conditions of Shannon's theorem apply, and hence there is very little we can say about the scheme. Despite all these criticisms, many experimenters have fitted the following equation to their data:

$$t = a - b \sum_i p_i \log p_i$$

where a and b are constants, t is mean reaction time, and p_i is the probability that on the next occasion the ith lamp will be lit. The fitting of such an equation may be more or less accurate, but no matter how good the fit there are many reasons as Laming has shown for rejecting an information channel scheme as the underlying explanatory model. If one does anything at all, Laming suggests the scheme shown in Fig. 8.6.,

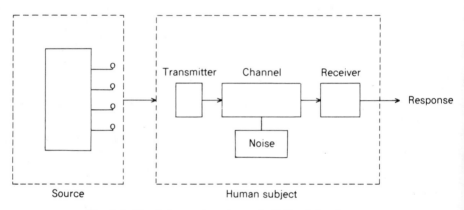

Fig. 8.6. The information channel of Fig. 8.5 redrawn.

where the transmitter and receiver together with the channel are all incorporated in the subject. This is theoretically easier to justify, experimentally harder to study.

Now let us consider the case of a geography student looking at a map. The map is not a discrete source transmitting information at a rate of H(Map) per second. There is no mention of encoders and transmitters. The student might not be paying attention, on the other hand he might. He might be trained in map analysis, he might not. Now let us suppose we have a television camera scanning a map. Light impinging on the camera generates a series of signals as the subject is scanned. This

information is transmitted to the television screen where it is scanned
back and forth to produce a picture. In this context we can talk about
the rate at which the television system is transmitting information,
whether the picture is held on a stationary map, or moved over a
countryside scene. A system with limited channel capacity will not give
a very good picture, a system with high capacity will give better pictures.
That much we can say, th..t much can be measured. But we still cannot
measure the effectiveness of the viewers reception — that is a level B
and level C problem. Suppose we show an unchanging picture, as in test
transmissions, as far as the system itself is concerned it is constantly
transmitting at the same rate. The viewer, however, soon sees what the
picture is, and begins to think that no new information is coming to
him. To the system all the information it is transmitting is constantly
new, it has no memory of what was shown one microsecond ago.

It would seem therefore that the application of information theory in
the form of studies of communication channels might be severely restricted in geography. However, there is an entirely different approach to
the subject which also gives us a measure H, but since it is based on different reasoning, the interpretation of it can also be different.

8.5 Second approach: information as surprise

We know that some event has a certain probability of occurring tomorrow. Let us suppose that the probability that it will rain is p_r. How surprised are we if it does rain? If we live in England and $p_r = 0.9$, then we
are not very surprised at all. If on the other hand we live in Utah and
$p_r = 0.1$, then we are very surprised when it rains. Information is therefore associated with the inverse of the probability of an event occurring.

$$I = f\left(\frac{1}{p_i}\right)$$ (8.23)

where I is Information, f is some function, and p_i is the probability of
the event. We also require that the information we receive when two
independent events are confirmed at the same time should be equal to
the information of each confirmation on its own added together. If the
probability p_i is statistically independent of the probability p_j then the
probability p_{ij} of both i and j is $p_{ij} = p_i p_j$. Hence if we desire that

$$f\left(\frac{1}{p_{ij}}\right) = f\left(\frac{1}{p_i p_j}\right) = f\left(\frac{1}{p_i}\right) + f\left(\frac{1}{p_j}\right)$$ (8.24)

we can satisfy the conditions by taking the function $f()$ to be a logarithmic function.

This is the *individual information* of a single message confirming a given event or given events. Before we receive the message we can attempt to work out how much information we would expect to receive on average, i.e. a statistical expectation of the information contents. The probability p_i is a member of an exhaustive set of probabilities so that

$\sum_i p_i = 1$. Each probability is related to an event, and each such proba-

bility has an information content if its respective event occurs. These statements can be shown to be true with the simple case already illustrated. The probability of rain, p_r, is a member of an exhaustive set of probabilities, even if the only other member we care to specify is p_n, the probability of it not raining. Before tomorrow comes we know that we will receive one of two individual information contents, i.e. $\log \dfrac{1}{p_r}$ and $\log \dfrac{1}{p_n}$. We also know that the probability of receiving the first is p_r, and of receiving the second is p_n. Our expectation is therefore

$$p_r \log \frac{1}{p_r} + p_n \log \frac{1}{p_n}$$

or in general

$$\sum_i p_i \log \frac{1}{p_i}$$

This is obviously the expression for entropy as defined above. The difference between this and the approaches above is simply in terms of assumptions and the mode of thinking. The above had a physical system as the basic model; here we have simply a formulation from the receiver's point of view. He has a prior expectation of the occurrence of some events, where these expectations are defined in terms of probabilities. If he receives knowledge of one of these events, no matter through what channels this knowledge reaches him, whether by letter, by voice, by code, he gains an amount of information depending on his "surprise". The concept is intuitive.

Perhaps, following Shackle (1969), we should query the use of probability as a surrogate for surprise. There are many occasions when the set of hypotheses to which surprise would apply are not mutually exclusive.

Suppose we ask for the probability that the weather will be muggy tomorrow, and the probability that it will rain. Clearly the two events are not exclusive, and there would be no point in averaging them. There are also occasions when an experiment is not repeatable, so that although there exists a set of rival hypotheses which are mutually exclusive there is no sense in averaging them. Shackle's example of this is the non-divisible experiment. We shall define divisible and non-divisible experiments as follows. Suppose we ask, "If I throw two dice 36 000 times, how often will they show a double six?" The question can be answered statistically with some degree of meaning. The experiment is divisible into many repeated analogous single experiments. Suppose, however, I ask what the weather will be like on Friday 13 June 1985. The experiment is non-divisible. In Shackle's words, in such a case, "the experiment and its answer are a unitary whole and actuarial principles are not able to give that answer". The idea of averaging in such a case is clearly dubious. Finally there is the caution that the surprise accord to some future event is clearly the potential surprise, now, which is equated with a hypothetical surprise that would occur if in the future the event were to take place.

However, these are philosophical problems about which the reader will only be cautioned. We will not mention them again in this text. Although the problems raised are worth deep consideration by anyone using the entropy expression, they do not automatically translate themselves into necessary assumptions about the derivation of the expression. In a communication channel the assumptions about the physical behaviour of the channel have to be spelt out. Here all we have done is define some quantity H which can be arithmetically calculated for any set of numbers x_i such that $\sum_i x_i = 1$. The interpretation of this arithmetic operation in the present approach rests on the fact that the numbers are said to be probabilities, and if they are probabilities, then we can interpret H in terms of an average expected surprise. Theil (1967) calls H in this context the *average expected information* content of a single message confirming the occurrence of one of the defined set of events.

8.6 The properties of entropy

The properties of the entropy formula are what make it so general and so useful in many very disparate contexts. We will examine here some of the major properties.

(a) The minimum value of H

The minimum value of H occurs when $p_i = 1$ for one value of i, and for all other values of i, p_i is zero. We then have

$$1 \log 1 + 0 \log 0 + 0 \log 0 \ldots = 0 \qquad (8.25)$$

Many students have queried the case where a probability of zero occurs. The log is minus infinity. Thus the individual expected information content of a zero probability event (which could be termed impossible depending on the confidence placed on the derivation of the probabilities) is infinite. On the other hand the information content of an event which is certain, with probability one, is zero. The above minimum value for H is clearly derived from considering, quite legitimately, that the product of zero and minus infinity is zero, but this is not always a sufficient answer to students who doubt the validity of averaging in a case such as this.

An alternative way of looking at this is to say that at any time the probability set under consideration refers to a subset of the universe of all events which might occur in the next time interval as a consequence of all actions now. Given one action now (an experiment) most of this universe of all consequences is completely irrelevant to our action, and all such consequences are excluded from our set of possibilities and are given probabilities of zero. If then the set of probabilities corresponding with the subset of possible outcomes of our action contains any zeros, then the consequences to which those probabilities refer should not logically be part of the outcome of our experiment but should belong to the rest of the universe of consequences. Put another way, if we have a set $\{p_i\}, i = 1 \ldots n$, and $\sum_i p_i = 1$, such that $p_i > 0$ all i, then to this set we can add another set $\{p_j\}$ $j = n + 1 \ldots \infty$, $p_j = 0$ all j, to form the set $\{p_n\}$ $k = 1 \ldots \infty$, still bound by the condition $\sum_n p_n = 1$; but the exercise is pointless.

(b) Maximum value of H

The maximum value of H occurs when $p_i = 1/n$, $i = 1, \ldots n$. This condition simply states that all events are equally probable, and in such a class the maximum average surprise occurs. The algebraic proof of this is not included here, but readers may refer to Theil (1967) for confirmation. We can demonstrate the result quite easily by graphs of H for specified values of p_i. We can only represent those cases of less than four dimensions on two-dimensional paper, hence Figs 8.7 and 8.8 only show

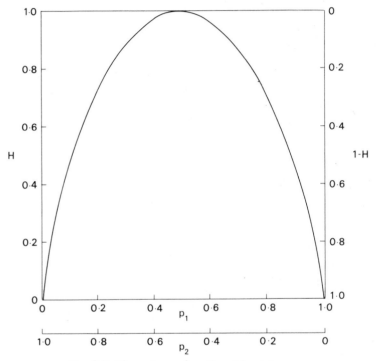

Fig. 8.7. The entropy function, bivariate case.

values of H for the case of a probability set with two members and the case of a set with three members respectively. In one case we have a line reaching a maximum when $p_1 = p_2 = 0.5$, and in the other case we have a surface reaching a maximum when $p_1 = p_2 = p_3 = 0.333$.

In general

$$H_{max} = \sum_{i=1}^{n} p_i \log\frac{1}{p_i} = \sum_{i=1}^{n} \frac{1}{n} \log\frac{1}{1/n} = \log n \qquad (8.26)$$

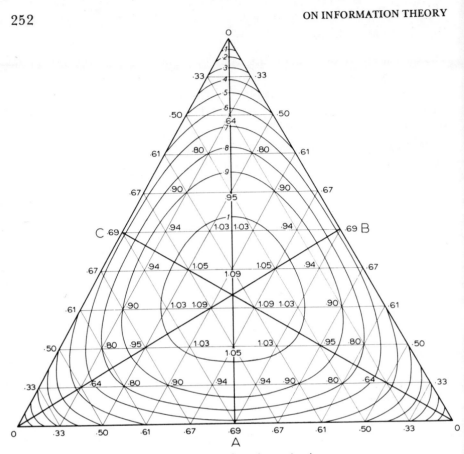

Fig. 8.8. The entropy function, trivariate case.

An alternative way of presenting visual evidence of the behaviour of H is suggested by Tideman (1967). H is a summation of the quantities $p_i \log \dfrac{1}{p_i}$, which are clearly quantities in two dimensions, that is they are the product of p_i and $\log \dfrac{1}{p_i}$. If we construct a graph with an x axis of unit length and a y axis marked in arithmetic intervals, we can plot these quantities as a series of rectangles as in Fig. 8.9.a. The summation is the total area of all the rectangles. Two cases are shown, one where maximum entropy is reached, the other where a lower value is reached. Note that the order of the p_i on the x axis is not fixed, but can be any desired, and note that if p_i = zero, then the interval p_i becomes a dimen-

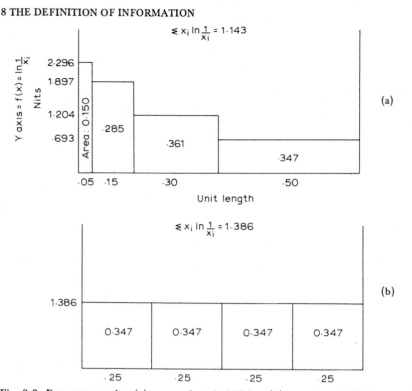

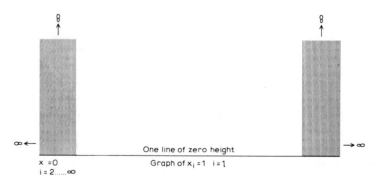

Fig. 8.9. Entropy graphs: (a) unequal probabilities, (b) equal probabilities, maximum entropy.

sionless point, and $\log\dfrac{1}{p_i}$ becomes a line parallel to the y axis and going to infinity. A line, having no breadth, has no area value. The case of $p_i = 1$ is represented by a line along the x axis, as in Fig. 8.10.

Fig. 8.10. Minimum entropy.

8.7 Interpretation of H

(a) Equality and heteorogeneity

H is explained in words in many different ways. If we go back to the telecommunications system, then H is usually used in the first instance to assess the source entropy. Then we can say that H is the uncertainty of the source. Note that although H was explained in terms of the number of questions that *would* have to be asked to identify *one* member of the source, the number of such questions on average is a function of all the members of the source and their relative frequencies. Hence H is a measure of *uncertainty* and is a property of the source.

Consider a different use. In a given country different persons share the total national space unequally: some are rich and have large gardens, some are poor and live in high-density flat developments. If each person has a share x_i of the national area, then $H(x)$ becomes *inverse measure* of *inequality*, or a direct measure of *equality*. As H is greater, so inequality is less and equality greater. There is also an informational interpretation of this case where H is also interpreted in terms of uncertainty, but we will come across this later. Next let us consider two adjacent fields, separated from each other by a hedge, but in the hedge there is a gate. One field has 50 cows in it, the other has 50 sheep in it. In terms of *categories* sheep and cows, we can measure separately the entropies of each of the fields, where p_c and p_s is the fraction of cows and sheep in field 1, such that these two fractions sum to unity. Then initially for field 1

$$H(p_{c,s}) = \sum_{i=c,s} p_i \log \frac{1}{p_i} = 0 \qquad (8.27)$$

But then a walker leaves the gate open, and the animals become mixed up between fields. We then find H has increased to H^*:

$$H^*(p_{c,s}) > H(p_{c,s}) \qquad (8.28)$$

A typical interpretation given to H in these circumstances is to say that H is a measure of heterogeneity, or mixing. This sounds opposite in meaning to H being a measure of equality, but note that in both cases the maximum of H occurs when $p_i = \frac{1}{n} = p_j$, all i and j.

The difference in meaning can be attributed to the difference in the derivation of the p_i, in other words what in reality the "probabilities" stand for. In one case they represent the fractional shares of a categorically defined property (e.g. land as opposed to income etc.) distributed amongst individuals (the interpretation of H as a measure of equality) and in the other case they represent groupings of individuals with the same categorical property, e.g. sheep or cows (H as heterogeneity).

(b) Entropy as a property of the observer and as a property of the system

If we consider thermodynamic entropy for a moment, we realize that it is in the sense described in Chapter 3, an immanent property, and one which is assumed to be independent of the observer's method of measuring it. As such we can hypothesize its existence as a quantity which dictates certain system behaviour characteristics, whether man is around or not. Without getting involved in the metaphysics of meaning when man is not present to think, it is clear that energy becomes degraded in river systems in accordance with the laws of thermodynamics whether the nearest man to observe it is a primitive hunter or a scientist. Entropy in this sense is a property of the system which is not dependent on the means of measuring it. The point is that a physical system exists. In the case of communication networks, if at any time we can point to an existing and transmitting system, such as the television screen depicting a map considered in the example above, then similarly we can talk of the entropy of the source in a manner independent of the observer and the means of measurement. The physical system exists.

In the two examples of the previous section, entropy as inequality, and entropy as heterogeneity, no physical system exists. In both cases we could construct systems to convey certain information, and if we did construct such systems we could then discuss their entropy, assuming that the system fulfilled the assumptions pertaining to the use of information theory in communications.

For example, in the first case, that of national area being split into individual shares, we can hypothesize that the land is composed of many small pieces, the size of such pieces being determined by the fineness of measurement we use (the resolution level or accuracy level). We then send out a message saying to whom each piece of land belongs. In the limit the area shares x_i can be seen as the probability that the mth unit of land will be allocated to individual i. If there are m units of land and

m is very large, we can conceive of the one message being split into many messages of some length s, such that all the coding assumptions apply. Then the entropy of the source per designated piece of land would be

$$\sum_i^N p_i \log \frac{1}{p_i}$$

which also means that the total amount of information would be

$$m \sum_i p_i \log \frac{1}{p_i} \tag{8.29}$$

to specify the land distribution totally. We note that the latter is a function of H and of m, that is, the more finely we measure the land surface, the more information we generate.

However, on the whole the system does not exist, and none is hypothesized. And if we were to hypothesize one, the importance of such a system from the engineer's point of view would be its performance in relation to channel capacity C. We, however, are interested in the source entropy. In the absence of even a hypothesized communication system we find that the entropy of the system does not exist as an immanent property — it exists as a property of some distribution of probabilities defined by the observer. It is thus a property of the observer's understanding of some aspect of the system. It has no basic roots in any objective reality.

In the second example similar reasoning applies. The entropy of field one in terms of cows and sheep is a property defined by the observer. If no communications system exists, which sends messages about sheep and cows, then we can ask any other questions about field one. What is the entropy of the set of the probability of finding any specific cow at the one-cow-at-a-time drinking trough? This might give us some idea of the extent to which cows were equally thirsty, or stronger than each other.

It is because of this freedom to define some probability set that we find "paradoxes" such as the definition of a regular point pattern as a pattern of zero entropy by Medvedkov (1967) and as a pattern of maximum entropy by Chapman (1970).

In such arbitrary circumstances it is obviously worthwhile trying to establish some basis for the choice of the probability set used. In Chapman (1970) each point is considered individually, and the fractions of the total area "allocated" to each point constitute the probability set. This fraction may be derived by observing in reality the areas of a set of farms for example, or by using Thiessen polygons if such data are not available. Maximum entropy then occurs when all points have the same area. We can hypothesize that given no information to the contrary, in some competitive situation where each unit is self-sufficient, then competition should produce this kind of area distribution. But suppose that cooperation existed, so that one man gave up farming to make shoes, and another man doubled his farming area to provide food for the cobbler. Entropy would decrease. Zero entropy would occur when all men except one no longer required space to work in, and one man farmed for all. Such a case is of course hypothetical, and there are many other ways in which cooperation can occur. But we can give some meaning to this extreme value. The same kind of meaning could be given to a set of towns. Note also that the actual geometrical layout is not given, merely area shares, so that distortion in the pattern can occur.

In Medvedkov's case, the area is divided into quadrats of equal size, and a frequency distribution is drawn up of a number of cells against points per cell. Regularity then is shown by an entropy of zero, where only one class of points per cell is recorded, as shown in Fig. 8.11. Note that this pre-supposes that the pattern is geometrically regular if the quadrat arrangement is regular. The most telling criticism of this approach is probably to ask "what is the meaning of maximum entropy"? In such a case the frequency of all points-per-cell classes would be similar. Such a distribution Fig. 8.11.b would be significant in the extreme, in that we know the expected random distribution of points in space expressed in quadrat counts conforms to the poisson, as in Fig. 8.11.c. The inability to give meaning to the case of maximum entropy weakens the usefulness of the approach.

8.8 T, a measure of information gain

Suppose that we are told that some field is being investigated in England, and that we will be told what sort of crop is grown there. How much information do we expect to receive? We could evaluate H using the probability set of the field being under crop A or crop B, or C . . . etc. Knowing only that the field is in England we assume that these probabilities are proportional to the number of fields in England under the

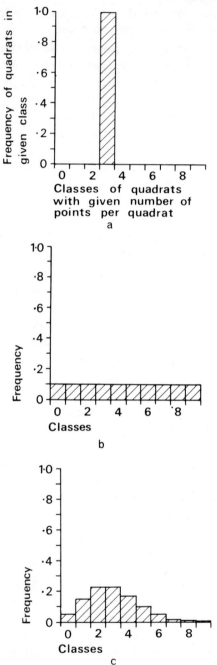

Fig. 8.11. The entropy of three probability distributions.

respective crops. But later we are told that the field is in Surrey. We have separate data for Surrey that tell us the numbers of fields under various crop types for that county only. We find that compared with the national probabilities, the probability of rough pasture has decreased, and the probability of good pasture has increased. What is our expectation of the amount of information we have gained? The amount of information we have gained for the ith land use type is the difference in the two information contents

$$\log \frac{1}{x_i} - \log \frac{1}{y_i} = \log \frac{y_i}{x_i}$$

where x_i is the national probability, i.e. the prior probability and y_i the Surrey probability, i.e. the posterior probability.

The terms are arranged in this way so that if $y_i > x_i$ then $\frac{y_i}{x_i} > 1$, and hence $\log \frac{y_i}{x_i} > 0$. Then a positive information gain has been made if the probability of the ith category has increased. On average we will gain this amount of information y_i of the time. We therefore define the Average Expected Information Gain, denoted by T, as

$$T = \sum_i y_i \log \frac{y_i}{x_i} \tag{8.30}$$

If one definite message is received then for one i, $y_i = 1$, and for all other i, $y_i = 0$. The right hand side of (8.30) becomes

$$1 \log \frac{1}{x_i}$$

Now let us suppose that the first probability x_i is a member of a set of equal probabilities. That is $x_i = x_j$ all i and all j, and $i = 1, \ldots N$. Then $x_i = \frac{1}{N}$ so that the expression above becomes

$$T = \log N$$

We find that when there is a known outcome and when the initial set of alternatives are equally probable that the information gained on the receipt of a message selecting one of the alternatives, or alternatively the amount of information necessary to specify one of the alternatives, is $\log N$.

We thus find that in the circumstances specified the value of T, a measure of information gain, is the same as H_{max}. The explanation of this state of affairs is quite simple. The specified circumstances under which T and H both become $\log N$ are in the first case certainty about an outcome, which is as much information as one could have, and in the other case maximum uncertainty about an outcome. It follows that if H_{max} specifies the maximum amount of missing information, that is the state where our average *expected* information is greatest, then if we have a gain from this state to a state of complete certainty, minimum uncertainty, then we *have gained* all that was missing. Thus the two have the same value.

Let us stress that although the two can have the same value, the interpretation of the two is different. I believe that a lot of the confusion about such statements as "information is negative entropy" or "author X uses the opposite meaning for entropy" derive from those cases where information gain at its maximum can be equated with maximum entropy.

The quantity T defined above has been explained from a viewpoint that assumes that there is some time difference between possession of the set x_i and the set y_i. Often this is in fact the case, but there are occasions when the time difference is not explicit. The formula T is often used as a kind of surrogate for a correlation measure since it measures the extent to which the x_i and the y_i match each other for any given i. In correlation, a time dimension is not necessarily assumed — we merely state that to some specified degree one variable is a good predictor of another variable. There are examples in the literature in geography where this kind of "correlative" use is made of T, and where the two data sets for x_i and y_i are presented simultaneously. The administrative areas of a country and their populations can be depicted on the same map. We can then define the quantities $a_i = A_{i/A}$ and $n_i = N_i/N$, $i = 1 \ldots m$, where a_i is the fraction of total national area A represented by the area A_i of the ith administrative unit, and n_i is the fraction of the national population N represented by the population N_i of the ith administrative unit, and where there are m such units. The a_i and the n_i are clearly fractions which sum to one, and can therefore be used in evaluating T. (Whether they can be considered probabilities is a question which will be dealt with later.) But we have to decide which of the data sets is the *a priori* set, and which the *a posteriori*. Since the weighting of the individual gain terms is by the *a posteriori* probability set only, T

will have two possible values depending on which set is the *a posteriori*, that is whether we predict area shares from population, or population from area shares. The answer to this example is given in terms of a philosophical attitude that says that space is relative to people (see section 2.2), but there are other cases where a decision might not be simple.

Since the time dimension is sometimes not explicit one wonders whether one could not define a quantity which used both probability sets in the weighting term. In fact a quantity known as the divergence has been defined by Kullback (1959) as

$$D = \sum_i (y_i - x_i) \log \frac{y_i}{x_i}$$

but I know of no use of this quantity within geography so far. The reason why T is used is found again in the history of information theory with its origins in physical communication channels. In such channels the time dimension can be explicit, and moreover, manipulation of the entropy equations to produce quantities which can be given conceptual meanings often gives rise to quantities of the form T. When the analogy between some given circumstance and a communication channel holds, T can be readily accepted, but when the analogy is not clear we might perhaps pay more attention to D. Kullback also finds that D has properties which are more easily associated with classical statistical concepts than T.

Finally, one can ask why T is used as the symbol. In those cases where the analogy with a communications channel holds, we find that the quantity T occurs in equations which associate the entropy of a source, the entropy of the receiver and the joint entropy of source and receiver in such a way that T can be explained as the quantity of *transmitted* information, i.e. what actually does get through. This is explained in detail in section 8.10 below.

8.9 The entropy of a function

The purpose of this section is to introduce some very general and very useful ways of handling entropy. We will show some general relationships that are mathematically true for a two-dimensional probability distribution, but everything that has been said above about the philosophical validity of using entropy and information theory outside their original fields still holds, although the reader will now find that the cautionary riders will disappear.

Consider a vector of probabilities p_k, $k = 1, \ldots 100$, and where $\sum_{k=1}^{100} p_k = 1$. Clearly we can use an entropy measure for assessing the inequalities or heterogeneity implied by this set, as we have detailed above. Now the set can be partitioned into 10 subsets, each of 10 members, and we can write down on a piece of paper 10 groups of 10 probabilities each in any way we like, and the sum of all the members will still be 1. Specifically, however we can arrange the 10 subsets neatly as follows:

$$
\begin{bmatrix}
p_1 & p_2 & \cdots \cdots \cdots \cdots \cdots & p_{10} \\
p_{11} & p_{12} & \cdots \cdots \cdots \cdots \cdots & p_{20} \\
p_{21} & p_{22} & \cdots \cdots \cdots \cdots \cdots & p_{30} \\
\cdots & \cdots & \cdots & \cdots \\
\cdots & \cdots & \cdots & \cdots \\
\cdots & \cdots & \cdots & \cdots \\
\cdots & \cdots & \cdots & \cdots \\
\cdots & \cdots & \cdots & \cdots \\
p_{91} & p_{92} & & p_{100}
\end{bmatrix}
$$

The original vector has now been laid out as 10 subvectors, which together make a square matrix. It is possible to use a coordinate reference system for members of the matrix whereby any probability in the matrix is located by its row number and its column number. So for example, if the first subscript refers to row numbers and the second to column numbers, then $p_{1,2}$ will refer in this case to the original probability p_2: similarly, $p_{10,1}$ refers to p_{91} and $p_{10,10}$ to p_{100}. In general terms we can write $p_{i,j}$ to represent the ith row and the jth column cell of the matrix. For convenience we shall drop the comma, and write p_{ij}.

In our example i can be any value between 1 and 10, and similarly for j. If we now write $\sum_{i=1}^{10} \sum_{j=1}^{10} p_{ij}$, we find that we are instructed to add together all the cells of the matrix. Conventionally we can read the instruction to mean: first take i with the value 1 and then add all p_{1j} together, with j equal to 1 to 10 successively (in other words add all the columns of row number 1); next take i to equal 2 and then add to the total we have so far p_{2j}, with j again going from 1 to 10; and so on until the whole matrix is added. Conventionally, we have "cycled" the second subscript for every time we have changed the first subscript, that is we have gone along all the columns every time we have changed to a new row. Note that the example above makes use of a square matrix, but what is said here can apply to any rectangular matrix, i.e. one where any one row is the same length as any other, and where, too, all columns have the same length.

The point of introducing the matrix at some length like this is partly for the benefit of those readers who have not used them before, but also to demonstrate that a "two-dimensional" entropy is in reality a simple entropy where the data have been rearranged for the convenience of the analysis.

Any measure we make on the whole set of probabilities p_k, $k = 1 \ldots$ 100 will be true also of the set $p_{ij}; i, j = 1 \ldots 10$.

Thus

$$\sum_{k=1}^{100} p_k \log \frac{1}{p_k} = \sum_{i=1}^{10} \sum_{j=1}^{10} p_{ij} \log \frac{1}{p_{ij}} \tag{8.31}$$

We will now take an actual example to show why the matrix mapping can be useful. Figure 8.12 shows a simple matrix of the number of people in a year migrating from towns A and B to towns C and D. There are in total 120 instances of migration. Now, if we assume that this is a fair and accurate representation of the relative strengths of migration flows between these towns and that these strengths will be maintained (i.e. we assume the basic probability characteristics are unchanging — we have statistical stationarity) we can convert these figures into probabilities as in Fig. 8.12.b. These probabilities then represent the probability that any single instance of interaction that can be observed will be from, for example, A to B ($p_{11} = 0.3$) or from B to D ($p_{22} = 0.4$) etc.

Clearly the set (p_{ij}) has an entropy value, which we will designate $H(ij)$.

$$H(ij) = \sum_{i} \sum_{j} p_{ij} \ln \frac{1}{p_{ij}} = 1.28 \text{ nits} \tag{8.32}$$

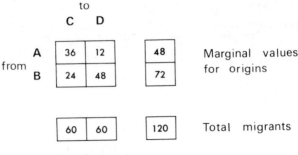

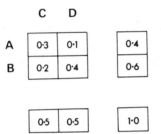

Fig. 8.12. A simple migration matrix.

We can ask the question, is there any particular significance in this value? To answer this, we will show that the overall entropy term can be shown to be made up of several terms that we can interpret.

We will now define $p_i. = \sum_j p_{ij}$ and $p._j = \sum_j p_{ij}$, which are known as marginal values.

These represent the probabilities in the first case, that any single instance of migration will start from town i, which in this case means town A or town B according to whether i has the value 1 or 2, irrespective of the destination of the migrants. In the second case, $p._j$ represents the probabilities that migrants will arrive at either town C or town D according to whether j has the value 1 or 2, irrespective of their origin. In other words, as the instructions implied by the definition state, total the row values to find $p_i.$ and the column values to find the $p._j$.

Now if we indulge in a little algebra we can expand $H(ij)$ as follows:

$$H(ij) = \sum_i \sum_j p_{ij} \log \frac{1}{p_{ij}}$$

$$= \sum_i \sum_j p_{ij} \log \frac{p_i . p_{.j}}{p_i . p_{.j} p_{ij}}$$

$$= \sum_i \sum_j p_{ij} \log \frac{1}{p_i .} + \sum_i \sum_j p_{ij} \log \frac{1}{p_{.j}} + \sum_i \sum_j p_{ij} \log \frac{p_i . p_{.j}}{p_{ij}}$$

$$= \sum_i p_i . \log \frac{1}{p_i .} + \sum_j p_{.j} \log \frac{1}{p_{.j}} - \sum_i \sum_j p_{ij} \log \frac{p_{ij}}{p_i . p_{.j}} \qquad (8.33)$$

We find that the total entropy can be decomposed into three terms. The first term is the entropy of the marginals corresponding to the origins of the migrants, and the second term is the entropy of the marginals corresponding to the destinations of the migrants. These terms tell us how sure we are of migrants' origins or destinations. The third term has a form which looks exactly like the form used for the definition of T in the section above. It looks like some kind of information gain term, and it measures how much information we have gained by knowing the probability p_{ij} of a migrant going from one specific town i, to another specific town j, compared with a "prior" expectation of $p_i . p_{.j}$. This prior probability is simply the product of the two probabilities $p_i .$ and $p_{.j}$, and from probability theory we know that the probability of both X and Y occurring if X and Y are completely independent of each other is simply the product of their individual probabilities. The proposition implied here is that if we had no knowledge at all about the connections between origins and destinations, but we did know the probability of someone originating from a certain town, or of arriving at a certain town, our best guess about the probability of a migration between these two specific towns would be the product of the probabilities of leaving from and arriving at the two towns involved. What we are doing is setting up some base state, the case of minimal prior knowledge, just as in section 8.8 above we measured information gain from the state of complete uncertainty in equation (8.30).

To simplify the discussion we will now define three terms of equation (8.33) as follows

$$\sum_i p_i . \log \frac{1}{p_i .} = H(i .) \qquad (8.34)$$

$$\sum_j p_{ij} \log \frac{1}{p._j} = H(._j) \qquad\qquad (8.35)$$

$$\sum_i \sum_j p_{ij} \log \frac{p_{ij}}{p_i. p._j} = T(ij/i .. j) \qquad\qquad (8.36)$$

and re-write as follows:

$$H(ij) = H(i.) + H(._j) - T(ij/i .. j) \qquad\qquad (8.37)$$

Now, following Rothstein, we may state the following. The purpose of any function is to map an input into an output. Any function has an entropy, the value of which is less than the sum of the entropies of the input and output by the amount of information introduced by the function. In this case we are observing some function, a migratory process, which is mapping migrants from their origins to their destinations. This mapping function may have introduced some level of information into the migratory process. If it has, we would like to know how much information, to see whether there is some organized process going on which we would like to investigate. But to answer the question "how much information has been introduced"?, we have to put the quantity of information gain in the function into perspective. In other words the answer is relative to other quantities. It is for this reason that we set about decomposing the original entropy value of equation (8.32) into its components.

In Table 8.I all the values for equation (8.37) have been worked out in full. We can see that the function has introduced some information since $T(ij/i .. j)$ has the value 0.0863, but in relative terms we can see that the amount introduced is so small that we could hardly count this as an organizing function. A useful way of expressing this would be to express the information gain term as a percentage of the sum of the two marginal entropies:

$$\text{Relative Organization} = \frac{T(ij/i .. j) \times 100}{H(i.) + H(._j)} = 6.32\% \quad (8.38)$$

What exactly do we mean by organization? First we have to make it clear that there are some scale distinctions involved. Any organization that we talk about in terms of these functions is at the level of the whole function, in other words in the case of the example of the migrants it is our view of the four towns and the migrants as one system of migration.

Table 8.I

$H(i.)$

$P_i.$	$\ln 1/P_i.$	$P_i. \ln 1/P_i.$
0.5	0.6931	0.3466
0.5	0.6931	0.3466
		0.6931

$H(.j)$

$P_{.j}$	$\ln 1/P_{.j}$	$P_{.j} \ln 1/P_{.j}$
0.4	0.9163	0.3665
0.6	0.5108	0.3065
		0.6730

$T(ij/i.j)$

P_{ij}	$P_i.$	$P_{.j}$	$\ln P_{ij}/P_i. P_{.j}$	$P_{ij} \ln P_{ij}/P_i. P_{.j}$
0.3	0.5	0.4	0.4055	0.1216
0.1	0.5	0.4	−0.6931	−0.0693
0.2	0.5	0.6	−0.4055	−0.0811
0.4	0.5	0.6	0.2877	0.1151
				0.0863

$H(ij)$

P_{ij}	$\ln 1/P_{ij}$	$P_{ij} \ln 1/P_{ij}$
0.3	1.2040	0.3612
0.1	2.3026	0.2303
0.2	1.6094	0.3219
0.4	0.9163	0.3665
		1.2799

$H(ij) = H(i.) + H(.j) - T(ij/i..j)$

$1.2799 = 0.6931 + 0.6730 - 0.0863$

At the individual level clearly every instance of migration will involve some degree of personal organization, but we know nothing about that and are not attempting to measure it. We are looking at one scale higher up.

Secondly, to understand organization at the system scale better we have to have a clear understanding of the maximum and minimum values of $H(ij)$ and the way that these are affected by the other three terms of equation (8.37). We will consider this in general terms in the next section.

8.10 Equivocation, transmitted information and noise

We will for the purpose of this section revert to the concept of a communications channel linking a source to a receiver. In Fig. 8.13 the

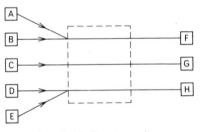

Fig. 8.13. Equivocation.

source has five possible states, but the receiver and the channel have only three possible states. For the moment we will assume that there is no coding, so that we know that the channel cannot transmit nor the receiver receive the full range of five states. Of course if we allow coding to occur and a transmission delay is possible then we know from above that it would be possible for the five states to be transmitted through a binary channel — but for the moment we will forget that.

Now it is clear that there will have to be some coalescence of some source signals in such a manner that more than one source signal will give rise to a specified receiver state, and coalescence is indicated in Fig. 8.13. Where exactly and how exactly this occurs is not of concern to us.

If we look at signals from the receiver's point of view then clearly for some of the received signals there is doubt about what signal was sent. If an F is received we are left in some doubt as to whether an A or a B was sent. This is what is known as equivocation.

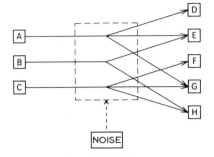

Fig. 8.14. Noise.

In Fig. 8.14. we see what is apparently the same diagram drawn the other way around. This time some disturbance in the channel may corrupt a signal. From the source's point of view, given say an A is sent we cannot be sure whether a D, E or G is received. Noise has corrupted the message.

Note that it is not necessary that the number of output states should be less than the number of input states for there to be equivocation, nor is the reverse necessary for there to be noise. A simple technical fault in a transmitter could cause equivocation, and a technical fault could even cause noise to be present. Indeed from the statistical point of view they appear almost to be the same thing, or the result of the same thing, but looked at from different ends of the systems.

If we forget about the channel and concentrate merely on the statistics, then again we can use graphic diagrams and matrices as above. If we take Fig. 8.15a as a starting point, clearly we can draw from this two diagrams representing firstly equivocation from the point of view of the outcomes and secondly noise from the point of view of the initial states, and these two cases are shown in Fig. 8.15b and c. We see that from the receiver's viewpoint there is doubt about the transmitted character whenever a 1 or a 3 is received, and from the source's viewpoint there is doubt about the received signal whenever a 2 is sent. Note how intimately and sometimes inextricably the two ideas can be linked together. In this example if we eliminate the noise from 2, and assuming that the intended transmission is a 2, then the equivocation will also disappear. In Fig. 8.12 above the extracted diagram for noise will look exactly like the original diagram, and so will the extracted diagram for equivocation. In other words the same diagram can be named as a diagram of the system, or as a diagram of the equivocation in the system, or as a

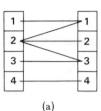

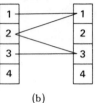

(a)   (b)

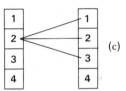

(c)

Fig. 8.15. Simultaneous equivocation and noise (a) combined, (b) equivocation abstracted, (c) noise abstracted.

diagram of noise in the system. But the two ideas are not always so dependent on each other. Figure 8.13 discussed first in this section portrays a noiseless system with equivocation, and the reverse is also possibl In large part the kinds of configurations possible depend upon the relative numbers of states available at the source and the receiver, and the behaviour of the channel.

So far we have assumed that the system that we are observing has no encoder. Now let us see how we would handle a system with an encoder. Figure 8.16 portrays a system where the channel has a binary capability, for example a dot or dash morse-code tapper, and where we are transmitting from a source of four states to a receiver of four states. Clearly,

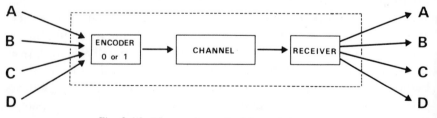

Fig. 8.16. Binary channel of four state source.

in order to say anything constructive about the behaviour of the system
we are going to have to reintroduce rate measurements, which we
touched on briefly above. To illustrate the point, let us imagine a coding
system as follows:

A transmitted by 00   (dot dot)
B transmitted by 01   (dot dash)
C transmitted by 10   (dash dot)
D transmitted by 11   (dash dash)

If the source transmits at one character per hour, even the doziest
human operator could keep up with it. If it transmitted at 60 000 characters a minute, no person acting as an encoder has a chance. Alternatively,
problems could come if the coding system were unnecessarily complicated. For example, each of the four codes above could unnecessarily be
preceded by extra 0's and 1's. The source would then overload the system quite easily.

Now let us enclose the whole system in a black box, represented by
the dotted line. All we know now is the correspondence between the
input and output, and the correspondence could be portrayed as in the
figures and matrices above. These figures would then represent the
average behaviour of the system over some length of time. Given this
information, we can now measure the noise and equivocation in the
system. What we can no longer do is ascribe any observed equivocation
to a particular reason — that is we no longer know if the channel transmitting capacity is too small or if the coding system is inefficient.

We now are in a position to see better the significance of Shannon's
11th theorem, quoted above. It says quite simply that if the source is
transmitting at some rate greater than channel capacity then there will
be equivocation of at least $H - C$, where C is channel capacity and H is
source entropy rate. There might be even greater equivocation than this
if the coding were inefficient. So the theorem also says something about
coding: that there exists some code which will enable the system to
transmit with an equivocation of about $H - C$, but it does not say what
the code is, nor how to find it.

In our black box case we do not even know the capacity C of the
channel which is used. We merely have information about the behaviour
of the system. But always provided that this is frequency information
which does accurately summarize the average performance of the system,
then we can use it for analysis, although usually we will not be able to

ascribe any measured equivocation specifically to an encoder, or to a channel capacity which is too small. Sometimes, however, we are concerned with systems where we deliberately hypothesize that there is no coding at all; in such circumstances we can still legitimately use information measures, and ascribe all measured equivocation to deficient channel capacity. The case study of Bihari farmers examined below provides examples.

So much for what equivocation and noise are; we now have to define them quantitively. Figure 8.17 shows a matrix representation of a

Receiver   States

		1	2	3	4	5
	1	0·09	0·01	0·0	0·0	0·0
	2	0·0	0·08	0·0	0·04	0·0
Signal	3	0·0	0·03	0·21	0·05	0·0
	4	0·0	0·01	0·33 ֽ	0·09	0·0
	5	0·0	0·0	0·0	0·0	0·6

Fig. 8.17. Matrix representation of transmission.

system with noise. What we mean in this context is that if we take any specific row of the matrix, representing the differing probabilities the receiver states for a given source signal, then we find that there is more than one non-zero entry in the row. In other words there is a specified probability that some receiver state other than the intended one can occur. If we take the first row of this specific example where there are two receiver states with non-zero probabilities and if we assume that state 1 is the intended state and state 2 is an infrequent error, then clearly with respect to that source signal there is a small amount of noise. If we had found that the receiver states had equal probabilities, then the noise level would have been much greater. What would we say if the intended signal was still 1 but in fact the system was so erroneous as to give 2 with a probability of 0.09 and 1 with a probability of 0.01? Would this be a case of greater noise than the 0.05 and 0.05 case just hypothesized? The answer is no, the noise level would sink again to the same amount as in the first case. The reason is that we can take advantage of the fact that it is nearly always wrong, and use the "wrong" information to indicate with a probability of 0.9 the right answer. In other words information is a quantity, and it is not concerned with semantics. It will measure something that can be used, but it is up to us as to how we use it. It is this kind of reasoning which goes into the answers to party questions such as, "Two men are standing at a junction in a road. One of them always lies, one of them always tells the truth. Can you find by asking one of them one question which road leads to the nearest town?". (If the reader does not know this question he is left to find the answer for himself.) In our case all we would have to do to make use of the information actually transmitted would be to relabel the two receiving states. This is not cheating, since at some stage source and receiver had to be in contact with each other to make sure the coding and decoding matched. All we are saying is, make sure you have the right decoder. In a matrix the erroneous coder can cause problems in other ways, since although the 0.01 and 0.09 case is no noisier than 0.09 and 0.01, equivocation may be increased none the less.

Given that the noise associated with one source signal and two receiver states will be at a maximum when the probability of either receiver state is 0.05, and given that it will also be at a minimum when one of them has a probability of 0.1, then clearly we can make use of a simple entropy measure to specify the noise associated with the transmission of the original source signal.

To make use of an entropy measure we need a set of probabilities that sum to 1. We therefore write for any row of the matrix

$$\text{Noise} = \sum_j \frac{p_{ij}}{p_{i.}} \log \frac{1}{p_{ij}/p_{i.}} = \sum_j \frac{p_{ij}}{p_{i.}} \log \frac{p_{i.}}{p_{ij}} \qquad (8.39)$$

since $p_{i.} = \sum_j p_{ij}$, and therefore by definition, $\sum_j \frac{p_{ij}}{p_{i.}} = 1$.

This is the noise for any one row of the matrix. What of the total noise in the whole matrix? Quite simply we take the weighted average of each of the individual row expectations of noise, where each row's contribution is weighted by the probability of the associated source signal. Thus

$$\text{Matrix noise} = \sum_i p_{i.} \sum_j \frac{p_{ij}}{p_{i.}} \log \frac{p_{i.}}{p_{ij}} \qquad (8.40)$$

which may by simple cancellation be reduced to

$$H_i.\,(j) = \sum_i \sum_j p_{ij} \log \frac{p_i.}{p_{ij}} \qquad (8.41)$$

We can argue similarly to define equivocation. This is the uncertainty of the source signal given the state of the receiver. So, for any specific receiver state, we look down its column in the matrix to see the varying probabilities of the original source signal. We then define equivocation as

$$\text{Equivocation} = \sum_i \frac{p_{ij}}{p.j} \log \frac{p.j}{p_{ij}} \qquad (8.42)$$

for any column of the matrix, and for the whole matrix the weighted average

$$H.j\,(i) = \sum_i \sum_j p_{ij} \log \frac{p.j}{p_{ij}} \qquad (8.43)$$

Algebraically the form of the definition of equivocation is the same as the form of the definition of noise. In fact this form is often used simply as a conditional entropy, in those circumstances where such a measure is useful, but where there is no necessary parallel with sources and receivers. It is conditional simply because it is the entropy of some set of probabilities given some prior condition. We will also meet this kind of usage of these terms below.

In this section it remains for us to show how these terms relate to each other. In probability theory we know that the probability of two events occurring, in those cases where there is some dependence between the events, is the product of the probability of one of the events occurring with the conditional probability of the second occurring given that the first has occurred:

$$P(A,\,B) = P(A)\,.\,P_A(B) \qquad (8.44)$$

where $P(A,\,B)$ is the probability of both A and B occurring, $P(A)$ is the probability of A occurring, and $P_A(B)$ is the probability of B occurring given that A has occurred.

We may also write:

$$P(A,\,B) = P(B)\,.\,P_B(A) \qquad (8.45)$$

Now one may often find parallels between the various entropy equations and equations relating probabilities, remembering always that because of the logarithmic form multiplication will be replaced by addition. In this case we may write

$$H(ij) = H(i.\,) + H_i.\,(j) = H(.j) + H._j(i) \tag{8.46}$$

and to prove it we can write it out in long-hand

$$H(ij) = \sum_i p_i.\log\frac{1}{p_i.} + \sum_i\sum_j p_{ij}\log\frac{p_i.}{p_{ij}} = \sum_j p_{.j}\log\frac{1}{p_{.j}} + \sum_i\sum_j p_{ij}\log\frac{p_{.j}}{p_{ij}}$$

$$= \sum_i\sum_j p_{ij}\log\frac{1}{p_i.} + \sum_i\sum_j p_{ij}\log\frac{p_i.}{p_{ij}} = \sum_i\sum_j p_{ij}\log\frac{1}{p_{.j}} + \sum_i\sum_j p_{ij}\log\frac{p_{.j}}{p_{ij}}$$

$$= \sum_i\sum_j p_{ij}\log\frac{1}{p_{ij}} = \sum_i\sum_j p_{ij}\log\frac{1}{p_{ij}} \tag{8.47}$$

These are useful relationships, as they enable us to show the following:

By substituting the first conditional relationships of equation (8.46) into equation (8.37) we obtain

$$H(i.\,) + H_i.\,(j) = H(i.\,) + H(.j) - T(ij/i\,.\,.\,j)$$

$$\therefore T(ij/i\,.\,.\,j) = H(.j) - H_i.\,(j) \tag{8.48}$$

which means that transmitted information is output minus noise.

By substituting the second conditional relationship of equation (8.46) into equation (8.37) we obtain in similar fashion

$$T(ij/i\,.\,.\,j) = H(i.\,) - H._j(i) \tag{8.49}$$

which means that transmitted information is also input minus equivocation. Both these results are of interest, firstly because of the way the concepts are related, and secondly because of the way it is possible to derive directly from each other the values of different concepts once a few basic values are known.

But we may go further to the most interesting result of all. Combining equation (8.48) and (8.49) we obtain

$$2(T(ij/i\,.\,.\,j)) = H(i.\,) + H(.j) - H._j(i) - H_i.\,(j)$$

$$\therefore T(ij/i\,.\,.\,j) + H._j(i) + H_i.\,(j) = H(i.\,) + H(.j) - T(ij/i\,.\,.\,j)$$

which by reference to equation (8.37) means

$$H._j(i) + T(ij/i\,.\,.\,j) + H_i.\,(j) = H(ij) \tag{8.50}$$

or, total information is equal to equivocation plus transmitted information plus noise. With these terms in hand we can analyse the efficiency of a system, the organization of a system, the determinacy of a system, and all the other manifold interpretations which can be placed on these indices.

Note that it is only by convention that we assume that transmission is from i to j, and therefore that it is only by convention that we term equation (8.43) as equivocation, and equation (8.41) as noise. It would be possible algebraically speaking for the system to be viewed as transmitting from j to i, in which case the names would be reversed.

We can also consider briefly the relevance of these concepts to the cybernetic approach of Ross Ashby noted in Chapter 10 (section 10.5). We can tabulate the canonical representation and draw a kinematic graph of systems with no equivocation and no noise, and also systems with equivocation and no noise, but we cannot do so for any system with noise.

9

Some Concepts Revisited in Terms of Information Theory

9.1 The entropy of functions

We have already in Chapter 3 (section 3.6) come across the concept of system determinacy expressed in terms of one : one, one : many, and one : all correspondence between input and output states. These three situations are shown here in Fig. 9.1. Note that these diagrams are simply graphic portrayals of the kinds of situations that can be shown in matrices. Thus the case of the migrants illustrated above by the matrix Fig. 8.12 can be shown by a graphic diagram like Fig. 9.1c, and the diagrams of Fig. 9.1 can be portrayed as matrices as in Fig. 9.2, where representative values have been included.

We will now show that case A represents the case of maximum organization and case C the case of minimal organization. The total entropy of the function for the case where we have one : one correspondence can be worked out, since in this case we know that $p_{ij} = p_i$. for one j, and, for all other j, p_{ij} is zero.

We can write the entropy function as

$$H(ij) = \sum_i \sum_j p_{ij} \log \frac{1}{p_{ij}} \tag{9.1}$$

Whence we know that in this particular case

$$H(ij) = \sum_i p_i. \log \frac{1}{p_i.} \tag{9.2}$$

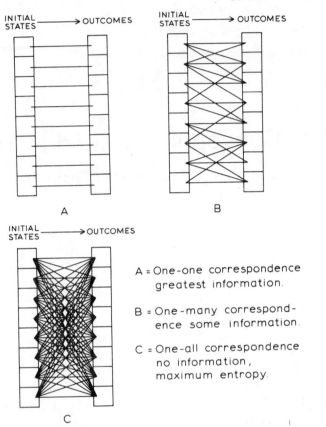

A   B

INITIAL STATES ⟶ OUTCOMES

A = One-one correspondence
    greatest information.

B = One-many correspond-
    ence some information.

C = One-all correspondence
    no information,
    maximum entropy.

C

Fig. 9.1. The entropy of a function: (a) one : one correspondence, (b) one : many correspondence, (c) many : many correspondence.

or in other words the entropy of the function has been reduced to the entropy of the marginal p_i. . Since there is a one : one correspondence, this is reasonable. We can also check the information introduced into the function. From equation (8.36) we can write

$$T(ij/i \ . \ . \ j) = \sum_i \sum_j p_{ij} \log \frac{p_{ij}}{p_i \ . \ p_{\ . \ j}}$$

$$= \sum_i \sum_j p_{ij} \ \log \frac{1}{p_{\ . \ j}} - \log \frac{1}{p_{ij}/p_i \ .} \tag{9.3}$$

(a)

to output states

from input states	1	2	3	4	5	6	7	8	
1	·25	0	0	0	0	0	0	0	·25
2	0	·14	0	0	0	0	0	0	·14
3	0	0	·12	0	0	0	0	0	·12
4	0	0	0	·20	0	0	0	0	·20
5	0	0	0	0	·05	0	0	0	·05
6	0	0	0	0	0	·03	0	0	·03
7	0	0	0	0	0	0	·13	0	·13
8	0	0	0	0	0	0	0	·08	·08
	·25	·14	·12	·20	·05	·03	·13	·08	1·0

(b)

to output states

from input states	1	2	3	4	5	6	7	8	
1	·10	·05	·10	0	0	0	0	0	·25
2	·03	·05	·01	·05	0	0	0	0	·14
3	0	0	·07	0	·05	0	0	0	·12
4	0	·06	0	·04	·10	0	0	0	·20
5	0	0	0	0	·02	·02	·01	0	·05
6	0	0	0	·01	0	·01	0	·01	·03
7	0	0	0	0	0	·10	·01	·02	·13
8	0	0	0	0	0	·04	0	·04	·08
	·13	·16	·18	·10	·17	·17	·02	·07	1·0

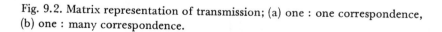

Fig. 9.2. Matrix representation of transmission; (a) one : one correspondence, (b) one : many correspondence.

to output states

		1	2	3	4	5	6	7	8		
	1	·010	·030	·040	·020	·050	·040	·020	·040		·25
	2	·010	·030	·010	·010	·010	·030	·010	·030		·14
from	3	·050	·010	·010	·010	·010	·010	·010	·010		·12
(c) input	4	·010	·060	·070	·010	·020	·010	·010	·010		·20
states	5	·005	·010	·010	·005	·005	·005	·005	·005		·05
	6	·002	·005	·001	·004	·005	·005	·004	·004		·03
	7	·001	·004	·060	·040	·010	·009	·005	·001		·13
	8	·010	·010	·010	·010	·010	·010	·010	·010		·08
		·098	·159	·211	·109	·120	·119	·074	·110		1·00

Fig. 9.2. Continued, (c) many : many correspondence.

The information gain will be maximized when the second term in the parentheses goes to zero. Now in the one : one correspondence case we know that $p_{ij} = p_i.$ for one j and all other p_{ij} are zero. When this occurs the second term in the brackets is log 1 = 0, for the non-zero p_{ij}, and for all other items is log 0 which is taken conventionally as zero. We know therefore that the minimum value of $H(ij)$, representing maximum organization, does occur when

$$H(ij) = H(i.) \text{ and } T(ij/i..j) = \sum_i \sum_j p_{ij} \log \frac{1}{p._j} = H(.j)$$

In the case of a square matrix it also follows that $H(i.) = H(.j)$.

The one : one correspondence function maximizes the amount of information introduced. Similarly we can argue from (9.3) that the amount of information introduced will be at a minimum when

$$\log \frac{1}{p_{ij}/p_i.} = \frac{1}{p._j} \tag{9.4}$$

whence

$$\log p_{ij} = \log p_i. - \log \frac{1}{p._j} \qquad (9.5)$$

$$= \log p_i.p._j$$

whence

$$p_{ij} = p_i.p._j$$

which means that the least information will have been introduced when the prediction of any final state from any initial state is simply made according to the combined probabilities of the input states and the output states. This is the case of the many : many indeterminate system.

In this case the value of $T(ij/i..j)$ is $\sum_i \sum_j p_{ij} \log \dfrac{p_i.p._j}{p_i.p._j} = 0$, and hence

$$H(ij)_{max} = H(i.) + H(.j) \qquad (9.7)$$

Note that the maximum and minimum values are therefore dependent on the entropies of the marginals, and it is for this reason that it is sometimes useful to use a relative measure of the amount of information introduced as we used above in (8.38). Note also that we can specify a trivial case where $H(ij)_{min} = 0$, if the marginal set $p_i.$ contains one member with the value 1 and similarly for the marginal set $p._j$.

Organization therefore means that the information is introduced so that

$$p_{ij} \neq p_i.p._j \qquad (9.8)$$

and any system that has some degree of organization will have some such information in it. Note that where there is some information introduced we can measure it, but the act of measurement does not necessarily tell us where the organization comes from. But, there are many cases where we construct models based on some organizing principle and in so doing we define a function where some information is introduced. A classical example of this is the gravity model, when we begin the construction of the model by saying that migration will be proportional to the product of the two cities' populations: thus far we have:

$$m_{ij} = ap_ip_j \qquad (9.9)$$

where m_{ij} is migration and p_i and p_j are the populations of the towns i

and j. To make the model work in computational terms for more than just two cities we have to deal with fractions or else introduce some coefficients, as in the case of Wilson (1970). The model thus far becomes

$$X_{ij} = X_i . X_{.j} \text{ where the } X\text{s are fractions} \qquad (9.10)$$

which is clearly portraying an unorganized system. However, a term for distance is then introduced so that

$$X_{ij} = \frac{X_i . X_{.j}}{f(D_{ij})} \qquad (9.11)$$

where D_{ij} is the distance between i and j. This is the constraint that specifies that

$$X_{ij} \neq X_i . X_{.j} \qquad (9.12)$$

and then clearly the system becomes organized.

It might seem curious to say that a system of migration based solely on population sizes is unorganized. However, we must stress again that what is or is not unorganized is the system defined by the observer, and in this circumstance the observer would have defined the marginal values, or the input and output of his system, but would not have defined anything else connecting the input and output, and therefore simply by our definitions he would not have defined an organized system.

In cases where we have a non-square matrix — or in other words either more input states than output states, or vice versa — evaluation of the situation will necessitate using corrective measures for the noise and/or equivocation in the system, following the procedures demonstrated in section 8.10 above.

9.2 Laws and entropy

Physical geography has some laws that are uniform in time and space. These are general because they describe general relationships which include not only observed cases but also other possible cases that have not been observed. If a cloud mass of a certain humidity and temperature is lifted over a mountain of a certain height, then we can state with some degree of accuracy when it will rain. There are laws which relate to the behaviour of gases and which will predict changes in certain conditions. Now, there are many such cases which could occur. We can think of an infinite number of permutations of humidity and temperature, but only a few out of this infinite number of possibilities have been observed. However, although only a few cases may have been observed, we have a general equation which enables us to predict for any state, and thus it includes the observed states. All predictions are based on one : one correspondences, in that a defined set of circumstances will yield one result (assuming the definition has been accurate enough). The general law provides a mapping between the initial set and the final set with single valued mappings in all cases.

In studies of the geography of economic development the usual procedure is to make generalized inductive statements from the observed cases. Given the course of history, however, we are keenly aware that at any time things might have developed in other ways. Now it would appear illogical, therefore, to insist that the observed states are representatives of all possible states. If we abandon historical determinism we have to conclude that the observed states are a few cases from a whole range of cases. In the example of cloud behaviour the observed few cases might occur at irregular intervals along the ordered set of possible initial and final states. To make a generalized inductive statement on these few would narrow the enquiry and might simply produce the statement that rain is more likely near mountains. It would not allow opportunity to derive the general predictive equation. In studies of economic development it might be better to widen the enquiry into the field of other possible states, rather than narrow it by restriction to the observed and to inductive generalization. Such a model involving a complete set of possible states and one : one correspondence between the initial set and the final set would be a meta-model as envisaged by Slobodkin (1958).

It becomes clear that a law is a function which can be described with the same equations as we introduced in 9.1 to describe the organization in a gravity model. A good law is one where the organization is so high that there is a one : one correspondence between input and output.

A general principle can come from this to explain Russell's interpretation of the sentence, "The golden mountain does not exist". The paradox in this sentence is clear, in that if the golden mountain does not exist, how can we specify that we know of its existence so that we can say it does not exist? Russell explained it by saying, "There is no entity c such that 'X is golden and mountainous' is true when X is c and not otherwise". This means that the X cannot be uniquely and unambiguously equated with a single entity c. If not, we have not specified uniquely and unambiguously what it is that does not exist, and hence we

have not made any paradoxical statement. Russell calls this the Theory
of Descriptions. It might also be called the Principle of Sufficient Information. If we do not have enough information to specify exactly and
unambiguously some entity, then we cannot specify what the entity is
in any given proposition, and hence the validity of the proposition cannot be tested. The principle of inductive generalization in geography is
the process whereby a model is constructed from several cases by a
process of information loss. A good model maximizes simplicity and
minimizes information loss. However, if there is no longer sufficient
information to specify some entity that exists, the truth or falsity of the
model can never be tested. It can only be subjectively more or less true
according to the user's conception of the parallelism between the model
and some real case. On the other hand the meta-model is specifically a
model where any case can be uniquely and unambiguously defined. The
defined case can then be tested for truth or falsity. Some particular circumstance of humidity and temperature can be tested in the model, and
if we do not find a unique result, then either the equations are wrong,
or we do not have sufficient information to specify the initial circumstance uniquely. Obviously this is begging the question about the definition of unique on a continuum scale. But defined levels of accuracy can
be introduced, such levels of accuracy determining the information
content of the successful model.

9.3 Hierarchies of objects

In the early chapters in this book mention was made of the existence of
hierarchies of objects, each comprising objects of the next lowest
order. We have also seen that organization results from the arrangement
of parts in a whole in a particular way. It will come as no surprise that
there are information theoretic means whereby we can assess the information we have in observing an object made of several parts.

It is necessary for these purposes to assume the existence of a clear
hierarchy. In this example I am going to assume that towns are real
constructs, meaningful classes into which people may be grouped. The
example is based directly on Margalef (1958), the only difference being
that I have substituted people and towns for animals and species of
animals.

The data in Table 9.I represent the sizes of all towns in the Gaya
District of Bihar, India, in 1961 and 1951. The population figures are

Table 9.I

Town sizes in the Gaya District of Bihar

Population in thousands	
1961	*1951*
151	134
23	12
17	10
14	10
13	10
13	8
10	6
8	7
7	6
6	
262	203

given in thousands to make the following calculations easier for the purposes of illustration, although it is clear that this should not in all strictness be done if we are interested in the *absolute* amount of information in the data. For comparative purposes between the two years, no harm is done.

How much information is represented by these data? There are many ways in which the data can be analysed, but here we calculate the amount of information we possess by virtue of having the following knowledge: *the number of towns, and the number of people in each town.* In geography we usually observe some event without knowing the number of alternative states that that event could have taken. Here we have to find out how many towns there could have been, to enable us to calculate the amount of information we have by knowing how many towns there are. In 1961 there were 262 people in total in all the towns. We consider that there could have been a number of towns which varies between 1 and 262, that is everybody in one town, or everybody in their own town. There are 262 alternative states. The reader is likely to object that it is not very likely that in some large area there is only one town, nor are towns of only one person allowed. In effect you, the reader, would then be saying that you have some information which narrows the range of doubt. How much of this information do you have? It varies from moment to moment as subjective thoughts pass through the mind. It is not a sure datum. The only sure datum is the stance of complete uncertainty and complete ignorance.

Then the amount of information we have is

$$I_1 = \log 262 = 2.4183 \text{ dits, and } \log 203 = 2.3075 \text{ dits.}$$

There is not a great difference from one year to the next. Part of this information is what the reader can already account for from his own judgement and experience, but that will not tell him how much information he already has in terms of hard dits.

The second question is, given that there are S towns, how much information do we have by knowing the actual sizes of the towns? Given that there are S towns and N people, how many ways are there of changing the number of people in each town? This is obviously a problem in factorials.

Assume all N people are distributed along a long line. There are $N - 1$ places where we can place divisions between the people, representing "borders" between the towns. To divide the people into S groups there have to be $S - 1$ divisions. The first of these could occur in any of $N - 1$ places, the second in any of $N - 2$ places, etc. We have therefore the first $S - 1$ terms of $(N - 1)!$ to consider. But the order of these divisions is of no importance. There are therefore the following number of possible town size distributions:

$$\frac{(N-1)!}{((N-1)-(S-1))!(S-1)!} = \frac{(N-1)!}{(N-S)!(S-1)!} \tag{9.13}$$

and the information content of knowing the actual size distribution which does occur is therefore, assuming that all of these states are equally probable, the logarithm of this number. For the purposes of calculation we write

$$I_2 = \log \frac{(N-1)!}{(N-S)!(S-1)!} = \log (N-1)! - \log (N-S)! - \log (S-1)! \tag{9.14}$$

and consult the logarithms of factorials found in any statistical tables.

We find that by knowing the town sizes we have 16.130 dits of information in 1961 as opposed to 13.777 in 1951.

The two other questions for which we can give numerical answers are now calculated, although we do not have the actual town name of each of the 262 people written in the data, nor do we have their unique locations.

To find the amount of information necessary to specify the town to which each person belongs, given the number and sizes of the towns, we reason as follows. Suppose the people of the towns are again arranged in a long line, only this time they join the line in town groups. In the first group are the N_1 people of the first town, and in the second there are the N_2 people of the second town, . . . up to the full line ending with the N_S people of the Sth town. Now how many ways could these people have lined up in these town sizes? The N people could have lined up in any of $N!$ ways. But it would not matter what order they were in inside each town group, since they would still have the same town name. The number of ways of naming these N people to S towns of given sizes is therefore

$$\frac{N!}{N_1!\,N_2!\,.\,.\,.\,.\,N_S!}$$

and assuming that all of these ways are equally probable, the amount of information we would have would be

$$I_3 = \log \frac{N!}{\prod_i (N_i!)} = \log N! - \sum_i^s \log N_i! \qquad (9.15)$$

Using this formula we find that in 1961 we would need 171.269 dits, and in 1951 108.828 dits. Both of these are very large amounts of information, in bits 568.9 and 361.5 respectively. This is for data which have been reduced by 1000. It is a reminder of the very large amounts of information that we handle in geography. It is also the reason why the actual message, i.e. the names of all the people and their respective towns, is not given here. To print that amount of bits would take a lot of space and money.

The percentage increase in our information between question 2 and question 3 for the two years is

$$\frac{171.2 \times 100}{16.1} = 1063\% \text{ and } \frac{108.8 \times 100}{13.8} = 773\%$$

which clearly shows that the rate of increase in information from I_2 to I_3 has increased between 1951 and 1961.

Also of course, we know that

$$\log \prod_i \frac{N!}{(N_i!)} \approx N \sum_i \frac{N_i}{N} \log \frac{N}{N_i} \qquad (9.16)$$

We find therefore that the amount of information *necessary to specify to which city all* N *individuals belong* is equal to N times the amount of organization or inequality of city sizes, as well as N times the amount of information necessary on average to specify one city name from a set of city names with unequal frequencies of occurrence. If we ask an Englishman, "From which city do you come?", we will not be very surprised if he answers, "London". The weighted average of surprise values will be weighted in favour of such large cities, which are cases when we get a low information content.

The final question is, if the towns are subdivided into unique locations (houses?) for each person, how much information is required to allocate each person to his correct house. This is simply $\log N!$, and we find that the respective values for this are

$$I_4 = 521.4 \text{ dits } (1961) \text{ and } 379.5 \text{ dits } (1951)$$

Paradoxes are continually apparent in Information Theory. We can illustrate this clearly by a question from Margalef on a paradox found when using I_3:

> Since in nature the number of species is very great, practically without limit, of many groups (i.e. ecosystems) composed of the same number of individuals the one including the smallest number of species, and the most unequal representation of the same, is the one representing the most intense selection or segregation (as a consequence of certain organizing forces — ecological and historical factors, competitive and complementary relations among different species) and is, in brief, the least probable. The presence of a single species to the exclusion of all others is the least probable type of natural community and, therefore, represents a maximum of information. But if we calculate its Information content by means of current procedures, on observing that there is no more than one species we say, *a posteriori*, that our study has not provided any Information at all, since all states and combinations are reduced to a single possible one.
>
> One of the most serious problems encountered in Information Theory, found at the root of the paradox that troubles us, is that of utilizing prior information to evaluate information received. The difficulty lies in the fact that very different systems may be involved and in the transfer or translation of information from one to another there is always a human element which must be eliminated in order to maintain the necessary scientific rigour.
>
> (Margalef, 1958)

The essence of this problem is prior information. Before the measure I_3 is made on the single species, we have gained the knowledge that there is a single species. Prior information can enter at every stage. The "rose-coloured spectacles" of observation are in fact prior information filters. Even by selecting a problem for study we have introduced the information necessary to specify the problem. In the urban population studies above the knowledge of what towns are has been introduced, and the size of the total population has been taken as a given.

One further comment is necessary in this section. We are considering hierarchies of objects, but we have only considered two levels — towns and their component people. But if we drop down another level, the whole analysis can be repeated in terms of the numbers and kinds of organs in the body, and then again to the number and kinds of cells in the organs. At all levels the same questions can be repeated. There are of course many other more complex questions that can also be asked, but in the terms that were suggested at the beginning of Chapter 3 and in Chapter 5 (section 5.4) in the discussion of Monod's work, these simple ones are enough to establish vastly different quantities of information in different circumstances.

Part IV

Energetic Considerations

10

Open and Closed Systems

10.1 Introduction

To my mind at least the parts of this book are all interrelated and form differing threads of one continuing argument, but to most systems theorists there is obviously one gap that still needs to be filled. I have not yet explicitly considered the distinction between open and closed systems, which for the General Systems purists would probably be the first chapter of any book. That I have not done so is because many of the ideas of systems theory can be considered in the abstract, even if in their commonest physical manifestation considerations of energy and thermodynamic entropy are involved. Equally, I think that the distinction does neatly sum up many of the remarks I have made about boundaries, external variables, control and the like, and it is as valid to use it as a summary as it is to use it as an introduction. But more than that, by virtue of its concern with energy, it opens up a whole new field of considerations which I do not wish to pursue in this book, and these omissions might have been more awkward following an early chapter.

10.2 Open and closed systems

The distinction between open and closed systems is important because of the difference in the modes of analysis which are adopted in the two cases. This, at least in theory, is why the distinction is made. However, particularly in the social sciences and to a lesser extent in physical geography the terms open and closed are used without any apparent differences in the following discussion. In physical sciences the differences are immediately apparent because the definitions are framed in terms of basic physical quantities which are the subject of investigation in systems. In the social sciences, on the other hand, an investigator does not always use such basic physical quantities, and hence the definition of open and closed systems based on such quantities is irrelevant, or misleading. But, just to confuse the issue, we then find definitions of "open" and "closed" based on quantities which have nothing to do with physical systems but which seem to be suitable surrogates in the social world. There are a number of people who conceive of money in a social system as the equivalent of energy in a physical system. One cannot argue that such analogies are wrong, but one can argue that they can be highly dangerous. As Georgescu-Roegen (1972) points out, economic systems have often been implicitly thought of as being closed because the money supply is restricted, and keeps recirculating endlessly from one hand to another. Such effortless recirculation would be impossible in an energetically closed system, which a physicist normally conceives of only in its terminal, i.e. dead state. Money only needs to keep circulating because the economic system continually imports matter and energy from its environment. The truth then is that money exchange is a regulatory mechanism governing the quantities of matter and energy in any given channel through the system. Despite what I consider to be the obviousness of this conclusion one still reads statements such as that by Katz and Kahn (1966):

> In many organizations outcomes are converted into money and new energy is furnished through this mechanism. Money is a convenient way of handling energy units both on the output and input sides, and buying and selling represents one set of social rules for regulating the exchange of money.

It seems to me that they agree with both views: that money is a regulator, and that money is energy. On the output side it seems reasonable that except with the power and fuel industries most economic organizations output materials rather than energy.

There is also a second source of confusion in the use of terms with respect to open systems in one discipline, which in another discipline only have meaning with respect to closed systems. The obvious example in this light is the concept of equilibrium. In physics this term applies to closed and isolated systems, ones which have reached maximum entropy or to the theoretical but fictitious concept of a reversible process. It is inert and dead. If one system is enclosed within another system, then when the whole has gone to maximum entropy, the inner system is in equilibrium with the enclosing system. In energetic terms it is then indistinguishable from its surroundings. This specific scientific meaning of the term is the basis for such remarks as Weiner's (1948): "For an organism to be in equilibrium is to be dead".

On the other hand one reads of open systems being in equilibrium, of dynamic equilibrium, and the like. Animals are often referred to as open systems in equilibrium with the environment. Such statements are anathema to many scientists. The reason why has been put succinctly by Koehler (1938):

> I have sometimes been asked why I refuse to call the standard state of the organism 'an equilibrium'. My reason is simply that this standard state is not an equilibrium in any sense which has as yet been defined by science — not even an *unstable* equilibrium. It is a *stationary* process; and we are just beginning to learn that there are two classes of stationary process, one with which a minimum, and another with which a maximum of energy is associated. Nothing could be more unfortunate than an attempt to hide such new essential distinctions behind an outworn general term.

It is a general truth that an adult man, in his years of maturity, i.e. after growth is completed and before the degeneration of senility occurs, has a much greater capacity to work than a child. The stationary state of the organism is characterized by a maximum of potential energy — and the crucial importance of this maximum potential energy has been clearly stated by Kremyanskiy (1960): "It is on the phenomenon of surplus external and internal work that is based the possibility of expansive reproduction of populations and species, and in society the possibility of using domesticated animals for work". For such reasons as these it is clearly dangerous to call the stationary processes of living organisms "equilibria". We shall attempt to avoid confusion between the strict physical meaning of this term and the looser meanings associated with it in socio-economic systems.

10.3 "System" in the physical and social sciences

The word system in physics refers to any portion of matter, arbitrarily delimited or not, around which one can *hypothesize* a boundary. I italicize this word because when for example in thermodynamics one imagines a gas enclosed in a cylinder by a frictionless piston, the cylinder and piston are not part of the system, but merely conceptual apparatus that surrounds it. The system is the gas. One instinctively thinks of a gas as being homogeneous in all respects within such a cylinder, that is it has a uniform temperature throughout, and a uniform pressure. On this basis it might seem that the idea of calling such a undifferentiated portion of matter a system does not correspond with the social scientist's intuitive view of a system as something with internal structure. However, the gas need not at all times be undifferentiated. If heat is applied to one small part of the enclosing cylinder a temperature gradient can be set up within the gas, even if for only a short time. Similarly if the piston is suddenly compressed then the pressure of the gas immediately in front of the piston can rise higher than the pressure at the back of the cylinder. But if after having had heat applied, and if after the cylinder has been moved in a specific amount, the system is left alone for a while, then the internal conditions will again become uniform. The point is, as Ramsay (1971) says, that thermodynamics is concerned with ends, not means. In other words it makes statements about these uniform states after a system has gone to equilibrium, but nothing about how long or in what way it will reach equilibrium. The differentiated heterogeneous system can exist, but within thermodynamics no lawful statement can be made about it, only about the state to which it will go if no matter or energy is added to or subtracted from it.

There is also another way in which we can look at the apparent dissimilarity between the physical definition of a "system" and the definition given in Chapter 4. The physical system *is* composed of parts, that is a gas is a collection of many molecules. Many of the phenomena of gas behaviour are explained with respect to these molecules — heat is a random movement of the molecules, pressure is the force of molecules striking a surface. Within statistical mechanics the relationship between the total energy of a system and entropy is expressed in terms of the distribution of molecules amongst different energy levels. Clearly we are dealing with two scales — the parts and the whole, local scale and system scale. This scale distinction gives rise to a distinction between micro-states and macro-states, which for the moment we will explain as follows. A micro-state is a state where the position of each molecule is known. A macro-state is a state which has unique system properties (i.e. no other macro-state has the same properties such as temperature, pressure) but which can be caused by any of several micro-states. Since the micro-states are unobservable, the empirical research on physical systems occurs at the macro-scale. Now, with systems of the scale studied in geography, we can observe the parts, and hence we can know what the micro-state is. Little concern is shown for macro-states study, because (an important point in physical theory) the most probable macro-state of a system is calculated on the basis of the number of micro-states that could give rise to it. But if we know what the micro-state is, the logic of such argument evaporates, unless of course we are building predictive models of a parsimonius nature.

10.4 Isolated, closed, and open systems

We will now be a little more precise, and make some definitions. An *isolated system* is a system which can exchange neither matter nor energy with its environment. It is completely and hermetically sealed. It exists by and for itself and quietly ignores the rest of the universe. By definition external activity cannot affect it.

A *closed system* is a system which is closed to the import and export of matter between itself and its environment, but on the other hand it can exchange energy with its environment, either as heat flow or as work. We can now see that the gas enclosed in the cylinder is a closed system, since we define the cylinder to be perfect and gas neither leaks from or into it, and since energy can be exchanged with the environment either by the work of the piston moving or by heat flows.

An *open system* is a system which can exchange both matter and energy with its environment. Note in passing that this might suggest that the identification of the system could be difficult since matter can enter and leave, and if the system is defined in terms of matter then the system can change itself. There is a rough analogy here with the question: is a city which grows over time the "same" city changed by degree, or is it a new city changed by kind? Within the field of biology the problem is not serious on the whole, since we can identify structures which are preserved even though matter is exchanged with the environment. The maintenance of form in a physical open system has been neatly demonstrated by Pask (1960), to whose work interested readers are referred.

There are several points that emerge from these definitions which have not always been accepted within the social sciences. The only distinction between the closed and the isolated system is that in one case energy can be exchanged with the environment, and in the other case it cannot. It follows that if energy is not a variable which enters explicitly into any given study, there is no point in making the distinction between closed and isolated systems. In such cases the closed system means the same as the isolated system. Further, if neither matter nor energy is involved, then the distinction between all three is lost. If neither matter nor energy enters the discussion, then obviously it is impossible to make any kind of thermodynamic sense out of such a system, and we do not have any guarantee that statements made by analogy with thermo-dynamic systems are tenable either. For example one hears of "socio-logical systems" which are often "closed" for some analysis. In such circumstances, the meaning of the term "equilibrium" has to be given some non-thermodynamic definition, and the system has to be assumed to reach it other than by the universal trend of all closed systems to maximum entropy, if at all. Within the field of management sociology Emery (1969) says,

> In the realm of social theory, however, there has been something of a tendency to continue thinking in terms of a 'closed' system, that is, to regard the enterprise as sufficiently independent to allow most of its problems to be analysed with reference to its internal structure and without reference to its external environment. . . . However, it (closed system thinking) has tended to be misleading on problems of growth and the conditions for maintaining a 'steady state'. The formal physical models of closed systems postulate that, as in the second law of thermodynamics, the inherent tendency of such systems is to grow towards maximum homogeneity of the parts, and that a steady state can only be achieved by the cessation of all activities. In practice, the system theorists in social science refused to recognise these implications but instead, by the same token, did 'tend to focus on the statics of social structure and to neglect the study of structural change'.

In other words, such theorists have tried to analyse functioning organi-zations in terms of static structure (as we noted above the analysis of change in a system is very problematical) or a closed system. If the sys-tem is closed without reference to energy or matter (whatever such closure would mean) then it is possible that conceptually some structure i.e. heterogeneity, may still exist. Clearly the value of such a concept can only be discovered empirically.

10.5 Cybernetic view of a closed system

There is one non-thermodynamic context which I have come across in which the idea of closure is given a very specific meaning. Ross Ashby has illustrated the canonical representation of machines within the field of cybernetics. The canonical representation is of the form of a transformation as shown in the simplest case in Fig. 10.1a. The transformation T merely says that from the states in the first line the machine always goes to states in the second line as indicated. The behaviour which this Transformation shows can also be demonstrated with the use of Kinetic Graphs, as in Fig. 10.1b. Now, the transformation T is said to

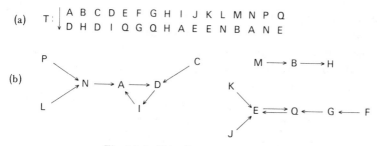

Fig. 10.1. Transformation function.

be closed if there is no state in the second line which is not also in the first line. In other words the application of T cannot "send" the machine to a state from which further transitions cannot be predicted. In terms of the kinetic graphs this means that a closed transformation will show the machine entering some state which then remains invariant with repeated application of T, or it enters some loop of states from which it will not leave.

This is a formal representation of behaviour, and of behaviour in time. We conclude that a closed transformation which is representative of some machine will over some time period cause the behavioural characteristics of the machine to adopt a steady state or a set of sequential states. It sounds very close to the kinds of conclusions reached about thermodynamic systems. But there is a very essential difference. The motive force behind the transitions is not identified and is irrelevant to a discussion of the pattern of behaviour. In other words the machine that exhibits this behaviour must be a machine which imports energy or energy and matter. If we consider the theory of ecosystems as an example, it is often held that the ecosystem goes to some stable climax state. If it is interfered with by some external agent and a plagio-climax is established, then when interference ceases, assuming that the interference has not been destructively large, the system will return to its original climax. In other words the transformation representing the behaviour of the ecosystem is closed and tends to a steady state. But even in this climax state the ecosystem constantly imports matter and energy from its environment. In a thermodynamic sense it is an open system, and we can make no statement about a trend to thermodynamic equilibrium.

Another obvious example of behavioural closure is the Markov chain applied within geography to the location of firms (Collins, 1970). Any state to which a firm can go has to be represented by a state from which a firm can come, even if its "coming" is to stay there, as with the absorbing state of death. In other words the Markov transition matrix has to be square. Then and only then can one make any predictions about the steady state that the chain will reach. It goes without saying that such a tendency to "equilibrium" is not necessarily a very realistic representation of firms in a growing economy, but that point need not concern us here.

In this context it should be noted that Ross Ashby does use the word equilibrium, but since it conflicts with the thermodynamic sense we will not use it to mean that in this book. There are no systems of functioning objects which are of interest to geographers in which energy and matter do not have their role. The central importance of energy in our societies can be seen by correlating GNP per capita with Energy Consumption per capita, as in Fig. 10.2. And even in agricultural societies of a primitive kind ecological energetics are a basic consideration behind the structure of the farming system, as Rappaport illustrates (Fig. 10.3). The World Power Conference of 1972 has also stressed our dependence on a rapidly depleting fuel base, and with respect to materials we know that we may be exhausting our supplies of economically workable iron and copper ores. The "Oil Crisis" that began in 1974 made the same point quite bluntly.

It seems then that energy and matter are as essential to our systems as to any other. In such circumstances it seems foolish to apply the concepts of thermodynamics by analogy to systems in which they have their own role to play. We have seen that a system may be behaviourally closed, and that in such a condition it achieves a time-independent steady state. But the persistence of that state through time depends very much on the continued supply of matter and energy to the system.

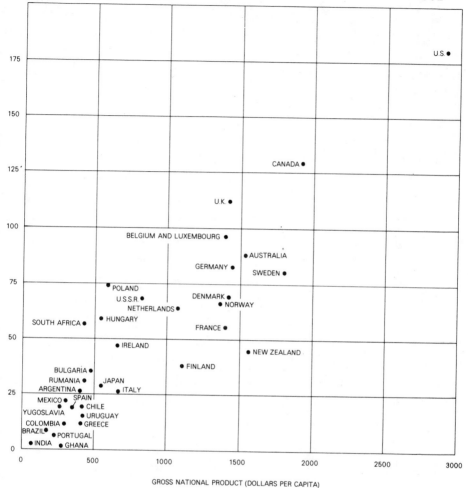

GROSS NATIONAL PRODUCT (DOLLARS PER CAPITA)

Fig. 10.2. Energy consumption and GNP. (From *Scientific American*, 1971)

10.6 The unstable equilibrium

The second law of thermodynamics says quite simply that the entropy
of the universe is increasing. This means that the useful quality of
energy, the capacity to do work, is being continually degraded. But
despite this fact, it is clear that the universe still contains a great deal of
useful energy. Dyson (1971) has constructed a table, reproduced here as

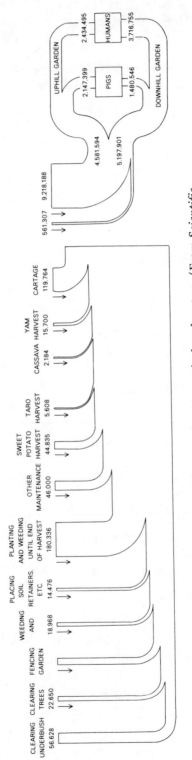

Fig. 10.3. Energy flow in a primitive agricultural system. (From *Scientific American*, 1971)

Table 10.I

Forms of energy	Entropy per unit of energy
Gravitation	0
Energy of rotation	0
Energy of orbital motion	0
Nuclear reactions	10^{-6}
Internal heat of stars	10^{-3}
Sunlight	1
Chemical reactions	$1-10$
Terrestrial waste heat	$10-100$
Cosmic microwave radiation	10^4

Table 10.I, indicating the usefulness of the main forms of energy in the universe, ranking the forms according to their associated entropies. He comments that although energy must always flow in such a direction that entropy increases, that as it flows "down the table", the main source of energy in the universe is still gravitational. Little has as yet ended up in the ultimate heat sink of cosmic microwave radiation. This obviously provokes one to ask, "Since the universe is on a one-way slide toward a state of final death in which energy is maximally degraded, how does it manage, like King Charles, to take such an unconscionably long time a-dying?". The answer is not easy, not completely understood. But Dyson considers what he terms accidental "hang-ups" as the main reason. The first hang-up is sheer size. The average density of matter in the visible universe is one atom per cubic metre, and the calculated freefall time for the universe to collapse, i.e. contract into itself, is of the order of 100 billion years. Apart from sheer size, there are spin hang-ups, such as preserves our galaxy from collapsing and the earth from collapsing into the sun. From there we progress to thermonuclear hang-ups in stars such as our sun, and from these we can come down to earth and consider another hang-up termed by Brillouin (1949) "unstable equilibria".

Let us for the moment briefly consider the nature of chemical energy. This is a kind of potential energy which takes the form of bonding between atoms because of their mutual attraction, known as their "chemical affinity". This affinity is specific to the pair or group of atoms which between which the forces are acting. Ubbelohde (1963) gives an example of what happens when these bondings change as coal or coke is burnt in oxygen, and some of the chemical energy of the previous bonds

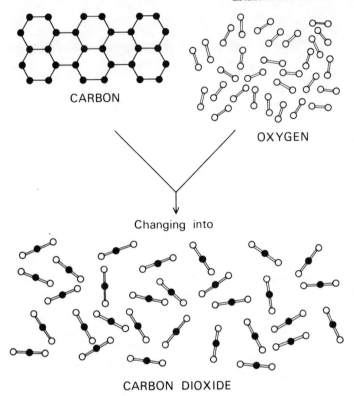

CARBON

OXYGEN

Changing into

CARBON DIOXIDE

Fig. 10.4. Degradation of a mouse in a closed system.

is released as heat, here shown as Fig. 10.4. The importance of this release of chemical energy to man can hardly be stressed enough, since
nearly the whole of our transport and power industries is based on this
kind of release of chemical energy. As an aside, we can note that part of
the search for a pollution-free car is directed to the perfection of a fuel
cell, where this chemical energy can be converted directly into electricity
without the intervening stage of conversion to heat.

Brillouin's point is that commodities such as coal and oil are in unstable equilibria. Their existence for some duration of time indicates that
as far as these resources are concerned there is no increase in entropy
for that duration of time. As he observes, "Such things would not be
permitted if the second principle were an active principle and not a
passive one". And again, "All our so-called power reserves are due to
systems in unstable equilibrium. They are really reserves of negative

entropy — structures wherein, by some sort of miracle, the normal and legitimate increase of entropy does not take place, until man, acting like a catalytic agent, comes and starts the reaction".

As yet science knows very little about these states. They can be cata-lysed into action, but nevertheless in the absence of a catalyst are dor-ment. Conceptually, if we can conceive of catalysts, even if we do not know much about them, then perhaps we can also conceive of negative catalysts. What is the nature of negative catalysts that preserve energy stores?

Within this context life itself is a kind of catalyst. "Life acts as a catalytic agent to help destroy unstable equilibrium, but it is a very peculiar kind of catalytic agent, since it profits by the operation. When black platinum provokes a chemical reaction, it does not seem to care, and does not profit by it. Living creatures care about food, and by using it they maintain their own unstable equilibrium". But they are not just catalysts themselves, they are also maintained by negative catalysts. Living organisms are highly elaborate, highly improbable structures, chemical systems in unstable equilibrium maintained by "some strange power of life, which manifests itself as a sort of negative catalyst".

The industrial revolution and the subsequent expansion of manu-facturing activity can in many ways be seen as the extension by "arti-ficial means" of man's capability to act as a catalyst to those unstable equilibria which are the resources of the environment. This is particu-larly true of the power industries, apart from hydro-power. The energy thus gained is usually used as an anti-catalyst to make new unstable equilibria such as cars and books, which subsequently break down under such actions as rusting and mould and termite activity. The total effect of this multi-stage process is a large general increase in entropy, both in the sense of the degradation of energy to waste heat, and in the sense of a general increase in the locational disorder of those atoms, such as iron and carbon, which we use. There is also the contradictory effect of the creation of unstable equilibria which are remarkably stable, that is the development of plastics and some forms of pesticides, whose persis-tence presents us with long-run problems. Since life in a pre-agricultural phase of earth history seemed to be well adjusted and balanced with respect to its use of unstable equilibria and the role of catalysts and anti-catalysts in controlling the rate of destruction and creation of such equili-bria, we can characterize man's present activity as one where the role of catalysts and anti-catalysts has been subject to vast arbitrary changes.

10.7 Examples of open and closed systems

The open system is the most commonly conceptualized case within geography. Matter, energy and information can be exchanged between the system and its environment. But there are at least two viewpoints from which the relationship with the environment can be considered. In one case the environment is considered to be isolated from the rest of the universe and hence the system and its environment together form one larger system which is constrained *in toto* by the energy and matter within it. This case will be considered below. In the other case, the environment is not considered to be closed or isolated, and the system operating within the environment can use matter and energy from the environment as some function of its own needs and the structure of the environment but is not limited by the environment *in toto*. For example an animal searching for food eats what it requires, and may have to perform a more or less exacting search procedure to find this food according to its pattern of distribution in the environment, but the extent of this environment is arbitrarily large. A good example of this approach is given by Simon's (1956) analysis of an organism searching for food in a structured environment, where he demonstrates that one of the critical factors associated with the organism's survival is the relationship between its storage capacity, range of vision, and the dispersion of food. In such a case the behaviour of the system in time is analysed as a function of some parameters of the environment, which affect the organism's exchanges with the environment, and the initial state of the system at the beginning of the period of observation.

If a system is isolated, then the performance in time of the system is not of interest, or, no statements can be made about its behaviour at least from the viewpoint of thermodynamics. The controlling parameters are the constraints put upon the macro-properties of the system, which will indicate the equilibrium which the system will reach after some arbitrary length of time, irrespective of the initial state of the system. It might seem confusing to say that the constraints have to be specified, while the initial state does not, but an example can make this clear.

Suppose we use a mouse as an example of an open system. Initially this mouse, like Simon's organism, is in an unrestricted but structured environment, as shown in Fig. 10.5. One of the inputs into the structured environment as it has been drawn here, is gravity, which enables us to denote a distinction between air and ground. The mouse will continue

ad infinitum  ad infinitum

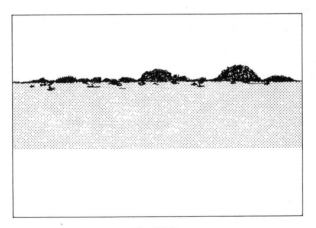

Fig. 10.5.

functioning in the environment, exhibiting some behaviour conditioned by the structure of the environment, its own abilities to search and digest, and the state of its fat reserves and its location in the environment at the start of observation. If now the mouse and some portion of its environment are enclosed within a hermetically sealed box, then irrespective of where the mouse is at the start of the period, how large its fat reserves etc., the isolated system will after some time interval go to an inert state, showing no forms of life. The mouse will die from oxygen starvation, or from hunger. Plants will fail for lack of solar radiation, and even though microbes may live for some long time on the residues, ultimately they will die too. By placing the open system in an isolated system in the end the open system ceases to exist, and we can make statements about the outcome as for a simple isolated system. Energy is maximally degraded and uniformly spread. Matter is reduced to a minimal structural level. The characteristics of this state, that is the total energy still contained within it in terms of heat motion and chemical bonding etc., still remain the same as was the case at the time of hermetic sealing, so does the total mass, and the total number of each kind of atom, and these are the constraints that will determine the nature of the final equilibrium state. In a case such as this, there do remain some conceptual problems. In a simple spatial sense the matter in the system will not be completely random, since if we assume a continuing gravitational input, the molecules will be segregated by weight. We can also get involved in far more difficult territory. Thermodynamics is usually concerned with some system in a single phase, e.g. a pure gas. Spatially a system with more than one phase, e.g. oil droplets in water, presents problems of another kind. But it is surprising to realize how "complete" an equilibrium may be. Schrödinger (1945) gives an example as follows:

> . . . if a glass filled with pure water and a second glass filled with sugared water are placed together in a hermetically closed case at constant temperature, it appears at first sight that nothing happens, and the impression of complete equilibrium is created. But after a day or so it is noticed that the pure water, owing to its higher vapour pressure, slowly evaporates and condenses on the solution. The latter overflows. Only after the pure water has totally evaporated has the sugar reached its aim of being equally distributed among all the liquid water available.

Despite that, it is fair to point out that not all the problems of order and disorder in science have been resolved. Purcell (1963) comments that it is only recently that anybody has come near to deriving a model of a gas which calculates the transition between liquid and vapour. "Previous models of a gas, from kinetic theory on, give only a hint that a thing like condensation can happen. This, too, is, in a sense, a transition from a disordered state to an ordered state".

The isolated system is, as far as we are concerned, a fiction which on occasion may have its uses. Mostly we deal with open systems within open systems, within open systems. A nation exchanges matter, energy, and information with its environment, which means *both* other nations *and* its own physical environment. The latter point is sometimes disregarded in present-day thinking, although it was the base of environmental determinism. The discussion about "spatial closure" of regional systems as seen on a two-dimensional map and the rush away from environmental determinism seems sometimes to have lead to a conceptualization of the environment of the system as being outside that area of earth space. But as has been stressed above, the object of study is a three-dimensional volume, and hence the environment exists on all sides of it in all dimensions. The bounding of open systems within open systems might lead us to think that the kinds of problem associated with the approach to thermodynamic equilibria of isolated systems is of no concern to us. In a strict sense this is true, but the rate of trading between different systems can still have severe constraining influences on the various systems. The trading between systems can be considered in terms of energy exchanges, matter exchanges where the matter represents a source of potential energy, and simple matter exchanges. The second of these three, matter as potential energy, is often simply expressed as "structure", and sometimes as "order".

In the example of the mouse placed in a hermetically sealed container together with some limited section of its environment, assuming that the oxygen supply is sufficient, the mouse may for a time survive by eating plants. These plants represent structure in the environment, and a source of potential energy. In general Schrödinger in a famous sentence has said: "Life consumes negentropy", which we may put here as meaning that life consumes structure. We may ask, where has this structure come from? The answer in terms of genetic inheritance is complex, but the answer in terms of the trading between systems is simple. The ecosystem takes energy from the solar system and uses it in photosynthesis to create plant structures from minerals and organic compounds in the ground.

10.8 Energetics of the ecosystem

A distinction is made in ecology between autotrophs and heterotrophs. Autotrophs are plants and algae which are independent of organic compounds in their environment, and which are capable of producing their own organic compounds by absorbing matter and energy from the environment. On the other hand, animals and plants (e.g. a venus fly-trap) which obtain their energy and matter from organic forms are heterotrophs, and in the food chain are obviously dependent ultimately upon the autotrophs.

The autotrophs can be divided into two types according to the source of their energy in the environment. The vast majority depend on the use of chlorophyll and a source of radiant energy for the process of photosynthesis. But some depend on the degradation of some compounds in the earth which have potential chemical energy. Phillipson (1966) remarks:

> The energy used by *Beggiatoa*, a blue-green algae, in synthesizing organic materials is produced by oxidation processes. Hydrogen sulphide is oxidized to elementary sulphur which is deposited within the cells: $2H_2S + O_2 \rightarrow 2H_2O + 2S + 126$ energy units (kcal). When the hydrogen sulphide is exhausted the sulphur is further oxidized to sulphate: $O_2 + \frac{2}{3}S + \frac{2}{3}H_2O \rightarrow \frac{2}{3}SO_4 + \frac{4}{3}H + 98$ energy units (kcal). The energy released is used to reduce carbon dioxide to bio-organic substances, the overall equation being: $6H_2 + 2O_2 + CO_2 + energy \rightarrow (CH_2O) + 5H_2O$. *Beggiatoa* is thus able to grow in the complete absence of organic substances, its energy sources being the low potential chemical energy of inorganic materials.

Let us repeat that these chemo-autotrophs are rare in the natural ecosystem. They are, in Brillouin's terms, the only catalysts for unstable equilibria at the autotroph level.

10.9 The environment of man

Man as a heterotroph has long occupied a position high up the food chain. As such he has depended on the structure available to him in the ecosystem as a whole, and this in turn has depended almost entirely on the photosynthesizing autotrophs. In general man as a component in the ecosystem has depended on the rate of emission of solar radiation to earth, as an ultimate constraint. In the case of the geological and geomorphological background, solar radiation is important in powering the

atmospheric and oceanic circulations on which nearly all geomorphological processes ultimately depend. There is additionally the heat source
of the molten centre of the earth as well. The most important point is
that these processes result in a structured earth. In the absence of any
constraints the most probable state of the atoms and molecules of which
the earth is composed is one of complete random mixing. But through
the complex interaction of the processes mentioned, they become sorted
and concentrated. We have coal deposits and iron ore reserves, as well as
scattered carbon and ferrous molecules. The economics of exploitation
depend upon this concentration. In this context it is well worth noting
that the geographer's constant pre-occupation with space has led him to
consider that resources are randomly distributed. In a spatial sense of
course the location of these concentrations of material may be random,
but nevertheless they represent the highly structured form of the earth
as a result of a vast history of processes of sorting and concentration. In
that sense they are very far indeed from being random.

Human societies on earth are open systems within open systems that
have a definite rate of useful energy supply available to them. If man
degrades the structure of his environment more rapidly than the structure can be replaced using this fixed rate of energy transmission, then
ultimately his systems cannot continue to survive in the same form.
With respect to ecological systems we cannot in the long run extract
more from them than solar energy will permit. In the short run we often
do extract more. Georgescu-Roegen (1976) approaches the same problem from the viewpoint of low-entropy resources (i.e. those which have
energy available for man's use):

> In the first place, by eliminating the traditional partner of the farmer — the
> draft animal — the mechanization of agriculture allows the entire land area to be
> allocated to the production of food (and to fodder only to the extent of the
> need for meat). But the ultimate and most important result is a shift of the low
> entropy input from the solar to the terrestrial source. The ox or the water
> buffalo — which derive their mechanical power from the solar radiation caught
> by chorophyll photosynthesis — is replaced by the tractor — which is produced
> and operated with the aid of terrestrial low entropy (e.g. oil). And the same goes
> for the shift from manure to artificial fertilizers. The upshot is that the mechani-
> zation of agriculture is a solution which, though inevitable in the present impasse,
> is anti-economical in the long run. Man's biological existence is made to depend
> in the future more and more upon the scarcer of the two sorts of low entropy.
> There is also the risk that mechanised agriculture may trap the human species in
> a cul-de-sac because of the possibility that some of the biological species involved
> in other forms of farming will be forced into extinction.

The point is that the industrial revolution has changed human societies as a whole from being heterotrophic to chemo-autotrophic to a large degree. We use the stored chemical potential energy of coal and oil. Chemo-autotrophs do exist in natural ecosystems, but nowhere is their importance great in overall terms, although they may play a part in the initial colonization of some new surface.

The reserves of chemical low entropy have been formed as the result of immensely long geomorphological and geological processes. That is to say we may conceive of the input to the earth's structure as being very small indeed, so small in fact that we may accurately represent society as existing within a closed system of mineral resource concentrations. Our total society to survive in its present form has adopted a consumption pattern where we must degrade and destroy our mineral resources. This is not vastly different from any other form of life which consumed ne-gentropy, or in other words destroys structure. But it is vastly different at the rate at which it does so. At present we are eating back through the history of our planet. We are consuming a reservoir of carefully sorted materials. There can be only one result for such activity: in the end our open system will no longer be able to survive. On this the prophets of doom are justified, but there still remains the possibility that there are other forms of open system for society to adopt, and of course the translation from what is loosely termed the economy of flow to the economy of stock. By this is meant that the materials taken from the environment must be held within the man system and re-used rather than dissipated after use into the earth environment.

At present we are accomplishing the opposite of the geomorphological processes. We extract from the concentrations of carbon materials, and after burning them distribute the waste to the four winds. We are tend-ing to create the isotropic plane beloved of the theoretician by diffusing and mixing what was previously localized and sorted.

11

Information Entropy and Thermodynamic Entropy

11.1 Introduction

Suddenly in the last chapter a word which had assumed one meaning all the way through the book assumed another. Entropy, a condition of uncertainty, suddenly came to mean the more concrete "availability of energy to do work". Here I attempt to clarify the distinction between the two terms, but also to show that at a sufficient level of abstraction, or, as a structuralist might say, at a deep level, they are basically the same thing.

11.2 Entropy as a primitive property

Jaynes (1957) notes that the idea of entropy was derived from consideration of the equations of motion supplemented by additional hypotheses, which were contrasted with the laws of thermodynamics. "Now, however, we take entropy as the starting concept, and the fact that a probability distribution maximizes entropy subject to certain constraints becomes the essential fact which justifies use of that distribution for inference." The importance of this "entropy-maximizing" approach is that it is maximally non-committal with regard to missing information.

Suppose we have a problem as follows. We have a quantity X, which can take one of a series of discrete values X_i, each such value having a probability p_i, which is not known. But we do know the expectation of $f(X)$ a function of X.

$$f(X) = \sum_i p_i f(X_i)$$

On this information, what is the expectation of another function $g(X)$?

The problem appears insoluble, because we do not know what the p_i are. What we need is a criterion of choice for giving the values of p_i on the basis of the information that we have. Laplace had a "Principle of Insufficient Reason" which stated that two or more events were to be assigned equal probabilities if there was no information to indicate otherwise. However, as Jaynes says, this is just as arbitrary as any other probability assignment. What is needed is a criterion which is unambiguously maximally non-commital with regard to missing information. Shannon's measure of Information or Entropy provides "a unique unambiguous criterion for the 'amount of uncertainty' represented by a discrete probability distribution, which agrees with our intuitive notions that a broad distribution represents more uncertainty than does a sharply peaked one, and satisfies all other conditions which make it reasonable". By "unique" is meant that there is, from an axiomatic viewpoint, only one expression which satisfies the properties required of it. Theil (1967) has a good illustration of this approach. Thus the problem above is solved by maximizing

$$-\sum_i p_i \log p_i$$

subject to the equation above, and $\sum_i p_i = 1$.

The importance of the approach cannot be explained solely in terms of the fact that it is maximally non-committal with regard to missing information. Its operational usefulness lies in the fact that it can give most worthwhile results. The item of interest is clearly the final probability distribution, which may indicate a strongly favoured alternative. When little information is available the approach might offer no help, as no really strongly favoured solution may appear. But whenever there is sufficient information the maximum entropy approach usually gives a strongly peaked distribution indicating the favoured alternative. This is discovered while knowing that we are being maximally non-committal with regard to missing information, so that the result is clearly founded on such incomplete information as we may possess. It happens that " . . for systems of very large number of degrees of freedom, the probability distributions of the usual macroscopic quantities determined from the equations above, possess a single extremely sharp peak which includes practically all the 'mass' of the distribution. Thus for all practical purposes average, most probable, median, or any other type of estimate are one and the same". Of course even when no such peak appears the approach is still logically valid, though the results are not as useful.

Jaynes demonstrates that the treatment of temperature, energy, etc. is possible by the same maximum entropy approach, the mathematical processes being exactly the same, although the interpretation will differ. Thus it appears that entropy becomes the primitive concept with which we work, more fundamental even than energy.

We can put this another way. Uncertainty is the most basic quantity, but this quantity can be given differing meanings in thermodynamic and information contexts. Historically it might appear that the evolution of the terms was sequential as in Fig. 11.1, but in terms of their philosophical relationship Fig. 11.2 gives a better understanding.

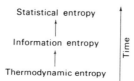

Fig. 11.1. Historical evolution of entropy concepts.

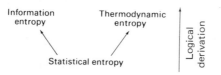

Fig. 11.2. Logical relationships of entropy concepts.

11.3 The most probable state in thermodynamics

Although we have alluded to it many times, we have not yet covered properly the concept of the most probable state of molecules in a gas.

The best introduction to the problem is to be found in Sonntag and Van Wylen (1971), upon whom this section relies heavily.

The problem is to find a distribution of molecules amongst various energy levels. The levels are ordered according to the amount of energy a particle has if it is at that level, and so in accordance with quantum theory we hypothesize the "existence" of these levels even if they are unocuppied. Figure 11.3a shows a distribution of molecules over several energy levels. Geographers would normally be accustomed to seeing their frequency distributions rotated 90° as in Fig. 11.3b, but we follow convention and use the arrangement of Fig. 11.3a.

The other data in the problem consist purely of a macroscopic property — either the intensive one of temperature (intensive means that it is independent of volume) or the extensive one of energy (extensive means that it is dependent on volume — and of course energy is a product of temperature and volume for the gas). Given knowledge of this macroscopic variable we wish to establish the distribution of the particles over the energy levels.

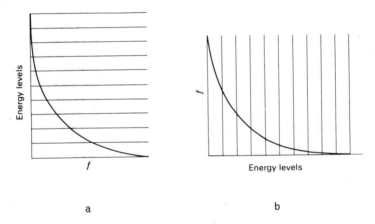

Fig. 11.3. Frequency distribution over energy levels.

Suppose energy $U = 3$. Suppose further that the energy levels are ordered with values 0, 1, 2, 3, etc. Suppose we have $N = 4$ molecules, N_i of which are to be found at the ith energy level.

Now we know that

$$\sum_i N_i \epsilon_i = U = 3 \qquad (11.1)$$

where ϵ_i is the energy of a particle at the ith level, since this is merely a restatement of all that we have said so far. But we do not yet know the N_i.

We now introduce the concept of macro-states and micro-states. A macro-state is a distribution showing the number of molecules at each level, and in this context, one which also satisfies equation (11.1). A micro-state depends upon the idea of distinguishable particles. Suppose all particles have their own names, e.g. A, B, C, and D. Suppose further that having no knowledge to the contrary we presume that they have an equal chance of going to any level they like. A micro-state is then defined as a distribution of identified individual particles over the various energy levels. Table 11.I shows three macro-states, each of which satisfies equation (11.1). One of these macro-states is macro I. Table 11.II shows

Table 11.I

ϵ_i	Macro I	Macro II	Macro III
3	1	0	0
2	0	1	0
1	0	1	3
0	3	2	1
$\sum_i N_i\epsilon_i$	3	3	3
W	4	12	4

Table 11.II
Four microstates to macro I

ϵ_i				
3	A	B	C	D
2				
1				
0	B, C, D	A, C, D	A, B, D	A, B, C

the four micro-states which can give rise to this macro-state. Now, I have said "the four micro-states", which implies that there are none other. Indeed we can calculate the number of micro-states for a given macro-state by:

$$W = \frac{N!}{\prod_i (N_i!)} \qquad (11.2)$$

which needs no introduction.

Now, note that in reality we cannot distinguish all particles uniquely, and we do not do so. We can, however, calculate this number. We take the number to mean the number of ways that this macro-state could have occurred by chance. We assume that since all particles have an equal chance of being anywhere, then all such micro-states have equal probability, therefore the probability of a macro-state is a function of the number of the micro-states.

Thus of the three macro-states shown in Table 11.I, number two is the most probable. It happens that, as we noted above, with large N the most probable distribution becomes overwhelmingly so.

To recapitulate, to find the most probable state of the N molecules of gas over energy levels e_i, we have maximized $\dfrac{N!}{\prod_i (N_i!)}$ subject to $\sum_i N_i \epsilon_i = U$. Note that if we are dealing with probabilities, then $N = 1$, and we can consider that we are maximizing in log form $\sum_i p_i \ln \dfrac{1}{p_i}$ subject to $\sum_i p_i \epsilon_i = U$.

In thermodynamics entropy measured macroscopically is usually calculated from the increments in energy imparted to a gas during a reversible isothermal expansion:

$$\Delta S = \frac{Q_1}{T_1} = R \ln \frac{V_2}{V_1} \tag{11.3}$$

where ΔS is change in entropy, Q_1 is an increment of heat at temperature T_i, R is the gas constant, V_i and V_2 are the volumes of the gas before and after expansion.

In general we may write

$$\Delta S = \int_x^{x'} \frac{dQr}{T} \tag{11.4}$$

where dQr is an increment of heat at temperature T, and x to x' indicates the change of state.

It is clear that entropy has the dimensions of energy divided by temperature.

Now, in the consideration of the most probable state, we have already defined entropy in terms of microscopic aspects of macro-states, and therefore we would expect some kind of correspondence between the two definitions we have now produced. If we write

$$p = \frac{N!}{\prod_i (N_i!)} \tag{11.5}$$

then we may also write entropy as

$$S = k \ln p \tag{11.5}$$

where k has the value of 1.38×10^{-16} ergs per degree Celsius, which is Boltzman's constant. Not surprisingly we now have an energy—temperature dimensionality.

We may also write the change in entropy between two observed states of probability p_i and p_j.

$$\Delta S = k \ln p_i - k \ln p_j \tag{11.6}$$

11.4 Information and thermodynamic entropy

We are now getting onto difficult ground, but one which nevertheless makes some interesting points. Let me caution the reader that the ground is controversial, and that not all authors are in agreement about it. I will point out later the areas where disagreement is strongest.

Let us consider a system comprising molecules of gas, and an initial macro-state with P_0 micro-states. Subsequently we observe a different macro state with P_1 micro-states, where $P_1 < P_0$. Since the second state is less probable, we must have gained some information to be able to specify or observe such a macro-state, and that information gain is given by

$$I = k \ln P_0 - k \ln P_1 \tag{11.7}$$

which is positive since P_1 is less than P_0.

We can also compute the entropy changes between the two states —

$$V = S_0 - S_1 \tag{11.8}$$

where the change V will be positive if the entropy has decreased, and negative if the entropy has increased.

But we may also write

$$S_0 = k \ln P_0$$

$$S_1 = k \ln P_1$$

whence $$S_0 - S_1 = I = V \qquad (11.9)$$

Thus entropy decreases if information gain is positive, and increases if the information gain is negative. We may also of course simply write

$$S_1 = S_0 - I \qquad (11.10)$$

which demonstrates that "information is a negative contribution to entropy" (Brillouin, 1964).

All of this seems too facile to be believable: indeed some corners have been cut. It seems that the circumstances of these manipulations, and in particular the value of k, need to be examined far more closely.

Firstly it is obvious that for this to have any meaning the P_0 and P_1 states must be referring to the same thing in the information and thermodynamic cases — probable distributions of molecules in this case. Then both information and thermodynamic entropy will be functions of probability. With respect to k we know that in the thermodynamic case it has the value 1.38×10^{-16} ergs per degree Celsius. In the information case let us for the moment use the symbol K. If we define information as $K \ln N$, where N is a number of equally likely states, then K can have any value we think fit to give us units of any kind we desire. Usually we use bits, or nits, or dits; for bits K has the value $1/\ln 2 = 1.4427$.

At this stage of the argument Brillouin (1962) asserts that clearly k and K are related by $k/K = 1.38 \times 10 \times \ln 2 = 1.38 \times 10^{-16} \times 0.693 \approx 10^{-16}$. Brillouin (1964) later does not worry about this step and simply says since we can use any units for information we can give k its thermodynamic value, hence the exact correspondence used in the equations above. Interestingly, he never actually says what the dimensions of the constant are: he never claims that they are ergs per degree Celsius, although implicitly they have to be.

Now it seems to me obvious that one can talk in information terms about the probable distribution of molecules of a gas, and it is also true that such probabilities are the basis of thermodynamics, hence it seems simple to accept that in this case they are related. If one accepts the argument as given then one also finds that there is a minimum small level of entropy increase and work expenditure to acquire information.

When talking of thermodynamic systems of molecules of gas, it is not possible to derive one bit of information for less than 10^{-16} ergs per degree entropy increase — which is a very small number indeed. I put this as an inequality, because clearly a bad experimenter could expend much more energy than that.

But there are still some nagging doubts. If information is now tied up irrevocably with entropy, is it not the same thing after all, so why give it a different name? To quote Fast (1970):

> Taking into consideration that information and negentropy are introduced as similar quantities by Brillouin, the whole quotation amounts to the tautology: when we know that a system has not yet reached its state of maximum entropy, then it is still possible for its entropy to increase.

The tautology appears to have been exposed. But Fast has used the words "when we know" which is the point of departure for an example given by Morowitz (1968). An isothermal box is divided into two compartments, one empty, the other containing a mole of gas. If the gas is allowed to expand to twice its volume by making some connection between the two parts of the box, then the maximum amount of work we could obtain from the gas by placing a pump inside the connector would be

$$\Delta W = RT \ln 2 \qquad (11.11)$$

But the box can be subdivided many times, always with half the cells full, and the other half empty. From Fig. 11.4 it is obvious that the distribution will ultimately reach the equivalent of a random one. But at any stage of the process there would always be half of the gas constrained, and half of the space void, and therefore at any stage someone with knowledge of which chambers were full and which were empty would be able to obtain some amount of work with the same maximum (11.11) as before.

This seems strange, since quite clearly the gas is all the time approaching the maximum entropy distribution anyway. Something has been left out of the accounts. What has been left out is the work that is necessary to know which boxes are full and which are empty. For Fig. 11.4a the observer needs one bit of information. For Fig. 11.4e he needs

$K \ln \dfrac{32!}{16!16!}$ bits of information, which is approximately 1.4427 ln

$6.0108 \times 10^8 = 29.16$ bits of information. Since $K \ln 2$ is one bit, we may

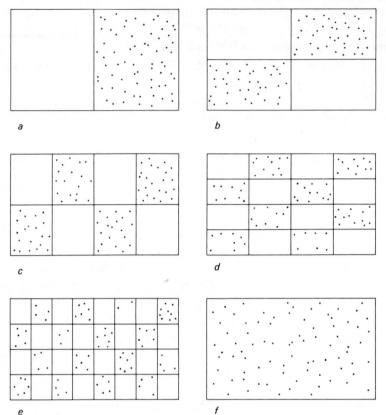

Fig. 11.4. Distribution of molecules.

write that he needs 29.16 K ln 2 bits. But this will generate entropy at the rate of k/K ergs per degree per bit, hence the entropy increase is

$k\ 29.16\dfrac{K}{K}$ ln 2 = 29.16 k ln 2 ergs per degree. The work required to

derive this information is the change in entropy multiplied by the temperature at which it occurs: he needs to expend 29.16 k T ln 2 units of work. Therefore he has only

$$RT \ln 2 - 29.16\ k\ T \ln 2 \qquad (11.12)$$

units of useful available energy. It can be seen that as the number of boxes, which affects the only variable quantity of (11.12), increases, ultimately the work done in identifying the full and empty ones will be equal to the amount of work available.

This is not such a strange result. If a car tyre has its pressure tested a sufficient number of times, it will go flat and be reduced to the ambient pressure. If a thermally isolated hot bath has its temperature taken by a large enough number of thermometers, each initially at the external ambient temperature, each of which is pushed through a small aperture in the insulation in succession, then the bath will ultimately reach the external temperature. It takes heat to make the mercury or alcohol expand.

It is much harder with this example to find the kind of tautological thinking about which Fast is concerned. The crux of the issue clearly lies yet again in the idea of observers of systems, and discussion of whether an observer is part of the system or not. It also arises because science is for once caught up in a notion of value — energy available for work, or useful energy — and explicitly one of the conditions of usefulness is that something can make use of it, i.e. "knowledge" in some form or other exists.

The link between information and energy may also give useful results. In a fascinating article Johnson (1970) examines the failures and possible future successes of information theory in biology. The link between information and energy is one that he highlights in a discussion of kidneys. The behaviour of these had for a long time puzzled scientists: for the amount of work they did they consumed far too much energy, being second only to the heart in oxygen consumption per unit weight. But when it was realized how much information the kidneys had to gain in sorting out molecule by molecule and ion by ion unwanted material from the blood stream, then it became obvious that although the amount of energy necessary to gain one bit of information is small, that necessary to generate information in the quantities here defined was by no means negligible. Calculations indicate that the energy requirements of the kidney may indeed be explained in part by this approach.

It is obvious though, that we are still at the level of molecules. Beyond this level the connections between information and entropy become speculative in the extreme. It is probably safer simply to say that analogies may be made, and that all information has a minimal energetic price, but that this price for most activities is so small as to be negligible in comparison with other costs.

Yet it is interesting to note that where costs of some kind can be shown theoretically to have a very low level, technology will work towards that realization. The computer is followed by the mini-computer, the by the micro-computer, and miniaturization seems to know no limits. The small amounts of negentropy corresponding to the large amounts of information is the reason why the transmission of information is cheap. Offices which decentralize from a major city because they can maintain telecommunications with it are acting on this principle. But apart from this, the possession of a certain amount of information is no indication of the energetic cost of acquiring it, nor of the energetic consequences which follow from possession. To acquire a certain amount of information one may read a book, or one may read the same book on the top of Mount Everest, having climbed it first, to clear one's mind ready for the task of reading. Similarly everyone is aware of the number of mistakes one usually makes when trying to carry out some simple statistical analysis. The information at the end is the same regardless of the number of mistakes and corrections necessary.

From the other viewpoint, the amount of energy that may be released by a control process dependent on the receipt of information is no indication of the amount of information received. For example a signal from a computer which says that b is greater than 1 can cause a steel blast furnace to open up, or a research student to make a celebratory cup of coffee. But quite clearly the signal could not occur without some energy input. In general we may say that no signal can occur, no information can be transmitted, which can be dissociated from energy, but the consequences of the signal may have any energetic form. We are back to the semantic problem of BLURB and the bomb in the Palace of Heaven.

Guilbaud (1959) observes upon this point that what circulates in any system must be studied from two viewpoints. These are the classical viewpoint of energy and the newer one of information. Information is not the same as energy, but it must be understood that there is no signal without some material embodiment, and that information can never be dissociated from energy.

Perhaps the most general remarks made in connection with information and energy are those of Rothstein and Brillouin. The field they cover is very wide, linking observations and measurement to the notions of hypothesis and law, and reducing all to a common information theoretic approach. Anything that is known to exist because of some observable measurement has an information content. Hypotheses and laws are interpretations of things that exist and also have information contents. A law minimizes the uncertainty of the outcome of a certain situation, and has therefore an implicit information interpretation.

There are several other aspects of information and energy that are not central to the theme of the argument here, but which are worth mention because of their general applicability. Information obeys the same laws as thermodynamics, which is not surprising in view of the remarks above. No more information can be obtained from a channel than is inherent in it, and in general in any process on the channel it will be degraded. Thus it is impossible to get out of a set of data more information than is represented by that set of data. In general any manipulations of the data represent a loss of information. For example the standard deviation has lost the original values of the data, and it is not possible to go back from the standard deviation to the original set of data. In most systems involving manipulation of data there are errors possible in coding and calculation even if these errors are as "normal" as rounding operations on a number in a computer store.

Information systems also have the same properties as open and closed thermodynamic systems. Our information about an isolated system cannot increase. It can only increase by measurement from without, i.e. by interaction with it. If information is lost or degraded as suggested above, then information loss can be thought of as analogous to the trend to maximum entropy, which is "time's arrow". It might be thought that as we progress through time information is being gathered, and therefore the arrow is the wrong way round. But when an observation is made our concentration is centred on one object of interest in the universe while we are increasing entropy because of the energy needed to make the observation, and while the remainder of the universe is at the same time tending to a state of less information. In essence this means that no isolated system can determine itself, i.e. observe what state it is in. Such an action would mean an increase in entropy. The system has to interact with its environment to gain the energy necessary for self-observation, and is therefore no longer isolated. This presupposes that the environment has structure, i.e. an energy gradient, so that in this wider system entropy will be increased. It becomes apparent that the isolated information system is as fictitious as a perfect gas or an isolated thermodynamic system. Systems enclose systems within yet more systems. Von Foerster (1956) touches on similar points in his observations on the self-organizing system.

11.5 Gravity models and the most probable interpretation

The gravity model is basically a predictive tool. If we know the flows between pairs of places then there is no need to predict them. There is, however, a need to predict the likely flows within a set of places if something in the set is altered — for example if a new town is added — or if a completely new set is to be connected. For an example of the latter case a telephone company installing connections for the first time between towns in an underdeveloped country has an urgent need to predict the likely level of traffic generation between places to make sure that the capital it has available for investment is distributed in optimal fashion over the various links. The usefulness of the gravity model derives from the fact that where it has been used to predict (some would say post-dict) flows which in reality are known, the correspondence between observed and predicted is often very good.

Generally the model is simply phrased as

$$I_{ij} \propto \frac{P_i P_j}{d_{ij}} \qquad (11.13)$$

where I_{ij} means the interaction between places i and j, $\propto$ means is proportional to, P_i and P_j are measures of "mass" or "attractiveness" of places i and j, and d_{ij} is some measure of distance between them, be it time, miles or cost. Phrased like this the model is purely conceptual — that interaction of some unspecified kind is proportional to the product of some kind of attractiveness and inversely proportional to some kind of distance. It is also quite avowedly mechanistic — based on an analogy with the mechanics of Newton's Laws of Gravity.

In any modelling situation concept has to be replaced by calculation. The proportional sign must be replaced by an equality. Immediately we will find that there are several variants of the model in practice; but we will begin with the simplest, the unconstrained case. The meaning of this term will become clear below.

Suppose we do wish to predict telephone calls from the population figures of towns, and from distance. The model becomes:

$$T_{ij} = K \, P_i^a P_j^b \, / d_{ij}^c \qquad (11.14)$$

Because we have used an equality, and the left-hand side now represents the number of telephone calls, a constant K is essential, to link the left-hand side units to the right-hand side units, people[a] [b]/miles[c]. The effects of P_i and P_j and d_{ij} are also supposed to be mediated by the exponent terms, which would inflate or deflate the relative strength of these variables in the predictive equation.

Mostly, however, we deal with constrained cases where the marginal subtotals of the interaction matrix have to correspond to some fixed figure, as well as the overall flow totals. In such cases we would have a vector of numbers acting as a constraint on the row totals and/or another vector constraint on the column totals. If only one such constraint applies, then the model is singly constrained: if both, then it is double constrained. By convention the singly constrained case is often split into the origin (row total) case, or the destination (column total) case, but this distinction is not of mathematical or operational importance. The computation for both cases is essentially the same.

I shall move straight to an example of the doubly constrained case. Suppose we are studying migration and we know the number of people who leave each town, and the number of people who arrive at each town. Suppose further we wish to use these values as surrogates for the repulsiveness and the attractiveness of each town. We can hypothesize the following case shown in Fig. 11.5. The problem is to find the number of

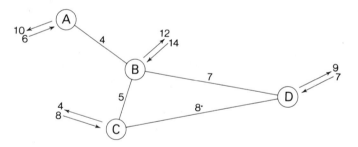

Fig. 11.5. Migration example.

people migrating in both directions between each pair of places. To make the calculation closed, we place some constraints on the numbers straight away: if O_i is the number leaving i and D_j the number arriving at j, and T_{ij} the number migrating from i to j, then

$$\sum_i \sum_j T_{ij} = \sum_j D_j = \sum_i O_i \qquad (11.15)$$

If this were not true we would have people wandering in and out of the systems from places unspecified to us, which lie beyond the borders of the system. This constraint can also be derived from the two separate constraints

$$\sum_j T_{ij} = O_i \qquad (11.16)$$

$$\sum_i T_{ij} = D_j \qquad (11.17)$$

which says that only people who leave all the i places to go to a specific j may arrive at j, and only those who arrive at all j places from a specific i place may in fact have left that place i. These two mean the same thing j places cannot receive Martians from outside the system, and i places cannot send migrants into orbit.

These two equations represent the two vectors of constraints in the doubly constrained case.

We can now attempt to build a model using equation (11.14) above, by writing:

$$T_{ij} = KO_iD_j/d_{ij}^2 \qquad (11.18)$$

In Fig. 11.6. this equation has been used to complete the values in the

		A	B	C	D	
		6	14	8	7	
A	10	0 $_\infty$	8·75 $_4$	0·99 $_9$	0·58 $_{11}$	10·32
B	12	4·5 $_4$	0 $_\infty$	3·84 $_5$	1·71 $_7$	10·05
C	4	0·30 $_9$	2·24 $_5$	0 $_\infty$	0·44 $_8$	2·98
D	9	0·45 $_{11}$	2·57 $_7$	1·13 $_8$	0 $_\infty$	4·15
						27·50

Fig. 11.6. Migration estimates.

matrix with K implicitly defined as 1. By relating the total flows obtained to those that should obtain, we derive a new value for K and deflate the whole matrix by that amount. The deflated matrix is shown in Fig. 11.7. Note then that if we sum the predicted values across the rows and down the columns to obtain new marginal figures O_i^* and D_j^* these new marginals do not agree with those originally given. In other words the model in equation (11.18) has failed to meet the constraints (11.16) and (11.17).

O_i \ D_j	6	14	8	7	
10	0	11·14	1·26	0·74	13·14
12	5·73	0	4·89	2·18	12·80
4	0·38	2·85	0	0·56	3·79
9	0·57	3·27	1·44	0	5·28
	6·68	17·26	7·59	3·48	35·0

(O_i^* on the right; D_j^* below)

Fig. 11.7. Deflated migration estimates.

The answers have not been satisfactory. We need to specify improved K values. We can attempt to do this by substituting (11.18) into (11.16) to derive

$$O_i = \sum_j K O_i D_j / d_{ij}^2$$

$$O_i = K O_i \sum_j D_j / d_{ij}^2$$

$$\therefore K = \frac{1}{\sum_j D_j / d_{ij}^2} \qquad (11.19)$$

This is not a consistent equation: the right-hand side has an i unspecified in it, therefore there must be as many Ks as there are is. The js are specified because of the summation. Similarly the other way round we would find

$$D_j = \sum_i K O_i D_j / d_{ij}^2$$

$$\therefore K = \frac{1}{\sum_i O_i / d_{ij}^2} \qquad (11.20)$$

and again there must be as many Ks as there are js.

Working backwards from these two discoveries we can specify two different models which we know would be consistent with respect to (11.19) and (11.20).

$$T_{ij} = K_i O_i D_j / d_{ij}^2 \qquad (11.21)$$

$$T_{ij} = K_j O_i D_j / d_{ij}^2 \qquad (11.22)$$

We also know we can calculate the quantities involved. The trouble is, though, that we have two models: in fact each corresponds to a singly constrained case, the first to the origin constrained, and the second to the destination constrained.

What we want is a model which satisfies both constraints simultaneously. Taking a leap in the dark, we can specify what we think the model should look like, and then we can see if we can derive some equations for calculating the K factors.

At this point it is wise to change the notation: for convenience's sake and for convention's sake, let us replace K_i and K_j by A_i and B_j. Now let us specify the model as

$$T_{ij} = A_i B_j O_i D_j / d_{ij}^2 \qquad (11.23)$$

from which it follows that

$$O_i = \sum_j A_i B_j O_i D_j / d_{ij}^2$$

$$= A_i O_i \sum_j B_j D_j / d_{ij}^2$$

$$\therefore A_i = \frac{1}{\displaystyle\sum_j B_j D_j / d_{ij}^2} \qquad (11.24)$$

and

$$B_j = \frac{1}{\displaystyle\sum_i A_i O_i / d_{ij}^2} \qquad (11.25)$$

These two equations can be solved by reiteration, to converge simultaneously on the two vectors of coefficients which will satisfy the constraints.

In Fig. 11.8. the reiterations have been pursued to a satisfactory solution, and the final flow values then entered in the matrix. We now have achieved a feasible doubly constrained gravity model.

There are two things worth remembering about the model. Firstly it

		A	B	C	D	1′	2′	3′	4′	5′
		6	14	8	7					
A	10	∞	7·14 ₄	1·20 ₉	1·65 ₁₁	0·26	0·25	0·25	0·25	0·25
B	12	4·37 ₄	∞	3·92	3·90	0·18	0·19	0·19	0·20	0·20
C	4	0·42 ₉	2·13 ₅	∞	1·45 ₈	0·29	0·29	0·29	0·29	0·29
D	9	1·22 ₁₁	4·70 ₇	3·07 ₈	∞	0·56	0·56	0·55	0·55	0·55
1		6·00	3·00	5·00	12·00					
2		5·24	3·19	5·06	11·92					
3		5·07	3·28	5·00	11·76					
4		5·00	3·32	4·98	11·69					
5		4·98	3·33	4·97	11·66					

A_i's

B_j's

Fig. 11.8. Reiteration to find doubly constrained estimates.

is still an exact mechanistic model; and secondly, the term that we have introduced to represent the deflationary effects of distance is purely arbitrary, and has been pulled out of thin air. We could put any function of distance into the model, and the model would still be feasible. This is easily seen since the function for distance turns up unaltered in equations (11.24) and (11.25).

By using entropy maximization we will now reinterpret the gravity model as a probabilistic phenomenon. It is necessary to stress that this will be a reinterpretation — basically the calculations will always remain an apparent mechanistic type similar to equation (11.23) anyway. But we will have a new reason for doing what we are doing. During the demonstration of this reasoning, we will make certain calculations that are not normally made, but which aid in the understanding of the basic concepts.

Nor surprisingly we start with flow matrices that must satisfy certain constraints. Firstly we must satisfy

$$\sum_i T_{ij} = D_j \qquad (11.26)$$

and

$$\sum_j T_{ij} = O_i \qquad (11.27)$$

at all times.

Beyond that we introduce a new constraint, namely that

$$\sum_i \sum_j T_{ij}C_{ij} = C \qquad (11.28)$$

or, that the total amount of money spent on travelling in the system is a constant. This constraint is clearly analogous with the energy constraint placed on the closed system in equation (11.1) in section 11.3 above. In Fig. 11.9 two matrices are shown which satisfy the constraint for $C = 29$

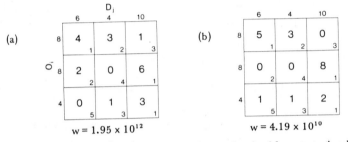

Fig. 11.9. Two unequally likely solutions to the doubly constrained migration problem.

and the marginal values shown. These two matrices were found simply by fiddling with numbers to find two solutions.

The question is now, given that there is more than one distribution which satisfies the constraints, which is the "best" one. The answer that is given is that the "best" is the "most probable".

We have to calculate how many ways each distribution could have occurred. We presume that all 20 persons are individuals, free at any time to conduct any particular journey (occupy any particular cell), completely independently of each other and the number of persons already in a cell of the matrix.

As in the thermodynamic case in section 11.3 above, the answer will be given by computing the ever-present factorial term:

$$w = \frac{T!}{\prod_{ij} (T_{ij}!)} \qquad (11.29)$$

We find that the matrix of Fig. 11.9a is the more probable of the two on this basis.

However, we do not know for sure whether there is still another distri-

bution which is even more probable than either of these two. It can be
shown algebraically that the distribution which maximizes (11.28) subject to (11.26), (11.27) and (11.28) is

$$T_{ij} = \frac{A_i B_j O_i D_j}{e^{\beta C_{ij}}}$$ (11.30)

where β is a coefficient that has to be specified. The proof of the maximization is given in any of the books on thermodynamics mentioned
above, or in Wilson (1970).

It is quite clear that equation (11.30) is a form of the gravity model,
as in equation (11.23), except that the function for the deflationary
effects of distance is explicitly given. The entropy maximization concept
has thus proposed an interpretation of the model which suggests a probabilistic origin of flows and determined a particular exponential distance function. When, however, in any particular circumstance the model
is needed for predictive purposes, equation (11.30) is evaluated in a
straightforward manner as for the gravity model of equation (11.23).

On the face of it we have achieved a system level allocation model of
admirable properties. No single flow may be explained in relation to any
other single flow: all flows have to be explained simultaneously with
respect to each other and the constraints. In this respect it is exactly like
a linear programming model. The organization which is achieved is also
attributable to an external variable, C. Ideally, if C changes over time, we
can watch how all the parts of the system change over time too, in the
manner of Fig. 5.6, providing always that the speed of change of C is
not too fast for the parts always to be in equilibrium with it.

In practice these rarified considerations carry little import. In practice
we do not know nor do we apply C to a town. C, instead of being applied
as a constraint, becomes a quantity which is known only by derivation:

$$C = \sum_{ij} T_{ij} C_{ij}$$ (11.31)

Since C is not known in equation (11.28), it is not possible to solve the
model for β either. Hence β is discovered only by calibration where we
have some real flows against which to check (11.30).

All of this is a little discomforting. The model may work in practice,
but the entropy maximization of (11.29) with respect to (11.26),
(11.27), (11.28), is the sole reason for using equation (11.30) as opposed

to (11.23). And now we find that the quantity necessary for the constraint (11.28) cannot be known in practice.

One might also suggest that in a world where people save as much as possible that (11.31) should be written as

$$\sum_i \sum_j T_{ij}c_{ij} < C \qquad (11.32)$$

which makes the mathematics nonsensical in the entropy-maximizing case, although this is exactly the objective function of a linear programming model, rather than the probability function (11.29).

In the real world of commuters the T_{ij} and the c_{ij} are not independent of each other. If a road is heavily used the chances are greater that it will be improved and that c_{ij} will come down, or in some cases possibly go up if congestion arises. Thus again there is another element of unreality in the thermodynamic analogy.

Finally, I would like to make some comments on the assumption of distinguishable particles free to occupy any cell of the matrices. Although this might be a reasonable first approximation for the simple thermodynamic case, it is less reasonable here — not on the grounds of distinguishability so much as on the grounds that distinguishable particles are hardly equally likely to turn up in any cell. If Mr Brown lives in zone i then most of his trips will be limited to those originating from zone i, i.e. entries in that row of the matrix only, or to those destinating in zone i, i.e. in that column of the matrix only.

Questions of restrictions on particles and on varying conditions of distinguishability do arise in thermodynamics. The simple expression of (11.29) is replaced by a variety of functions under such names as Fermi-Dirac, Bose-Einstein, Boltzman etc., none of which is alarmingly difficult. I feel that there is considerable scope for investigating these in geography as well as the simple case investigated so far.

11.6 Concluding remarks

It might seem strange that Wilson's work on traffic flow should be mentioned in a chapter on energy, but I feel that the analogy between his basic model and that of thermodynamics is so close that the two are best handled together. It also forces one to pay close attention to the ideas of closure in a system, and a demonstration of the purposes for which closure is achieved.

We have also looked very closely at the link between energy and information. It is not a matter of paramount importance to geography, but one of which we should be aware. I tend to think rather like Georgescu-Roegen (1972), that we have spent far too little time considering the real physical limitations on our economic and social systems. Thus both in a direct sense, and as models in probability, the thermodynamic concepts discussed here are overdue for a much closer examination in geography than they have so far had.

Part V

Some Empirical Examples

12

Empirical Examples: Measures of Relative Space, Redundancy in a Townscape, Regulation in Farming

12.1 Introduction

There are so many books which are full of exhortatory theory, but no practice, that I am determined that this should not be yet another. However, I must admit that I have come across many difficulties in pursuing this aim. There were no published examples elsewhere of these ideas worked out in practice, and upon which I could draw. Therefore I have had to provide them myself, and in so doing have come into every researcher's problems of insufficient or unsuitable data, and of course inadequate time to do more than the smallest amount of empirical exploration. I am not satisfied with the three studies considered here; they have been produced at different stages over the last 8 years at different stages in the evolution of my thinking. Nevertheless they do show that the ideas in this book are not purely abstract.

The first study is a study in relative space. Part of this assumes that cities are meaningful units — something against which I have argued quite strongly in the early part of the book. My defence is the inevitable one: it is the way that the data has been produced. I ask the reader then not to concentrate so much on the concept of city, as on the idea of relative space positions which has been explored.

The second study is of redundancy in a city landscape. The study embraces a smaller area than I had originally hoped would be the case — but the extraction of the kind of data I needed was difficult, and I was relying on the very kind offices of a busy student to provide me with it. The results too are negative ones, in the sense that they show that spatial contiguity of the kind considered is not important; but I happen to believe that negative results are useful ones, and certainly this study suggests that general surfaces (e.g. potentials) may be of more use than definitions based on contiguity.

The third study explores the concept of regulation, in the setting of man—environment relationships in India. I think that the study is basically successful, and that it could potentially lead on to some very useful ground. It also exemplifies the fact that most of the ideas of this book are far from being culture-specific.

12.2 Relative space: and the population distributions of England and Wales, and the United States of America

Let us conceive of a naïve model of the development of a geographic system. Here we will restrict ourselves to a consideration of the spatial properties of the components of the system. Initially there is a "society" of primitive food gatherers in an area. It is called a "society" because the social organization is at a minimum, since such activities as food gathering require a minimum of such organization. If the area has reasonably uniform resources then a stable position is found when competition between groups (families or extended families) reduces all to the same size of territory. Each family is in the only state possible for it: it is a food-gathering group. There is no set of alternatives, and each is a static cog. The larger system of interchange between the families does not exist, as, each being the same, there is little complementarity and virtually no division of labour. The advent of agriculture releases more energy into the society and a division of labour occurs. A small urban settlement is founded, occupied by the priests and artisans of the society. The groups no longer have the same spatial properties, the farmers having more area attached to them than the artisans, so that an increase in spatial organization occurs as a division of labour occurs, all of it depending on an energy supply both for the production of the extra goods and for their interchange. As development proceeds, then more towns are founded and their sizes and functions are differentiated.

The economies of scale possible in some functions exceed extra transport costs, and so these are found in fewer towns in greater distances from each other than towns producing goods which have a less beneficial ratio between economies of scale and transport costs. Thus the development of the towns shows organization with respect both to size and to location. The whole process depends on energy availability and the efficiency with which it is used, and ought to be observable in the real world. The higher states are more organized.

This simple model suggests three indices which we could consider for the analysis of organization in a population distribution: (1) an index of the inequality of space defined around each person as a result of his competitive needs in society; (2) an index measuring the degree of organization represented by the way that the urban component of these people is organized into a variable number of places of variable size; (3) an index which assesses the organization implied by the location of the urban places relative to each other. In practice I have been able to define what seems to me to be satisfactory indices for (1) and (3), but not, unfortunately, for (2). For a fuller discussion of these points the reader is referred to Chapman (1970, 1973b).

For Index 1 we may measure the inequality of the use of space by people by the use of the equation for Information Gain:

$$I_1 = \sum_{i=1}^{N} x_i \log \frac{X_i}{1/N} \tag{12.1}$$

where x_i is the fraction of the total national area occupied by the ith individual and N is the number of individuals in the nation. In effect we derive the information gain between the assumed datum where every person would have an equal share of the national territory, and the case where they are observed to have their shares x_i. Note that $\sum_i x_i = 1$.

In actual practice data are not available for individual people. People are therefore classed in areal units. Equation (12.1) then becomes

$$I_1 = \sum_{i=1}^{C} x_i \log \frac{x_i}{p_i} \tag{12.2}$$

where x_i is the fraction of the total national area of the ith areal class, and p_i is the fraction of the total national population in the ith areal class, and there are C such classes.

Grouping of the areal classes into sets enables us to derive a further but equivalent formulation of equation (12.2) in which the total inequality of space usage by people in the areal classes is shown as the sum of two components, firstly the inequality between sets, and secondly the weighted average inequality between classes within each set:

$$I_{1S} = \sum_g x_g \log\frac{X_g}{P_g} + \sum_g x_g \left(\sum_{i \in S} \frac{x_i}{gX_g} \log\frac{x_i/X_g}{p_i/P_g} \right) \qquad (12.3)$$

where $X_g = \sum_{i \in Sg} x_i$ and $P_g = \sum_{i \in Sg} p_i$

In the analysis of population data from the U.S.A. this two-level aggregation was used. The basic areal classes are the urban and rural areas of each state, and the sets are the state areas.

Figure 12.1 plots the values of the two components of equation (12.3) for the U.S.A. for the seven dates involved, and also the total of the index value. It should be remembered that the interest of these figures is based mostly on the fact that what is normally presented as a map of population density, has now been summarized as index figures at each

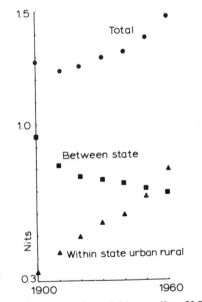

Fig. 12.1. Index of spatial inequality, U.S.A.

year. In terms of organization, the decreases in the between-set term represents a decrease in the organization of settlement between the states over this time period. Such an interpretation is valid in view of the spread of settlement out from the Eastern Seaboard. Interestingly enough, it would appear that this trend is nearing fulfilment, indicating that some macro-scale adjustment is now being reached over the whole of the U.S.A., balancing the legacy of historical forces against the natural advantages of the different areas of the U.S.A. The within-set term is consistently increasing. This represents the micro-scale adjustment of the population to the forces of urbanization, resulting in the continued concentration of the population in small areas. Since these terms are relative, it does not preclude the possibility of the rural population density increasing, but merely reflects that in proportional terms the rural population per head has a greater share of territory than the urban.

The interpretation of the composite effect of these two trends is that at the macro-scale settlement has been more evenly spread over the U.S.A., while at the same time such settlement has been increasingly nucleated, so that one would surmise that the effective spread of settlement to the west has been increasingly of an urban nature, and not of a widespread rural and areal nature.

The analysis of data for England and Wales was initially made using I_{1S} as for the U.S. data. This time the between states component becomes a between-county component, while the within-county component is still based on urban and rural areal classes. The results for the overall index figures for the years 1861, 1871, 1901, 1931, 1951, and 1961 are shown in Fig. 12.2. Some decennial dates are not included because of data problems. In 1941 there was no census.

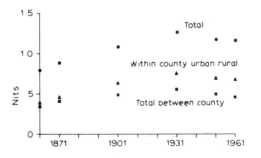

Fig. 12.2. Index of spatial inequality, U.K.

Further analysis for the years 1861, 1931 and 1961 used a decomposition of I_{1S} into three components:

$$I_{1SS} = \sum_a X_a \log\frac{X_a}{P_a} + \sum_a X_a \left[\sum_{g\epsilon_a} \frac{X_g}{X_a} \log\frac{X_g/X_a}{P_g/P_a} + \sum_{g\epsilon_a} \frac{X_g}{X_a} \right.$$
$$\left. \left[\sum_{i\epsilon_g} \frac{x_i}{X_g} \log\frac{x_i/X_g}{p_i/P_g} \right] \right] \qquad (12.4)$$

In this case the counties have been grouped into two categories: peripheral and central. The x_a and p_a, $a = 1, 2$, refer respectively to the central and peripheral shares of the national area, and the central and peripheral shares of the national population. The between-county inequality can thus be split into the two components between centre and periphery, and average within-centre and periphery. The values resulting from this analysis are given in Table 12.I. The peripheral counties were

Table 12.I

Index 1. Total inequality for given years from given
components, England and Wales

	1861	Nits 1931	1961
Within centre-periphery inequality	0.2880	0.3493	0.2592
Between centre-periphery inequality	0.0992	0.2033	0.2280
Total between county inequality	0.3872	0.5526	0.4872
Within county inequality	0.3950	0.7345	0.6732
Total inequality	0.7822	1.2871	1.1604

designated as those which were "extensively empty" in 1961, i.e. those names in column 1 of Table 12.II. All other counties were taken to be central. The same grouping was used for all three dates.

An interpretation of these results suggests that in overall terms England and Wales have passed a peak of density differentiation. But this trend is composed of several components. The between-centre and periphery component is always increasing. We assume that settlement

Table 12.II

Counties designated as extensively empty

1961	1951	1931
Cornwall	Cornwall	Cornwall
Cumberland	Cumberland	Cumberland
Devon	Devon	Devon
Herefordshire	Hereford	Herefordshire
Lincolnshire	Lincolnshire	Lincolnshire
Norfolk	Norfolk	Norfolk
Shropshire	Shropshire	Somersetshire
Suffolk	Suffolk	Suffolk
Westmorland	Westmorland	Wiltshire
North Riding	North Riding	North Riding
Breconshire	Breconshire	Breconshire
Caernarvonshire	Cardiganshire	Pembrokeshire
Cardiganshire	Pembrokeshire	
Pembrokeshire		

1871	1861
Cumberland	Cumberland
Devon	Devon
Lincolnshire	Lincolnshire
Norfolk	Norfolk
Northumberland	Northumberland
Westmorland	Westmorland
North Riding	North Riding

has therefore emphasized the central counties more and more during this period. The overall between-county component increased till 1931 and then fell, a trend which is clearly based on the density difference between the counties in the centre, given the average centre density, and between the counties at the periphery, given average periphery density. In other words, the between-county differentiation is largely based on trends within the centre and within the periphery rather than between the centre and periphery. At the same time the urban—rural differentiation also passed a peak in 1931. The total picture at these three scales suggests that settlement has retracted from the peripheral counties of England and Wales in favour of the centre, but since 1931 within the centre this settlement has been more evenly spread between all counties, and within counties the peak of differentiation has been passed as urban settlement has sprawled and as semi-urban densely settled villages have grown in the orbit of large urban centres. Whether this feature is a result of increasing commuter mobility within a small country or simply the result of overall population pressure where all nuclei are growing and spreading, or a combination of the two, is of course left open to interpretation.

The total between-county score is the result of the summation of individual values for all counties. Such an individual value would be computed as

$$X_g \log \frac{X_g}{P_g} \tag{12.5}$$

The values of X_g do not change over time, since the counties always have the same share of the national total area. The value of P_g can vary. If the county population share is in exact proportion to the county area share, then X_g/P_g is 1, and the whole term goes to zero. If all counties had the same population density, i.e. the national average density, then for all counties $X_g = P_g$, and the total between-county differentiation would be zero. If the county share of people is less than the area share, then the value will be positive. If a county has a greater share of people than of area, the values will be negative. But the total value will depend on both this ratio and the actual value of X_g by which the logarithm of the ratio is weighted. Because of this a large positive score will result as a balance of both a low population share and a large area share.

On the basis of this reasoning we may designate counties with a large positive score as "extensively empty". Not only is their density markedly different from the national average, but such a difference exists over a large area. In a way, one may appeal to a loosely probabilistic argument which would suggest that "extensive emptiness" was significant. The larger a statistical unit is, then the more the averaging of its internal densities to give to its overall density figure, and hence the less likelihood that a large density difference should occur. Similar reasoning enables one to interpret large negative scores for any county as an indication of "extensive high density".

As an arbitrary definition all scores greater than 0.02 are taken as being indicative of "extensive emptiness". The counties which qualify at the various dates are shown in Table 12.II. The table gives a clear indication of the increasing retraction of settlement from peripheral areas.

Table 12.III

Counties with extensive high density

1961	1951	1931
Lancashire	Lancashire	Glamorgan
West Riding	West Riding	Lancashire
Durham	Durham	West Riding
Essex	Essex	Durham
Kent	Middlesex	Essex
Middlesex	Staffordshire	Staffordshire
Staffordshire	Surrey	Surrey
Surrey	Warwickshire	Warwickshire
Warwickshire		

1871	1861
Lancashire	Lancashire
West Riding	West Riding
Staffordshire	Middlesex
Surrey	Staffordshire
	Surrey

Taking as an arbitrary definition all scores less than −0.01 as an indication of "extensive high density" the list of counties so qualifying is also seen to increase over the dates shown in Table 12.III. The two counties which are clearly remarkable in this respect are Lancashire and the West Riding of Yorkshire. London does not feature, although London County itself has the highest density in England and Wales, because the county area is so small. The counties around London, for example Essex, Middlesex, Surrey, Kent, do feature, but none has as high a value as Lancashire — not even Middlesex, which in 1951 and 1961 has no rural population.

Since we have a set of two-dimensional values, we may, following Tideman (1967) plot these results as "entropy diagrams", as in Fig. 12.3. The horizontal scale is of unit length, and is divided according to the values of X_g of each county. The vertical scale records the values of log $\frac{X_g}{P_g}$. The arrangement of the individual counties along the line is arbitrary. In this instance all those which have been designated as peripheral have been placed at the left of the line. All the central counties are to the

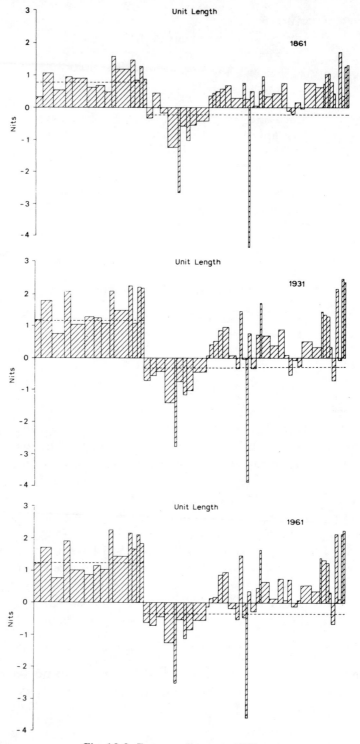

Fig. 12.3. Entropy diagrams, U.K.

right. The distinction is made clearer by the superimposition on the
diagram of the dotted lines representing the two values of X_a by $\log\dfrac{X_a}{P_a}$.
Visually one has the impression of the much lower degree of differentiation in 1861 than in 1931, but it is not so easy to see a clear distinction
between 1931 and 1961. The actual values of the figures in Table 12.II
do of course show that the changes since 1931 have been smaller, and
less associated with a dramatic large-scale change such as occurred
between periphery and centre between 1961 and 1931.

The index values for these two different national cases show how different their patterns of development have been over the last 60 or more
years. Both countries are "developed" and predominantly urban. But in
terms of their national areas at the largest scales it is clear that in the
U.S.A. settlement is only now achieving some kind of adjustment within
its new lands. It is a new country. On the other hand, in England and
Wales the adjustment has been to withdraw settlement from the long-
settled disadvantaged periphery as the nation has urbanized and industrialized. It is the reverse of expansion into new lands. In terms of
urban—rural differentiation in the U.S.A. there is a clear and continuing
trend of increasing nucleation. In England and Wales such a trend exists
only until 1931, and since then as urban areas have expanded these
countries have passed the "hump" of maximum differentiation. The
differences could be accounted for in part by the slightly higher urbanization of England and Wales compared with the U.S.A., but it would
seem most likely that the greater part of the difference has to be connected with the fact that England and Wales have much smaller territories and are much more densely settled. It is suggested that visual
inspection of population maps would hardly show the extent to which
these differences have been revealed by these index figures.

One may suggest ways in which one can interpret the extent to which
the patterns have been shown to be "improbable". Clearly we have
assumed that a uniform distribution is the most probable, and that patterns with dense urban concentrations are improbable. In an energetic
sense, therefore, the improbable states would have to be maintained by
a continuous source of negentropy. This is indeed the case. The maintenance of urban populations depends upon the daily flow of food,
materials, water etc. These flows in the end mostly depend on fossil fuels or
nuclear power. If these energy sources were turned off the populations
of the cities would have the choice of starving or walking out to where

the food was grown. Either way the dense concentrations would disappear off the map.

In the case of the U.S.A. such an attitude towards the urban—rural inequality measure is perfectly possible; in the case of England and Wales this measure passes a peak about 1931, so it might appear less easy to make such an interpretation. However, this is clearly a scale problem in two senses: firstly the nature of the reporting area, e.g. the city boundaries become less representative through time; and secondly, these two countries are improbable at a world scale, relying on massive food and material imports. The analysis has not been conducted at this scale.

Index 3 is a measure of the relative location of cities within some total system of cities. The data needed for the calculation of the index are the distance between all pairs of cities in the system and the population of each city.

For the U.S.A. the number of cities included in the system varied from 205 in 1900 to 298 in 1969, these figures being dictated by the data available. These cities were located on the railway network of the U.S.A. The network was digitized by using a D-Mac pencil follower, and the data was then converted by a computer program into the lengths of the edges of the network. These lengths were then supplied to another program which worked out the shortest route distance between all pairs of cities.

These distance data were then combined with population data at each date to give a matrix of "predicted flows" between all cities based on a simple gravity model

$$F_{ij} = \frac{m_i m_j}{d_{ij}^2} \tag{12.6}$$

where F_{ij} is the predicted flow from city i to city j, m_i and m_j are the populations of cities i and j, and d_{ij} the calculated distance between them.

For 1900 this gives us a matrix of 205 x 205. In effect this matrix is a listing of coordinate locations of the cities in a 205-dimension interaction space. The inverse of the level of interaction could be taken as a coordinate measure of the nearness of cities to each other in an interaction space.

The problem is, however, to convert these 205 coordinates into some simpler form so that we may comprehend better their significance. A full explanation of the following procedure is given in Chapman (1970).

In fact two interaction matrices are constructed. One matrix is as described above, and a second matrix is calculated where the distance between all cities is assumed to be 1, or in other words there is no distance decay in interaction levels. For each matrix the entries are then converted into fractions such that the sum of all entries is 1. For each row of each matrix we may then compute

$$I_{3i} = \sum_j \frac{p_{ij}}{p_{i.}} \log \frac{p_{i.}}{p_{ij}} \qquad (12.7)$$

where p_{ij} is the fractional value of the predicted interaction between city i and city j, and where $p_{i.} = \sum_j p_{ij}$.

This information measure will be high where the all predicted flows tend to be the same, and low where some flows are large and others comparatively small. These two cases are seen to represent centrality and eccentricity. Centrality results when the interaction of one city is not predominantly with a few others, i.e. when it appears accessible to all members of the system and not to be highly specialized in its interactions with only a few. For such a condition to prevail, the larger centres would have to be more widely spaced than the smaller, on average. The final index figure used for each city is then a percentage value

$$\frac{I_{3di}}{I_{31i}} \times 100 \qquad (12.8)$$

where I_{31i} is the information value calculated from the matrix where distances are assumed to be 1, and where I_{3di} is the information value calculated from the matrix where distances are included. The percentage change then indicates the extent to which the position on the transport network, given all urban populations, is such as to make interaction specialized or general. The actual locations of the cities in absolute space on the transport network do not of course change from year to year. But the change in the urban population at the various node locations will cause changes in the "interaction" location of cities.

We may additionally compute one overall national value

$$\frac{I_{3d.}}{I_{31.}} \times 100 \qquad (12.9)$$

where
$$I_{3d\,.} = \sum_i p_i . I_{3di}$$

and
$$I_{31\,.} = \sum_i p_i . I_{31i}$$

These values can either be interpreted simply as index values, or in fact it is possible to put an information interpretation on them. The quantities I_{3di} and I_{31i} are conditional entropies. If we hypothesize that the fractional interaction values represent a frequency distribution resulting from many individual cases of single instances of interaction, then these conditional entropies specify the amount of information on average which we would need to specify the destination of any single instance of interaction which originated in the given city. In this context centrality then means that a large amount of information would be needed to specify the destination of any single instance of interaction originating from a "central" city. The quantities $I_{3d\,.}$ and $I_{31\,.}$ are average conditional entropies for the whole set of cities.

The results of the relative location index for some individual cities are given in the graphs shown in Fig. 12.4. Additionally maps of the whole U.S.A. have been prepared plotting the results for the cities in class intervals. Extracts of these maps are shown in Fig. 12.5. The overall national index value is shown plotted in Fig. 12.6.

In 1900 most of the cities have a high value. Most of them are accordingly not specialized within some local region of cities, but are central. Most of the cities with lower values are found in the north-east manufacturing belt and on the Pacific coast, whereas the cities with higher values are found in the Midwest and the South. Some cities are highly eccentric, or specialized — but this mostly occurs where "twin" cities are found, for example the two Kansas cities, the two St Louis, and Minneapolis St Paul. In effect one may consider that the interaction that has been defined here is more of an "intra-urban" kind, because two distinct administrative names are given to what are in effect single cities.

Change by 1920 is slight. In general it seems that most change is in the direction of increasing eccentricity. But the pattern of centrality in the southern states still contrasts with the pattern of eccentricity in the north-east.

The major changes in 1940 seem to be associated with the growth of satellite cities. The pattern of isolated and central cities in the south

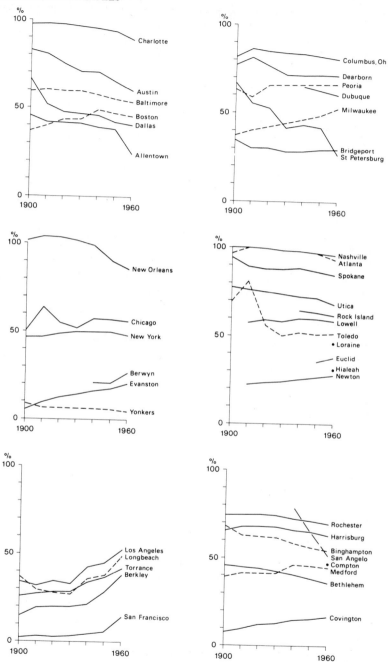

Fig. 12.4. Individual location values for U.S. cities.

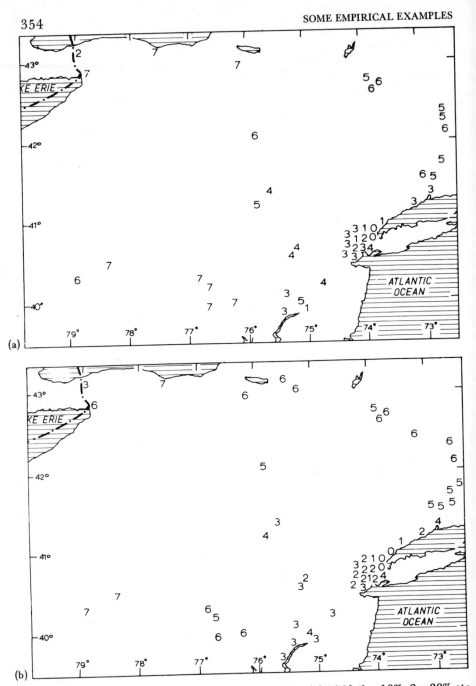

Fig. 12.5. Maps of relative location, U.S.A. (a) 1900, (b) 1960. 1 = 10%, 2 = 20% etc.

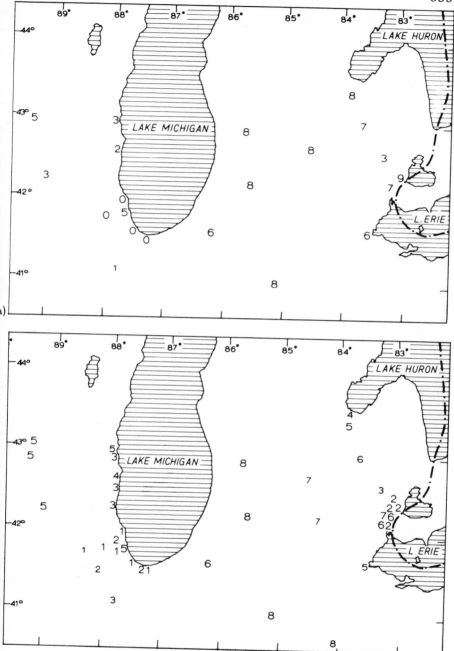

Fig. 12.5. Maps of relative location, U.S.A. (a) 1900, (b) 1960

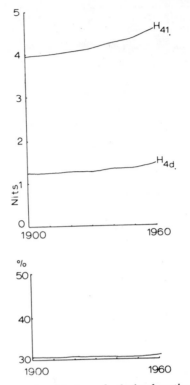

Fig. 12.6. National index of relative location, U.S.A.

seems to be changing. Birmingham now has a lower figure, mostly because of the group of satellites. Around New York, there is little "new entry" of new cities, and most cities show increasing eccentricity. Chicago and its region offers a contrast. The entry of new satellites seems to be associated with rising values, presumably because interaction is less dominated solely by Chicago. An opposite trend is shown by a group of cities in the Carolinas. These cities, the subject of a book entitled "Urban Growth Dynamics in a Regional Cluster of Cities" Chapin and Weiss (1962) show over time increasing eccentricity, with no single dominant central city in the group.

By 1960 there are only a few areas of "central" cities left. These are to be found in the western fringes of the Ozarks, the southern Appalachians, and in western and northern Michigan. The first two areas correspond with regions of backwardness, the third with a resort region placed between the industrial areas west and south of Lake Erie, and in Illinois.

The highest centrality values seem associated with isolation, and usually with areas of lower economic wealth. It would seem to corroborate the hypothesis that wealth is generated within regional clusters of cities.

One may also suggest different patterns of change with time in the East, the Midwest, and the West. In the East, the most central cities seem to have static values with time, while the satellites become increasingly eccentric; in the Midwest the central cities seem to be static while the satellites become less eccentric: in the West both central city and satellites have rising centrality values. One may interpret this as follows. Population growth in significant relative terms has not occurred in the East, has occurred in the satellite cities of the Midwest, and has occurred in all cities in the West. The "newer" urban regions would suggest that the old East-coast pattern of central city surrounded by eccentric satellites has been replaced by uniform regional urban growth.

The overall national index Fig. 12.6., has a steady time-independent value. That it is quite low, around 30%, can be explained by the weightings p_i. used in calculating I_{3d}. . Such weightings favour the interaction within the urban clusters, most of which is associated with cities with low centrality values. The nature of the stability of the value would appear to be explicable in general terms in that the different changes with time observable in the East, Midwest, and West, clearly balance each other. I can offer no comment on the significance or not of the stability of the value.

The analysis of cities in England and Wales followed the same method. 300 cities were included in 1961, and the same number in 1861, although in that year some towns, particularly the planned new towns dating from the 1940s onwards, have purely notional populations measured in 100s. Some sample extracts of the national maps are shown in Fig. 12.7, and individual city values in Fig. 12.8.

The pattern in 1861 clearly shows that the majority of high centrality values are associated with isolation, although London, Wolverhampton, Birmingham, Liverpool and Manchester do also have quite high values within their own urban clusters. Newcastle and Gateshead have low values owing to the twin-city effect noted in the case of the two Kansas cities in the U.S.A.

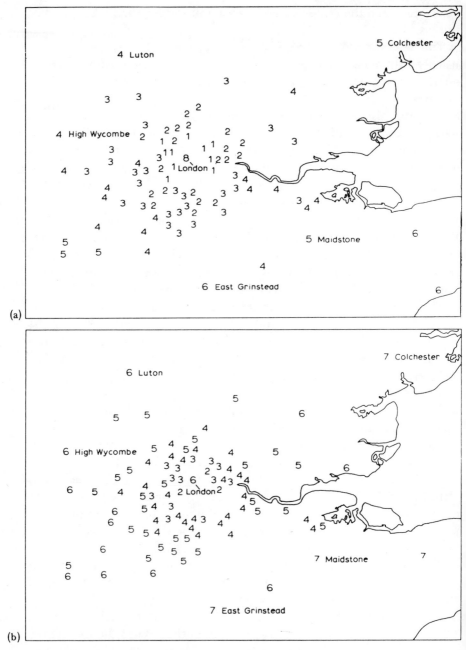

Fig 12.7. Relative location maps, U.K. (a) 1861, (b) 1911. 1 = 10%, 2 = 20% etc.

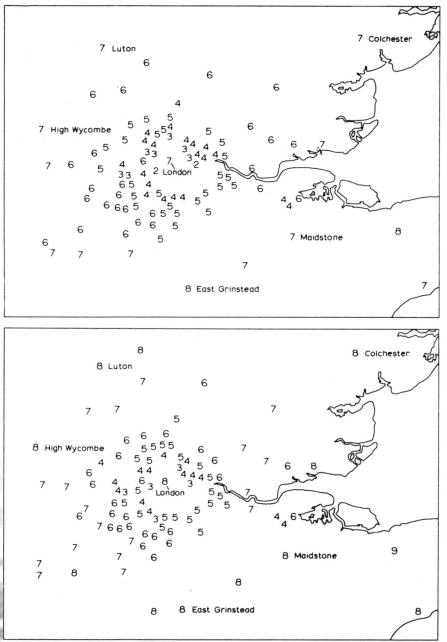

Fig. 12.7. Continued, (a)1931, (b) 1961

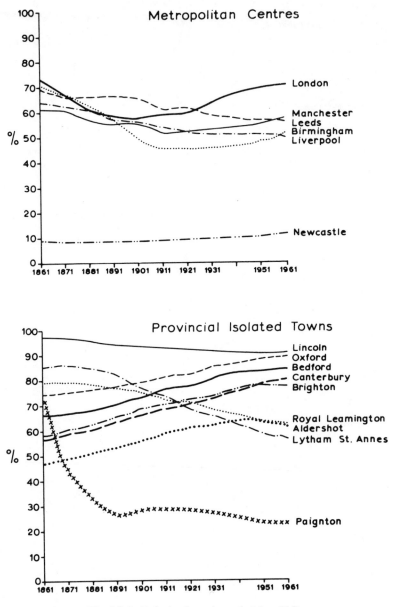

Fig. 12.8. Relative location of cities, U.K.

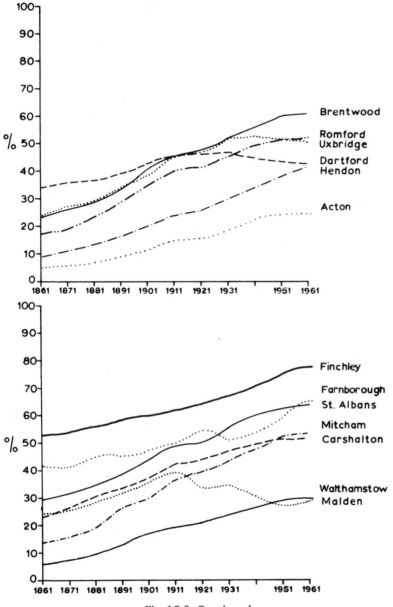

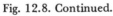

Fig. 12.8. Continued.

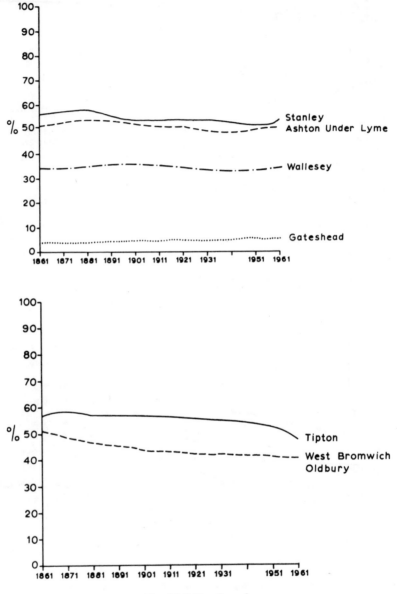

Fig. 12.8 Continued.

There is a clear distinction between the urban regions of Manchester and Birmingham on the one hand, and London on the other. Concentric rings with centrality values starting low and increasing further away from the central city can be discerned around London. The satellites of Manchester and Birmingham have higher values and show no such clear patterning.

Over time fewer very high centrality values occur. But on the other hand around the outer ring of satellites of the London region centrality values have risen. The value of London itself declines slightly till about 1911, then rises again. The pattern around Birmingham shows declines, whilst around Liverpool and Manchester little change occurs.

The distinction between the London region and the other urban regions is quite clear. Over time there has been a constantly higher proportionate rate of growth at further distances from London, whereas the same has not occurred at the other regions. It would seem that the reason for such growth around London is simply membership of the London cluster, whereas in the other areas cities which have as their basic *raison d'etre* a high basic activity content, and have not grown because their basic industry has not grown. Over time a rippling wave of centrality seems to have spread out from London. It even seems possible to identify in the case of some of the closest suburbs of London an increase in eccentricity in the last years as the centrality wave has passed further out and away from them.

The overall national index shows a U-shaped curve over time (Fig. 12.9). This is a weighted average of the individual city terms. The cities may be crudely classed in one of three categories: those showing U-shaped curves like the national curve, e.g. London, those showing overall declines, e.g. Manchester, and those showing overall gains, e.g. Bedford. It would then appear that the weighting of individual terms in the total term has, in relative terms, emphasized lowering values more than rising values initially, and then rising values more than lowering values, if we take the U-shaped curves as having a "neutral" effect on the total index. An analysis of the actual cities with these characteristics suggests a time-lagged change from Northern urban regions, to the Midlands and South-east in terms of total predicted interaction, concomitant with a change in the nature of the urban regional growth.

The results in the two case studies are rather different, but an analysis of the differences can only suggest some possible reasons for this, in view of many fundamental differences in the scale of consideration and the number of cities considered. The 298 cities considered in the U.S.A.

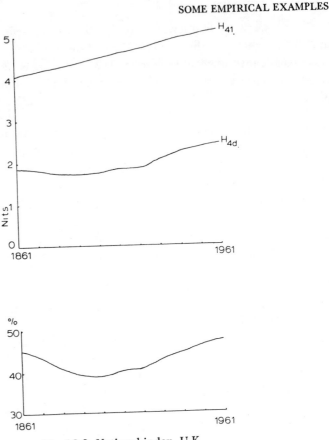

Fig. 12.9. National index, U.K.

represent a smaller fraction of all urban places than do the 300 in England and Wales.

The ratio of average distances within an urban region to distances between urban regions is higher in England and Wales than in the U.S.A. This scale difference may account for the fact that the overall index value in the U.S.A. is smaller than in the U.K. In other words the scale difference would mean that in the complete set of all national cities no city in the U.S.A. could achieve the same level of centrality as a city in the U.K.

The fact that the index in one case is stable, but in the other case shows a U-shaped curve would seem to indicate a major difference between the two. In the U.S.A. there has been change which has in part been accomplished by the development of new urban regions on new locational bases. In particular the most recent growth has not been around a pre-existing dominant centre on the west coast, which contrasts sharply with the growth pattern around London.

Clearly there are many avenues that could be pursued. Firstly as with the case of Index 1 the analysis of other countries would be interesting. But there are also a number of changes that could be made to the data used in this index. The exponent used in the gravity model can be changed as a kind of filter. The higher the value of the exponent, the more that the index reflects local rather than national influences on centrality values. Again, a completely revised predictive interaction formula may be used. The effect of changing the transport links, of improving some and increasing the friction in others, could be tested. Alternatively real interaction data could be used.

Lastly, one comment is necessary on the way the results were presented. The results of the third Index were used to prepare maps of the relative space value of different cities. These maps were used for a discussion of the meaning of the index results. Such a procedure is in many ways illogical.

A map using coordinate space, such as the maps in Figs 12.5 and 12.7, is based on the principle that there is more information in such a presentation of the results than would be obtained by a mere listing of the results in tabular form. In tabular form the names of the cities could have been listed with the index value alongside. The map gives a meaning to a location by showing a position which can be compared with others. The mapping is not made solely to identify the place. The comparison gives some idea of a relative position. In this particular case the index values that have been mapped at these relative positions are themselves relative positional values. The procedure appears therefore to be paradoxical. The term satellite city can be applied equally to a city with a low locational index value and to one which on the map is near another large city. In the English and Welsh results there was mention of the notion of a "wave of centrality" moving outward from London, particularly to the west. The notion of centrality is based on the relationship of these places to all other places within the urban system, and therefore the knowledge that it is moving westward is completely irrelevant, except that it helps as a memory aid for people used to thinking in map terms in identifying those places which at any date have a high centrality value. The position on the map gives some information about the place in relation to others, but the location index value is used to show that this is not the "true" positional value. The place is not what it seems, but is another place, and some mental gymnastics are involved in interpreting the maps.

12.3 Redundancy in the landscape of Acton

(a) An illustration of redundancy in a regular landscape

The reader will remember that the concept of redundancy was introduced in Chapter 4 (section 4.7). In linguistic terms we could define redundancy as the generation of a good estimation of the next letter in a sequence of letters — this of course means that the letters of a language convey less than the maximum information possible, but we also found that the reason for this lower information content was that redundancy counteracted against errors in transmission.

As a simple illustration of redundancy in a spatial sense consider the diagram in Fig. 12.10. Here we have three classes of places — metropolis,

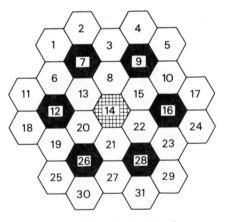

Fig. 12.10. Central place landscape.

town, and village — each with six neighbours, except of course for the peripheral villages. The arrangement of these places shows some kind of order: there is a recognizable symmetric pattern in the whole. To measure this pattern we take each of the 31 objects in turn, and record the type of its neighbours at one step removed, at two steps removed etc. up to the maximum of six steps removed. At each step length we then have a frequency distribution over the three types of place that could be found. For each of these frequency distributions it is possible to compute a simple entropy expression to indicate how uncertain we are of the type of place to be found at that number of steps away from the given origin. Suppose we take object 14 as the origin, then we can compute

$$H_{14}(i) \text{ at one step from } 14$$

$$H_{14 \, .}(i) \text{ at two steps from } 14$$

$$H_{14 \, ..}(i) \text{ at three steps from } 14$$

There is no point in calculating beyond this step length for object 14, since clearly we will have reached the edge of the landscape from the centre.

Entropies calculated in this way are shown in Fig. 12.11 for four of

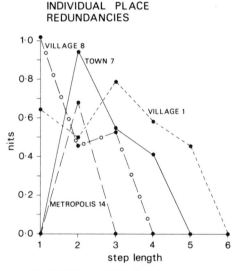

Fig. 12.11. Individual redundancies.

the objects, plotting the redundancy values in nits against the step length. A low entropy value indicates low uncertainty and a high redundancy. We can see from the diagram that the peripheral village 1 has the lowest overall redundancy (it is hardest to know how the world is organized from the viewpoint of this place), whereas the metropolis has the highest redundancy. Village 8 has a lower value than town 7 at step lengths two, three, and four, but its total value for all step lengths is slightly higher — 2.015 as opposed to 1.928 nits — which suggests a less central position overall.

In Fig. 12.12 the aggregated redundancies are given — these are cal-

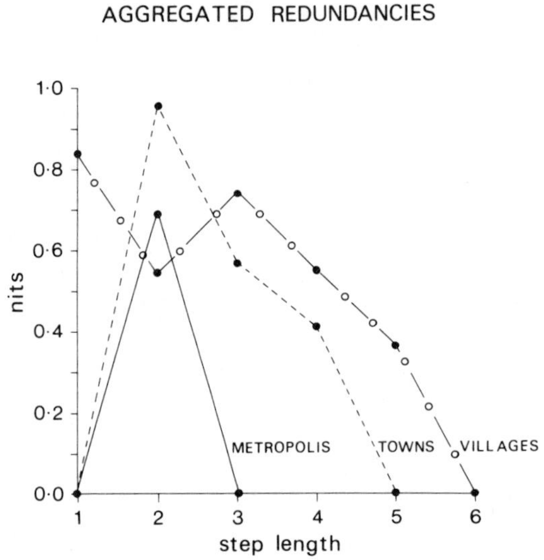

AGGREGATED REDUNDANCIES

Fig. 12.12. Aggregated redundancies.

culated for the metropolis, for the towns and for the villages. We are now no longer considering the places to be unique, but replicable in relative space. With respect to the value for towns it will be seen that this is the same as for the individual town 7 in Fig. 12.11. That the value for all towns is the same as the value for one town means of course that in information terms all six towns are in the same place — as suggested in Chapter 2. Overall we can see that the metropolis is the vantage point from which the landscape is best known, but even then there is still uncertainty at step length 2. To explain this, we must for a moment digress into central place theory, upon which this example is based.

The organizing principle in central place theory is spatial competition but this does not provide enough information alone to "fix" completely the resultant output. On this principle alone we can have any number of nets of functions of the same rank in any number of orientations, and it is not even necessary that functions should coincide with functions of a lower order to create places. Thus some extra information has to be given to the model as input data: in Christaller's case it is that the metropolis contains all functions, and that functions are then allocated to places, not vice versa. In Losch's case it is that the metropolis contains all functions, that all other functions are spaced in multiples of the smallest spaced function, and that the nets are revolved to maximise the accordance of functions. But even then with both models the overall orientation of the landscape is still undefined. In our particular case this is reflected in the uncertainty still prevailing at step length 2 from the metropolis, which reflects the fact that we are not sure whether at that distance we shall encounter a town or a village. This uncertainty can be removed by knowing the orientation of any one town or any one village from the metropolis, and comparing this with the orientation of the objects at step length 2.

Thus the analysis of these redundancy values has confirmed quantitatively several aspects of pattern which we could perceive by eye.

(b) Time-space redundancy

In the linguistic examples of redundancy given in Chapter 4 (section 4.7) the concept of "next" was bound in time by the one-dimensional seriality of language. In the example above the concept of "next" is defined in terms of spatial contiguity. We now come to consider the case of next in time-space. We can obviously bind an object in time quite simply: we can define those other objects which are before or after in time. To this we can ally the spatial concept of contiguity in space, to produce a time-space contiguity in which we can search for redundancies. However, the concept of contiguous in space is very limiting: it takes a very highly ordered landscape to produce the kinds of redundancy measured in the example above, and in general the measurable redundancy for a landscape such as that shown in Fig. 4.11. is rather low.

Nevertheless, working with these limitations in mind, we can define various rules to guide us in assessing the frequency distributions that we need. The rules which were used in the empirical time-space investigation were those already illustrated in Fig. 4.11, but for both the antecedent and the descendent cases. There were some difficulties with the actual data set for Acton, in that it included only commercial concerns, and

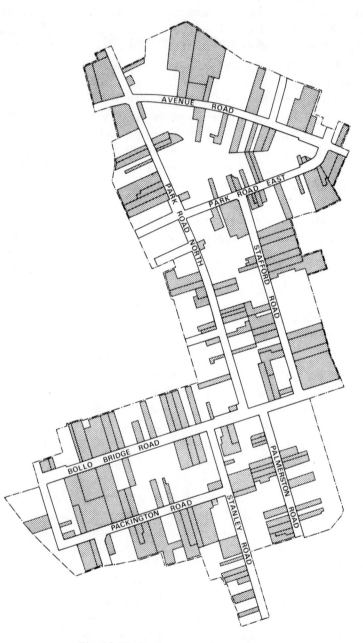

Fig. 12.13. Business premises in Acton.

not residential housing units. This necessitated the generation of further rules to define spatial contacts consistently.

(c) The data set for Acton

The data set used in the analysis is concerned with industrial and commercial objects in the Acton area of London over the period 1900–1965 approximately. The map in Fig. 12.13 indicates the 166 locations used for the analysis. It will be appreciated that finding a data set which met the rather stringent requirements laid out here was not easy, and I am deeply indebted to N. P. C. Waloff of Emmanuel College, Cambridge, for providing me with one (Waloff, 1973).

I hoped that the set would also include information on the residential sector, indicating the date of every change of ownership of each house, but this was not possible. The reason for wanting such information is simple. Figure 12.14 illustrates schematically the data set used with no

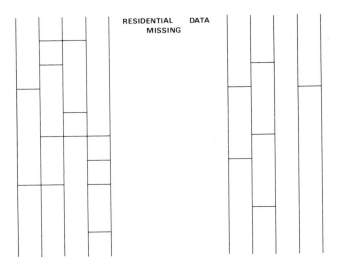

Fig. 12.14. Schematic data set.

information on change of ownership for residential purposes. Each residential block is also a complete time-space blockage prohibiting the development of contacts across the missing data. This reinforces the idea that control should be important in the definition of object, since a change of control also indicates a potential change of object type.

In the absence of residential data the definition of a neighbour is extended to mean the next commercial/industrial location in the street concerned. Again, to be non-arbitrary, or rather to have replicable results, we find we need rules to define neighbours spatially. The rules used were:

1. In all cases adjacency (direct contact) with neighbours on the same side of a street or on opposite sides of the street. (The street was defined as a single line in the middle of the road and locations were projected to meet this line) but excluding back-to-back adjacency (two locations adjacent but fronting on different streets).

2. Corner-to-corner contact counts as adjacency.

3. There has to be a minimum of one right hand (facing the street) and one left hand contact for every location; corner adjacencies can count as right or left hand contacts, but if there are no adjacent right or left hand contacts then the nearest location in the relevant direction on either side of the street is taken as a neighbour.

4. All contacts around street corners have to be two-way, i.e. reciprocal.

Figure 12.15 shows the contact pattern defined for locations in one part of the data area.

The locations are not the objects of interest, though. What we are investigating are the actual concerns that function at different points in time. As is consistent with what was written in the early chapters, a basic part of the definition of objects is control. Thus as an object changes control, then even if the same function remains, a new object exists. Hence it is possible for a butcher to follow a butcher at the same site.

The data are of course relative: we have relative space and relative time, where adjacency in time, but not duration of time, is important. However, this is not quite enough to produce the kind of replicability which enabled us to aggregate the results of towns and villages in the above example. We need also to define what constitutes the same kind of function in our context. Given a total of only 517 objects at the 166 locations, a detailed classification of objects would have too many classes with very low frequencies. A classification was devised of 21 types of business. This meant including as the same kind of thing both clothing shops and tobacconists, to give but one example.

The classification is not a standard one. Having looked at several such, I came to the conclusion that none were suitable. Most were based on

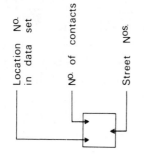

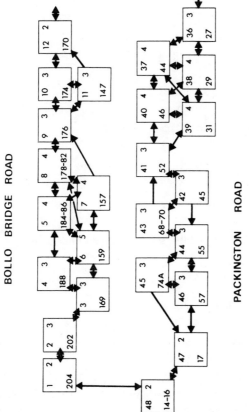

Fig. 12.15. Sample contact pattern.

some kind of consideration of the material involved in a process, not the function of the process in society. In this context I refer the reader again to Chapter 2 (sections 2.4 and 2.5). Hence the scheme used here envisages several functioning objects, with different kinds of needs in terms of structural maintenance, and structural growth. A diagram on which the classification of Table 12.IV is based is shown in Fig. 12.16. I would

Table 12.IV
Object classification

: : LEVEL 1

Residential
    1. Houses
    2. Flats

Fabric
    3. Builders, decorators, fire protection, heating engineers, plumbers

Durables support
    4. Carpet cleaners, car repairers, removal contractors

Durables retailing
    5. Furniture, hardware, electrical, toys

Perishables, food
    6. Food shops, off-licences, restaurants, dairies

Perishables, non-food
    7. Newsagents, tobacconists, chemists, clothing

Perishables support
    8. Laundries, boot repairs

People support
    9. Betting shops, pubs, clubs, schools, playgrounds, churches

: : LEVEL 2

Fabric
    10. Builders' merchants, timber yards

Durables
    11. Manufacturers, wholesalers of furniture, toys, electrical consumer goods

Perishables
    12. Manufacturers, wholesalers of food, food products
    13. Manufacturers, wholesalers of non-food perishables, clothing, buttons, pharmaceuticals, coal merchants

Table 12.IV — *cont.*

: : LEVEL 3

Business durables
  14. Office equipment, furniture, filing cases, sign manufacturers, catering equipment, shop fittings

Business support
  15. Shop fitters, printers, book binders, haulage contractors

: : LEVEL 4

Materials supply
  16. Electrical engineering
  17. Mechanical engineering and metal working
  18. Chemical engineering

: : LEVEL 5

Recycling
  19. Scrap metal
  20. Scrap clothing, paper
  21. Unoccupied

---

caution that this scheme is not well tested, but nevertheless I think it can offer several ideas for discussing classifications of this sort.

(d) Results of the analysis

For convenience, three kinds of results will be considered in order: (i) we will consider the overall redundancy values of the different adjacency rules; (ii) we will consider the values for certain business types only; and (iii) we will consider the spatial spread of contacts through time. Some conclusions follow in (iv).

(i) The simply entropy of the overall frequency distribution of the objects, shown in Table 12.IV, is 2.437 nits. This is a datum alongside which all other figures can be compared. It shows the degree of uncertainty we would face if we had to guess the business type of one object without any other additional information. The distribution of the business types is clearly remarkable for the preponderance of type 8 — people support services. The area was the main laundry district of London at the beginning of the period, and this figure reflects the enormous number of laundries. Over time the laundries decrease in number,

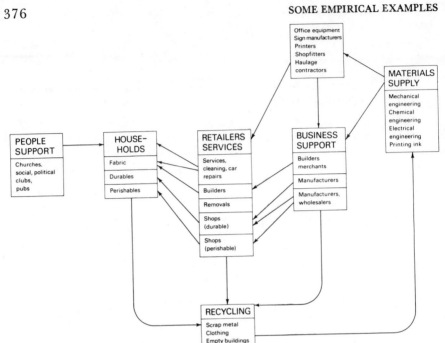

Fig. 12.16. Diagram of classification scheme.

and other businesses of more varied time supplant them.

The entropy values obtained given some knowledge are displayed on the graphs shown in Fig. 12.17. The letters A or D1 refer to the generating rules used, as in Fig. 4.11. Thus A cases are temporal only, and D1 cases are time-space cases. The word antecedent refers to those cases which look back from a later time to earlier times in an attempt to find redundancy in the causes; the word descendant refers to those cases which look forward in time to the effects of an earlier cause. The words full and short refer to changes made in those circumstances in which there are more than one objects at a location through time. If, for example, we are considering the location of objects B, L, M and R in Fig. 4.10 it is clear that the antecedent contact patterns of L, M, and R are also subsumed within the pattern of B. Unless otherwise mentioned, and where the word "full" is used, the contact patterns of all four such objects at the one location would be used in assessing frequencies. Where the word "short" appears, only the first object of the location would be used for estimating the contact frequencies — in this case B.

The "short" case in descendant rules is obviously the converse: instead of only the most recent object at a location being used, only the earliest object is used.

Next I have to explain the meaning of ADD ALL and ADD1. There are many ways by which V in Fig. 4.10 may be reached from B in, for example, four steps. When calculating the frequency of objects of the same type as V at four steps from B we could either add 1 to the frequency count no matter how many ways V is reached, or we could add 1 for each different way that V was reached. Those who are accustomed to powering connectivity matrices will be aware of the very large numbers of ways that routes may be defined between two points at great step lengths from each other. Because this inflationary problem seems somewhat arbitrary, and will obviously affect the redundancies calculated, in all runs except the one marked ADD ALL it was decided to add 1 to a frequency no matter how many ways that an object could be contacted. The problem is rather a good example of the way that an increase in dimensions increases other problems more than proportionately. In one-dimensional language, not only is "next" unambiguous, but so is "next-but-one". In spatial terms we may define "next" simply, but the definition of "next-but-one" is not unambiguous, since it may also simultaneously be the next-but-two, or -but-three, etc.

The first obvious comment to make is that in nearly all cases, and certainly in overall terms, the A rules produce much lower entropies, i.e. greater redundancies, than the D rules. Put simply, if a person needed to predict forwards or backwards in time from a certain business type at a location to its likely successor or predecessor, he would be better to base his estimate only on the existing type at that location, and not to use the other information of what is nearby. To put it another way, spatial information added to the historical information blurs a previously better estimate.

Temporally, all cases show assymetry. This can be seen in the lower values for the antecedent cases than for the descendant cases. In this data set it is easier to know the past from the present than the present from the past. This result is not unexpected, since, as was pointed out above, the area was predominantly covered by laundries at the turn of the century, but as that industry has become large-scale and mechanized, there have been a number of successor industries of increasing variety.

But in other ways the graphs show some unexpected results. Rather than finding uncertainty increasing with increasing step length, in all

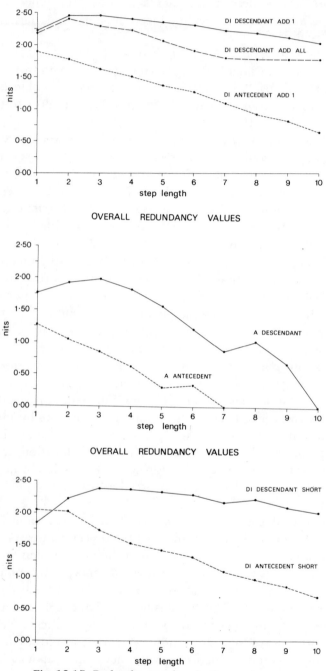

Fig. 12.17. Redundancy values in time and space.

OVERALL REDUNDANCY VALUES

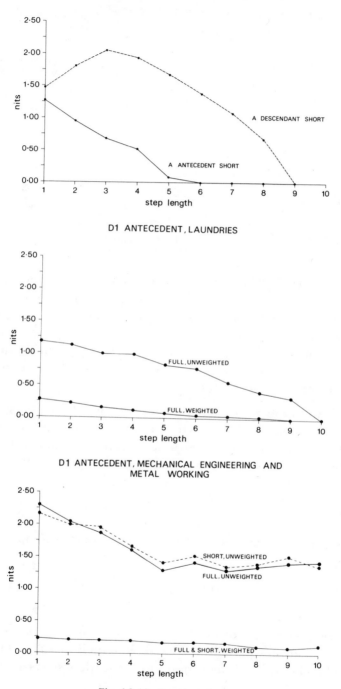

D1 ANTECEDENT, LAUNDRIES

D1 ANTECEDENT, MECHANICAL ENGINEERING AND
METAL WORKING

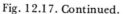

Fig. 12.17. Continued.

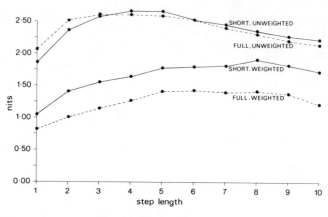

Fig. 12.17. Continued.

cases it decreases. This is explicable in terms of the rather small data set used. Since there are progressively fewer and fewer objects which have connections of the greater and greater number of steps, then the estimates of the frequency of contacted business types becomes biased more and more in favour of a few types. This effect unfortunately negates some of the value of the study, and can only be cured by using a much larger data set.

(ii) Two of the more common industries have had individual graphs prepared in Fig. 12.17. The extra terminology to be explained here merely concerns the words weighted and unweighted. It will be recalled that for the ith business type we can compute an entropy

$$H_i(j) = \sum_j \frac{P_{ij}}{P_i} \log \frac{P_i.}{P_{ij}} \qquad (12.10)$$

and that for the whole set of business types we may compute the overall entropy

$$H_i(j) = p_i . \sum_j \frac{p_{ij}}{p_i.} \log \frac{p_i.}{p_{ij}} \qquad (12.11)$$

In these diagrams the unweighted term is the entropy of that business type's redundancy pattern, the weighted term is that term multiplied as in (12.11) to give the contribution of the ith business activity to the total figure. It can be seen that the contribution of the mechanical, engineering and metal-working industries is small compared with the contribution of the laundries.

In weighted form the descendants of the laundries show the continuously increasing redundancy that one would expect, and the same pattern is observable at least for the first five steps of the unweighted form.

Again, in both the laundry and the engineering cases, the A cases give better results than the D1 cases. In the case of the laundries, however, a word of caution is necessary. There are very few laundries with any antecedents in the data set — hence the A antecedent case is giving suspect results; and in the case of the A descendants there are few laundries with more than four or five successors at the same location.

(iii) In the set of maps shown in Fig. 12.18 I have plotted a number of objects at their locations and with their dates. The other shaded locations then represent those locations which were contracted from the initial object up until 1972 according to the D1 descendant rules.

Obviously, given the length of time involved, the spread of "effects" seems very small. Very few patterns spread even beyond their own street. The same kind of restricted spatial contacts also appear from the converse case of the D1 antecedents. Nearly all recent businesses had antecedents within a very short range.

None of this appears to be very "real", in that we know that businesses in these streets would have been affected by other activities spread over an area certainly measured at the least in miles. Such longer-range influences are not calculated in our generative rules of contact in time-space, although from the data it is possible to find related business concerns operating several streets apart. This clearly reflects on the considerable problems of defining nearness in the time-space continuum.

(iv) Overall, the results show that space, in the way that it has been introduced in this study, is not informative. History alone is much more informative. It may be objected that that is not basically true, that it is the fault of the way that space has been introduced. But, on the other hand, how is it to be introduced? I rather imagine that the only satisfactory way of involving space in such an analysis is by some kind of potential map of related business concerns and market opportunities. Then clearly the spatial scale of the problem changes, to the idea of this as one area within London. But that just proves the point anyway — at the micro-scale there is no point in looking for any pattern in the loca-

1907-1940

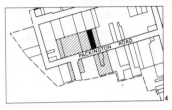
1927-1929

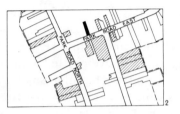
1907-1972

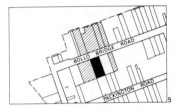
1910-1931

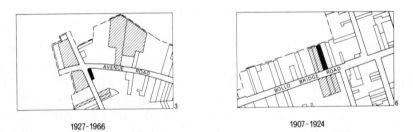

1927-1966   1907-1924

Fig. 12.18. Maps of contact patterns in Acton.

tion of the shops and business in the streets of Acton, for the simple reason that there is no real pattern in the sense of a pattern with a discoverable order in it.

To put it another way — we have considered before the concept of a complexion in a landscape, and we have said that an organized landscape occurs when the ensemble of the complexions is considerably reduced. In this case there is no evidence to suggest a small ensemble of complexions: the little amount of spatial redundancy suggests that any arrangement in space is as good as any other, and will work just as well. Of the many possible alternative landscapes, most would be as good, and could have happened just as easily.

12.4 Regulation in Indian farming

(a) Technical

We can suggest a very simple model of the functioning socio-economic landscape of an agricultural area. This landscape might be seen visually as a continuum surface. For example a rice-producing landscape at the time of plant growth suggests a continuing area much greater than any individual farm which is given to the production of rice. But in reality, it is composed of many units, the farms, each of which is controlled by a separate decision maker, the farmer. The landscape is not continuous, but is composed of a whole set of subsystems operating within and linked to, a wider system. We can see this when we consider the problems of villages within India. These are often classified as backward, or advanced, and yet within each village the problems of crop production are not the responsibility of the village but of the individual farmers, some of whom may be advanced, some backward. In fact present literature on village India often suggests that the villages are not wholes, but are divided within themselves by religion, caste, and factions. Therefore we identify the individual farmer as the prime decision maker within the agricultural system of any area.

The farmer is faced with a total operating environment which may be thought of as comprising two parts: the physical environment which affects his crops, and the human environment, often simplified to the economic environment, which provides him with the opportunity of acquiring inputs and the opportunity for disposing of any surplus product. Neither of these is known to him completely, and they therefore provide a continuous source of uncertainty to which he has to respond in some fashion (even if his response is, "do nothing").
Within a traditionally largely self-sufficient agricultural sector as in India the importance of the physical environment may be seen as being greater than the importance of the human environment. As a country develops, the importance of market factors increases, and the proportion of a farmer's production which enters into an exchange mechanism also increases.

The farmer operates within these two environments, and is aware to a given degree of the factors that can affect his operational ability, and the responses that are open to him. Within this context he makes his decisions. He decides which crop or which crop combination, or even combination of animals and crops, to grow on his farm, in the light of this expectation. However, for the purposes of this study we have proceeded to the next stage, where we have assumed that this decision has already been made, and that the farmers are all going to grow rice. Yet, even when this decision has been made there are further management decisions to make during the course of crop growth, whether to irrigate or not, whether to spray or not. Such decisions are made in response to the actions of the environment and the state of the crop. However, both the actions of the environment and the state of the crop are very much personal assessments by individual farmers, based on their experience of weather conditions affecting their crops, and on their own expectation of their crops.

The problem can be seen as one of management with a defined objective and defined disturbance and responses. The farmer may decide, where it is possible for him to do so, to intervene between the environment and the crop to stop the former transmitting disturbances to the latter. If there is a drought, then by irrigating the crop he can stop the crop "sensing" the drought. Farmers and their equipment can constitute a regulator, in the sense defined in Chapter 6.

The aim of this study is to make a quantitative assessment of the farmers' capacity to regulate. This measurement is dependent on the farmers' own definitions of environmental variability and their own expectations of crop yields. (These yields are in fact the "central" variable in the presentation of data for analysis.)

The measurements that are derived should ultimately be useful in comparing farmers with different crops and in different regions, even to the extent of making meaningful comparisons between the performance of farmers in for example India and the United Kingdom.

In the particular example outlined here no data have been collected on the human environment. This limitation was necessary to restrict this pilot study to reasonable proportions, and it was decided that the physical environment is probably still of greater importance for farmers in the study area of South Bihar, where the great bulk of production is for home consumption.

We are concerned with a system where there are three principal information sources. These are: the physical environment, the farmer and the crop. These can be treated as information sources since each can be in a number of alternative states. These states may be summarized by appropriate vectors whose elements are the values of specified variables.

There is nothing to prevent us including the human environment in the model as well. Although this has not been used in the practical work, the theory of it is simple. In Fig. 12.19b S has been placed between the

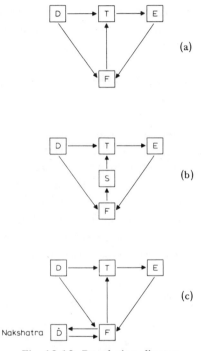

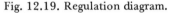

Fig. 12.19. Regulation diagram.

farmer and T. S then represents a regulator introduced by the human environment. Suppose a pest attack occurs and the farmer receives information about it (either from D or F) and he wishes to spray. However, S states that no sprays are available in the market, then R cannot actuate T to spray, so that S has blocked R's intended move.

We will now consider the actual method used in this study. The crop has a history as it grows. A sequence of disturbances and a sequence of responses may affect it. However, the matrix shown in Fig. 6.4 cannot portray a history, since it merely details a result for any combination of actions. It is of course possible to keep referring to the matrix as events occur to find out what happens to the crop, and in a rather restricted way, that is in fact what was done.

By questioning agricultural experts in the study area it was found that the crop had three significant growth stages, these being the period after germination, the middle growth period, and the flowering period. Every farmer was asked about his date of planting and of harvesting, and from these dates we can approximate the germination period, middle growth and flowering of his crop.

Three basic matrices are used. The first of these, the matrix for germination, is shown in Fig. 12.20a. The four actions of the environment with which the study is concerned are shown on the J axis. On the I axis are four possible responses of the farmer.

Figure 12.20b illustrates the second matrix, this time for the middle growth period. Again we note that the I axis has been subdivided to allow for the frequency distribution of transitions to the states a, b, and c, but we also note that the J axis has also been subdivided by the divisions a, b, and c. We remember that this second matrix is the second matrix in a three-stage history of plant growth, and that the first matrix has already been applied to determine plant transitions. The states to which the crop was transformed by the first matrix were the states a, b

| | | | Rain | | No rain | |
			No Pest	Pest	No Pest	Pest
No irrigation	No Spray	a	1.00	0.01	0.00	0.00
		b	0.00	0.29	0.72	0.03
		c	0.00	0.70	0.28	0.97
	Spray	a	1.00	0.25	0.00	0.03
		b	0.00	0.61	0.72	0.28
		c	0.00	0.14	0.28	0.68
Irrigation	No Spray	a	1.00	0.01	0.60	0.03
		b	0.00	0.30	0.37	0.28
		c	0.00	0.68	0.03	0.68
	Spray	a	1.00	0.27	0.60	0.42
		b	0.00	0.59	0.37	0.48
		c	0.00	0.14	0.03	0.10

(a)

Fig. 12.20. Transition matrices.

| | | | Rain | | | | | | No rain | | | | | |
| | | | No pest | | | Pest | | | No pest | | | Pest | | |
			a	b	c	a	b	c	a	b	c	a	b	c
No irrigation	No Spray	a	1.00	0.00	0.00	0.01	0.00	0.00	0.01	0.00	0.00	0.00	0.00	0.00
		b	0.00	1.00	0.00	0.24	0.10	0.00	0.68	0.20	0.00	0.13	0.01	0.00
		c	0.00	0.00	1.00	0.75	0.90	1.00	0.30	0.80	1.00	0.87	0.99	1.00
	Spray	a	1.00	0.00	0.00	0.16	0.01	0.00	0.01	0.00	0.00	0.02	0.00	0.00
		b	0.00	1.00	0.00	0.61	0.57	0.00	0.70	0.21	0.00	0.29	0.15	0.00
		c	0.00	0.00	1.00	0.23	0.42	1.00	0.29	0.79	1.00	0.68	0.85	1.00
Irrigation	No Spray	a	1.00	0.00	0.00	0.01	0.00	0.00	0.57	0.03	0.00	0.03	0.00	0.00
		b	0.00	1.00	0.00	0.25	0.11	0.00	0.37	0.74	0.00	0.34	0.15	0.00
		c	0.00	0.00	1.00	0.74	0.89	1.00	0.07	0.23	1.00	0.63	0.85	1.00
	Spray	a	1.00	0.00	0.00	0.16	0.01	0.00	0.58	0.03	0.00	0.38	0.02	0.00
		b	0.00	1.00	0.00	0.61	0.57	0.00	0.37	0.75	0.00	0.47	0.72	0.00
		c	0.00	0.00	1.00	0.23	0.42	1.00	0.05	0.22	1.00	0.15	0.26	1.00

(b)

| | | | Rain | | | | | | No rain | | | | | |
| | | | No pest | | | Pest | | | No pest | | | Pest | | |
			a	b	c	a	b	c	a	b	c	a	b	c
No irrigation	No Spray	a	1.00	0.00	0.00	0.04	0.00	0.00	0.04	0.00	0.00	0.01	0.00	0.00
		b	0.00	1.00	0.00	0.30	0.09	0.00	0.55	0.23	0.00	0.15	0.04	0.00
		c	0.00	0.00	1.00	0.65	0.91	1.00	0.40	0.77	1.00	0.84	0.96	1.00
	Spray	a	1.00	0.00	0.00	0.33	0.00	0.00	0.04	0.00	0.00	0.04	0.00	0.00
		b	0.00	1.00	0.00	0.47	0.53	0.00	0.55	0.25	0.00	0.36	0.17	0.00
		c	0.00	0.00	1.00	0.21	0.47	1.00	0.40	0.75	1.00	0.60	0.83	1.00
Irrigation	No Spray	a	1.00	0.00	0.00	0.04	0.00	0.00	0.53	0.03	0.00	0.12	0.00	0.00
		b	0.00	1.00	0.00	0.30	0.09	0.00	0.39	0.71	0.00	0.51	0.35	0.00
		c	0.00	0.00	1.00	0.65	0.91	1.00	0.08	0.26	1.00	0.37	0.65	1.00
	Spray	a	1.00	0.00	0.00	0.33	0.00	0.00	0.53	0.03	0.00	0.50	0.08	0.00
		b	0.00	1.00	0.00	0.48	0.53	0.00	0.39	0.73	0.00	0.37	0.67	0.00
		c	0.00	0.00	1.00	0.20	0.47	1.00	0.08	0.24	1.00	0.13	0.25	1.00

(c)

Fig. 12.20. Continued.

and c. Thus at the start of the middle growth period we have to make allowance for the fact that the crop may already be in a less desirable state than state a. We have in fact a simple demonstration of error-controlled feedback, but we also note that from the farmer's point of view the state of the environment and the state of the crop form a composite state (on the same axis in the matrix) which is the disturbance against which he is reacting. It might seem strange that the present state of the crop is part of the "environment" of the crop, but obviously in such a model as this the definitions are devised according to the concepts involved in calculation. However, there is still a simple explanation of why the two aspects, crop state and environment, should be on the same axis. The present crop state is an information source, which is in fact a "memory" — a memory, that is, of previous disturbances and the farmer's actions.

The third matrix (Fig. 12.20c) has the same form as the second, and no further comment is needed here on what it looks like. However, it is wise to remember that the third matrix will lead to the final state of the crops after applying the first and second stages, so that it is only after applying the third that we have an "end result" embodying the legacy of the history of growth.

We will now comment on the exact data required. First consider the germination matrix of Fig. 12.20a, and look at the axis for the environment. We need frequency estimates of the occurrence of the four states concerned. Firstly we need to know the frequency of drought.

Drought is not solely a property of the environment, but a property of the environment in relation to the requirements of a plant, and these requirements themselves are not defined solely by a plant, but by a farmer's expectation of his plant. Thus the same climatic environment can represent completely different disturbance patterns to two neighbouring farmers growing the same crop. For the purposes of this study drought is defined as some number of consecutive days without rain. The farmer is asked to state how many days without rain will harm his crop, and to which state it will go in such an event. Ideally, we should be more crop- and state-orientated than that. The states of the crops are defined by the farmer in terms of yields, so that we know what each farmer considers an a, b and c state to be. Having discovered this we should in fact ask for three drought figures, those which will send a crop to b from an a, to c from an a, and to c from a b. This refinement was not incorporated in the pilot study. Note that figures of 1.00 are recorded in the transition matrix. These appear under the best conditions, and would seem to be suspicious. However, they result by definition, since for any farmer the environmental state "no pest — no drought" is defined by him as that state which causes no harm to his crop.

Having discussed the farmers' definitions of drought, these figures are compared with daily climatic data for, in our case, a 15-year period. From this we can assess the frequency of drought that farmers will face given their definitions of drought, in each of the three growth periods. (The definitions of drought are defined by the farmers for these three periods separately.)

In a similar way the farmers are asked about the frequency of pest attacks under two conditions, one is of sufficient rainfall, and the other is drought. We then have the data required for the calculation of the marginal environmental frequencies.

$$P(R) = 1 - P(D)$$
$$P(R,P) = P(R)P_R(P)$$
$$P(R,NP) = P(R) - P(R,P)$$
$$P(D,P) = P(D)P_D(P)$$
$$P(D,NP) = P(D) - P(D,P)$$

Where: $P(D)$ is the probability of drought and calculated by comparing drought definitions with climatic data; $P(R)$ is the probability of rain (i.e. no drought) and is calculated; $P(R,P)$ is the probability of rain and pest together, and is calculated from $P(R)$ and $P_R(P)$ which is the conditional probability of pest given rain (taken from the data); $P(R,NP)$ is the probability of rain and no pest, calculated from the previous values; $P(D,P)$ is the probability of drought and pest, and is taken from $P(D)$ and $P_D(P)$ which is the conditional probability of pest given drought (from the data); and $P(D,NP)$ is the probability of drought and no pest. The four marginal probabilities of the J axis are: $P(R,NP)$, $P(R,P)$, $P(D,NP)$, and $P(D,P)$ which sum to unity.

Given that these are the conditions that can occur, we have to observe how the farmers will respond to them. Not all farmers can spray, nor can all irrigate. Therefore we ask the farmers what they can do and whether they do so for each of the environmental states. From these data we can derive a reaction matrix. Such a matrix is illustrated in Fig. 12.21. For each of the four environmental states we have a frequency distribution against the four possible responses of the farmer, where in each column the sum of frequencies adds to one, so that all farmers have in fact responded.

For each of three periods we now have three sets of data. These sets are the transition frequency matrix (Figs 12.2a, b, and c), the vector of probability of environmental disturbance (the probabilities $P(R,NP)$, $P(R,P)$, $P(D,NP)$, $P(D,P)$ which are calculated separately for each of

ENVIRONMENT

		Rain		No rain	
		No Pest	Pest	No Pest	Pest
FARMER	No Spray No Irrigation	1.00	0.84	0.93	0.83
	Spray No Irrigation	0.00	0.16	0.00	0.11
	No Spray Irrigation	0.00	0.00	0.07	0.01
	Spray Irrigation	0.00	0.00	0.00	0.05

Fig. 12.21. Reaction matrix.

the three periods), and the reaction matrix (Fig. 12.21). The same Reaction Matrix is used in this example for all three periods, and is based
on the equipment that the farmers have, i.e. those who have said that
they can irrigate are assumed to irrigate during each drought which is
calculated to occur in the vector of probability of environmental
disturbance.

For each period all three of these data sets are combined to make one
matrix, in exactly the same way as in Chapter 6. After the derivation of
the germination period terminal state of crops, the terminal values,
which sum to one, will be multiplied with the four elements of the next
Vector of Probability of Environmental Disturbance, to make a frequency vector of 12 elements, which will be used in conjunction with
the Middle Growth Period Transition Frequency Matrix and the Reaction
matrix to derive the Middle Growth period terminal crop states.

For each of the three periods we now have in one matrix the results
of the combined effects of the environmental disturbance, the farmers'
regulation, and the transition frequency. We can suggest a remodelling
and re-phrasing of Fig. 12.19 as shown in Fig. 12.22. In Fig. 12.22 D is
now the Vector of Probability of Environmental Disturbance. R is now
the Reaction Matrix, T is the Transition matrix, and E is the Resultant
matrix. In Fig. 12.22b the situation at the beginning of the Middle
Growth period is indicated, now with a link from the Germination Stage
Resultant Matrix to the Environmental Disturbance matrix, instead of
direct to the farmers' reaction matrix. The three Resultant Matrices are
shown in Fig. 12.23.

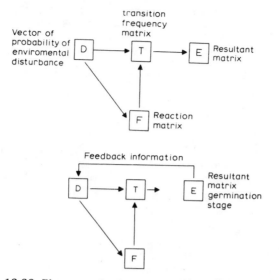

Fig. 12.22. Elements of calculation and regulation diagram.

We now wish to analyse the Resultant matrices to see what they can tell us about regulation. It soon becomes apparent that we need some measure of uncertainty. The environment can be in one of four states, but the importance of regulation increases if the uncertainty increases as to which of the four states will occur. If for 99% of the time there is no

				Rain		No rain	
				No Pest	Pest	No Pest	Pest
No irrigation	No Spray	a		0·75	0·00	0·00	0·00
		b		0·00	0·01	0·13	0·00
		c		0·00	0·03	0·05	0·00
	Spray	a		0·00	0·00	0·00	0·00
		b		0·00	0·01	0·00	0·00
		c		0·00	0·00	0·00	0·00
Irrigation	No Spray	a		0·00	0·00	0·01	0·00
		b		0·00	0·00	0·00	0·00
		c		0·00	0·00	0·00	0·00
	Spray	a		0·00	0·00	0·00	0·00
		b		0·00	0·00	0·00	0·00
		c		0·00	0·00	0·00	0·00

(a)

Fig. 12.23. Resultant matrices for farmers in Pihar, (a) after germination.

			Rain						No rain					
			No pest			Pest			No pest			Pest		
			a	b	c	a	b	c	a	b	c	a	b	c
No irrigation	No Spray	a	0.40	0.00	0.00	0.00	0.00	0.00	0.00	0.00	0.00	0.00	0.00	0.00
		b	0.00	0.08	0.00	0.04	0.00	0.00	0.09	0.01	0.00	0.00	0.00	0.00
		c	0.00	0.00	0.05	0.13	0.03	0.02	0.04	0.02	0.02	0.01	0.00	0.00
	Spray	a	0.00	0.00	0.00	0.01	0.00	0.00	0.00	0.00	0.00	0.00	0.00	0.00
		b	0.00	0.00	0.00	0.02	0.00	0.00	0.00	0.00	0.00	0.00	0.00	0.00
		c	0.00	0.00	0.00	0.01	0.00	0.00	0.00	0.00	0.00	0.00	0.00	0.00
Irrigation	No Spray	a	0.00	0.00	0.00	0.00	0.00	0.00	0.01	0.00	0.00	0.00	0.00	0.00
		b	0.00	0.00	0.00	0.00	0.00	0.00	0.00	0.00	0.00	0.00	0.00	0.00
		c	0.00	0.00	0.00	0.00	0.00	0.00	0.00	0.00	0.00	0.00	0.00	0.00
	Spray	a	0.00	0.00	0.00	0.00	0.00	0.00	0.00	0.00	0.00	0.00	0.00	0.00
		b	0.00	0.00	0.00	0.00	0.00	0.00	0.00	0.00	0.00	0.00	0.00	0.00
		c	0.00	0.00	0.00	0.00	0.00	0.00	0.00	0.00	0.00	0.00	0.00	0.00

			Rain						No rain					
			No pest			Pest			No pest			Pest		
			a	b	c	a	b	c	a	b	c	a	b	c
No irrigation	No Spray	a	0.07	0.00	0.00	0.00	0.00	0.00	0.01	0.00	0.00	0.00	0.00	0.00
		b	0.00	0.04	0.00	0.00	0.00	0.00	0.17	0.04	0.00	0.00	0.00	0.00
		c	0.00	0.00	0.05	0.00	0.00	0.01	0.12	0.14	0.24	0.01	0.01	0.01
	Spray	a	0.00	0.00	0.00	0.00	0.00	0.00	0.00	0.00	0.00	0.00	0.00	0.00
		b	0.00	0.00	0.00	0.00	0.00	0.00	0.00	0.00	0.00	0.00	0.00	0.00
		c	0.00	0.00	0.00	0.00	0.00	0.00	0.00	0.00	0.00	0.00	0.00	0.00
Irrigation	No Spray	a	0.00	0.00	0.00	0.00	0.00	0.00	0.01	0.00	0.00	0.00	0.00	0.00
		b	0.00	0.00	0.00	0.00	0.00	0.00	0.01	0.01	0.00	0.00	0.00	0.00
		c	0.00	0.00	0.00	0.00	0.00	0.00	0.00	0.00	0.02	0.00	0.00	0.00
	Spray	a	0.00	0.00	0.00	0.00	0.00	0.00	0.00	0.00	0.00	0.00	0.00	0.00
		b	0.00	0.00	0.00	0.00	0.00	0.00	0.00	0.00	0.00	0.00	0.00	0.00
		c	0.00	0.00	0.00	0.00	0.00	0.00	0.00	0.00	0.00	0.00	0.00	0.00

Fig. 12.23. Continued, (b) after middle growth, (c) after flowering.

drought and no pest attacks, then the uncertainty of the environment is slight, and on the whole it probably pays a farmer to do nothing. If for 99% of the time there is both drought and pest attack, then the farmer can indulge in a modified environment of the type seen in the acres of glasshouses in the Lea Valley in London. He irrigates all the time, and he always uses preventive sprays, in what may be called a "blanket response". A Game Theory solution is in fact a blanket response.

Similarly we wish to curtail the uncertainty of the final crop state. It is assumed that the farmers wish to achieve an a state as often as possible, and that a distribution of final states with great uncertainty indicates that they have failed to block the uncertainty transmitted from the environment.

Finally we wish to know the uncertainty of the farmers' actions. This may sound a strange concept. However, if the farmer's response is certain, what we mean is that he lacks flexibility. If for example it is certain that he will do nothing, we assume he is unable to irrigate or spray when it is necessary for him to do so. Except in those conditions where the farmer creates a new environment, as with a blanket response where he is in fact not regulating against the environment but creating a new one, a constant response such as continuous irrigation can be harmful. (Although paddy often grows standing in water the height of the water is critical: the crop can be drowned.) Another limiting condition on a blanket response, though not one which enters explicitly in this study, is that it is economic nonsense to indulge in regulatory activity which is not needed.

Using data from the resultant matrices we can then calculate the following values:

$$H(D) = \sum_j p_{.j.} \log \frac{1}{p_{.j.}}$$

$$H(E) = \sum_k p_{..k} \log \frac{1}{p_{..k}}$$

$$H_E(R) = \sum_k \sum_i p_{i.k} \log \frac{p_{..k}}{p_{i.k}}$$

$$H_D(R) = \sum_j \sum_i p_{ij.} \log \frac{p_{.j.}}{p_{ij.}}$$

$$H_{DR}(E) = \sum_i \sum_j \sum_k p_{ijk} \log \frac{p_{ij.}}{p_{ijk}}$$

$$H_{RE}(D) = \sum_i \sum_j \sum_k p_{ijk} \log \frac{p_{i.k}}{p_{ijk}}$$

In all these formulae the dot . refers to summation over the index that is replaced. For example:

$$p_{.jk} = \sum_{i} p_{ijk}$$

The various H values represent the following:

$H(D)$ is the uncertainty in the environment.

$H(E)$ is the uncertainty of the outcome.

$H_E(R)$ is the uncertainty in the farmers' effective responses.

$H_D(R)$ is the accuracy of the farmer's response to D.

$H_{RE}(D)$ is the uncertainty in the environment given that we know which move the farmer has made and which outcome results, and is a measure of equivocation.

$H_{DR}(E)$ is the uncertainty in the outcome given that we know both the state of D and the farmers' responses, and is a noise term.

There remains only one further theoretical problem that needs to be clarified, and this is the problem of aggregation. It will be seen that all the farmers contribute in each period to the transition frequency matrix. That is, we have pooled the results at each stage, and assumed that the answers in terms of a, b and c frequencies are representative of the a, b and c frequencies which all farmers might face at the end of the first stage, although the a, b and c refer to different yields in absolute terms from farmer to farmer. The reason this pooling has occurred is that we need transition frequencies. If we were to choose to make a transition history for each farmer separately, then each farmer, having answered only one question for each transition from a given D state with a given R response, will have an $H_{DR}(E)$ of zero, that is the answer will be deterministic. This is an unreasonable assumption, and the only way to avoid it in practice, so as to avoid the very real conceptual problems of aggregation, would be to observe the same farmer on many different occasions with the same D and F states. In other words we would need more information.

In practice some disaggregation does occur, with the splitting of the total group of farmers firstly into tribal and non-tribal farmers, and secondly into large and small farmers.

(b) The study area

The study area lies in the hilly country of South Bihar, around the city of Ranchi. Geologically the area is rather old, although younger igneous rocks have been intruded into the surface rocks. These have formed great domes of rock, which have in places been exposed and exfoliated to dot the landscape with the little rock mountains that are the hallmark of the region. More significantly this kind of rock formation continues below the surface deposits, forming many impervious rock basins where ground water collects. The region suffers drought periodically, but there are no large surface-water reserves for canal and ditch irrigation, nor is the terrain, uneven as it is, suitable for a supply network from a major scheme. The only source is the ground water, which may be exploited through conventional wells, or tube wells. The problem is that the hard bed-rock subsurface is unpredictable, and before a well is sunk there is no way of knowing whether it will hit a rock peak near the surface, or sink into a reservoir of suitable size. Local people constructing conventional wells have no idea when they begin to dig of whether they will or will not reach an adequate supply of water at a reasonable depth.

The area is also interesting from a sociological and anthropological point of view. It is peopled by Biharis, and by Adivasis, the tribal non-Hindu indigenous people of the area who have survived with their own non-Sanskritic languages. Many of these have been converted by both Catholic and Protestant missionaries to the Christian faith, so that the tribes are not only divided by language, but also by religion (their own religions are animist, in some areas currently with Hindu embellishments). The area also have a significant number of Muslims who are, however, mostly urban or in urban-orientated villages.

No matter what ethnic origin or what faith, the majority of farmers devote most of their land to rice production, initially for their own consumption.

The area is intrinsically interesting for the study proposed here. There are opportunities to contrast the abilities of tribal and non-tribal farmers, the former being held in low general esteem by the Bihari population, and to some extent we can attempt to measure whether this contempt is justified. Additionally there is the question of providing irrigation. The cost of such provision must be high and to some extent uncertain, but after a sufficient number of drilling attempts, no doubt it would be possible to give a statistically likely cost of providing various percentages of irrigated areas within the total farmed area. The question on the other side then revolves around the likely benefits. It is here that the present study can be adapted for simulating likely returns as they are perceived by the farmers, and this must be crucial in any argument, since it is they who in the end will have to pay back the credit which might be made available. Obviously, to assess the likely benefits one simply changes the frequencies of irrigation responses in time of drought within the three successive matrices used.

About 110 farmers were interviewed, but checking of the question-naires showed some to be incomplete, and others to be inconsistent. In the end 92 were accepted for incorporation into the analysis. Of the 92 farmers, 42 were tribal. In addition 23 were classed as large farmers, in this context meaning that they had more than 10 acres of land. In general they seemed quite happy with the quality of the land, although on a state-wide basis this is not a particularly renowned soil region.

(c) Results of the pilot study

The various uncertainty values required for discussion and analysis are shown in Table 12.V, each such value being shown by stages for the whole set of farmers, and for two cases where the whole set has been divided into two subsets, firstly tribal and non-tribal, and secondly large and small farmers. If one considers $H(D)$ for a moment one important factor is made clear. The values for $H(D)$ for both the middle period and the flowering state (completed history of growth) are much higher than those for the germination period. This is because in the first stage the environment has only four possible states, whereas in the next two stages it has four possible states, where the crop state from the previous period has been incorporated into the uncertainty against which the farmer regulates. The maximum value possible for $H(D)$ in nits for four stages is $\ln 4 = 1.38629$. For 12 states the maximum value is $\ln 12 = 2.4891$. The increase in uncertainty of D is therefore in great part a measure of the inclusion of feedback information.

The H values refer to the various states of components in the informa-tion system which has been modelled around the growth history of the rice crop. It is pertinent, therefore, before discussing the H values to have some general background on the history of plant transitions for the set of farmers and the four subsets. The histories are plotted in Fig. 12.3 which represents the distribution of outcomes a, b and c at the end of

Table 12.V

	$H(E) =$	$H(D)^*$	$-$	$H(R)^*$	$+$	$H_{DR}(E)$
	$H(E) =$	$(H(D) - H_{RE}(D))$	$-$	$(H_E(R) - H_D(R))$	$+$	$H_{DR}(E)$

GERMINATION

Complete	0.7062 =	0.5898	−	0.0404	+	0.1568
	0.7062 =	(0.7018 − 0.1120)	−	(0.1120 − 0.0716)	+	0.1568
Tribal	0.8081 =	0.6381	−	0.0253	+	0.1953
	0.8081 =	(0.7780 − 0.1399)	−	(0.0776 − 0.0523)	+	0.1953
Non-Tribal	0.6063 =	0.5358	−	0.0482	+	0.1187
	0.6063 =	(0.6163 − 0.0805)	−	(0.1224 − 0.0742)	+	0.1187
Large	0.4476 =	0.4083	−	0.0470	+	0.0863
	0.4476 =	(0.4233 − 0.0150)	−	(0.1118 − 0.0648)	+	0.0863
Small	0.7717 =	0.6242	−	0.0282	+	0.1757
	0.7717 =	(0.7547 − 0.1305)	−	(0.0831 − 0.0549)	+	0.1757

MIDDLE GROWTH

Complete	1.0793 =	0.8786	−	0.0698	+	0.2705
	1.0793 =	(1.7646 − 0.8860)	−	(0.2424 − 0.1726)	+	0.2705
Tribal	1.0820 =	0.8853	−	0.0419	+	0.2385
	1.0820 =	(1.7899 − 0.9146)	−	(0.1548 − 0.1129)	+	0.2385
Non-Tribal	1.0766 =	0.8774	−	0.0931	+	0.2923
	1.0766 =	(1.7070 − 0.8296)	−	(0.3127 − 1.2196)	+	0.2923
Large	0.9900 =	0.8535	−	0.1234	+	0.2599
	0.9900 =	(1.4358 − 0.5823)	−	(0.3346 − 0.2112)	+	0.2599
Small	1.0912 =	0.8720	−	0.0485	+	0.2677
	1.0912 =	(1.8306 − 0.9586)	−	(0.1892 − 0.1407)	+	0.2677

FLOWERING

Complete	0.8680 =	0.4997	−	0.0329	+	0.4012
	0.8680 =	(1.7592 − 1.2595)	−	(0.2520 − 0.2191)	+	0.4012
Tribal	0.8259 =	0.4391	−	0.0237	+	0.4105
	0.8259 =	(1.7666 − 1.3275)	−	(0.1383 − 0.1146)	+	0.4105
Non-Tribal	0.8992 =	0.5560	−	0.0407	+	0.3839
	0.8992 =	(1.7634 − 1.2074)	−	(0.3262 − 0.2855)	+	0.3839
Large	0.9804 =	0.6037	−	0.0778	+	0.4545
	0.9804 =	(1.7450 − 1.1413)	−	(0.4582 − 0.3804)	+	0.4545
Small	0.8233 =	0.4638	−	0.0338	+	0.3823
	0.8233 =	(1.7505 − 1.2867)	−	(0.1532 − 0.1304)	+	0.3823

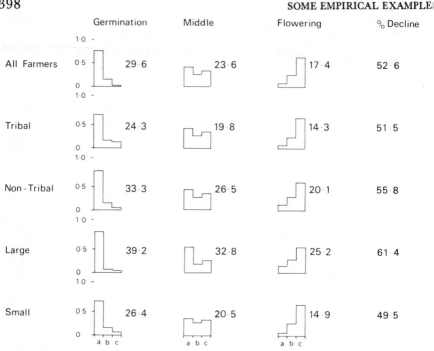

Fig. 12.24. Histograms of predicted yields.

each stage. At the end of the germination period the non-tribal farmer have a greater frequency of *as* and a smaller frequency of *cs* than the tribal, and similarly, the large farmers have a greater frequency of *as* and a smaller frequency of both *bs* and *cs* than the small farmers. Given the initial potential of staying at *a* throughout, the non-tribal farmers and the large farmers have both lost less ground.

The difference between the tribal and non-tribal farmers is not so apparent at the end of the middle stage, but the difference between the small farmers and the large farmers is marked, the former having lost far more potential yield. By the end of the last period the tribal farmers have more *cs* and fewer *as* than the non-tribal ones, and the large farmer similarly have more *as* and fewer *cs* than the small farmers.

However, one point is well worth noting. It was said earlier that we were seeking to minimize the uncertainty in the outcomes of the crops, that is to say to maintain as many at *a* as possible. We now come across one of the crucial problems of information theory which we mentioned in Chapter 8. Information theory can give us a measure of the uncertain in a set of states. All that is necessary is that the states be different. No value-ordering of the states is implied whatsoever. However, in our case we have defined the states according to a value-ordering of probable yields. That is to say, c is less desirable than a. Information theory does not recognize this semantic problem and so we find in analysing the value of $H(E)$ for the last two periods, in all cases except that of the large farmers that $H(E)$ actually decreases between stages 2 and 3. In other words, the uncertainty of outcome is less in the last stage than in the previous stage. The reason for this is that by then the crop has gone "over the hump" of uncertainty, and is progressively more and more certainly a c crop. We are becoming as sure of ending with a c as we were with starting with an a.

In our case the answer to the problem might be to weight the final uncertainty value by some figure of the average yield, but there is no rigid methodology for saying which weighting we should use.

To return to $H(D)$, there are some results which are unexpected. It was assumed that the more successful farmers, who on an analysis of Fig. 12.24 would seem to be the non-tribal and the large farmers, would be more perceptive of their environment, and would see more disturbance and act more against it than the other farmers. However, these two groups have the lowest uncertainty value in the environment even at the first stage. At the second two stages it may be more understandable, in that if their crops have suffered less in the first stage the feedback component of uncertainty at the next two stages would be lower than for others. Since $H(E)$ is in fact low for large and non-tribal farmers at the end of the first stage, their feedback component at the next stage will be low. At the time of writing the exact reason why the uncertainty in the environment should be less for these farmers is not known. The distribution of $p_{.j}$ for the first period shows that they suffer less drought, and also fewer insect attacks, although the latter effect might be as a result of the small statistical sample, particularly for the large farmers. The ideas that will be investigated are that they use more drought and pest-resistant varieties of rice, or that they plant at better times, thus avoiding early drought.

An analysis of $H(R)^*$ is simple. Those farmers who regulate most are the large farmers and the non-tribal farmers, and as in the later stages the regulation increases then the regulation by these two groups increases far more rapidly than for the other groups. In fact, the tribal and small farmers actually record a decrease in regulation in the last period, presumably not only because their ability to respond is more limited than the others, but also because by the start of the last stage more of their crops are at state c, irrecoverably beyond regulation. But more than any thing else, in all cases the amount of regulation achieved is very small, and it is clear that the environment $H(D)^*$ accounts for most of $H(E)$.

$H_{DR}(E)$ records the variation in outcomes, given which D and R have occurred. It measures how deterministic the outcomes are, given the variables we have chosen to use, in other words how good the variables (choice of states for D and R) are in a predictive sense. In the first stage large farmers have the most predictive outcomes, but by the last stage they have the least predictive outcomes. It is not known whether it will be possible to give an exact reason for this, since after all this is a measur of missing information. All we know is that as the history of the crop lengthens, then increasingly there are more factors we should take into account than we do (which is reasonable enough), and that we should d this most for the large farmers, who might perhaps be those who have greatest variation in farming technique.

$H_{RE}(D)$ measures the amount of information in D that cannot be transmitted to E. This quantity is initially small, but does increase greatly (in most cases by a factor greater than 4) as the growth progresses. Obviously we should expect this, since in the last two stages we have moved from 4 to 12 environmental states, while we still have only three states of the crop to which these 12 states can transmit information. The large farmers start and end with the smallest values. Perhaps because the small farmers regulate less than the large, there is more chance that environmental disturbances will be transmitted but more of the "potential" disturbance is blocked by the choice of only three resultant states.

The last comment on the results belongs to the prediction of final yields. We know the definition of a, b and c yields for each farmer in terms of maunds per acre. Simple averaging enables us to give the mean estimates of yields in each crop state for the various groups of farmers as shown in Table 12.VI. We see yet again that large farmers have higher expectations than small farmers, and that non-tribal farmers have higher expectations than tribal farmers. These figures are then used to ascertain the likely expected yield of the crop based on the distribution of crop states at each stage of growth. The mean a, b and c yield figures in each group are multiplied by the respective a, b and c frequencies, and the resultants added — in other words we derive a weighted mean figure.

Table 12.VI

Means of stated crop yields in mounds per acre of
best, average and worst yields

Farmer group	Best (a)	Means yields Average (b)	Worst (c)
All farmers	33	22	13
Tribal farmers	28	19	11
Non-tribal farmers	36	25	15
Large farmers	41	29	19
Small farmers	30	20	11

These figures are plotted with the histograms in Fig. 12.24. As expected the smaller farmers and the tribal farmers have the worst predicted resultant yield. However, when the final resultant yield is expressed as a percentage of the best yield (the assumed starting point for each group) we also find that tribal and small farmers in relative as well as absolute terms move further away from the desired target. This merely confirms what we know from the analysis of $H(R)$ values, namely, that they regulate less than the other groups.

It would be quite possible with this model to change the regulatory capacity of the farmers and assess the impact on final yields. Its uses therefore extend beyond a quantitative assessment of the farmers at present to the testing of policy implications for planners. However, it might be possible to improve it further by using it with actual rather than perceived values. In the present study, although few farmers have experience of irrigation or sprays, they are nevertheless asked about the likely crop transitions when these are used. To measure their perception of advantage is itself important, but side by side with this data we should ideally collect observations on what actually does happen under these varying conditions. This would have necessitated a field organization beyond the capacity of this study, but hopefully the value of doing so in the future has been demonstrated.

The results of using such a model for simulation would be more useful for policy testing. However the difference between such a model and the present one based on perceived advantage could show a great deal about the accuracy of perception and the requirement for agricultural education through demonstration and extension services.

(d) Conclusions

It is believed that this study has achieved the aims set for it. It has shown that it is possible to define separate decision units and the process whereby regulation is achieved, to maintain as far as possible some target variables within given bounds. The sources of variation in this process are defined in quantitative terms of useful generality. A similar study in Britain, for example, could show the variation in the environment which farmers there perceive, and the amount of regulation against it, in terms that would be comparable with the present study of Indian farmers.

In specific terms the results suggest (though since the sample is small the confidence of the results is not high) that there are differences between large and small farmers, between tribal and non-tribal farmers, in terms of their expectations of the benefits of regulation, and in the crop yields they are likely to obtain on the basis of their expectations.

The major problems of using the technique are concerned with the data-expensive nature of the model, and with careful interpretation of the results until such time as the problem of value-ordering of information states is unambiguously resolved.

13

Conclusions

I do not like writing conclusions. At the end of the book one has said what one wanted to, and the rest must seem something like repetition. Besides, some of the Preface was the conclusions. But, in the manner of the negro preacher who was asked how he preached, and who answered "I tells 'em what I'm gonna tell them, then I tells them, then I tells 'em what I told them", I feel I may be required to say what I said.

Mostly this is a book which represents a methodological position. It seems to me that academics go through life cycles, and one of their seven stages is that stage when they emerge from the comfortable cocoon of student learning to do some research themselves. At this stage they need to know what their own methodological position is: if they can take as given most of what they have just been taught, they simply spread their wings and take off. But some people take a little longer — perhaps they are just born sceptics, or perhaps there are real reasons why they feel the wings that academic evolution gave them are not good enough for flight. It seems to me that methodological statements by individuals are often made early in their academic life for this reason, and once they have got themselves sorted out, they then embark on some real research. I intend from this point on to concern myself less with this basic methodological position, and more with the development of its application.

But it has been a very necessary stage for me to go through, and one which I regret not in the least, even if the reader has.

One of the motivations for leaving these topics to do other things is quite simply the feeling that unlike many specialists, I have felt that I was beginning to know less and less about more and more, which is of course the classic description of the journalist as opposed to the expert. But I have felt it necessary to get some overall grasp of the complex problems of interdependence in studies of the kind that geography attempts. Interestingly enough, there is of course a defence for doing so that has at least some aura of trendy respectibility — namely General Systems Theory, mentioned for the first time in this book. I have never been persuaded of the value of what G.S.T. is trying to do, but I now find I have accidentally persuaded myself because it is what I have been doing. Hence, the book itself has become more and more ways of looking at systems, no matter their subject origin, and ways of thinking about systems, than a discussion of any particular system. The more that this has happened, the more I have come to realize that Von Bertalanffy is right in believing that science in general, and in this case geography, can learn enormously by seeking the isomorphisms between the systems studied by different disciplines. It does not really matter whether the gravity model in geography is a physical analogy or not, it just happens that in thermodynamics and geography we are confronted with an estimation problem that can be defined in similar terms based on general concepts like the amount of the observer's information.

Note again the clue laid bare by the word — the observer. In a real sense the unity of G.S.T. is not to be found in the towns and molecules that different subjects study, but in the way in which the observer structures his understanding of what he observes. The reason why we move up and down scales of analysis, using the same ideas, is that our focus of understanding has changed. The focus has to change because of the limits to the amount of information that we can absorb and use at each level.

In using the word "level" I have returned to the starting point of the book — the definition of "objects" as an act of entitation.

There will be some objections that I have proposed a definition of objects that is "too clean". The real world is not composed of objects as simply identified as I may have implied — but this does not invalidate the principles by which one attempts their definition. The significance o the boundary lies in the way in which it is impermeable to something or things: that is, we maximize the internal interconnections between the components of an object, and minimize the cross-boundary connections. This is essential to a behavioural and functional approach. Similarly, the

alert reader will have noticed that although I remark upon the usefulness
of the concept of control in defining objects, the justification for the
identification of a complex system does not rely upon the known existence of a control centre: the justification is in more general terms —
that is in the concepts of emergent behaviour and the constraint implied
by diminishing degrees of freedom.

In these concepts lies the rejection of the reductionist analysis, an
implicit and unconscious act that geographers now must bring out into
the open, on ground of their own choosing. Then we may understand
why the idea of systems has taken such a hard knocking over the years,
since the basic cause of the dissent is, I believe, easy to identify. The
triumph of rational thinking and experimental science has left a strong
imprint on the social sciences. It matters not so much what you know,
as how you know it. For the first triumphs of empirical science this was
no problem, since the observed phenomena belonged to the inanimate
realm, of, at the most, complex aggregates. Explanation could then
proceed at the level of an idealized individual. These same viewpoints
have been accepted by much of classical economics. The assumption of
perfect competition is basically a statement that any one firm has no
marginal impact on any other. That being the case, then it is possible to
conceptualise its behaviour in isolation, and the total behaviour of a set
of firms as a simple aggregation or multiplication of this individual
statement. But, in this situation, we begin to find that the framework of
theory is not compatible with the framework of observation. Intuitively
we observe complex wholes of interdependent parts which do not
exhibit behaviour that can be explained by a reductionist logic applied
to idealized components, and for a long time in this unhappy struggle
it has been the theoretical requirements which have triumphed. The inexplicable observation becomes inadmissable: the epistemology van-
quishes the ontology, the test of what you know becomes not just how
you know it, but how you can communicate it.

The geographers have found themselves trapped in a defensive position. Intuitively they feel that they know that such things as growth
poles do exist, that the behaviour of these poles is a result of complex
interaction, and that the whole is more than the sum of the parts.
Reference to external economies and urban economies in part assuages
the criticisms of those who need to have a detailed process model explained to them, who need to know the role of the individual firm in
reductionist fashion. But these references are not enough to defend

growth pole theory: indeed it becomes demoted to a loose assemblage of vague sub-concepts. A successful defence lies in applying new theoretical perspectives, and in denying the validity of applying the established logic of relata to these observations. This new perspective is for me systems theory, and for others structuralism. Its present demerit lies in the fact that the rigorous outline for its application is only now emerging. But the tightening of the necessary concepts of order, of emergence, of constraint and degrees of freedom, of arrangement, has begun.

It seems to me that a further fatal flaw in the reductionist attitude is that it fails to make a distinction between two kinds of predictive statements. The first kind of statement can be summarized, as "If an X meets a Y a Z happens", which is often obscured by a more lawful sounding generality "Xs and Ys interact to cause Zs". The great point is simply that these statements always rely on some kind of implied "if", and it is of course the hallmark of the experimental sciences to contrive those circumstances in which the "if" is true and the statement can be verified. In the great non-experimental world, we cannot take it for granted that the "if" will happen.

In predicting the state of the world tomorrow, we need to know not only those rules which state "If X and Y then Z", but also the basic factual information as to whether or not Xs will interact with Ys. We cannot predict the state of all oxygen and carbon molecules of the universe tomorrow from simple knowledge of the fact that if they are adjacent to each other at a high enough temperature they are rearranged and combined. The state of the universe tomorrow will depend upon how many of them meet in the defined circumstances.

Now it seems to me entirely plausible that an omniscient mind could know the whereabouts of each atom of the universe, and from knowledge of physical laws alone predict the state of the universe tomorrow. Even human behaviour could by such a mind be interpreted according to the physical interaction of atoms and molecules in the neurons of the brain. But, equally, I find it implausible that any human brain could contain all the information as to the whereabouts of all the atoms of the universe. In terms of crude calculations it seems quite obvious that the number of cells in one brain is so small that they could devise no coding system to store information about all the atoms in the universe. This being the case, there is no point in assuming that we can use physical law to predict any phenomenon of any scale.

If this is the case, then the higher the scale of the object we observe, the less of the detail of the lower scales we preserve. We observe at a high scale and then explain at a high scale; and in doing this we admit the necessity of the emergent properties which I have talked about in the main text not merely as some reality of behaviour but as a reality of our understanding of behaviour. In doing so we shall also admit the value of laws of a non-physical kind.

The operationalization of all these ideas is obviously not going to be easy. In the later parts of the book I have begun to delve into one of the more promising avenues — that of information theory and many allied cybernetic concepts. I realize that many readers of this book will not find the connections as immediate and obvious as I do: that is because I see in them the promise in the furure of hard answers to big questions, but to date only the laying of a few operational foundation stones like entropy-maximizing procedures. But the promise is enormous: within this text I have been able to give quantitative expression to such concepts as organization, loss of degrees of freedom, and uncertainty itself as a limit, and this is only the beginning. Increasingly it is becoming possible to derive by deduction new information concepts that can guide the crystallization of intuitive ideas. We are beginning to find a theoretical perspective of precision and power to match the level of empirical observation.

At this stage I am now encroaching on material which I have come across since writing the main text, but I wish to make reference to it here for obvious reasons. Conant (1976) has been able to show by pure deduction using information concepts the kinds of relationships which have been observed in complex systems. I hope the reader will remember the ecological example in the text where I comment on the finding that there is a contrary relationship between the efficiency of an individual species in an ecosystem, and the stability of the system as a whole. Efficiency means reducing the variety of inputs — but the stability of the whole requires widening the variety of inputs. Conant is able to affirm "the common observation that general-purpose systems, which are expected to deal with a wide variety of problems, are slower and less efficient than special-purpose systems operating on a narrower variety of problems, if the comparison is made between systems of equal size". He further notes that in evaluating the terms of his Deterministic Partition Law of Information Rates, it is not possible to ascribe the activities of blockage, throughput, and coordination to specific variables, since the terms he uses are global measurements on the whole system and cannot, in general, be localized. Another insight, by Ashby (1971), proves the need, by deduction, for the local use of symbols in the decomposition of decision making in a complex whole of many parts. For example, the planning of the invasion of Normandy in the Second World War was based on the use of dates described as D-day minus 1, or 2 etc., which is thus a local calendar and not a global one. Later when the date for D-day is fixed, it is possible to coordinate the whole plan within the global calendar with other spects of the war. That one can prove deductively the need for local symbols, is a marked step forward. The exactly similar basis of D-day planning and the local use of variable names in a FORTRAN subroutine becomes apparent, and it also becomes apparent that the usual predilection in model building in geography for using a set of global variables which are partitioned between the various subsystems is unrealistic.

The generality of the information viewpoint and its relevance to geography can best be summarized in one of Conant's paragraphs:

> If each variable in a system is viewed as a message source which sends information about its values to the other variables that are 'listening', then what is conveniently seen as a network of causes and effects can be viewed as a network of transmitters, channels, and receivers. The strength of the causal relations can then be quantified by information rates $\bar{T}$ between variables or over sets of variables. These rates can be bounded by channel capacities. Information theory can therefore be used in the analysis of constraints or dependencies in multivariable systems, where it has peculiar advantages for dynamic systems and systems with hierarchical structure.

The next small part of the book concerns energy. Although it is apparent that the abandonment of reductionism leads one directly into the laws of cybernetics and information in complex systems, and I have noted the necessity for laws other than physical and chemical ones, it remains true that none of the activity of social systems can transgress basic physical and chemical laws. Thus I have included a small section on energy and thermodynamics not merely for comparative conceptual purposes, but because there are constraints that apply to our social systems from this direction too, and in recent years as the debate on the environment and the limits to growth has grown, many geographers have increasingly turned their backs to these issues, and concentrated on social behaviour.

It seems curious to me that it is not until recently that we have begun to think in terms of the energy efficiency of our society, and that we have begun to think of the integration of ecology and economics. For all the denials, economics is a very limited subject, particularly with relation to the real engines of economic growth, that is innovation and energy consumption. It is probably as true to say that invention is the mother of necessity as it is to say the converse: and then economics merely guides in the choice from amongst the set of known alternatives. Hence it may have something to say about the choice between the wooden-wheeled, wooden hub-bearing, Indian ox-cart and a modern heavy lorry: but the best long-term solution may well be in terms of the physical efficiency of the ox-cart. A better designed one, with rubber tyres and metal ball bearings may enable an ox to pull twice the weight, thereby halving fodder demands, but at the same time still relying on a renewable energy resource rather than depleting a capital one. The pursuit of intermediate technology is a quest for increasing the range of choice from which one may select.

Everyone can of course list the major omissions within a subject, as he sees them. But it seems to me that most of those that I would like incorporated fall under two major headings, one concerned with observation, and the other with understanding. Firstly, since geographers always insist on theorizing about some billiard-ball planet in which everyone has perfect information, it seems to me that we need a period in which we try and develop a consensus on what in empirical reality we are trying to study, and how we go about it. We need a theory of empirical enquiry that embraces entitation and observation, and one which will help us in comparative studies far more than any that currently exist. Since it also seems likely that such a theory will call our attention to complex interdependent systems, the second major heading obviously has to be methods of understanding and explanation that are not partial and reductionist. The traditional Chinese curse to a bastard child, "May you live in interesting times", applies to us. The hurdles we will have to cross are ominous. Most of them belong to the basis of human thought patterns and understanding. To take but one of them: I believe that human language, far from being one of the great achievements of our species, is an inhibitor not so much of thought as of explanation and communication. Language is one-dimensional and serial, but the concepts of arrangement are multi-dimensional. Language may well be an inferior field within which to explain what one does. For generations geographers have said exactly that, and thought in terms of maps as an answer to holistic explanation: but unfortunately the maps have been limited like their adjacent concept, the region, by inferior concepts of space and arrangement. Frequently too geographers have argued on foreign ground in answering the question, What does the map say? If the answer is in ordinary language, then the answer is reductionist, sequential and partial. The map says nothing: it exists as the most embracing statement. In this example, what we have to do is to improve on this most embracing statement, as Tobler and others have tried to do in recent years.

It becomes apparent that the integrity of geography, and its intellectual survival, depends upon assisting now in the rapid development and application of systems ideas. It is not merely for us to await the development of these ideas elsewhere and then to apply them. The subject has existed for a long time on an intuitive appreciation that there are complex interacting phenomena — but neither inadequate concepts like the region, nor the breaker's-yard technique of synthesis from other subjects, have substantiated the subject in other's eyes. For too long we have been content with soft answers to big questions, and in the last decades have succumbed to our intellectual inferiority complex by mimicking others in producing hard answers to small questions. The resultant self-vivisection has been apparent for all to see.

The road to hard answers to big questions is not and will not be easy, but there is no alternative.

References

Abler, Ronald, Adams, J. S. and Gould, Peter (1971). "Spatial Organization". Prentice-Hall, Englewood Cliffs, New Jersey.

Ackerman, E. A. (1963). Where is a research frontier?, *Annals of the Association of American Geographers*, 3, 429—440.

Ackoff, Russell L. (1957—58). Towards a behavioural theory of communication, *Management Science*, 4, 218—234. (Reprinted in Buckley, 1968, pp.209—220.)

Angyal, A. (1941). A logic of systems, from Ch.8 of "Foundation for a Science of Personality". Harvard University Press, pp. 243—61. (Reprinted in Emery, F. E., 1969.)

Ashby, W. Ross. (1956). "An Introduction to Cybernetics". Chapman and Hall, London. (Reprinted 1964, Methuen and Co.)

Ashby, W. Ross. (1960). Adaption in the multistable system, from Ch.16 of "Design for a Brain", 2nd edition, Wiley, New York. (Reprinted in Emery, 1969.)

Ashby, W. Ross. (1971). Systems and their informational measures. *In* Klir, George R. (ed.) "Trends in General Systems Theory". Wiley Interscience, New York.

Berry, B. J. L., Goheen, Peter and Goldstein, Harold. (1968). "Metropolitan Area Definition: A Re-evaluation of Concept and Statistical Practice". Working Paper 28, Bureau of the Census, U.S. Department of Commerce, Washington.

Boudon, R. (1971.) "The Uses of Structuralism". Heinemann, London.

Boulding, K. E. (1955). The Malthusian model as a general system. *Social and Economic Studies*, 4(3), 195—205.

Boulding, K. E. (1956). General Systems Theory — the skeleton of science. *Management Science*, 2, 197—208. (Reprinted in Buckley, 1968.)

Brillouin, León (1949). Life, thermodynamics, and cybernetics. *In* Buckley (1968) pp. 147—156, reprinted from *American Scientist*, 37 (Oct. 1949) pp. 554—68.

Brillouin, León. (1962). "Science and Information Theory", 2nd edition, Academic Press, New York.

Brillouin, León. (1964). "Scientific Uncertainty and Information". Academic Press, New York and London.

Buckley, Walter (ed.) (1968). "Modern Systems Research for the Behavioural Scientist". Aldine, Chicago.

Bunge, W. (1962). "Theoretical Geography". Lund Studies in Geography, Series C, General and Mathematical Geography I. Gleerup, Lund.

Bunge, W. (1973). Ethics and logic in geography. In Chorley, R. J. (ed.) "Directions in Geography". Methuen, London.

Carter, Harold. (1971). "Wealth". Penguin, Harmondsworth.

Chapin, F. S. and Weiss, S. F. (eds) (1962). "Urban Growth Dynamics in a Regional Cluster of Cities". Wiley, New York.

Chapman, G. P. (1970). The application of information theory to the analysis of population distributions in space. *Economic Geography*, 46(2), 317–331.

Chapman, G. P. (1973a). The Green Revolution: a gaming simulation. *Area*, 5(2), 129–140.

Chapman, G. P. (1973b). The Spatial Organization of the Population of the United States and England and Wales. *Economic Geography*, 49(4), 325–343.

Chapman, G. P. (1974). Perception and regulation: a case study of farmers in Bihar. *Transactions, Institute of British Geographers* No.62, 328–343.

Cherry, C. (1966). "On Human Communication". M.I.T. Press, Cambridge, Mass.

Childe, V. Gordon (1936). "Man Makes Himself". Watts and Co., London.

Chomsky, Noam. (1972). "Problems of Knowledge and Freedom". Fontana, London.

Chorley, R. J. and Kennedy, B. K. (1971). "Physical Geography: A Systems Approach". Prentice-Hall International, London.

Cliff, A. D. and Ord, K. (1970). Spatial autocorrelation: a review of existing and new measures with applications. *Economic Geography*, 46(2), supplement, pp. 269–292.

Cohen, S. B. (1964). "Geography and Politics in a Divided World". Methuen, London.

Collins, Lyndhurst. (1970). "Markov Chains and Geographical Applications". Paper presented to the I.G.U. Commission on Quantitative Methods Conference at A. Michiewicz University, Poznan. Mimeo, Department of Geography, University of Edinburgh.

Conant, Roger C. (1976). Laws of information which govern systems. *IEEE Transactions on Systems, Man and Cybernetics*, SMC–6(4), 240–255.

Curry, Leslie. (1970). Univariate spatial forecasting. *Economic Geography*, 46(2), supplement, pp. 241–258.

Dacey, M. F. (1965). "Some Observations on a Two-dimensional Language". Technical Report No.7, Geographical Information Systems, Department of Geography, Northwestern University, Evanston, Illinois.

Darby, H. C. (1962). The problem of geographical description. *Transactions, Institute of British Geographers*. No. 30, 1–14.

De Bono, Edward. (1969). Playback 8 analysis. *Science Journal*, 5A(4), 35–37.

Dyson, Freeman J. (1971). Energy in the Universe. *Scientific American*, 224(3), 50–59.

Ellis, Brian. (1968). "Basic Concepts of Measurement". Cambridge University Press, London.

Emery, F. E. (ed.) (1969). "Systems Thinking". Penguin, Harmondsworth.

Fast, J. D. (1970). "Entropy". Macmillan, London.

Feibleman, J. K. (1954). The Theory of Integrative Levels. *British Journal for the Philosophy of Science*, V, 59–90.

Forrester, Jay W. (1969). "Urban Dynamics". M.I.T. Press, Cambridge, Mass.

Forrester, Jay W. (1971). "World Dynamics". M.I.T. Press, Cambridge, Mass.

Furth, R. (1952). Physics of social equilibrium. *The Advancement of Science*, VIII(32), 429–434.

Galbraith, J. K. (1970). "The Affluent Society". Penguin, Harmondsworth.

Garfinkel, D. (1962). Digital computer simulation of ecological systems. *Nature*, 194, 856–859.

Georgescu-Roegen, Nicholas (1971). The Entropy Law and the Economic Process". Harvard University Press, Cambridge, Mass.

Georgescu-Roegen, Nicholas. (1976). "Energy and Economic Myths". Pergamon Press.

Gerard, R. W. (1957). Units and concepts of biology. *Science*, 125, 429–33. (Reprinted in Buckley, 1968.)

Gould, P. (1963). Man against his environment: a game theoretic framework. *Annals of the Association of American Geographers*, 53, 290–297.

Grigg, David B. (1965). The logic of regional systems. *Annals of the Association of American Geographers*, No.55, 465–491.

Guilbaud, G. T. (1959). "What is Cybernetics?". Heinemann, London.

Haggett, P. (1965). "Locational Analysis in Human Geography". Arnold, London.

Hall, A. D. and Fagen, R. E. (1956). Definition of Systems. *General Systems Yearbook*, 1, 18–26.

Hall, E. T. (1965). "The Hidden Dimension: Man's Use of Space in Public and Private". The Bodley Head, London.

Harvey, David. (1969). "Explanation in Geography". Arnold, London.

Hoffmann, Banesh. (1959). "The Strange Story of the Quantum". Dover Publications, New York.

Ions, Veronica. (1967). "Indian Mythology". Hamlyn, London.

Jaynes, E. T. (1957). Information theory and statistical mechanics. *Physical Review*, 106, 620–621.

Johnson, Horton A. (1970). Information theory in biology after 18 years. *Science*, 168. 1545–1550.

Johnson, J. H. (1967). "Urban Geography: An Introductory Analysis". Pergamon, Oxford.

Katz, D. and Kahn, R. L. (1966). Common characteristics of open systems. Chapter 2 of "The Social Psychology of Organization". Wiley, New York. (Reprinted in Emery, 1969, pp. 86–104.)

Koehler, W. (1938). Closed and open systems, from Chapter 8 of "The Place of Values in the World of Fact". Liveright. (Reprinted in Emery, 1969, pp. 59–69.)

Kowal, Norman, E. (1971). A rationale for modelling dynamic ecological systems. *in* Patten, B. C., (ed.) "Systems Analysis and Simulation in Ecology", Vol.1. Academic Press, New York and London.

Kremyanskiy, V. I. (1960). Certain peculiarities of organisms as a "system" from the point of view of physics, cybernetics and biology. "General Systems Yearbook", 5, 221–230. (Reprinted in Emery, 1969.)

Kullback, Solomon. (1959). "Information Theory and Statistics". Wiley, New York.

Laming, D. R. J. (1968). "Information Theory of Choice–Reaction Times". Academic Press, London and New York.

Langton, John. (1972). Potentialities and problems of adopting a systems approach to the study of change in human geography. *In* Board, Christopher, Chorley, Richard J., Haggett, Peter and Stoddart, David R. (eds) "Progress in Geography". Vol. 4. Arnold, London.

Lassiter, Ray R. and Hayne, Don W. (1971). A finite difference model for simulation of dynamic processes in ecosystems. *In* Patten, B. C. (ed.), "Systems Analysi and Simulation in Ecology", Vol. 1. Academic Press, New York and London.

Laszlo, Ervin. (1971). Systems and structures: towards bio-social anthropology. *Theory and Decision*, 2, 174–192.

Lyons, John. (1970). "Chomsky". Fontana, London.

Margalef, D. Ramón (1958). "Information Theory in Ecology". *General Systems Yearbook*.

Margalef, D. Ramón. (1968). "Perspectives in Ecological Theory". University Press, Chicago.

MacArthur, R. (1955). Fluctuations of animal populations and a measure of community stability. *Ecology*, 36, 533–536.

McLoughlin, J. B. (1969). "Urban and Regional Planning: A Systems Approach". Faber and Faber, London.

Medvedkov, Y. V. (1967). The regular component in settlement distributions as shown on a map. *Soviet Geography, Review and Translation*, VIII(4), 150–168.

Melton, M. A. (1958). Geometric properties of mature drainage systems and their representation in an E_4 phase space. *Journal of Geology*, 66(1), 35–56.

Minshull, Roger. (1967). "Regional Geography: Theory and Practice". Hutchinson, London.

Monkhouse, F. J. (1959). "A Regional Geography of Western Europe". Longmans, London.

Monod, Jacques. (1974). "Chance and Necessity" (trans. Austryn Wainhouse). Alfred A. Knopf, New York.

Morowitz, H. J. (1968). "Energy Flows in Biology". Academic Press, New York and London.

Murphy, R. E. (1965). "Adaptive Processes in Economic Systems". Academic Press, New York and London.

Pahl, R. E. (1965). Sociological models in geography. *In* Chorley, Richard J. and Haggett, Peter (eds), "Models in Geography". Methuen, London.

Pask, G. (1960). The natural history of networks. *In* Yovits, M. C. and Cameron, S. (eds), "Self-Organizing Systems". Pergamon, Oxford.

Paterson, J. H. (1965). "North America: A Regional Geography". Oxford University Press, Oxford.

Patten, B. C. (ed.) (1971). "Systems Analysis and Simulation in Ecology", Vol.I. Academic Press, New York and London.

Patten, B. C. (ed.) (1972). "Systems Analysis and Simulation in Ecology", Vol.II. Academic Press, New York and London.

Philbrick, A. K. (1957). Principles of areal functional organization in regional human geography. *Economic Geography*, 33, 299–336.

Phillipson, John. (1966). "Ecological Energetics". Arnold, London.

Piaget, Jean. (1971). "Structuralism". Routledge and Kegan Paul, London. (Translated from the French).

Purcell, Edward. (1963). Parts and wholes in physics. *In* Lerner, Daniel S. (ed.), "Parts and Wholes". The Free Press, New York. (Reprinted in Buckley, 1968, pp. 39–44.)

Ramsay, J. A. (1971). "A Guide to Thermodynamics". Chapman and Hall, London.

Rappaport, Roy A. (1971). The flow of energy in an agricultural society. *Scientific American* 224(3), 116–133.

Robinson, M. E. (1974). Cloze procedure and spatial comprehension tests. *Area*, 6(2), 137–141.

Rothstein, J. (1958). "Communication, Organization and Science". Falcon's Wing Press, Colorado.

Rowe, J. S. (1961). The level of integration concept and ecology. *Ecology*, 42, 400–427.

Sahlins, M. D. and Service, E. R. (eds) (1960). "Evolution and Culture". University of Michigan Press, Ann Arbor.

Sarley, R. M. (1971). "MIKEGASIMO". Department of Social and Environmental Planning, Central London Polytechnic (Mimeo).

Schrödinger, Ervin. (1945). "What is Life?". Cambridge University Press. (Extract from "Order, Disorder and Entropy", reprinted in Buckley, 1968.)

Shackle, G. L. S. (1969). "Decision, Order and Time in Human Affairs", 2nd edition. Cambridge University Press, London.

Simon, H. A. (1956). Rational choice and the structure of the environment. *Psychological Review*, 63, 129–38. (Reprinted in Emery, 1969.)

Slobodkin, L. (1958). Meta-models in theoretical ecology. *Ecology*, 139, 550–551.

Sommerhof, G. (1969). The abstract characteristics of living systems. In Emery, F. E. (ed.) "Systems Thinking", pp. 147–202. Penguin, Harmondsworth.

Sonntag, R. E. and Van Wylen, G. J. (1971). "Introduction to Thermodynamics". Wiley, New York.

Theil, H. (1967). "Economics and Information Theory". North-Holland, Amsterdam.

Tideman, T. N. (1967). "Graphical Representation of Some Concepts from Information Theory and Its Economic Applications". Report No. 6708, Department of Economics and Graduate School of Business, Chicago University.

Ubbelohde, A. R. (1963). "Man and Energy". Penguin, Harmondsworth.

Von Bertalanffy, L. (1962). General systems theory, a critical review. *General Systems*, VII, Society for General Systems Research, Ann Arbor, Michigan.

Von Foerster, H. (1960). On self-organizing systems and their environment. *In* Yovits, M. C. and Cameron, S. (eds) "Self-Organizing Systems", pp. 31—50. Pergamon, Oxford.

Waloff, N. P. C. (1973). "A study of intra-metropolitan industrial mobility and the dynamics of premises: manufacturing industry in west London". Unpublished B.A. Dissertation, Department of Geography, University of Cambridge.

Wärneryd, O. (1968). "Interdependence in Urban Systems". Göteborg, Sweden.

Warntz, William. (1965). "Macro Geography and Income Fronts". *Monograph Series*, 3, Regional Science Research Institute, Philadelphia, Penn.

Weiner, N. (1948). "Cybernetics". M.I.T. Press, Cambridge, Mass.

White, L. A. (1949). "The Science of Culture: A Study of Man and Civilization". Farrar, Strauss, and Cudahy, New York.

Whitehead, Alfred North. (1964). "Adventures of Ideas". Cambridge University Press, London.

Williams, Richard B. (1972). Steady state equilibriums in simple nonlinear food webs. *In* Patten, B. C. (ed.) "Systems Analysis and Simulation in Ecology", Vol. II, pp. 213—240. Academic Press, New York and London.

Wilson, A. G. (1970). "Entropy in Urban and Regional Modelling". Pion, London.

Yovits, M. C. and Cameron, S. (eds) (1960). "Self-Organizing Systems". Pergamon, Oxford.

Index

Numbers in italics are Chapter numbers, or numbers of paragraphs within chapters